# Islamic

## Fundamentalism

## *Myths* & Realities

# Islamic

## Fundamentalism

## *Myths*
## & Realities

### Edited by Ahmad S. Moussalli

# ITHACA
### PRESS

ISLAMIC FUNDAMENTALISM
*Myths and Realities*

Ithaca Press is an imprint of Garnet Publishing Limited

*Published by*
Garnet Publishing Limited
8 Southern Court
South Street
Reading
RG1 4QS
UK

ISBN 0 86372 232 6

First Edition

British Library Cataloguing-in-Publication Data
A catalogue record for this book is available from the British Library

*Jacket design by* Michael Hinks
*Typeset by* Samantha Abley

Printed in Lebanon

# Contents

# Part I

## Theoretical Studies

# 1

# Introduction to Islamic Fundamentalism: Realities, Ideologies and International Politics

*Ahmad S. Moussalli*

Islamic fundamentalism has obviously been on the rise and is most likely to continue. While the term "fundamentalism" itself is subject to criticism or approval it has become part of the literature on Islamic thought and could safely be used as a descriptive – and not necessarily as an evaluative – term of Islamic movements that seek to establish the Islamic state in accordance with the Islamic *shari'a*. Sadik al-Azm deals at length with the denotations and connotations of the term as well as its origins and discourse in both Islam and Christianity.[1]

Islamism is not a better term, for this term is loaded with extra concepts, like fundamentalism, which change Islam into political ideology or an "ism". But fundamentalism changes political concepts into religious ones. The question is then "do Islamic movements change the religious into the political or the political into the religious or both?" However, before answering this question, think also about this. Some scholars prefer to use the term "political Islam" instead of Islamism or fundamentalism, but then the question becomes: is there non-political Islam, or secular Islam, economic Islam or social Islam? The whole issue of preferring one description to another relates not only to the phenomenon itself, but to the perspective of the analyst as well as his/her discipline of knowledge and method of inquiry. To a religious scholar, it is most probably fundamentalism; to a political scientist it is most likely Islamism or political Islam.[2]

In this book, all of these terms and others are used interchangeably and when Islamic fundamentalism is employed it is not used necessarily as a comparable term to Christian fundamentalism. For the difference between

Islamic fundamentalism and Christian fundamentalism is comparable to the differences between Islam and Christianity. For religion means different things to different adherents, and fundamentalism in itself is not indicative of specific substantive principles but relates essentially to understanding of religion. For fundamentalists want to resurrect their religions in terms of their "fundamental" sources or original "fundamentals". This does not mean however that the fundamentals are necessarily similar.

This is why the Middle Eastern and the Western press as well as scholars of anthropology, sociology, political science, history and other disciplines differ in denoting the phenomenon of Islamic activism and the journey to return to the roots of religion. Thus, some call it renaissance or fundamentalism, others, awakening; for yet others, it is radicalism or renewal, or for many, it is simply a return to Islam. Because of the comprehensiveness of the Islamic movements and the diversity of their concerns, one may find that one description may fit a movement in Egypt or Algeria under certain circumstances or may account for an aspect of the movement in a specific period. But the too concentrated emphasis only on the political aspect of the movements misses much of the significance of religious movements in the modern world. That these movements are treated as only political dilutes the metaphysical role of Islam in its making and development. The truth of the matter is that these movements are not limited to political action but deal with a diversity of aspects and issues that make them a way of life and a philosophy and a critique of existing ways of life and philosophies. The following points are essential elements for understanding the movement and its maintenance of activist momentum and expansion.

## Islamic Fundamentalism: Western Perspectives

Two basic trends in the Western world have emerged over how to understand and deal with Islamic fundamentalist movements; a division which spilled over into policy making processes and institutions. For instance, the American Administration has had within it different attitudes. While the State Department was generally more prone, in theory at least, to co-opt Islamic political movements, the Defense Department looked at Islamic fundamentalism as an ideological and geopolitical threat that had to be eliminated. The trend that opposes inclusion of

Islamic fundamentalism is the largest and includes most of the American press. )

Even in research institutes, a lot of discussion is going on about the nature of the Islamic movements. A study, "The Green Threat", published by the Cato Institute in Washington by Leon Hardar, Bureau Chief for the *Jerusalem Post*, summarizes the need for creating a new enemy. The end of the cold war made the American Administration look for new enemies, including instability in Europe, the revival of European powers, new modern Russian imperialism and new nuclear terrorism. The "yellow threat" comes on the top of the new list of enemies, because of the economic threat that East Asia represents. Next comes the "green threat" which is represented by Middle Eastern Islamic fundamentalism. Furthermore, *The Economist* invented, for instance, the term "fundie" as a creature who looks like Ayatollah Khomeini armed with radical ideology and equipped with nuclear weapons with the full intention of declaring war against Western Civilization.[3])

Also George Will, whose political commentaries smack of hatred not only of Arabs but of Islam as well, says that a major war between Islam and Christianity might well start again. This was part of his response to a question whether the West might in the future celebrate the Prophet's birthday. It is obvious from these three instances – and there are many other similar comments[4] – that most of the Western press attempts to instil in the Westerners hatred for Islam and to market Islamic movements as worse than Marxist-Leninism. )

The rise of political Islam in North Africa and in Egypt, as well as the establishment of Muslim states in Central Asia, in addition to Iranian and Sudanese foreign policies, has fuelled the push to picture Islamic fundamentalism and, along with it, Islam, as the new enemy of democracy, the United States and the West. A political commentator in the *Washington Post* said that Islamic fundamentalism is revolutionary and aggressive, similar in its radicalism to the movements of Bolshevism, fascism and Nazism in the past. It is authoritarian, anti-democratic and anti-secular and cannot be absorbed in the secular Christian world. Because its objective is to establish the authoritarian Islamic state, the United States should smother it at its inception.) This picture of total confrontation and non-conciliation between Islam and the West is now being strongly positioned in Washington, D.C. The developments in the Western press before the second Gulf war show clearly how public opinion was being charged to accept any action against Saddam Hussein. Suddenly, Saddam Hussein became the most dangerous man in the world and one of the most important enemies of the United States after the cold war was over. Iraq was portrayed as aiming at controlling all of the Middle East, a portrayal that prepared the way for public acceptance of the war as a strategic necessity.

However, Saddam Hussein's threat was not identical to the "green threat", for while Saddam was considered as a wild thug – probably among other thugs – who broke the rules of the game and consequently endangered Western interests, he could be finished off. But he did not threaten the Western lifestyle. On the other hand, the threat of political Islam is different in its nature. The struggle with political Islam is treated as a zero-sum game: if political Islam wins, the West loses and vice versa. The Islamic Republic of Iran is considered as a non-rational state that cannot be brought into line by traditional military threats and political co-option. The struggle is therefore supposed to last for a long time since it is also viewed as cultural. As it was with the "red threat" during the cold war, the "green threat" is seen as a cancer that destroys Western values. This is why the American people are being prepared for a relentless struggle and for imposing containment and, therefore, why a new class of foreign policy experts on Islam is needed.

There seem to be many indications that the sporadic acts of terror as well as the practices of radical groups are being used in order to develop such a threat. The bombing of the World Trade Center was portrayed as the action of international terrorism. Tehran has been replacing Moscow as the centre of ideological and physical terrorism and military expansion; and Islam is replacing communism. A political commentator shows how Islam has been seen to be well suited to play the role of the bad guy after the cold war, for it is large, frightening and anti-Western and thrives on poverty and anger. It is spread over vast tracts of the world, and so the countries of Islam could be shown on TV as large maps in green, as the communist countries used to appear in red.[7]

Experts on foreign policy have already started since 1992 using cold war terms to describe the struggle with Islam. There have been discussions about containment of the Iranian threat all over the world, especially in Central Asia. Now, Iran and Iraq are subject to the "double containment doctrine". The US secretary of state visited some central Asian countries in order to draw the red lines that Islamists should not cross. Also, a diplomatic communiqué in 1992 demanded that the Sudan stop its export of revolution and terrorism.[8] Washington has also welcomed the Algerian government's iron-fist policies towards the Islamists and its suspension of the elections(The notion that Islamists or fundamentalists should be stopped somewhere and not allowed to spread is becoming stronger and stronger because of the readoption of the domino effect theory. Arnold Beichman, a researcher at Hoover Institute, argues, for instance, that Iran aims at geopolitical expansion through controlling the states of Central Asia, North Africa and Egypt and also the Gulf area. According to him, the basic strategic role for Iran is the control of Saudi Arabia. Therefore he concludes that the inability of the Arabs to control this challenge leads to the creation of a green barrier around the Middle East and the states of Central Asia which will become satellite states for a new Iranian order whose basic policy tool is terrorism.[9]

(The bombing of the World Trade Center publicized further the danger of the green threat in many quarters of policy-making institutions. What encourages this view is that many states like to see the United States immersed in a struggle with Islam – any Islam. The compelling question that must be answered therefore relates to the nature of the factors that give credibility to the cultural and ideological instruments that the anti-Islamic trend employs to discredit anything Islamic, be it fundamentalism, reformism or even traditionalism.)

Many factors can be identified; first among them are most of the Arab regimes and the Israeli regime. Most Arab states are afraid of some kind of rapprochement between the United States and some fundamentalist groups, since quite a few fundamentalists have posited the non-contradiction between the rise of Islamic states and the maintenance of Western interests in the area. The Arab regimes were chilled by the idea that the US had given a safe haven to Shaykh 'Omar 'Abd al-Rahman and a political platform to Hasan al-Turabi in the US Congress; the former is now in prison implicated in the bombing of the World Trade Center, and the latter is identified with Islamic terrorism in North Africa and even Egypt.[10]

The Egyptian regime has long called for curbing Iranian influence in its encouragement of Islamic fundamentalists. But the US has instead, and for a short period, opened up a dialogue with moderate fundamentalist groups in the Islamic world. But when the New York bombing took place, Shaykh 'Abd al-Rahman denied any involvement, and his Jama'a saw in that bombing as well as in another bombing earlier that week in a coffee shop in Egypt an attempt to discredit it inside and outside Egypt and to eliminate any possibility of a US–Islamist dialogue.[11] After the security apparatuses in Egypt accused the Shaykh and his group of being behind the attacks on tourists in Egypt and therefore implicated 'Abd al-Rahman personally, they raided the Jama'a's strongholds. Immediately after the bombing, the Egyptian President reminded the international community that he had already warned it of the dangers of Islamic radicalism inside and outside Egypt. For the same reasons, the Council of Arab Interior Ministers held a meeting on 5 February 1993. The Egyptian minister of the interior asked the conferees to be aware of the dangers of Islamic radicalism that beset their countries, for all of them are in the same boat. The Tunisian minister of the interior condemned Islamic radicalism because it posed a danger to the Arab and Islamic nation and because it aimed at destabilizing all states and halting the progress of their nations. The Algerian minister of the interior affirmed that the radical movements had chosen Tunisia, Egypt and Algeria as their targets. It was for this reason that the three countries put the issue of religious radicalism at the top of the list of their priorities regarding the difficulties that Arab governments should confront. On 4 March 1993, the Tunisian minister declared that his country took steps with regional and international organizations in order to contain radical groups. In order to convince their peoples and the international audience of the real danger of Islamic fundamentalism, Tunisia, Egypt and Algeria have publicly coordinated their efforts to curb the dangers emanating from Sudan and Iran. These three countries are also trying to market their views about Islamic fundamentalism and radicalism in other Islamic and Arab countries as well as in the West in general. They have been trying to propagate the notion of the existence of an international network of Islamic fundamentalism, where the Arab fundamentalist groups are organized by the Sudanese fundamentalist state which is connected to an Arab fundamentalism and secondly to an international fundamentalism based in Iran. An earlier summit of the leaders of North Africa put its finger on the nature of the danger: it threatens the stability of all North African states and its "democratic development".

The newly established Palestinian Authority is not far removed from the attitude of the other Arab regimes towards Islamic fundamentalism. The United States halted its dialogue with the movement of Islamic resistance (Hamas) which considered that such a decision was unwarranted and irrational. This happened again after the New York bombing when Hamas was said to be implicated in it. Yet the PLO announced on 6 March 1993 its satisfaction at the news that the US had discontinued its relations with Hamas. The PLO justified its position on the ground that the US wanted to split the unity of the Palestinian people and to force the PLO to give more concessions to Israel! In a meeting with the Israeli prime minister, the US secretary of state justified that act on the ground that Hamas had been committing terrorist acts.

Again, under pressure from Arab governments, Pakistan announced on 4 February 1993 that it would expel all illegal residents, meaning the Arabs who fought the Soviet Union in Afghanistan. This declaration was supplemented by a vicious campaign to expel most of the Arab fundamentalists.

Western strategists and policy makers have therefore been concerned with the role attributed by Arab countries – especially Egypt, Algeria and Tunisia – to Iran which is portrayed as the fountain of international Islamic fundamentalism and the source of and support for all Arab fundamentalist groups. Iran is now pictured in the West, especially in the United States, as leading an Islamic alliance that aims at destabilizing the pro-Western regimes. For Iran's arm extends to very strategically sensitive places: Hizbullah in Lebanon, Hamas and Islamic Jihad in Palestine and Israel as well as Islamic movements in Egypt and North Africa. Furthermore, what added to this danger is the CIA director's testimony that Iran is developing its nuclear capabilities in order to control many important areas in the world.[12]

While Egypt is leading the campaign against Islamic fundamentalism, it has long accused Sudan of supporting and even setting up Islamic fundamentalist groups, radical and moderate. But any observer of the modern history of Egypt knows that Egypt, and not Sudan, is the cradle of fundamentalism since the 1920s and up till the present as embodied first in the movement of the Muslim Brotherhood and later in its splinter groups. However, the Egyptian regime wants to put the blame on others in an attempt to receive more aid from the West and to claim that its problems, including fundamentalism, are imported. Sudan has become for the Egyptian regime the easiest target and scapegoat. Even at a time when the Ethiopian government announced that the attempt on the life of the Egyptian President in 1995 was made by Egyptians, the Egyptian regime still insisted on attributing it to Sudan. In fact, since 1992, the Egyptian regime has ordered its troops to be deployed in Wadi Halfa just south of the border with Sudan. But what is amazing then and now is that the Egyptian condition for withdrawing from Wadi Halfa, settling the conflict over Halayib and for restoring normal relations with Sudan is the removal of Hasan al-Turabi's influence and informal power. The US has also accepted the logic of the Egyptian regime and has threatened to isolate Sudan and to put it on the state terrorist list. US assistant secretary of state for African affairs announced as early as 11 March 1993 that his government is reconsidering its policy towards Sudan because it has become a refuge for the terrorists of Hizbullah, Hamas and Islamic Jihad and because the Iranian–Sudanese relationships make Khartoum a contact place for terrorist groups.

Within the Arab world, only Syria has escaped such incriminating charges towards Sudan and Iran because it has considered that the challenges the Arab world is facing go beyond the internal Arab differences and those with Iran. For this reason, it has shown its willingness to mediate in these conflicts, because its strategic relations with Iran help Syria focus on the Arab–Israeli conflict.[13]

The second and more important factor in inflating the danger of Islamic fundamentalism is Israel which is inciting the Western world not only against Islamic fundamentalism but also against Islam. It has redrawn its strategic role, after the elimination of the red threat, to become the only power that can halt the green threat from expanding. In the first summit meeting between the US president and the Israeli prime minister, the former said on 16 March 1993 that the discussion focused on security matters of the region and the proliferation of nuclear weapons in addition, of course, to peace negotiations and the economy. President Clinton underlined the importance of curbing terrorist and violent activities. Rabin, on the other hand, spoke after the president and focused on the importance of "confronting all sorts of bigotry that create destructive terrorism" similar to the terrorism that landed on the American shores, and this was made in reference to the bombing of the World Trade Center. He called on all the free nations to find a viable way to contain the danger of radicalism, meaning, of course, Israel.[14]

( As a matter of fact, for Israel such propaganda serves as a justifying vehicle for repressing Islamic political movements in the occupied territories and Israel itself. For Israel has for a long time, especially since the collapse of the Soviet Union, shifted the focus of the strategic danger from communism to Islam in order to maintain its strategic value in the Western world and so preserve its special position in the Middle East. It wants to maintain its image as an advanced Western entity that serves Western interests, while at the same time showing that Islamic movements – along with Islam – are new world threats that must be contained once and for all. The starting-point of containment is, needless to say, in the Middle East. Furthermore the president of Israel announced in Europe that the fundamentalist Hamas forms the main destructive force against the peace process in the Middle East, not the Arab–Israeli conflict, though that is important too.[15] )

The Israeli prime minister condemned Islamic movements and called for the containment of radical Islam as represented by Iran, Hizbullah, and Hamas; before then he focused on the containment of Iraq long before it actually happened. He added that Sudan, which harboured many Iranians, became the base for the fundamentalists of Egypt, Algeria and Tunisia. He warned that the Jordanian order might fall if the fundamentalists were to be allowed to come to power which would lead – again, the domino effect theory – to the fall of the Egyptian regime.[16] The bombing of the World Trade Center gave the opportunity to some radical Jews headed by a Rabbi in New Jersey to launch a demonstration in front of the Peace Mosque with slogans condemning Islam. Zionism is now using Islam as the new ideology threatening the West, and its culture and orders.

( It has therefore become clear that the slogan of the green threat is gradually gaining ground thanks to the efforts of two sets of groups, which are seemingly at odds with each other, but in this regard supplementing each other in highlighting the danger of Islamic fundamentalism and political Islam. On the one hand, Israel, with its "strategic importance in the Middle East", is making itself the carrier of the "banner of Western civilization". On the other hand, many Arab regimes are in fact inflaming Western hatred of political Islam in order that the West continues to prop up these regimes.

In addition to these two groups, there are of course many others including numerous think-tanks. These institutes, which are basically research organizations, feed the US administration with analyses and policies. Most publications of these think-tanks form part of the hearings in Congress and at general scholarly conferences. In turn, the ideas put forward find their way into the press, academic and journalistic. Many articles on the emerging green threat or the clash of civilizations have been put out in very well-known publications such as the *Wall Street Journal*, the *New York Times* and the *Washington Post* and *Foreign Affairs* (see the section below). Imagine the impact that the following image published on the cover of *Newsweek* on 15 March 1993 would have on forming a stereotype of Muslims. It shows a bearded man carrying a copy of the Qur'an, with the caption: "cold anger and terrorism today"; and one of the main headings inside the issue reads: "The Wrath of Islam".[17]

## Islamic Fundamentalism: Radical and Moderate

While many influential Western media and scholars have focused their interests on the dangers of Islamic fundamentalism, they have neglected the unending oppression of the peoples of the area as well as the dialogues and debates that have been going on among diverse political trends about political theories, ideologies, political life and, surprisingly, human rights. Again, sensational titles in magazines and newspapers such as "Will Democracy Survive in Egypt?" or "The Arab World where Troubles for the US Never End" or "The Clash of Civilizations" have further frightened and pushed the West away from the East. While quite a few Western academics concerned with the Middle East deal with the real problems of the peoples there, the West generally looks at these problems, such as oppression and human rights, as being peripheral and negligible when it comes to the Arabs and Muslims.[18]

However, current events in the Muslim world, particularly in Egypt, Algeria, Tunisia, and Sudan, have produced political and academic discussions on the compatibility of Muslim fundamentalist discourses, especially the doctrines of an Islamic state, with democracy, human rights and pluralism as well as the "the emerging world order". Any serious and objective study of the area shows that modern Islamic fundamentalist discourses are seriously discussing the issues of democracy and pluralism and their relationship to Islam. While a majority of Western media and scholars along with a majority of their Middle Eastern counterparts treat fundamentalism as exclusivist by its nature and definition, and while a few widely publicized fundamentalist groups are truly exclusivist and adhere to the notion of change through radical programmes and uncompromising revolutions, most mainstream and major fundamentalist groups are pluralistic, democratic and inclusivist indeed. For the origins of exclusion are neither Islamic metaphysical perceptions of the universe nor developed abstractly from the theological doctrines of Islam. Furthermore, exclusion is not limited to Islamic fundamentalist groups and includes the champions of the new and the old world orders. But it is only with Islamic fundamentalism that the doctrine of exclusion is transformed into part of a new theology of metaphysical perceptions and abstract doctrines of belief.

Islamic fundamentalism is however an umbrella term for a wide range of discourses and activism that tends to move from a high level of moderate pluralism, and thus inclusive democracy, to extreme radicalism, intolerant unitarianism, and thus exclusive majority rule. While some fundamentalist groups are pluralistic in terms of inter-Muslim relations and between Muslims and minorities, others are not. Again, while some fundamentalists are politically pluralistic but theologically exclusive, others are accommodating religiously, but direct their exclusivist programmes at the outside, the West or imperialism. Even at the scientific level, Western science and technology are regarded by some fundamentalists as Islamically sound, while others exclude them, because of their assumed un-Islamic nature. While the majority of fundamentalists call for pluralistic democracy and argue for it as an essentially Islamic point of view, the radicals brand it as unbelief.

Why? Why then do the fundamentalists, given their agreement on the usage of the *fundamentals* of religion, the Qur'an and the *sunna*, as well as a philosophical superstructure, have these basic, substantive and divergent views? The answer is that the inclusive democratic and exclusive authoritarian policies of most Middle Eastern states, and of whatever international powers exist at the time, reinforce and in fact create that dual nature of fundamentalist political behaviour While Arab regimes hold the international order responsible for harsh situations they find themselves in, the fundamentalists attribute economic, social and political failures of the states to the regimes themselves. They view the regimes as conductors of multi-layered conflicts between the dominant world powers against the ambitions and hopes of the indigenous populations, in this case the Muslims and their most vibrant spokesmen, the fundamentalists.

Fundamentalists in general believe that their governments do not serve the ideological, political or economic interests of their peoples but those of the dominant world powers. Imperialism, colonialism, exploitation, materialism – all these are charges brought against the West. Liberalization, whether economic, political or cultural, as well as social justice, political freedom, and democracy are major demands of both radical and moderate fundamentalist groups Modern national states have been considered by fundamentalists as the link between what is unacceptable and inhumane in both Western and Eastern civilization, namely Western materialism and Eastern despotism. An Islamic state, they believe, can withstand and even correct Western materialistic domination and Eastern political authoritarianism. This notwithstanding, the way a fundamentalist theoretician or movement creates its discourse and argues for the active method of setting up that state, the manner of conducting politics therein, and the basic ideology of the state can provide us with leads to classify one theoretician or movement as the exclusivist, non-liberal, radical antagonist of pluralistic democracy or the inclusivist, liberal and moderate protagonist of pluralistic democracy.

Both fundamentalist theoreticians and activists, in addition to Muslim and Western academic and press circles, have discussed the issues of exclusion, liberalism and democracy under the rubric name of liberal democracy, which is assumed to be, more or less, inclusive.[19] In *New Perspective Quarterly*, pluralism and tolerance in Islam are discussed under sensational titles that reinforce stereotypical understanding of Islam.[20] The editor of the journal argues that Islam remains monotheistic in faith and in practice. In today's globalized cultural space, Islam will face a host of challenges that will pit "the word not only against the mere language of Western literature, like Salman Rushdie's novel, but also against non-dogmatic, for example, of Hindu beliefs, not to speak of the radically free-style tolerance of Europe and America." The important question is then "will Islam turn toward pluralism and the West back toward faith?" [21]

In the same journal Akbar S. Ahmad is posited as saying no. For he argues that only one civilization, Islam will stand firm. "Only the Muslim world, poised both to implode and explode, offers a global perspective with a potential alternative role on the world stage/ Islam, therefore, appears to be set on a collision course with the West." For the West is based on secular materialism, the scientific reason of modernity, and the absence of moral philosophy; but Islam, argues Ahmad, is based on faith, patience, pace and equilibrium. He draws up, like many other Westerners and Muslims, a picture of non-conciliation between Islam and the West; it is "a straight-out fight between two approaches to the world, two opposed philosophies".[22]

Ahmad's exclusionary idea is not just Islamic but has its equivalence among prominent Western intellectuals – in addition to the press – such as Samuel Huntington who argues that the future will witness the clash of civilizations. In his "The Islamic-Confucian Connection" as well as his "The Clash of Civilizations", Huntington considers the conflicts that took place since the peace of Westphalia in 1648 up till the Cold War as "Western civil wars". Now the "cultural division of Europe among Western Christianity, Orthodox Christianity and Islam has re-emerged. Today the most significant dividing line in Europe may be that identified by the British scholar William Wallace – the eastern boundary of Western Christianity in the year 1500."[23]

Disregarding any diversity about interpreting Islam as well as its historical schools and modern different tendencies in religion and politics, Huntington, who served at the White House under President Carter in security and planning for the National Security Council and witnessed the collapse of the Iranian regime under the Shah and the establishment of an Islamic state, proclaims that Islam is a militant religion that does not make a distinction between the religious and the secular. "This theocratic proclivity makes it extraordinarily difficult for Islamic societies to accommodate non-Muslims. It makes it very difficult for Muslims to easily fit into societies where the majority is non-Muslim."[24]

Thus, in addition to showing very little knowledge of Islamic history and philosophy, he disregards the comparison of Islam with other religions, which, though looking at politics and religion as Islam does, nonetheless are included in Western culture and not Eastern. Although Judaism, for instance, is more like Islam, it has nonetheless been included, accepted and incorporated into Western culture. The West until recently excluded and persecuted Jews politically and culturally with Zionism being a direct consequence of this fact. Actually, exclusion was mutual, i.e. the Jews did not want to be assimilated by Western culture. After Hitler, "anti-Semitism" became an insulting term in the West and Zionist propaganda gave further impetus to this. Again, Protestant America, with its emphasis on the Old Testament as an integral and very important part of the Bible, was potentially very receptive to Zionist propaganda, as opposed to the Vatican's position.

In general, the Islamic world has been included, but only in a negative way, that is to say by military force employed in the past by the colonial powers and now by dominant world economic powers that use the threat of economic sanctions and the employment of sophisticated weaponry if need be. Why then do not these powers try to genuinely include the Islamic world economically, morally and philosophically, especially if one of the features that distinguishes the West is its inclusive pluralism? Or is the non-Islamicity of Muslims the condition for being included?

Judith Miller advocates a non-democratic exclusivist attitude towards the Muslim world since Islam is incompatible with the values of pluralism, democracy and human rights. This means that Western policy-makers should not support democratic elections since they might bring radical Islamic fundamentalists into government. She exhorts the American administration and others to reject any sort of conciliation with, or inclusion of, radical political Islam. 'For Western governments should be concerned about these movements, and, more importantly, should oppose them. For despite their rhetorical commitment to democracy and pluralism, virtually all militant fundamentalists oppose both. They are, and are likely to remain, anti-Western, anti-American and anti-Israeli.'

She further rejects indirectly Edward Djerejian's distinction between good and bad fundamentalists. Accepting Martin Kramer's idea of the non-compatibility of militant Islamic groups with democracy insofar as they cannot be by nature "democratic, pluralistic, egalitarian or pro-Western" and Bernard Lewis's argument that liberal democracy and Islam are not bedfellows, Miller concludes along with Lewis that autocracy is the norm, and postulates that "Islamic militancy presents the West with a paradox. While liberals speak of the need for diversity with equality, fundamentalists see this as a sign of weakness. Liberalism tends not to teach its proponents to fight effectively. What is needed, rather, is almost a contradiction in terms: a liberal militancy, or a militant liberalism that is unapologetic and unabashed."[25]

Fortunately, not all American thinkers, policy-makers and diplomats think similarly. Edward Djerejian, former assistant secretary of state and US ambassador to Israel, puts the matter differently. He states that "the US government, however, does not view Islam as the next 'ism' confronting the West or threatening world peace. That is an overly simplistic response to a complex reality." He goes on to say that the Cold War is not being replaced with a new competition between Islam and the West. The crusades have been over for a long time, and the ecumenical movement is the contemporary trend. Americans recognize Islam as a world faith for it is practised everywhere and counts among its adherents millions of citizens of the United States. "As Westerners we acknowledge Islam as a historic civilizing force among the many that have influenced and enriched our culture. The legacy of the Muslim culture which reached the Iberian Peninsula in the 8th century, is a rich one in the sciences, arts, and culture and in tolerance of Judaism and Christianity. Islam acknowledges the major figures of Judeo-Christian heritage: Abraham, Moses, and Christ."[26]

However, the US differs, according to Djerejian, with those groups that are insensitive to political pluralism, "who substitute religious and political confrontation with engagement with the rest of the world" and who do not accept the peaceful resolution of the Arab–Israeli conflict and pursue their goals through repression.[27]

Some scholars of the Middle East and the Islamic world go beyond this general statement. Augustus R. Norton in his "Inclusion Can Deflate Islamic Populism" argues that democracy and Islam are not incompatible since it is the demand of the people of the area to be included in the political system. While sceptics deny the usefulness of democracy for the people, because the regimes are inefficient and suffer from legitimacy claims and because the fundamentalist political movements are anti-Western, anti-Israeli and anti-democratic, Norton pins down the claims against the sceptics by saying that "to argue that popular political players are irremediably intransigent and therefore unmoved by tenets in the real world is at best naive, and, at worst, racist." He argues further that so long as the fundamentalist movements are not given any voice in politics, no surprise then that their "rhetoric will be shrill and their stance uncompromising. In contrast, well-designed strategies of political inclusion hold great promise for facilitating essential political change."[28] He concludes that while the rulers have no intention of stepping aside, they nonetheless have to be encouraged to enlarge "the political stage and to open avenues for real participation in politics. For the West, and especially the United States, the issues are complex and vexing, but the basic choice is simple: construct policies that emphasize and widen the cultural barriers that divide the Middle East from the West, or pursue policies that surmount the barriers."[29]

Another scholar, William Zartman, argues that the two currents of political Islam and democracy are not necessarily incompatible. The Qur'an might be interpreted to support different political behaviours. A synthesis might emerge between Islam and democracy where constitutional checks can be employed. He suggests five measures to democratize and make sure that democracy will triumph, including "to practice the forms of democracy whenever scheduled, let the most popular win, and let them learn democracy on the job."[30] Again, in "Democratization and Islam," John Esposito and James Piscatori argue that the process of liberalization and democratization in the Muslim world requires, as happened in the West, a process of reinterpretation of the divine texts. While Islam lends itself to different interpretations, some important fundamentalist thinkers have already started the process of accommodating Islam with democracy and liberalism.[31]

While the aforementioned discussion indicates the existence and emergence of a fundamentalist tendency to include some principles of Western civilization of liberalism and democratization as well as a free economic system, which in themselves represent features of an inclusionary mentality of political Islam, it also shows that there is a major and influential tendency among Western politicians and scholars as well as the press to reject the "Islamization" of democracy and liberalism and, on the other hand, insist on the "Westernization" of raw materials and markets in the name of national security or the clash of civilizations. The same tendency that stands opposed to the ascendancy of fundamentalism through democracy, because of the assumed authoritarian nature of fundamentalism, supports authoritarian regimes for the sake of maintaining a non-existent democracy – an indication of an exclusionary attitude and intolerance directed at Islam under the guise of fundamentalism.

So far, it seems that most international and regional actors have vested interest in pushing away fundamentalists from any legitimate role in internal, regional or international affairs. The argument against the fundamentalists outlined above has its counterpart in the Middle East. In "Liberalization and Democracy in the Arab World", Gudrun Kramer shows why Arab regimes are not yet ready for democracy. However, democracy is now one of the common themes among political movements and differs in nature and extent from one movement to another, ranging from the adoption of a liberal pluralistic Western model to "an Islamic model of participation qua consultation". However, the two movements "converge on the issues of human rights and political participation". And although some regimes have adopted certain classic mechanisms to liberalize and democratize such as the *infitah* (open door policy) and the multi-party system in Egypt, the limitations are nonetheless classic as well. "Formal constraints also limit the scope of legitimate political expression and action, usually a party law restricting the bases of party formation and a national charter defining the common and inviolable intellectual and political ground." Thus, for instance, the moderate Muslim Brotherhood in Egypt are not legally allowed to form a party, but nevertheless are allowed to participate informally by the regime. Kramer goes on to say that "even an Islamic political order may be able to incorporate Western notions of political participation and human rights". Furthermore, liberalization will have to give more room for manoeuvre to political actors critical of the West and openly hostile towards Israel. "While the public demands a greater distance from the West and a tough stand *vis-à-vis* Israel, the socioeconomic crisis intensifies dependence on Western governments and international agencies."[32]

It is obvious today that Middle Eastern regimes are no longer capable of relying mostly on repression. The Egyptian government, for instance, has decided to intellectually counter-attack the current tide of political Islam by having the General Egyptian Institute for Books publish a series of books under the general title "Confrontation" (al-Muwajaha). The series focuses on republishing books of scholars and intellectuals that have in common the goal of refuting the doctrines of radical groups by using the moderate religious and political thought prevalent in Egypt in the late 19th and early 20th centuries such as that of Jamal al-Din al-Afghani, Muhammad 'Abduh, 'Ali 'Abd al-Raziq, Taha Hussein, 'Abbas al-'Aqqad and others. The specific objectives are to circulate the opinions of the pioneers of "enlightenment" (al-tanwir), to positively focus on more moderate views, to refute radical ideas in relation to Islam's view of government and state and the application of the shari'a.[33]

However, this "intellectual" governmental activity is only a belated and subsidiary supplement to the doctrine of confronting the fundamentalists, i.e. the "security confrontation" doctrine that has been officially adopted by the Arab and Foreign Affairs Committee of Majlis al-Shura (Consultative Council), the highest judiciary council in Egypt. The solution, to be developed through the consolidation of security apparatuses, comes first and foremost, followed, secondly, by a religious confrontation to be launched by religious officialdom, and, thirdly and most surprisingly, legislature which must produce a state-of-the-art law against terrorism. But no substantial mention is made of rectifying the severe economic conditions of poverty, loosening political manipulations through liberalization and democratization or respecting human rights. But when the report of the Committee suggests paying greater attention to the social development of poor rural and isolated areas with special focus on youth, the objective is to control the hotbed of fundamentalists. The committee also proposes a further supplement to the law, already passed by the Egyptian Parliament, restricting the multiplicity of professional unions and the communication of local parties with foreign parties without official permission.[34]

The "religious confrontation" which is being led by Shaykh al-Azhar seems both to give credit to the measures taken by the government but simultaneously to provide indirect legitimacy to political Islam in addition to weakening the modernist and secular tendencies in Egypt. In a long interview, Shaykh Jad al-Haqq Ali Jad al-Haqq, the predecessor of the current Shaykh al-Azhar Muhammad Tantawi, categorically rejected the separation of the state from Islam. He argued that Islam is made up of both *din wa dunya* or, loosely translated, a religion and a way of life – basically identical to fundamentalist interpretation. The Prophet Muhammad did not differentiate the political from the religious. Again, the ruler should be appointed by *shura* (consultation) that may be conducted through different methods and techniques. After accepting the ideology of the Muslim Brotherhood as being Islamic, he only objects to the use of violence by some radical groups. However, the Azhar considers the Egyptian government's policies as Islamic and defends its actions against criticism by radical and moderate fundamentalist groups. Shaykh Jad al-Haqq convened in 1994 the First General Conference for those shaykhs in charge of the official mosques for the specific purpose of counter-balancing the activities of the radical groups. Some 1,500 shaykhs attended the conference and participated in its sessions along with, very interestingly, the ministers of foreign affairs, the interior, religious endowments, information, housing and agriculture. The interior minister emphasized the organic link between the security confrontation and the religious one through cooperation between the mosques and the media to curb terrorism. The information minister affirmed that the media had plans to uncover terrorism, but that depended on the "true" explanation of Islam. While refusing to lift media censorship and to license private TV stations, he affirmed the role of the Azhar as an "information authority" to confront "foreign fundamentalist" dangers, for an information revolution has been going on – especially now since fundamentalists outside Egypt correspond with those in Egypt by fax.[35]

The Azhar plays – with the tacit approval of the government – the role of a modern "Court of Inquisition". Naguib Mahfouz, a Nobel Prize winner for literature, has announced his readiness to withdraw his book, *Awlad Haritna* (The Children of our Neighbourhood) if the Azhar convinced him that it contained any blasphemous remark against Islam. Although Rif'at al-Sa'id, a secular leftist intellectual, condemns the fundamentalists for banning the book – in fact it was banned 34 years ago by the Azhar under Abd al-Nasser's presidency – he asks the government to face "the terrorists" not only by security measures but also by curbing their media. As one of the "enlightened thinkers" – a term used by Sa'id to describe himself and his intellectual colleagues – he calls for the suppression of whatever media freedom is left to Islamic thinkers, because radicalism starts initially as an idea,[36] though he forgets that inclusion, tolerance, pluralism and democracy started as ideas as well.

Again, the case of a university teacher Nasr Hamid Abu Zayd, brought to a "secular" – and not a fundamentalist – court in Egypt because of his heterodox views, shows how the government fights not only intellectual "terrors" of fundamentalism but also those of modernism. He was convicted of the charge brought against him and was "excommunicated" and separated from his wife on the ground that the marriage of a Muslim woman to a non-believing man is not valid. After his case was reviewed by the Court of Appeal he was exonerated from all charges, and Cairo University promoted him to the position of professor. However, he still lives abroad. The charge focused around his books which showed "animosity to the texts of the Qur'an and the *sunna*," "non-belief" and "recanting Islam".[37]

While the government uses its legal apparatus to exclude major modernist figures and trends, it uses it as well to exclude moderate fundamentalism. An Egyptian newspaper, *al-Sha'b*, published an article on capital punishment stating that the Egyptian government has moved from civil and penal law to emergency laws allowing the employment of the "iron fist" policy for the containment of fundamentalists. During Mubarak's presidency, the policy has resulted in the "political" execution of 48 individuals between 1981 and 1993, almost double the number (27) of those who were executed for similar political reasons during a whole century in Egypt, from 1882 to 1981, a period which in the previous 30 years included the presidencies of both Nasser and Sadat. In 1996, the number has gone up to 58.[38]

A member of Parliament stated in a parliamentary session that Egypt lives on the margin of democracy, for democracy means the peaceful and voluntary handover of power, a feature that does not exist today. The President of the Consultative Assembly (Majlis al-Shura), Hilmi Surur, unconvincingly responded that President Mubarak does not say that Egyptians have reached democracy but rather that democracy should be deepened – as if Mubarak's remark makes the absence of democracy any easier. Hilmi went on to say that democracy is represented by the existence of thirteen political parties that are free to associate and publish. The State Minister for Parliamentary Affairs added that it is unbelievable that the parliamentarians talk about the succession of power because it is elections and not governmental decrees that bring about political authority, a remark that insulted the intelligence of the parliamentarians. The party that receives the highest votes becomes the ruling party, he added. It is well known, however, that the truth is otherwise: the ruling party gets the highest votes. This notwithstanding, both officials forget, for instance, that one of the most popular movements, the Muslim Brotherhood, is excluded from official representation in government, parliament or party systems, though at times it is tolerated when running under the labels of other parties.[39]

Again, when the Egyptian government wanted to conduct a national dialogue, it basically did so with itself. Thus, 26 of the 40 individuals who were "appointed" by President Mubarak as a preparatory committee to set the agenda for the conference on political dialogue were drawn from the ruling party, al-Hizb al-Watani. Worse still, 237 out of the 279 conferees were from the ruling party; major political blocs were excluded. Though one might understand the exclusion of the radical groups that rejected "inclusionary" policies, one cannot really understand the government's exclusionary policies towards the Muslim Brotherhood, which has exhibited both intellectually and politically inclusionary tendencies through its acceptance of pluralism and democracy as well as the legitimacy of the regime. So who is dialoguing with whom? The Muslim Brotherhood (al-Ikhwan al-Muslimun) sought to be included in the much publicized national dialogue during 1994. While the government refused to allow official representation of the Muslim Brotherhood in that dialogue, the Brotherhood tried to participate through its unofficial representatives in professional unions such as lawyers, medical doctors, and engineers. The Muslim Brotherhood's view on the dialogue can be represented by what Ahmad Sayf al-Islam Hasan al-Banna, the general secretary of the Lawyers' Union and the son of the late Hasan al-Banna, the founder of the Muslim Brotherhood, had said about the national dialogue, namely that the Muslim Brotherhood would be willing to participate in the dialogue if the government were to include them. But the government denied them participation and pressured political parties to disassociate themselves from the Brotherhood. The Brotherhood's view was that though excluded as a political party, it could still be included as a representative of civil society. Instead, the government resorted to sweeping security measures; which also targeted the Muslim Brotherhood; these resulted in the death of a pro-Ikhwan lawyer while in police custody, an incident that provoked a strike by the Lawyers' Union and direct confrontation with the security forces in 1994.[40]

Ma'mun al-Hudaybi, the spokesman for the Egyptian Muslim Brotherhood, said in an interview that the exclusion of the Muslim Brotherhood from the dialogue along with independent fundamentalist thinkers, such as Muhammad al-Ghazali, was an example of the exclusion from public life of those who did not adopt or conform to governmental views. While the government does permit some thinkers to attack religion, it does not allow any open criticism by "slanderers" who attack religious thought and religious figures. He characterized the cause for violence in Egypt as being the result of governmental policies; for when the individual "finds no door open, he will destroy the wall [to get out of prison]. The one who thinks of destroying the wall is the prisoner. But those who find the door open but try to break the wall are very rare." In other words, being excluded from peaceful participation in political and public affairs, some groups were bound to be turned into radicals, because of the "closed-door policy". He expressed the Brotherhood's opinion that they were oppressed because of governmental prohibition on holding public meetings, an act the government considers a mutiny against the state.[41]

Following the same line of thinking, Muhammad Salim al-'Awwa, a moderate fundamentalist thinker, lawyer and university professor, puts the problem of exclusion in the following way: the government imposed novel kinds of laws such as the law against terrorism, emergency laws, the Law of Shame (al-'ayb), and the Values Court (for the violation of social norms) in order to hinder society from moving ahead. Again, political parties in the Arab world have been of two sorts: governmental parties that were made by and serve the government but did not represent the majority, even when claiming to do so, and the other kind of party, which may be unlicensed such as Egypt's Muslim Brotherhood or one that is recognized by an Arab government such as the Muslim Brotherhood in Jordan. The latter kind had to be encouraged and sorted out. However, this was not the case. But would the establishment of a recognized fundamentalist party in Egypt resolve the problem of radicalism? 'Adil al-Jawjari argues that the concept of *shura* provides the Islamic movement with a method that allows for peaceful coexistence between the government and an Islamic party. The alternative to radicalism must be a party where fundamentalists can vent their grievances and participate in the political life of Egypt. The containment policy that is being imposed from above by the government has proved futile, and the only meaningful and peaceful solution is the establishment of a legal fundamentalist party where the rights of minorities and political pluralism and other essential issues are part of its constitution.[42]

Though the Muslim Brotherhood published a manifesto in Islamabad – rather than Cairo because the Brotherhood's name could not be undersigned publicly in Egypt – condemning violence and terrorism, which has been its proclaimed public policy, it seems now that neither dialogue nor a political life along with it are developing or leading to any positive changes. The Muslim Brotherhood is being excluded more and more from normal public life, and the prospect of including them under the present regime seems non-existent.[43]

## Outline of the Arguments in this Volume

The objective of this volume is then to analyse certain theoretical and ideological issues brought up in the discussion above as well as a few case studies. It is very clear from the following chapters that Islamic fundamentalist thought and movement must be contextualized internationally, regionally and locally. A mere process of abstraction without due attention to the socio-economic conditions and intellectual and religious milieu leads to the creation of a myth: the "fundie", or "the Muslims are coming", or the East/West divide. While Muslims have their religious particularities, their collective actions are not beyond intellectual, economic, political and cultural analyses. Most chapters converge on the view that much of the popularity and strength of Islamic fundamentalism is mainly socio-economic in nature. They also concur that the intransigence and repression of Arab regimes stoke up radicalism which is a result of desperation and hopelessness. Islamic movements are shown to be capable of being turned into both moderating and reforming forces when the political space is open or radical and destructive forces when the space is blocked. Representative and just governments can go a long way in mitigating socio-economic and political conditions, while more repression and injustice certainly lead to more radicalism and uncertainty. |

Part I of this volume deals with basic theoretical issues that have not been so far treated in depth. In her "*New* New Orientalism: Political Islam and Social Movement Theory", Kristin Wolff shows that the studying of Islamic culture and movements has been mostly based on Eurocentric observations of the "other" The modernized European nation state made itself the centre of the universe, because of its monopoly of power, and therefore claimed to be the owner of "knowledge". The *otherness* of Muslims allowed Europe to dominate the Muslim world; "European knowledge" of the other was derived from its domination. This knowledge of the other arose from prejudice, patriarchy and other unequal power relations – such characteristics are not acknowledged by modern social science theories.

She goes on to show how Western social science is basically founded on Western contexts which are irrelevant to the Muslim world. This left Islamic social movements outside the main structural analysis. The Iranian revolution, for instance, is attributed to Khomeini's power or the Shah's ineptitude. Islamic movements are analysed outside "the global power of structures which made this crisis [the Iranian] possible in the first place". She insists on the need to understand the knowledge-power relationships in order to understand Islamic movements and suggests that orientalism is not a binary variable which can be observed in a few things but is a value-laden process which affects Western studies on Islamic movements. Scholarship and public policy have been carried out in an environment of prejudice and bias. Thus, for instance, she argues that this attitude has viewed Islamic fundamentalism as something inherent in Islam and separated from its context. Media coverage of Islam reinforces the prejudice of scholarship and stereotype of Muslims.

Also, Wolff attributes the problems in studying Islam to the inability of modernization theory and the like to look into contexts other than the Western, and therefore social scientists have failed to live up to their standards. For science has removed itself from its historical context and labelled itself as absolute, but in fact science is historical and subject to the problems that social science suffers from. Thus Islam is given a marginal status in the "scientific" environment, and political activism in the Islamic world is looked at not from a particular social theory point of view but as being Islamic or something beyond analysis. She argues that Islam has been dealt with as if it is outside the realm of rational investigation. She concludes by arguing the point that there is a need now to lift disciplinary boundaries in order to understand religious activism. She suggests employing a few basic concepts for understanding Islamic activism such as contestation, globalization, and empowerment. While criticizing what she called the "development-civil society paradox", she suggests identity-oriented paradigms as being more appropriate to study actors in different contexts and takes the social movements in Algeria as a case study. Algeria's problems could not be understood outside the actor's identity as well as its history. The studying of Islamic movements requires the insights of different social science theories which make the discourses of Islamism easier to understand and, in turn, it might influence theoretical and public issues in the West.

In his "Discursive Contentions in Islamic Terms: Fundamentalism versus Liberalism?", Armando Salvatore argues that while Islamic fundamentalist discourses could be studied from within models of Western modernity, it must not be reduced to its categories. For an analyst must ground such models in "the framework of universal reference" of Islam. The fundamentalist formula, or what he labels as "conflationist", looks at Islam as both a religion and a state, whereas the Muslim reformist formula, or the "deconflationist", rejects the idea that Islam is a blueprint for government and instead looks at the overall purpose of religion. Thus, the hermeneutics of those who perceived Islam as the solution, the fundamentalists or the "solutionists" in Salvatore's new categorization, are compared and contrasted to the reformists or the "neutralists". He compares and contrasts the discourse of the solutionist Yusuf al-Qaradawi, who is intellectually a follower of Sayyid Qutb, with that of the neutralist Muhammad Khalafallah, more or less a follower of 'Ali 'Abd al-Raziq. Salvatore shows that for the solutionist the definition of "true" Islam must be the product of a publicly ordained discourse based on *shura*. The legitimacy of the discourse is derived from public acceptance of the jama'a. For Islam unites theory and practice, and the call for the Islamic state is a call for the implementation of the *shari'a*. In fact, the interpretation of the *shari'a* becomes central in understanding modern fundamentalist discourses since it is not precisely defined but publicly called for. It is "the symbolic medium of Islam's unfolding in human history". Fundamentalism is therefore a natural phenomenon of Islam precisely because it brings to Muslim consciousness a coherent vision. The Islamic state is viewed therefore not as a disruption in history but the logical consequence of the call for the implementation of the *shari'a*. The call for the *shari'a* "functions as the discursive medium for envisioning Islam as the solution".

On the other hand, the reformists or the neutralists use the term "political Islam" to give the impression that Islamic movements corrupted the essence of Islam. Sa'id Al-'Ashmawi, following 'Abd al-Raziq's line of thinking, argues that Islam is a religion and a way of life. Khalafallah denies further that attributional Islam like *al-sahwa al-Islamiyya* (Islamic awakening) or the Islamic state has a solid basis in Islamic scripture. The basis of Islam is faith, which is the sacred essence of religion, while all other issues, especially the social and the political, must relate to the conditions of the interpreter and the community. Thus, a distinction must be made between what is sacred and what is not. For the neutralists see that man cannot really represent God's will on earth, whereas for the solutionist communal will replaces, or acts on behalf of, the divine will. Thus, religion for the neutralists could not be postulated against any form of government or constitution.

Salvatore expounds the fine differences between the neutralists and the solutionists and shows that although these two discursive trends differ immensely, they are nonetheless grounded in the "Arab–Islamic framework of universal reference" where Islam provides the necessary basis of a system of thought. On this both Islamic fundamentalism and Islamic liberalism converge; the essential difference however is that the former view the state as related to the religious and metaphysical, the latter, to the human and historical.

In his chapter on "Islamiyya and the Construction of the Human Being", Ronald A. T. Judy argues that Islam could be included in the sources of a practical philosophy of the New World Order, which is going through a process of reformulation. In particular, Judy shows the fine lines of convergence between Islamism, as particularly advocated by Dr Hasan al-Turabi of Sudan, and Western policies, as envisioned by Western strategists, particularly Brzezinski. Both want to give to the non-material and non-nationalist factors some role in the formulation of politics.

Judy finds no real reason for considering Islamism any more a threat to the New World Order. For Islamism is a development of a mixture of different civilizations, and is led by intellectuals trained in the West, like al-Turabi. While al-Turabi tries to think of Islam as an epistemology, he develops a metahistorical narrative and links Islam epistemologically to modernity. For al-Turabi, Islamism is based on the freedom of individuals to submit to the divine law in light of objective possibilities. Thus a collective process of re-reading history, based on consensus of Muslims, led to the necessity of including capitalism into the modern interpretation of Islam, which al-Turabi and others do.

Part Two of the book deals with case studies. In "State, Civil Society and the Question of Radical Fundamentalism in Algeria" Yahia Zoubir shows that the Algerians' adherence to Islam and to concepts like *jihad* pre-dates the establishment of the new national state and could be found in Algeria's long history of and fights with French colonialism. However, the disruption between the state and civil society is the consequence of the inability of state institutions to truly replace civil groups, functionally and theoretically. Among the problems he deals with are arbitrariness, favouritism and corruption as well as the central issues of legitimacy and social justice. The state, in his view, has failed to deliver the goods it has promised to the people. While the state has also tried to integrate Islam into a revolutionary perspective and has therefore included it in all its constitutions as a source of legitimacy, fundamentalists have infiltrated the state's apparatus.

Zoubir then explains in detail the history and development of Islamic movements, starting with influential thinkers like Malek Bennabi's gradualist and intellectualist approach, to Mahfoudh Nahnah's *harakat al-mujtama' al-Islami* to Abbasi Madani and Ali Benhadj's Islamic Salvation Front (FIS) and the Armed Islamic Movement. Zoubir deals also with the factors that have led to the popularity and radicalization of the Islamic movement in Algeria, which include issues of modernization, repression, defeat of Arab nationalism, economic reforms, redistribution of wealth, the rise of the *nouveaux riches*, the state of Israel, relations with the West, the legitimacy of the regime, the role of the mosques and the *imams*, the Iranian revolution, Afghan mujahidin and others.

He then shows the actual steps in the development of the Islamic movement and its splinter groups and other parties of opposition and their splinter groups. The 1988 events ushered in a period of moral and actual disintegration of the political system into an irreparable phase of legitimacy crisis and economic hardship. The Algerians lost all faith in the elite and pointed to it as the source of corruption and exploitation; and the FIS capitalized on the marginalized groups of the population: in fact the majority. Thus, ideological and social differentiation was overshadowed by religious solidarity and diluted the true nature of the conflicts between state and society. The democratization process by which the state tried to co-opt society benefited the Islamic movement, for FIS took the FLN's ideological discourse of egalitarianism, dignity and independence and re-argued it from an Islamic perspective, claiming that it is the only power that can save the Algerians. Zoubir also goes into an elaboration of the ideology, structure and leadership of the Islamic Salvation Front in order to show that it is not a theological movement but sociological in its call to reorganize society along a set of principles found in the *shari'a*. Its ideology is linked to influential fundamentalist thinkers like Hasan al-Banna, Sayyid Qutb, Muhammad al-Ghazali and al-Mawdudi. It includes also doctrines like the *jahiliyya* and the *hakimiyya* and, of course, the Islamic state. The question of democracy and *shura* and the views of FIS are discussed, and Zoubir argues that one must pay attention to the different democratic and non-democratic groups and elements among FIS. He concludes that the political culture is not conducive to tolerance and civility, it is still patriarchal. Transition to democracy is going to be long and painful, and the concept of civil society must be redefined to include the diverse groups of society along with a just and viable economic policy. The possibility of compromise between the regime and the Islamic movement is steadily becoming greatly reduced, and the possibility of comprehensive civil war is widening. The present political elites cannot any more save Algeria; they are now a major component of the crisis.

While Algeria has failed in its attempts to liberalize and democratize, Glenn Robinson argues in "Islamists under Liberalization in Jordan" that Jordan has succeeded, to an extent, in doing so. He provides us with Jordan's political liberalization programme and outlines the performance of the Muslim Brotherhood and its Islamic Action Front and analyses their major policy announcements. He shows that they have greatly adapted to democratic politics and underscores the problems that the fundamentalists have been facing under the monarchy.

He shows that while the fundamentalists' programme is Islamically argued, the fundamentalist bloc in parliament still played by the rules of the game, but the relationship between the government and the fundamentalists worsened since the 1991 Madrid peace conference. The National Charter acts as a blueprint for the process of democratization, for the fundamentalists accepted Jordanian nationalism, Arab nationalism as well as universal norms which were given somehow equal weight to Islam as sources of legitimacy – this is, theoretically speaking, quite an achievement. However, the state is still capable of manipulating the political system by, for instance, changing electoral laws in order to reduce the number of fundamentalist representatives in the parliament or forcing policies related to education and issues against the fundamentalist agenda. Nonetheless, the fundamentalists keep their own policies open and absorb the pressures from the state. Even on basic questions that relate to Palestine and Israel, Robinson argues that the fundamentalists are opposing the Jordanian policy from within the system. In other words, the politics of inclusion has its positive dividends for the regime and the movement.

Robinson analyses in depth the development of fundamentalist ideology along with the process of liberalization which shows the responsiveness of the Islamic movement to well-directed policies of inclusion. He further shows the root development of its calls for change in the economy, social life, human rights, personal freedom. But still it calls for *jihad* for liberating Palestine and its campaigns against peace with Israel, and the implementation of the *shari'a* might be the most difficult policy problem that both the regime and the fundamentalists must transcend. Nonetheless, Robinson concludes that the Islamic movement has been a force of democratic development and then deals with the issue that might radicalize the moderate Islamic movement.

In his "Islamism and Civil Society in the Gaza Strip", Michael Jensen outlines the modern history of the Islamic social institutions in the Gaza Strip and their proliferation; paradoxically, however, they are not heterogeneous, though the common belief is that the reform of the individual is a prerequisite for the transformation of society.

In "The Development Programmes of Islamic Fundamentalist Groups in Lebanon as a Source of Popular Legitimation" Hilal Khashan shows that the popularity of Islamic movements is due to religious tenets that are seen as relevant to socio-economic actions, which allowed them to attract, through offering essential services, a wide public in the state of Lebanon. After introducing the objective of fundamentalist groups as well as their usage of Islam as constituting a weapon against ruling elites, Khashan considers the pattern of popular legitimation as being basically linked to the ability of fundamentalist Islamic groups to provide services badly needed in the Lebanese community. He discusses the ideological affinities of the two major fundamentalist groups in Lebanon, the Sunni al-Jama'a al-Islamiyya and the Shi'ite Hizbullah. Thus, while the Sunni movement aims essentially at restoring the Islamic caliphate, Shi'ite movements emerged as protest groups along the line of similar Shi'ite groups in Iran and elsewhere. Again, notwithstanding its link to Iran, Hizbullah's popularity is derived from its ability to mobilize the Shi'ites in socio-economic terms, which allowed it to expand beyond other secular Shi'ite groups like Amal, an acronym of Afwaj al-Muqawama al-Lubnaniya (The Lebanese Resistance Detachments).

Khashan conducts an empirical study in order to substantiate the view that the basic popularity of Islamic movements is derived from the socio-economic conditions of the populace, the inadequacy of the state's delivery of essential goods and its inability to satisfy the needs of the people. For instance, he finds out that seventy five percent of Sunnis and ninety percent of the Shi'ites rated the governmental services "less than satisfactory"; ninety percent of the Shi'ites credit Hizbullah with the aid that they receive. From many other similar findings, Khashan concluded that it is very likely that more dissatisfaction with the political system would lead to increased support for fundamentalist groups – which is the present status with the Lebanese system. Then Khashan discusses the reasons behind the real commitment of more Shi'ites to fundamentalism than Sunnis, though, as he found, the percentage of the Sunnis who support fundamentalist groups is higher. What feeds into this dissatisfaction is political instability and bureaucratic corruption. Furthermore, political leaders of Islamic fundamentalist groups are more accessible to the people. Then when compared with other fundamentalist groups in the Arab world, Khashan finds out that they are "relatively quiescent in Lebanon". But he warns that the resolution of the Arab–Israeli conflict will shift the focus of Islamic demands from regional issues to local politics.

On the other hand, A. Nizar Hamzeh argues in "The Future of Islamic Movements in Lebanon" that there are three factors that will shape the future of the movements in Lebanon. These are the socio-economic conditions, relations with Syria and Iran, and the Arab–Israeli peace process. He starts his chapter by drawing attention to the catalysts for increasing the popularity and strength of Islamic fundamentalism such as political and economic stagnation and the Arab–Israeli conflict. However, the Islamic movements in Lebanon are not monolithic and show a high complexity in terms of both ideology and structure, and therefore some distinction must be made between activist militant movements such as Hizbullah and Tawhid and activist non-militant movements such as al-Ahbash. The two sorts of movements differ immensely in terms of looking at concepts and doctrines like *jihad* and *shura* and the relation between state and religion. Also, the complexity of the relationship between Islamic movements and non-Lebanese actors such as Syria and Iran are discussed. Hamzeh shows how the Islamic movements are trying to establish the Islamic state not by revolution but by evolution and by using elections for introducing the desired changes.

The participation of the Islamic movements in the 1992 elections shows both the benefits of inclusion for both the movements themselves and the Lebanese regime; it has simply reduced the radicalism and the uncompromising attitude that Hizbullah, for instance, followed for a long time. The settlement of the Arab–Israeli conflict should further reduce radicalism, but does not necessarily mean the fall of or weakness of Islamic fundamentalism. The roots of Islamic fundamentalism are grown at home but supplemented by external factors. Then Hamzeh elaborates the relationships among Islamic movements and Syria and Iran and concludes that the concerned parties are aware of the possible clash in the future, especially after the completion of the Arab–Israeli peace process. For it is in the interest of all to keep Islamic fundamentalism active in the Lebanese formula in order to balance out, for instance, anti-Syrian feelings. But radicalism would seem in the future less appealing to all, including Hizbullah. Still, the fate of radicalism in Lebanon depends to a large extent on fundamentalism in the religion; a fundamentalist takeover in Syria would change the Lebanese political formula and the role of the Islamic parties. Also, the weakening of President Rafsanjani's wing of Kawadır al-Bina' in Iran may mobilize the radical wing which has been neutralized for some time. However, the election of Muhammad Khatami as president signifies, for the time being, the continuation of

Rafsanjani's moderate line. For the time being, the fundamentalists have shifted grounds from ideological confrontations with other Lebanese to pushing for social and economic reforms as part of their political platform. Therefore Hamzeh concludes that real stability in Lebanon will depend on charting a just economic policy.

The state of the economy seems to be also focal in Michel Nehme's chapter "The Islamic–Capitalist State of Saudi Arabia: Surfacing of Fundamentalism". Nehme analyses the course of actions and reactions by both the "religious fundamentalists" who still demand the total application of the *shari'a* and the "Muslim Liberals" who are essentially materialist in terms of their political conduct and are the product of capitalist modes of economic development and consumption. The two trends are jockeying for status within the political establishment in Saudi Arabia. The gap between the two is growing wider, which is creating for the royal family tension in all spheres: economic, political and social.

Nehme starts out by indicating the impact of ideology and history of Wahhabi fundamentalism on the Saudi state and shows that the early revolutionary zeal of Wahhabism is still lurking in some tribes and groups, as evident from their attempt to take over the Grand Mosque and their actions during and after the Second Gulf War, from opposition to the United States to the introduction of consumerism and bank interest. Such hard core Wahhabi fundamentalist groups could use the regime's ideological legitimacy to topple it. What makes Wahhabi fundamentalism more appealing for many is that the rapid and sudden socio-economic transformations and weakening of tribal affiliations might lead to strengthening the religious symbolism as a force for expressing opposition and for checking Saudi development along Western lines.

The difficulty lies also, according to Nehme, in the royal family's inability to amalgamate Islamic values with capitalist modes of production and development. The capitalist mode has instead alienated quite a few members of tribes, which could become the hotbed for revolutionary fundamentalists. Nehme sees that the establishment of the Consultative Council and the promulgation of the Basic System of Rules in 1992 is crucial for understanding anxiety within the royal family at the growing public demand to participate in the decision-making process. While such a demand is still argued in Islamic terms, it stems from economic modernization. For instance, many young Saudis who are educated abroad or inside the Kingdom demand a greater say in running the state. In other words, the exposure to the West is leading both the fundamentalists and the reformers to ask for more say in the decision-making process. Then Nehme analyses major articles in the Basic Rules and finds that while they ignore many rights such as those of expression and association they do in fact raise expectation of political participation. What adds to this tension is that the Saudis suffer a collective sense of insecurity, notwithstanding their material achievements. While the two trends do not challenge the powers of the king, and are not at this point in time revolutionary, the royal family seems to be more geared towards placating the fundamentalists, because of the legitimacy issue. Nehme concludes that while there is no imminent takeover, the royal family has been put in a difficult position trying to balance the modern and traditional forces: the well-being of Saudi Arabia requires modernization along capitalist lines while its legitimacy needs stricter adherence to Wahhabi fundamentalism.

In "Causes for Fundamentalist Popularity in Egypt" Mirna Hammoud explains the factors that have been helpful in the rise of fundamentalist movements in Egypt, which are of socio-economic, confessional, religious, and political nature. On the other hand, she examines the regime's attempt to confront the fundamentalists by following policies that range from liberalization and co-option to extensive repression in addition to extending the use of patronage and the exploitation of differences among radical and moderate fundamentalists.

( Hammoud traces first the origins and nature of Islamic movements and discusses in particular the ideological discourses of two main fundamentalist thinkers of the Brotherhood, Hasan al-Banna and Sayyid Qutb, as well as central fundamentalist concepts of state, *shari'a* and legitimacy. She finds out that the popularity of fundamentalism is due to many internal factors such as the state's retreat from helping society, its adherence to open-door economic policies and the fundamentalists' move to fill the gap by easing socio-economic tensions. Also, fundamentalists have used the rhetorical power of Islam promising a better future, while the state's discourse has been incapacitated by its inability to deliver what it has promised. Moreover, repression has not eased tension or reduced violence, but has produced radical groups) The author concludes that the nature of the Egyptian political system is an important factor in the appeal of Islamic fundamentalism. While the state claims religious law as a basis for its legitimacy, it nonetheless refuses to apply the *shari'a*.

Then Hammoud considers the factors that are working against the rise of an Islamic state. The state, for instance, pursues a policy of liberalization of society and co-option of the moderate fundamentalists, all the while using repression with the radical groups and attempting to divide Islamic groups along the lines of doctrinal differences and political manoeuvring. Also, because it controls the essential and important resources of the country, the state employs a patronage system that forces many groups to pay allegiance to the state; the army, for instance, is a state within a state. She concludes that the fundamentalists are going to be a constant in the Egyptian political equation. However, the Egyptian political order is held firmly. While the Islamic movements have shown a strong capability to mobilize the people and to challenge the prevailing political order, still the viability and longevity of the state depends on its capability of providing the people with their essential needs and becoming more representative. A fundamentalist takeover is not, according to Hammoud, imminent.

## NOTES

1 Sadik al-Azm, "Islamic Fundamentalism Reconsidered: A Critical Outline of Problems, Ideas and Approaches", *South Asia Bulletin*, Comparative Studies of South Asia, Africa and the Middle East, Part I, Vol. XIII, Nos. 1 & 2 (1993), pp. 93–121, Part II, Vol. XIV, No. 1 (1994), pp. 73–98.

2 See Ahmad S. Moussalli, "Two Tendencies in Modern Islamic Political Thought: Modernism and Fundamentalism", *Hamdard Islamicus*, Vol. XVI, No. 2, Summer 1993, pp. 51–78 and "Hassan al-Banna's Discourse on Constitutional Rule and Islamic State", *Journal of Islamic Studies*, Vol. 7, No. 4, 1993, pp. 161–74.

3 "Fear of Fundie", *The Economist*, 15 February 1992, pp. 45–6.

4 "Abraham's Other Children: Islam as Enemy of the West?" *Policy Review*, no. 50. "Is Islamic Fundamentalism a New Red Scare?" *New York Times*, 26 January 1992.

5 "Washington's Algerian Dilemmas", *Washington Post*, 6 February 1992.

6 *Washington Post*, 19 January 1992. For a refutation of such a widespread argument, see Augustus Richard Norton, ed., *Civil Society in the Middle East* (Leiden: Brill, 1995), especially Chapter Three, "Modern Fundamentalist Discourses on Civil Society, Pluralism and Democracy".

7  David Ignatius, "Islam in the West's Sights: the Wrong Crusades?" *Washington Post*, 8 March 1992.

8  *New York Times*, 26 January 1992.

9  *Washington Post*, 28 February 1992.

10 *Current Affairs*, February 1993.

11 *Al-Hayat*, 9 March 1993.

12 *Al-Safir*, 10 March 1993.

13 Ibid., 7 February 1993.

14 Ibid., 16 March 1993.

15 *Al-Hayat*, 6 March 1993.

16 *Al-Hayat*, 13 March 1993 and Ahmad Moussalli, *Islamic Fundamentalist and World Order* (in Arabic) (Beirut: Center for Strategic Studies, 1992), pp. 94–5.

17 For similar images see also *New York Times*, 1 January 1992, "Muslim Militant Big Concern"; *Washington Post*, 31 January 1992, "US Fears Sudan Becoming Terrorist"; *Wall Street Journal*, 16 March 1992, "Islamic Fundamentalism's Rise in Sudan Sparks Concern over Movements' Spread"; *New York Times*, 6 February 1992, "US to Counter Iran in Central Asia".

18 "Will Democracy Survive in Egypt?" *Reader's Digest*, Canadian edn, December 1987, Vol. 131, No. 788, p. 149; "The Arab World where Troubles for the US Never End", *US News and World Report*, 6 February 1984, Vol. 96, p. 24; "The Clash of Civilizations", *Foreign Affairs*, Vol. 72, No. 3, Summer 1993, pp. 22–49.

19 This second section is largely based on my Introduction to *Islamic Fundamentalism: Radical and Moderate Theories of Knowledge, Ideology, Society and Politics*. See also Timothy D. Sisk, *Islam and Democracy* (Washington, D.C.: United States Peace Institute Press, 1992), p. vii.

20 *New Perspective Quarterly*, Vol. II, No. 2, Spring 1994, pp. 20–37. The articles are: Kanan Makiya, "From Beirut to Sarajevo: Can Tolerance be Born of Cruelty?"; Hahar Ben Jelloun, "Laughing at God in North Africa"; Farida Faouzia Charfi, "When Galileo Meets Allah"; Tariq Aanuri, "Justice is the Strife"; Naguib Mahfouz, "Against Cultural Terrorism".

21 Ibid., p. 3.

22 "Media Mongols at the Gate of Baghdad", *New Perspective Quarterly*, Vol. 10, No. 3, Summer 1993, p. 10.

23 "The Islamic-Confucian Connection", Ibid., p. 19. See also, "The Clash of Civilizations", *Foreign Affairs*, Vol. 72, No. 3, Summer 1993, pp. 22–49. For similar attitudes see "Will Democracy Survive in Egypt?" *Reader's Digest* Canadian edn, December 1987, Vol. 131, No. 788, p. 149 and "The Arab World where Troubles for the US Never End", *US News and World Report*, 6 February 1984, Vol. 96, p. 24.

24 Ibid., p. 21.

25 Judith Miller, "The Challenge of Radical Islam", *Foreign Affairs*, Vol. 72, No. 2, 1993, pp. 54–5 and see the complete article, pp. 43–55. In the same vein see

Bernard Lewis, "Islam and Liberal Democracy", *The Atlantic Monthly*, February 1993, pp. 89–98.

26 "One Man, One Vote, One Time", *New Perspective Quarterly*, Vol. 10, No. 3, Summer 1993, p. 49.

27 Ibid.

28 "Inclusion Can Deflate Islamic Populism", Ibid., p. 50.

29 Ibid., p. 51. For studies that deal with similar issues and on the relationships between political elites, Islamists and the West, see Ghassan Salame, "Islam and the West", *Foreign Policy*, No. 90, Spring 1993, pp. 22–37. See also Dale Eickelman, "Changing Interpretations of Islamic Movements", *Islam and the Political Economy of Meaning*, ed. William Roff (London: Croom Helm, 1987), pp. 13–30.

30 William Zartman, "Democracy and Islam: The Cultural Dialectic", *Annals, AAPSS*, 524, November, 1992, p. 191.

31 John Esposito and James Piscatori, "Democratization and Islam", *Middle East Journal*, Vol. 45, No. 3, Summer 1991, p. 434. Along the same lines of argument, see Gudrun Kramer, "Islamist Democracy", *Middle East Report*, Vol. 23, No. 4, July-August, pp. 2–8.

32 Gudrun Kramer, "Liberalization and Democracy in the Arab World", *Middle East Report*, Vol. 22, No. 1, January–February, 1992, p. 25 and see also pp. 22–4.

33 *Al-Hayat*, 24 April 1993, p. 19. See Alexander Flores, "Secularism, Integralism and Political Islam", *Middle East Report*, No. 183, July–August, 1993, pp. 35–8.

34 *Al-Safir*, 2 April 1993, p. 8.

35 *Al-Hayat*, 3 June 1993, p. 8. See also Flores, "Secularism", pp. 32–3. See also *Al-Diyar*, 22 July 1994, p. 14.

36 For details on this issue see *Al-Safir*, 10 June 1993, p. 1 and *Al-Safir*, 16 June 1993, pp. 1 and 10. On the views of the Mufti of Egypt on violence, see *Al-Wasat*, 11 November 1993, No. 94, pp. 21–9.

37 *Al-Safir*, 10 July 1993, p. 10. His books include *Al-Imam al-Shafi'i and the Foundation of Moderate Ideology* and *The Concept of Text: A Study in Qur'anic Sciences*.

38 Ibid. On the latest figures, see *Al-Wasat*, 25 July 1994, pp. 4–5. All sentences are not given by the regular courts; 56 of the 58 death sentences are given by martial courts; the other two by the higher courts of national security (emergency court).

39 *Al-Safir*, 3 April 1993, p. 10. Muhammad Salim 'Awwa, *Fi al-nizam al-siyasi li al-dawla al-Islamiyya* (Cairo: Dar al-Shuruq, 1989), pp. 85–113.

40 *Al-Hayat*, 4 February 1994, p. 7. See also the five long and diversified articles and dialogues that *Al-Hayat* serialized, from 2 August–5 August, under the title "Civil Society in Egypt and the Arab World". On interest in democracy in the Arab world and the resistance of the governments to such a society, see for instance, *Al-Hayat*, 4 August 1993, p. 19, and 25 September 1993, pp. 14 and 17.

41 *Al-Shu'la*, No. 26, March 1993, p. 38; see also pp. 39–40.

42 *Al-Hayat*, 3 August 1993, p. 19 and, *Al-Hayat*, 3 February 1994, p. 17. On the democratic changes that have been taking place in the Arab world and North Africa, see Lisa Anderson, "Liberalism in Northern Africa", *Current History*, Vol.

89, No. 546, April 1990, pp. 145–6, 148 and 174–5. See also on the state of democracy in the Arab world, Hilal Khashan, "The Quagmire of Arab Democracy", *ASQ*, Vol. 1, No. 1, Winter 1992, pp. 17–33. Consult also John Esposito, "Political Islam: Beyond the Green Menace", *Current History*, Vol. 93, January 1994, pp. 19–24. Al-Jawjari's views are contained in his book *al-Hizb al-Islami* (Cairo: The Arabic Center for Journalism and Publications, 1993).

43 *Qira'at siyasiyya*, Vol. 3, No. 2, Spring 1993, pp. 197–8. *Qadaya dawliyya* published the manifesto in its March issue of 1993.

# 2

# *New* New Orientalism: Political Islam and Social Movement Theory

*Kristin E. Wolff* *

A fundamental problem with which theorists and analysts of social phenomena are confronted is that of identifying the "object" of study. When social activity occurs, is it better explained as a function of human agency, such as a charismatic leader arousing a torrent of nationalism among his or her followers, or as a function of structural incentives/constraints, such as a fundamental change in the organization of the means of production? To what degree do these variables interact? The agent/structure decision is a fundamental one because it shapes the questions which logically follow from the characterization of social phenomena, impacts the method with which such phenomena can be analysed and, by extension, bounds the range of conclusions to which the analysis might lead. Theorists of Islamic or Middle Eastern social phenomena, no less than other theorists, confront this issue, but it is situated in the context of cultural differences and unequal power relations which are highly relevant to knowledge production *vis-à-vis* non-Western cultures.

Edmund Burke observes that "[s]*cholarly* concern with the Islamic roots of culture and politics is very recent."[1] (Emphasis added.) All knowledge, and, in fact the criteria with which we identify knowledge as knowledge, is a product of a particular historical moment. The "scholarly concern" to which Burke refers is "very recent" in that while Islam has existed (indeed flourished!) for centuries, it was associated with colonized

* The author would like to thank Dr Gerold Green, Dr V. Spike Peterson and Dr John Voll for their insights regarding the issues addressed in this paper and for their overall support, and Dr Ahmad Moussalli for his editorial patience and perseverance.

[41]

peoples and backwardness at the particular time Western (scientific) knowledge was being constituted, and the spread of Western capitalism was institutionalizing its brand of global hierarchy, rendering processes of industrialization/modernization seemingly inevitable. This situation produced "interests" on the part of those at the top of hierarchies which became, at least in part, constitutive of "knowledge" because knowledge was defined by those in dominant positions. Such a dialectic is important because of the specificity of the knowledge it produces in a context which represents such knowledge as universal. For example, the colonial era (recent memory for much of the world) witnessed the advent of rather arbitrary borders which indicated what territory (and which people in it) was controlled by which European power. Such borders served external interests, but the indigenous populations who so frequently (and often "illegally") transgressed them were identified as uncivilized because they did not acknowledge the legitimacy of such constructions. This Eurocentric observation, one of many, informed European "knowledge" with respect to many indigenous peoples, and served to justify their respective dominant and subordinate positions. Moreover, it illustrates an instance wherein a particular norm, the modernized European nation-state, could be represented as universal (i.e. those lacking such institutions are backward), because the monopoly of technological and industrial power was maintained by those who claimed to "know".[2]

This knowledge–power connection has manifested itself in the "otherization" of indigenous peoples, which, in turn, has justified the exercise of Western dominance over them. Such power relations are intrinsic to our understanding of the "other" and are embedded in the knowledge which informs both our theory and our theorizing with respect to the non-Western world. While much of what constitutes recent "scholarship" with regard to the Islamic world and other non-Western areas may at present be genuine and reflective, it has nonetheless emerged out of a foundation of prejudice, patriarchy and other forms of unequal power-relations which are too easily obscured in the claims of modern social science to objectivity. How does this context colour current research on social phenomena?

### Informing the research question

Because the foundation of social science was constructed in the Western world, continued research on Western social phenomena can assume certain characteristics of structure and agent when analysis occurs in a Western context.[3] Since such a context cannot be assumed to exist outside the Western world, our methodology must change in fundamental ways. Social movement research, for example, is dominated by structural analysis[4] in a Western context. Typical[5] social movements include labour union activism, the civil rights movement and anti-nuclear protests. These movements are assumed to (a) operate in the context of a liberal democracy;[6] (b) challenge the degree of "liberal-ness" in democracy (or its particular manifestation), but not the structure and constitution of democracy *writ large*; and (c) maintain a limited scope – they rarely transgress the boundaries of the nation-state or treat their particular predicament as part of a larger global crisis.

### Informing the method

Such topics lend themselves to structural analysis because the *fundamental* differences between them are relatively few. Research questions arising out of such topics in such contexts are likely to range from issues relating to objectives and strategies, to degree of success and rigour of methods, and are likely to involve comparisons of structural resources.

When we shift to non-Western contexts, however, we are forced to rethink what we mean by "social movement" (the more difficult task) or shift to questions of agency (the simpler and more popular one). For example, despite the plethora of analysis on the Iranian Revolution of 1978–79, little work addresses the question of how this event might be implicated in, or indicative of, a larger crisis related to the maldistribution of resources worldwide or the nature of community in a changing (industrializing) society. Instead, the focus remains largely on specific agents.[7] Common explanations became the charisma of Khomeini, the ineptitude of the Shah or the susceptibility of Iranians to particular ideologies. Even where we do find historical specificity, rarely do we see analysis of the *global* power structures[8] which rendered such crises possible in the first place. Because it is particular knowledge which informs not only our selection of subjects, but also the very questions we ask, power relations are embedded even at the most basic levels of seemingly apolitical research. While such observations do not invalidate current social science research and methods *en masse*, they do contextualize them, and in doing so, create discursive space for "others" (subjects and perspectives), which add depth and significance/value to the project of social scientific inquiry. Moreover, the acknowledgement of the knowledge–power relationships which create the need for such space serve as an important backdrop for an evaluation of social movement theory as a lens through which to view Islamic movements. Why a new lens?

When Edward Said published his now famous critique of Orientalism[9] and those who practise it, a critic in the *Jerusalem Post* noted that Said's work was "bound to usher in a new epoch in the world's attitude to Oriental studies and . . . scholarship". There was reason for optimism. Said's work, even if at times overstated, rendered *overt* the previously obscured connection between knowledge and power. Said argues:

> Orientalism [is] ultimately a political vision of reality whose structure promoted the difference between the familiar (Europe, the West, "us") and the strange (the Orient, the East, "them"). This vision . . . created and then served the two worlds thus conceived.[10]

He then points out that this dichotomous characterization tends to "polarize the [East–West] distinction – the Oriental becomes more Oriental, the Westerner, more Western – and limit the human encounter between different cultures, traditions and societies."[11] Said demonstrated the various ways in which the phenomenon of Orientalism became a self-fulfilling prophecy, creating and reinforcing dichotomies between "us" and "them", and informing *attitudes* on every social issue from health to international relations, and by extension, scholarship and public policy.

While Said's work had a profound impact in particular branches and sub-fields of the social sciences (even beyond those associated with Middle East studies), we did not witness a new epoch. Instead, a discourse emerged around *the existence of the notion Orientalism* itself, entirely ignoring Said's call for critical reflection in scholarship. Orientalism is not a binary variable by which we can test for presence or absence; it refers to the *process* by which value-laden descriptions are "bought and sold" as objective truths, and become implicated in prejudices and biases which inform scholarship and public policy. I argue that this discourse has changed shape during the last decade and currently manifests itself in what might be called "Islamism", or, the tendency to perceive the rise in Islamic political activism as something inherently or essentially rooted in the religion of Islam.

One scholar of Islamic studies, Dr Ralph Braibanti, lectured on this topic in the spring of 1994. Dr Braibanti displayed a four-foot by six-foot enlargement of the 19 November 1990 cover of *The National Review* magazine as an illustration of the kind of misinformation about Muslims which is pervasive in much of mainstream media and scholarship. This cover depicted what appeared to be an army of white-robed Muslim warriors on camels and proclaimed, "The Muslims are Coming! The Muslims are Coming!" The picture invoked symbols of every negative stereotype of Muslims, Arabs, Middle Easterners, which comes to mind; and the message was clear: these people are dangerous, irrational and unpredictable *because* they are Muslims. The picture had been taken at a camel race.

There are countless other examples of this kind of distortion in the popular media,[12] but there are also too many examples in academia. Emmanuel Sivan's *Radical Islam*,[13] for example, identifies the current state of Islam, "doom and gloom", as the precursor to Islamic activism – Islam, not economic deprivation, not social stagnation or global power relations – Islam is seen as the variable which is responsible for recent political activism. "The Islamic wave is sweeping over every nook and cranny," he notes[14] as if there is one Islam and without noting the object: every nook and cranny *of what?* While he acknowledges Said's notion of Orientalism in a chapter on authenticity, he dismisses the complexity of the *process* to which I referred to above.

Bernard Lewis's *Islam and the West*[15] is similarly disappointing. Lewis offers a scathing critique of Said and *Orientalism*, but he employs the same kind of (problematic) essentialism to which Orientalism speaks. He argues that although "Europe and Islam" (the title of his first chapter) do not at first appear to be symmetrical terms, they really are because of the way Muslims perceive Islam. Similarly, the "West", he notes, is the secularized (i.e. "modern") term for Christendom, rendering the terms in the title similarly symmetrical.[16] These clever justifications allow Lewis to establish dichotomy between the West and Islam and employ it throughout the book, thereby reifying differences and essentialist identities (even where he claims otherwise) and laying the foundation for the civilizational discourse brought to the fore by Samuel Huntington.

Huntington's original piece entitled, "The Clash of Civilizations – Or, the West Against the Rest", was published, in its short form, on the OP-ED page of the Sunday *New York Times*, 6 June 1993. Later, it was published in full in the Summer edition of *Foreign Affairs*. In this work, Huntington draws evidence from recent ethnic conflicts in an attempt to argue that these cultural divisions will be the source of conflict in the new world order. "The fault lines between civilizations", he notes, "will be the battle lines of the future."[17] His thesis is of particular interest to scholars of Middle Eastern studies because he specifically cites Islam[18] as a threat to Western interests. While providing little evidence that the increased violence we have seen since the break-up of the former Soviet Union (in Muslim regions) can be attributed to Islam itself, Huntington nonetheless carves out what he identifies as the geographic region in which we find the "Islamic civilization", informing us that "Islam has bloody borders."[19]

Despite the numerous (and well deserved) critiques Huntingon's piece provoked,[20] his civilizational discourse has infiltrated mainstream media and public policy.[21] He has again lent credence to the idea that there exists some "essence" of Islam which is conspiratorial, dangerous and utterly different from "the West". This is an old debate. The more relevant issue involves moving from debates over "Orientalism-or-not" to those involving issues and literature specifically focused not on the Middle East or Islam, but on issues which scholars of the Middle East and Islamic world are concerned with.

While the extent to which early 20th century social science, particularly modernization theory and the like, was (is) Western and Euro-centric is well-documented, there is a serious lack of interdisciplinary communication and cooperation which might lead to the development of better theories. Why? One reason, as I have implied, is that social science disciplines were defined and constructed *in* the Western world and utilized methods appropriate *for* the Western world. More importantly, as Western social science embraced the methods of the behavioural revolution, it eliminated, however inadvertently, issues, topics and contexts for which quantitative research methods were difficult or inappropriate, including many of those addressing the Middle East and Islam. A critical look at science reveals its biases.

## The "Scientizing" of the Social

The behavioural revolution sought to transfer scientific method to the social sciences in an effort to increase the precision of the meaning and use of terminology and the reliability and validity of social science data, and to expand the discipline's explanatory power and predictive capability. While the process of creating social "science" did produce new insights and better data, its practitioners were not sufficiently critical of the scientific method itself or of its capacity to explain social phenomena. New research questions became increasingly limited because of the need for objective data.

Paul Feyerabend points out that "the sciences especially are surrounded by an aura of excellence which checks any inquiry into their beneficial effect . . . [this aura] ennobles [science] but . . . also remove[s] it from the domain of critical discussion."[22] That is, science assumes[23] the existence of the subjectivity/objectivity dichotomy, and claims that objectivity, which it pretends to represent, will, by definition, reveal "truth". It then excuses itself from the same rigorous analysis to which it subjects everything else, because science believes, and has successfully convinced other fields to believe, that it sets the standard by which the quality of methodological/theoretical inquiry should be judged.

Feyerabend is not the only critical thinker to express such a view. Harding asks, "Is it ironic that natural science, presented as the paradigm of critical, rational thinking, tries to suffocate just the kind of critical rational thought about its own nature and projects that it insists we must exercise about other social enterprises?"[24] Dallmayr and McCarthy refer to the "claim of empirical science to absolute supremacy".[25] Such claims emanate from science's efforts to "know" the objective world through collection and interpretation of data. The content of this "data", however, reflects a particular bias which privileges one kind of knowledge: that which is "scientific".

Science, too often, assumes data to be objective. Scientists' claim to truth rests on their accumulation of proof based on that data which is *observable*. There are at least two unstated assumptions in this claim: first, that there exists a distinct subject/object separation which allows the scientist to observe reality without affecting it; and second, that observable facts – those which can be seen, smelled, tasted, touched, heard or counted – represent truth.

Sandra Harding is not alone, however, in pointing out that the identity of the observer often *determines* what he/she observes. Critical theorists refer to this notion as *standpoint epistemology*.[26] Rooted in the Hegelian idea that the "slave" sees more than the "master" because of his/her structural location, standpoint theory offers a critique of both the subject/object dichotomy (as well as dichotomies more generally), and the claim of the existence of empirical proof. Standpoint assumes the existence of an observer, and that the observer possesses an identity. Such an identity is constituted both in biology and environment. The latter is not static, but constantly evolving. The identity of the observer, therefore, changes with each new experience. Such changes affect the observer both in terms of what he/she looks for and what he/she sees. Standpoint theory (re)introduces relativity to science, thereby undermining its claims to seeking/finding "truth", and disputing the existence of an Archimedian position.

In claiming objectivity, science removes itself from the very historical context in which it was produced, thereby denying that it is, at least in part, a social construction. Modern science emerged from a particular set of historical conditions which directly impacted both its practice and practitioners, and, by implication, the direction it would take.

Moreover, as science becomes increasingly specialized, fewer people in the social world are able to critically evaluate its findings, thereby contributing to the creation of the "aura of prestige" which surrounds it. In an effort to gain access to the same privilege afforded the natural sciences, latter 20th century social scientists adopted the methodology of the "hard" sciences, including the use of rational, deductive reasoning under conditions of assumed objectivity.

As we have just shown, however, science *itself* fails to live up to its own standards. The social "sciences" are, in part, "ideologically constituted in the sense that they [are] based on false beliefs about what the physical sciences [are]".[27] The *social* "science" tradition, therefore, is subject to the same structural critiques articulated above, but to an even greater degree because of the following particularities: (1) the subject matter is a complex weave of mutually constituted (and constituting!) agents and structures, of which the social scientist is a part; (2) whereas some degree of control is possible in the physical sciences, the laboratory of the social scientists is without boundaries, making efforts at establishing control groups an exercise in futility; and (3) simple observation will not reveal some of the most important human characteristics, many of which belie "rational" interpretation, determining political behaviour in a given environment.

Such a critique of science reveals the multiple ways in which the Middle East and Islam were relegated to marginal status in an increasingly scientific environment. First, "hard" data about the developing world is considerably more difficult to come by than that which describes the industrialized West; such data also tends to be less accurate. Second, and more importantly, the scientific method tends to be more effective in revealing how actors *act* than how they are *acted upon*. This places constraints on the research questions social scientists are capable of investigating with positivist methodologies. In the case of Islamic political activism, data reveals the increased numbers of people appearing to adhere to Islamic movements and the increased frequency of such activity, but is unable to account for the Islamic variable.

More often than not, the result is that the *non*-Middle East specialist (Huntington) *assumes* political activism in Islamic countries to be *Islamic*,[28] (read "irrational", or "to be feared"), while the Middle East specialist either provides a religious context using Qur'anic passages and the work of Islamic scholars (Bassam Tibi) or provides a social/economic/historical context which addresses mainstream disciplinary debates, but does so in a way which explains one or more anomalies, leaving wider theoretical discourses unaffected (James Piscatori/John Esposito). The ways in which the topic of Islamic political activism is restricted to primarily Middle Eastern scholarship is, at least in part, a direct result of disciplinary reliance on the rationalism of the scientific method. This rationalism, while appropriate in many contexts, is inadequate for *comprehensively* addressing complex, critical issues, including Islamic political activism.

## Removing Disciplinary Boundaries

In addition to these (external) epistemological arguments *against restricting* the disciplinary boundaries within which we "locate" the study of Islamic political activism, a case can be made *for expanding* these boundaries based on characteristics intrinsic to the movements themselves and the contradictions in which they arise. In a comprehensive five-volume study[29] referred to as the "Fundamentalism Project",[30] editors Marty and Appleby compare ninety-five cases across seven religious traditions. Although the analytical comparison will be published in the fifth volume, there is at least a strong implication in the nature of the project itself that such movements do have certain themes in common, regardless of whether or not they happen to be Islamic. While their work brings the topic of Islamic political activism into mainstream literature on religious movements, other scholars argue that *religious activism*[31] *itself* should be placed within the domain of analysis on social movements/activism. Robertson and Chirico posited, in 1985, the existence of a global religious resurgence:

> In recent years we have witnessed a remarkable occurrence of religion-connected sociocultural phenomena across the globe; notably, a resurgence of religious "fundamentalisms", many of them emphasizing the intimacy of religious and political issues . . . It is argued [here] that the globality of the resurgence of religious and quasi-religious concerns can only be understood in sociological terms by establishing an analytical schema which grasps . . . global circumstances . . .[32]

What is so remarkable about this piece is that it addresses the same issues as do numerous accounts of Islamic "fundamentalism", (i.e. *How are socio-economic circumstances implicated? Of what significance is group identity? How does tension between the secular and non-secular versions of the good society affect political life?* etc.), but it does not once, to my knowledge, employ the word Islam. In fact, the authors clearly have Christian fundamentalism in the US and Europe in mind as these serve as the main referents. The closest the authors come to Islam or the Middle East is to mention each of Iran, Pakistan and Israel in the same sentence. Moreover, despite its critical perspective, the piece lies well within the sociological analytical tradition even though its specific subject matter, religious "fundamentalisms", crosses multiple disciplinary boundaries.

In 1988, Richard Falk argued that "ours [is] a period of unexpected, varied, and multiple resurgence of religion as a political force".[33] He posits that politicized religion is a form of post-modern[34] protest against the mechanization, atomization and alienation of the modern world. Religion, he argues, provides the materials with which to move beyond purely instrumental rationality and address "core issues of the current human situation".[35] What is important about Falk's piece, in addition to its theoretical insight, is that he does cite Iran as an example of the kind of religious movement to which he refers,[36] and he *compares these movements to the new social movements as discussed by Boggs, Cohen,*

*Touraine and other sociologists.*[37] Falk's work is a further contribution in the effort to add the subject of "religious" politics, more specifically *Islamic* politics, to interdisciplinary discourse on political activism.

William Swatos argues that a new sociological approach to what has been called "religion"[38] is required. Swatos identifies three specific limitations: "the *a priori* association between the concept of religion and that of social solidarity"; the failure to contextualize, from the actors' perspective(s), the meaning and actions associated with religion; and the uncompromising divide between what is associated with secularism and its antithesis.[39] He advocates a "situational" approach to the study of the sociology of religion which would acknowledge the diversity of the individuals studied, yet permit integration of structural ingredients, including culture, and go beyond "positivistic scientism" as a method for accounting for all human experience. Under such conditions, the task of the sociologist would not include defining religion, but would instead be to "observe and explain how and why people think and act religiously".[40] Such an emphasis would greatly increase potential shared discursive "space" between sociologists of religion, social movement theorists and scholars of Islamic political activism.

Echo Fields also forges connections between religious activism and structural context. In his analysis of "the New Christian Right", he argues that such activist fundamentalism arises "in response to efforts to deal with contradictions within social systems and to struggles among the state, economy, family and religion to control those efforts".[41] Using Habermas's notions of "legitimation crisis"[42] and "colonization of the lifeworld",[43] Fields argues that activist fundamentalisms can be understood as responses to the structural threats posed by crisis and colonization: they are attempts to reject such colonization and to "create" (whether literally or spiritually) a new "lifeworld". Although Fields's case is an American (Christian) fundamentalist movement, the international dimension of Habermas's capitalist critique speaks to the same issues against which many Muslim fundamentalist groups currently protest.

John Hannigan proposes that "[c]urrent religions and social movements . . . increasingly, have much in common, both structurally and ideologically."[44] He identifies three axes, *contestation*, *globalization* and *empowerment*, along which modern religious and social movements tend to converge. In terms of *contestation*, religious and social movements overlap where they aim to effect change beyond that which can be accommodated by traditional administrative apparatuses. That is, the issues of contestation are not simply matters of policy and procedure, they involve fundamental "lifeworld" questions. Ultimately, activist groups are wrestling for control not over "reigns of power" (although this may occur as a part of the project), but over the process of meaning-making itself.[45]

In identifying *globalization* as an aspect of convergence between religious and social movements, Hannigan is pointing to the challenge such groups pose to the "basic paradigm of an international world order structured on the exclusive relations between states, blocs and military superpowers".[46] This challenge arises as a result of contemporary movements redefining the problems they address in "transnational"[47] terms, and pursuing intervention strategies in similarly international ways.

The "space" which social and religious movements share in terms of the concept of power is the idea that their members can be influential ("empowered") in multiple ways through direct collective action. In contrast to the idea that religious institutions provide *incentives* for their members to participate in collective action as defined by the religious establishment, Hannigan's notion of empowerment[48] "implies a more proactive and emergent view of social and religious movements"[49] than traditional perspectives, and one which can accommodate more than specifically Western, Judaeo–Christian phenomena. Hannigan's conclusion is worth quoting at some length.

> Contemporary social and religious movements . . . can and must be considered within the same theoretical framework. Both are structural by-products of the erosion of boundaries between private and public domains, intrasocietal and transocietal. Both involve the active contestation both of new societal fields and of existing ones that have not been reformulated (e.g.: security, poverty). Both extend beyond any single society or social system and thus cannot be explained by . . . homeostatic approaches.[50]

Marty and Appleby, Robertson and Chirico, Falk, Swatos, Fields and Hannigan are certainly not the only scholars working toward a more meaningful understanding of the phenomenon of religio-political activism, but they do address fundamental issues in ways less Western-centric than others, thereby providing scholars of Islamic political activism with material for building bridges between and across disciplines.

Thus far, I have argued that religious movements, including Islamic political activism, resemble other kinds of collective action, and should not therefore remain a separate category of analysis. Rather, religious activism should be included in the range of topics which theoretical discourse on social movements addresses. But what issues *does* such literature address? And from what methodological perspectives? (Where) is there space for convergence?

## Social Movement Theory

It is the sociologists who have developed the most sophisticated literature on social movements.[51] Classical theoretical perspectives on such movements are of two basic types:[52] the structural-functional approach, the most popular manifestation of which is resource mobilization theory, and the agent-based approach to which Cohen refers as the "identity-oriented paradigm".[53]

### Resource mobilization theory

Because resource mobilization theory (RMT) changed the focus of research on social movements[54] away from the number and intensity of "grievances" of actors to the availability of resources with which actors might address those grievances, it was seen as a radical break from earlier work. As Zald correctly points out, the shift was partly a response to the theoretical challenge presented by the collective action of the 1960s, including student protests, the civil rights movement and feminist struggles.[55] It was also, however, part of a larger shift of the social sciences towards increasingly scientific methods – for structural/functional "resources" were more amenable to quantification than "ideologies" or "grievances".

RMT is rooted in the rational choice framework articulated by Mancur Olson in *The Logic of Collective Action* (1965). Olson's model, based on the economic man-as-actor of classical economics, involves measuring the propensity of a given sample to engage in collective action by employing a cost-benefit analysis of the acquisition of public goods. Olson demonstrates that it is irrational, at the individual level of analysis, for an actor to participate in efforts to secure collective goods because he[56] could reap the rewards of such goods without effort if others are able to secure them on behalf of the collectivity. The central problem in Olson's model, then, is how and why individuals act collectively *at all* if it is irrational for them to do so. This paradox, known as the "free-rider" problem, prompted a shift in focus away from the (internal) individual and his motives to the (external) structures in which the individual acts. The scope of the new research questions became limited to the location, availability and organization of external resources and the mechanisms through which states (and/or other authoritative institutions) facilitated or impeded collective action.[57]

While the rational choice perspective of RM theorists does provide some insight as to the effect(s) of the availability of structural resources such as the media and telecommunications, and the levels of institutional organization (of groups engaged in collective action), the degree to which such a perspective has become dominant far exceeds its (potential) contribution with respect to understanding collective behaviour.[58] The capacity of rational choice to explain social phenomena is self-limited as a result of at least three of its characteristics: (1) the highly individualistic and strictly utilitarian character of the rational man; (2) the centrality of the free-rider problem; and (3) the ethnocentrism (specificity) of the actor and his structural surroundings.

The rational man in Olson and in the work of subsequent RM theorists is far too autonomous and (arguably) entirely void of social context. He is without a sense of personal or civic responsibility or an understanding of the notions of "fairness" or "justice", both of which lie outside the bounds of his decision-making calculus. He evaluates potential activity on the basis of an absurdly limited cost-benefit analysis, for which he is assumed to possess perfect knowledge, and he operates in a competitive and anarchic social "order" in the company of other rational men. The assumptions upon which such a model is based, particularly when it is invoked in social movement theory, beg examining, for "these criticisms are not 'merely methodological'. They have concrete consequences for our understanding of social movements . . . Olson-type models, [although they] claim to *explain* collective action . . . actually make its occurrence a mystery."[59]

With regard specifically to social movements, Myra Feree[60] points to at least three ways in which rational choice presence in RMT obscures our conceptual understanding of social phenomena. First, with the notion of a constitutive "self" absent in each actor, the most effective means of mobilization for collective action is through coercive social control.[61] In contrast, Hirschman[62] points to loyalty – a human trait – as a more effective mobilizer because the level of commitment to the group and/or its goals is not dependent solely on the degree to which an actor secures individual rewards. Second, because RMT/rational choice carries an inherent bias toward the *output* of a given decision, it cannot accommodate ambiguity in the decision-making process itself. This means, for example, that two actors, one blindly devoted to the cause of a given event, and the other coerced into attending the same event, not only are assumed to possess identical levels of commitment to mobilization, but are also assumed to be operating within the same resource-context which presumably prompted such activity. Third, the rational choice model encourages the interpretation of attitudes in ways which preclude growth or change. Preferences are viewed as "pre-existing and stable structures, logically prior to and predictive of behavior".[63] Such logic implies a limited growth potential for formal organizations because of the lack of learning, growth or discovery in which their constituents are assumed to engage. Normatively, this static view of the individual runs directly counter to every trait associated with what it means to be *human*. It denies the importance and effectiveness of all strategies of recruitment from the consciousness-raising efforts of feminists to the letter-writing campaigns of human rights activists. More empirically, it is difficult to envision how strictly goal-seeking individuals could ever mobilize within the logic of RMT because many of the "resources" to which RM theorists point are *learned*. That is, resources must *become* useful; they are rendered useful only through human action because resources themselves are not actors. This rendering of "usefulness" is, at least in part, derivative of human cognition and learning.

RMT/rational choice theorists have become obsessed with trying to explain how this could possibly occur. Multiple internal strategies have been invoked[64] for overcoming this problem. The "free-rider", however, is *only* a problem under a very specific set of circumstances. As Feree points out, for example, "[i]f mother [or parent] and child rather than adult male is seen as the basic human unit, creating community does not seem so fraught with difficulty nor does competition seem the archetypal human emotion."[65]

Kahneman, Knetch and Thaler[66] found that the perception of "fairness", and its importance to the individuals tested, was of particular significance *vis-à-vis* economic behaviour. In fact, Isaac, McCue and Plott found that 25 to 35% of individuals tested *consistently refused self-interested behaviour* at the expense of the group, citing "doing the right thing" as their motive.[67] Sears and Funk[68] find that identification with a particular ideology explains the positions of individuals on specific policy issues better than does an analysis of the cost or benefit which accrues from such policies.

From empirical evidence supporting the existence of "reciprocal altruism"[69] to the fact that a majority of people *still* vote (do not "free-ride") – despite Olson's conclusion that voting, on the individual level, is irrational – there are powerful challenges to the theory of rational choice. The rational man must be contextualized, or everything that is human about him disappears and the central problematic in collective action analysis becomes explaining why individuals are motivated to *enter* a community, rather than explaining how individuals are affected by their associations with multiple communities of which they are *already a part.*[70]

## The Development–Civil Society Paradox

I have already argued that the concept of rationality assumed by RM theorists is overly strict;[71] it is also, in fact, steeped in Western liberalism. When RMT is invoked to explain social movements, it explains only *specific* social movements – namely, those which occur within the confines of the Western liberal democracies of Europe and North America. Because it is then more difficult to ascertain whether or not behaviour is "rational", we are forced into a position of injecting Western bias into our analysis by assuming behaviour which is *different* to be *irrational*, or we undermine the rational actor model as the crux of mainstream social movement theory.

In addition to the resources/means dilemmas discussed above, a spatial/temporal problem also arises when we attempt to transpose Western RMT to non-Western (in this case Islamic) societies. I have called it the *development–civil society paradox.* RMT takes as its structural starting point the existence of civil society.[72] It is precisely this structure which renders the utilization of resources and the mobilization of individuals possible. Civil society, however, varies from non-existent to only semi-institutionalized in most of the world, and is, in fact, the *objective* of the vast majority of recent sustained political activity, worldwide. RMT cannot explain such activity as social movement, because it takes as given precisely what many activists identify as the *goal* of their political activism. Overcoming this problem entails RM theorists' considering that social movements in developing areas might look, sound and behave *differently*. Again, however, such an endeavour risks "othering" such movements or undermining the entire RMT model.

Because RMT only normalizes those forms of collective action which it is able to identify as social movements, it leaves collective action outside this domain (primarily non-Western collective action), to retain, whether implicitly or explicitly, the negative stigma of the non-rational, aberrant-behaviour label associated with Le Bon. If non-Western collective action occurs in a "civilizing society" but retains its negative characterization, then it begs the question "what is *supposed* to occur within the space of civil society?" If not social movement (change), then what? As Alain Touraine points out, "[s]ocial movements are not exceptional and dramatic events [although they may manifest themselves in dramatic ways;] they lie permanently at the heart of social life."[73]

This cultural specificity is indicative of RMT's overall inability to explain the collective action that poses a fundamental challenge to the structure[74] in which it is situated, even though we know that it is precisely such social action which has (historically) given rise to (progressive) social change more generally.

## New Social Movements and "Identity-Oriented Paradigms"

The identity-oriented paradigm represents a range of perspectives including those of Cohen, Boggs, Touraine and Habermas, to name a few. Such perspectives are rooted in the earlier collective action model of Durkheim, but represent a reformulation which is less essentialist with regard to both agent and structure. Modern identity paradigms emerged as a result of the same challenges to which RMT responded – the social unrest in North America and Europe during the 1960s and 1970s. A fundamental difference, however, is that RMT responded to the challenge with new *theories* aimed at better explaining social movements in general, while identity perspectives saw such activity as a significantly *different kind of collective action*, and theorized on the basis of that difference. While both have been characterized as "current", "recent", "modern" and even "new", in Social Movement Theory, as in the case of RMT, "new" refers to "theory", while in terms of the identity perspectives, new refers to the social movements themselves. Henceforth, however, new social movement theory will refer only to identity perspectives.

Although the identity perspectives, like RMT, have been concerned primarily with Western social movements, their theoretical positions render them amenable to multiple contexts. I will discuss the identity perspectives and their potential incorporation of the strengths of RMT, and theorize the development as a lens through which the recent (so-called) Islamic "fundamentalist" movements can be observed.

Identity paradigms are concerned *holistically* with the process of identity formation in social movements. Theorists associated with such work were not interested simply in the interests, motivations and characteristics shared by the members of social movements, but also how such phenomena are developed, communicated and integrated into the identity of the group in a given socio-cultural context. These theorists began to argue that the social movements which were occurring in Europe and North America in the 1960s and 1970s had more in common with each other than with prior social movements. Such an observation prompted a reevaluation of the term "social movement" and its analytical utility.

While it is difficult to sort out the multiple and overlapping ways in which the concept "social movement" is employed, Mario Diani has provided a comparative analysis of the term in which he argues that despite the many varied approaches, there is convergence on at least three points. Social movements can be described as "networks of informal interactions 1) between a plurality of individuals, groups, and/or organizations, 2) engaged in political [and]/or cultural conflicts, 3) on the basis of shared collective identities".[75]

There is significant convergence as to what is *new* about new social movements.[76] Touraine points to the increased socio-*cultural* (emphasis added) aspect of modern social movements.[77] He argues that, at one time, there was some continuity between social movements and political parties because parties could absorb and articulate the demands of the movements; such continuity has broken down because of the state's intrusion into the private sphere and obstruction of the process of extra-state identity formation. Parties can no longer absorb demands because they (along with the state) are implicated in the crises to which social movements are responding.

Habermas identifies cultural reproduction, social integration and socialization as three areas at which the energies of new social movements are directed.[78] Habermas also points to the inability of parties and more conventional channels to accommodate the demands of these movements; but he goes a step further than Touraine and insists that the politics of new social movements will manifest themselves in subinstitutional, extra-parliamentary forms of protest.[79] That is, not only are the *concerns* of new social movements (NSMs) unconventional, but so, too, are their *means of protest*. Even Schmitt-Beck, a more empirical theorist than Touraine or Habermas and a sceptic of the "newness" of social movements, points to the potential social and political innovation of NSMs, implying that such innovation serves to distinguish them from other forms of protest.[80]

While this literature is complex and difficult, Carl Boggs provides a remarkably clear and comprehensive account of NSMs. He argues that NSMs, while rooted in earlier conflicts, are different because they are not primarily grounded in labour struggles or issues of small-scale, tangible distribution.

> [They are] situated within the unfolding contradictions of a rapidly changing order, as part of the historic attempt to secure genuine democracy, social equality and peaceful international relations against the imperatives of exploitation and domination.[81]

Boggs identifies three "shared characteristics" of NSMs. First, NSMs are extra-institutional in that they arise outside the public sphere, rooted instead in "civil society", and usually bypass or de-emphasize traditional power structures; second, they attempt to expand the popular conception of the political sphere to include social, cultural and material interests; and third, they have polarizing tendencies: in attempting to define themselves, they oppose themselves to the "other" (system or ruling party), leaving little room for moderation.

## A Practical Application: The Case of Algeria

While my comments about Algeria are not detailed enough to constitute a "case study", they are nonetheless illustrative of the ways in which a particular lens can serve, or not serve, as a self-fulfilling prophecy. According to Michael Dunn of the International Estimate, Algeria has crossed the threshold from civil unrest to civil war.[82] How is it that a state touted, only three years ago, as among the Arab world's brightest hopes in terms of establishing widespread political participation[83] now finds itself on the brink of civil collapse? What does this situation tell us, or *not* tell us, about how Islam is implicated in such political crises?

While it is difficult, and somewhat arbitrary, to identify exactly when Algeria's current political activism began, such activity gained international attention in the autumn of 1988 as a result of widespread rioting over food shortages. Prior to that time, Algerian politics had been dominated by the FLN (Front de Libération Nationale). For over two decades after the establishment of an independent Algerian state in 1963, the FLN-controlled government had carried out intensive industrialization programmes, while supporting policies which it identified as targeting social modernization (educational expansion programmes, etc.). Although the most powerful state institutions, the military, the party and the state bureaucracy, used rhetoric laden with Islamic symbolism, they were predominantly secular in orientation and permitted the religious establishment considerable autonomy.

This unofficial separation between state and religion had two consequences: it permitted (early on) considerable autonomy in decision-making at the state level; and it facilitated the evolution of an extensive Islamic power base, which operated within the mosque network and was left largely unchecked by state authorities. Such a separation did not constitute a threat during the immediate post-independence period, but the decline in the export value of oil and natural gas in the early 1980s severely restricted the Algerian government's ability to provide basic goods and services. The government began deficit-spending and introduced austerity measures including wage freezes/cuts, reductions in government subsidies and cutbacks in domestic investment. These resulted in such visible manifestations as nationwide food shortages and a suspension of construction, thereby exacerbating the already grave problems of urban hunger and housing shortages.

As Pfeifer[84] points out, however, not everyone suffered equally from belt-tightening. Economic elites were well-insulated from economic hardship, causing an increase in the gap separating the "haves" from the "have-nots". Because there were relatively few economic elites who benefited from government policies that severely threatened the economic health of the vast majority, they were popularly seen as unfairly privileged, and represented, for the masses, an abrogation of the principles of state socialism and Islam which the regime rhetorically advocated in its attempt to secure internal support. Such policies jeopardized the legitimacy of the regime.

Popular discontent culminated in the October 1988 riots. President Chadli Benjedid was forced to institute fundamental change. He legalized competitive political parties through constitutional reform in order to promote such change and to dampen further conflict. The process was clearly ahead of him. Within a few months, seventy parties were in the midst of registering for legal status – clearly, many had been institutionalized prior to official recognition – and over 12,000 political, professional and cultural associations were in place by May of 1990.[85] It was the FIS (Islamic Salvation Front) which benefited most from the change in state (FLN) policy.

## The Popularity of the FIS

The strength of the FIS lies in part in its internal legitimacy. First, despite its short *legal* history, the FIS is not new. Islamic political movements have existed as long as Islam itself.[86] In its modern[87] form, Roberts (1988) suggests that political Islam emerged along with the nationalism of the 1930s and that the precursor to the Algerian FIS emerged in the early 1970s.[88] Algerian Islam has a history considerably longer than that of the modern Algerian state. This fact alone accounts for a good portion of the party's institutional legitimacy.

Second, through the mosque network, the Islamists associated with the FIS were active in the trenches of communities in crisis, and often responded effectively to pressing needs when the government dragged its feet or failed to respond at all. As the ties between the Islamists and the local communities were strengthened, those between the government and local communities faded. Such relationships manifested themselves on several fronts. First, the mosque had always played a central role in the community: it served as a shared public space, a mediator of local conflict and a crisis centre for those in need. As the Algerian government failed (increasingly) to provide, the scope and magnitude of needs grew. In response, the mosques established small bureaucracies in the form of "charitable associations",[89] which became increasingly specialized, eventually providing local employment, education and social services in addition to emergency food and shelter.

The government initially supported such activity; after all, the mosques and associations were only minimally or not at all government funded, but were providing needed services. As the mosque/association network became increasingly institutionalized, it became increasingly efficient in completing visible tasks in the community – from trash collection and construction to education and child care – in order to meet the needs of an increasing, (and increasingly) young, urban population.

Another perspective holds that the Algerian government was initially supportive of FIS activity because it counteracted what the government perceived as a growing Berber threat.[90] This is evidenced by the Arabization legislation passed by the Parliament during the Gulf conflict of 1990/91. While the international media characterized this change as anti-French, local papers carried stories and cartoons about the Berber language/dialects.[91] As the Algerian government began to open the political process, its internal weaknesses were revealed and the FIS began to fill the political void.

I have outlined the structural reasons for the failure of the FLN and the ensuing popularity of the FIS as an economic determinist or an RM theorist might, and have provided a partial explanation. But what about the fact that the FIS claims to be Islamic? Are the mosques simply instrumental networks through which political opportunists work? Or are there other dynamics at work? Structural perspectives tell us much about the incentives which might prompt action, but if they were the only answer, then we should see such activity wherever structural factors are similar; we do not. Moreover, current Islamic political activism is neither confined to Algerians who bear the greatest hardships nor to the state borders which separate Algerians from other Arabs, Africans and Muslims.

Even Mahfoudh Bennoune, former Director of the Algerian Institute of Planning and Applied Economics, admits that "Algeria's current crisis cannot be pinned only on the collapse of oil prices or the three-year drought. It is . . a . . . crisis engendered by [the] regime's policies and practices."[92] "Policies and practices" which de-emphasized the very "values and cultural traditions" to which Brumberg points as one of three factors upon which prospects for a democratic "bargain" will ultimately depend.[93]

## What Role for Islam?

First, it is also crucial to note that the FIS has never been, nor is currently, a monolithic organization. In order to gain widespread support in the 1990 elections, the party managed to accommodate both of its major groups of constituents. Professor Abbasi Madani led the reformist *'ulama'* and intelligentsia in a movement which advocated modernist Islam, calling for pluralism and accommodation. Ali Benhadj advocated a radical Islam which appealed to the concerns of the urban youth.[94] The two leaders coexisted in a corporatist arrangement which emphasized that Islam provides a moral basis upon which to create a new social order on the foundation of a new egalitarian[95] society. This strategy proved successful as the FIS won 32 of 48 regional assemblies, a majority of the municipal councils, and was poised for national victory immediately prior to the military takeover. Whether or not the FIS coalition represents political pluralism is more than debatable, but the differences between various "Islams" reveal the FIS to be an alphabet soup of religio-political perspectives. Theory (NSMT) is useful in sorting out such important dynamics. Second, the complex relationship between Islam and politics reveals that social science has been unable to theorize "the spiritual". While certainly there are rational choice variables at work in social movements, by ignoring the spiritual dimension we miss what is most human about the social world: the quest for meaning and search for order. NSMs' emphasis on the identity of the agent and the dynamics of group cohesion is one theorization of "the spiritual" in a way that might be accommodated by "rational" social science. A related point flows from Fred Halliday's claim that the "right to difference must apply as much *within* as *between* cultures, religions and ethnic communities".[96] Fundamentalist movements may be, in part, manifestations of efforts to create identities from "the inside" of groups which, from "the outside", are presumed to already exist. NSMT provides the theoretical tools with which such complexities might be sorted out, thus linking the problem of Algerian (or other) identity within Islamic political activism to the larger debate surrounding identity and difference.

Third, because NSMT addresses "grievances" in fundamental rather than specific ways, the discontent manifested by SMs can be understood as a response to issues which may or may not be contained within state borders. The emphasis on crisis situations reveals that Algeria's economic, social and human disaster is not solely Algeria's creation, nor do such phenomena stop at Algeria's borders. One area of inquiry which would most certainly benefit from an exploration of the links between sets of grievances in relation to social conditions and the means through which such grievances are expressed is that relating to women (and gender) in Algeria. Susan Slymovics noted, in a recent *Middle East Report*, that women in Algeria have become a primary target in the battle over social space for *both* the Islamic and secular radical groups. This is not new; but how do we place this struggle in a context which imbues it with meaning? NSMT is helpful because it reveals multiple agents in complex settings. While numerous women, precisely *because* they are women, have been victims of utterly senseless violence, such violence is a manifestation of the present state of Algerian social (dis)order. It is the (dis)order which should be problematized, not the dichotomous oppressor/victim to which such (dis)order gives rise. The oppressor/victim scenario obscures the agency of the victim (women), and assumes the complicity of the category of men, leaving little possibility for the construction of bridges between them, and removing this particular category of violence from larger debates within and without Algerian society. NSMT is not dependent upon such dichotomies; rather it is focused on the theoretical space between them.

## Algeria's Current Impasse

Since October 1992, there have been intermittent reports that the military regime has been faltering.[97] Whether it remains, or does not, Algerians stand to lose progressively more as the impasse drags on and further polarizes different social groups. The military coup ended the state's role as mediator or "referee", instead pitting antagonists directly against one another.[98] Constant military harassment of, and outright violence toward, the Islamists, including the random "disappearances" and arrests of the leadership of the FIS, Benhadj and Madani, have only further radicalized the religious establishment, ending any prospects for a more moderate FIS. Tens of thousands of Algerians have lost their lives.

While (Western) social science seems far from the tragedy of the political situation on Algerian soil, if such theory informs public policy, as I have shown it has, then the two are intricately connected. I offer NSMT's "situational" emphasis on the actor's identity in a specific context as one way to bridge the gaps between agent-based and structural perspectives, while maintaining the insights of both. It can accommodate structural variables by sorting out the relationships between those variables and how they affect an actor's perception of him/herself and ability to engage in collective action. While NSMT is perhaps less concrete than structural perspectives alone, it might imbue our results with greater meaning. At the very least, such new perspectives would open the subject of Islamic political activism to multiple discourses; it might even yield insight which could inform both theoretical debates and public policy, ultimately helping to alleviate civil strife such as that which plagues Algeria.

## NOTES

1 Edmund Burke III, "Islam and Social Movements: Methodological Reflections", in *Islam, Politics and Social Movements*, ed. Edmund Burke III and Ira Lapidus (Berkeley: University of California Press, 1988), p. 17.

2 Such processes varied hugely, but I am trying to illustrate a point. I acknowledge that I run the risk of vastly over-generalizing, especially with regard to the East–West dichotomy (which is really a fiction), but I do so for analytic purposes only.

3 Feminists, of course, remind us that these assumptions are often not only culturally specific, but also gender-blind. My point, however, is that mainstream topics and methods are more appropriate to "Western" subjects than "non-Western ones".

4 I put Resource Mobilization Theory (RMT) – which I will introduce later in this paper – here because although a charismatic individual might be considered an agent in terms of my earlier reference, RMT assumes the individuals who would respond to such an agent are rational – equally rational. This implies that such individuals might really be responding to a structural grievance or circumstance which the agent addresses. This example also points to the thin line (I would argue "continuum") which separates (characterizes) structure and agent in terms of social movements.

5 New Social Movement Theory (NSMT) challenges this notion that social movements work within "state" or other insitutions/organizations; I will address this later in the paper.

6 I acknowledge the multiple and multi-faceted critiques of liberal democracies in theory and in practice (one excellent one which speaks to both issues is Carole Paterman's *Participation and Democratic Theory* (1970). Merits aside, however, in all liberal democracies, we can, at a minimum, point to some degree of institutional support for widespread participation in decision-making processes.

7 See, for example, Marvin Zonis, *Majestic Failure: The Fall of the Shah* (Chicago: University of Chicago Press, 1991), in which he proposes a psychoanalytic model for studying the Shah (and, by implication, Iranian politics). Richard Cottam noted in a review of the book in *Middle East Journal*, 46:1 (1992), p. 100 that it does not reveal "the dozens of poorly understood but critical episodes in Iranian history", which would have had a profound impact on Zonis's thesis. I am not arguing that Zonis's thesis is "wrong" or even that it is typical in its perspective. Zonis's work does, however, like much analysis on Iran, focus on a specific agent and *not* the the global circumstances to which the Khomeini phenomena responded.

8 Many have pointed to the role of the US in the Iranian modernization experience, but I refer here to larger crises, such as those described by Habermas, Fields, Adams and other critical theorists. These will be introduced later in the paper.

9 Edward Said, *Orientalism* (New York: Vintage Books, 1979).

10 Ibid., p. 43.

11 Ibid., p. 46.

12 Judith Miller's piece (and the accompanying front cover of the *New York Times Magazine*) entitled, "The Islamic Wave"; the countless books published during the Gulf War connecting the brutality of Saddam Hussein with Islam; the emphasis since early 1992 on the Algerian FIS's (Islamic Salvation Front) use of terrorism rather than the military's illegal takeover, etc.

13 Emmanuel Sivan, *Radical Islam* (New Haven: Yale University Press, 1985).

14 Ibid., p. 175.

15 Bernard Lewis, *Islam and the West* (New York: Oxford University Press, 1993).

16 He does not mention that the "West" is now comprised of such a plurality of religions – indeed religious freedom was the primary reason for the original migration to the Americas – that it would be inaccurate to refer to the area as "Christendom". He also does not mention that the (European and American) "state", as an insitution, is thought to command considerably more legitimacy than most Middle Eastern or Islamic states. It is reasonable to suspect that Islam carries more appeal as a label (for Muslims) precisely because it subsumes state legitimacy rather than being subsumed by it.

17 Samual P. Huntington, "The Clash of Civilizations – Or, the West Against the Rest," *Foreign Affairs*, 72:3 (1993), p. 22.

18 More precisely, he cites Islamic and Confucian "civilizations" and the military connection between them.

19 Huntington, "Clash of Civilizations", p. 35.

20 While a discussion of these critiques lies outside the scope of this paper, I feel compelled to cite a few. Ajami states that "Huntington is wrong", and offers a critique of Huntington's cultural determinism; Mahbubani does not quarrel with the idea of civilizations, but he reverses perspectives and addresses the plight of the 4.7 billion "rest" rather than the "paranoia" of the 800 million West; Bartley implicates the practitioners of foreign policy and their advisors (and the elites who read *Foreign Affairs*) in what becomes of the future; Binyan critiques Huntington's idea that "civilizations" are as uniform or as isolated as he assumes thay are; and even Jeane Kirkpatrick identifies Huntington's thesis as "dubious" (see *Foreign Affairs*, Vol. 72, September/October 1993). B. A. Robertson offers a comprehensive critique of the notion of the "Islamic threat" (see *Middle East Journal*, Vol. 48, Spring 1994). Leon Hadar addresses this same issue in his piece, "What Green Peril?" (see *Foreign Affairs*, Vol. 72, Spring 1993). John Esposito places the idea of the "Islamic threat" in a multiple-layer context (social, economic, historical, etc.) in his scholarly work, *Islamic Threat: Myth or Reality?* (Oxford: Oxford University Press, 1992).

21 While I had hoped such a perspective would attract only ivory tower academics, Huntington's piece has been referred to as this generation's "article X"; President Clinton has invoked the language of civilizations; dignitaries such as Vaclav Havel have addressed this topic in public forums inside/outside "the West"; numerous foreign policy experts have drawn from this discourse in forums such as *National Public Radio*, *The McNeil-Lehrer Newshour*, *Good Morning with David Brinkley*, and countless other news programmes and on-air (and on-line) discussion groups.

22 Paul Feyerabend, "Consolations for the Specialist", in Imre Lakatos and Alan Musgrave, eds., *Criticism and the Growth of Knowledge* (Cambridge, U.K.: Cambridge University Press, 1970), p. 209.

23 While I acknowledge the critique that I presume science to have agency, when, in fact, it is merely a concept, in order to alter the language of my argument, I would be forced to identify the systemic powers (elites) which perpetuate the myth of science as truth.

24 Sandra Harding, *The Science Question in Feminism* (Ithaca, NY: Cornell University Press, 1986), p. 35.

25 Fred Dallmayr and Thomas A. McCarthy, *Understanding and Social Inquiry* (Notre Dame, Indiana: University of Notre Dame Press, 1977), p. 3.

26 See Harding, *The Science Question in Feminism*, Chapter 6.

27 Peter T. Manicas, *A History and Philosophy of the Social Sciences* (New York, NY: Oxford University Press, 1986), p. 4.

28 The term "Islamic" in this context implies relating to or emanating from the religion itself rather than a function of the religious establishment.

29 Although there will be five volumes and two shorter monographs in the Fundament-alist Project, for this paper, I referred primarily to volumes 1 and 3, *Fundamentalisms Observed* and *Fundamentalisms and the State* (Chicago: University of Chicago

Press, 1991–93). Volumes 4 and 5 were not yet available at the time I wrote this section.

30 I have serious reservations about the term "fundamentalism" because it is rather "loaded", carrying an enormous number of connotations, many of which are intentionally misleading. In fact, most "fundamentalist" Islamic movements are not fundamentalist at all (in the Christian sense of returning to conservative, literal interpretations of holy scriptures). They are, as I will argue, mass-based responses to the political, economic and social failure of the state; they advocate radical *change* and tend to resemble the Latin American liberal theology movements of the 19th and 20th centuries more than any movement identified as fundamentalist in the Western sense. Marty and Appleby discuss this controversy in the introduction of their first volume. For additional debate, see Ali E. Hillal Dessouki, "The Islamic Resurgence: Sources, Dynamics and Implications", in *Islamic Resurgence in the Arab World*, ed. Ali E. Hillal Dessouki (New York: Praeger, 1982), p. 4; John L. Esposito, *Islamic Threat: Myth or Reality?* p. 7; Bruce B. Lawrence, "Muslim Fundamentalist Movements: Reflections Toward a New Approach", *The Islamic Impulse*, ed. Barbara Freyer Stowasser (Washington, D.C.: Center for Contemporary Arab Studies, 1987), pp.15–20; and Barbara Freyer Stowasser, "Introduction" in Stowasser, p. 7.

31 To my knowledge, none has yet specified that Islamic political activism should be integrated; it is usually relegated to "other" status. The analysis herein demonstrates that such an integration is in order.

32 Roland Robertson and JoAnn Chirico, "Humanity, Globalization, and Worldwide Religious Resurgence: A Theoretical Explanation", *Sociological Analysis*, 46:3 (1985), p. 219.

33 Richard Falk, "Religion and Politics: Verging on the Post-Modern", *Alternatives*, 13 (1988), p. 379.

34 The literature on post-modernism is at present extensive and rather like a minefield. The term resists definition, but for our purposes it is important to note that such a perspective challenges assumptions and rethinks the "taken-for-granted". It is critical of dichotomies and categories, instead of revealing connections and relationships. What could be identified as post-modern discourse/language appears throughout this paper, but debates over *its* essence are beyond my current scope. For a concise (and accessible!) treatment of post-modernism, see Barry Smart, *Postmodernity* (New York: Routledge, 1993). For post-modern debates on specific issues, see Barry Smart, *Modern Contradictions, Postmodern Controversies* (New York: Routledge, 1992). For good general theory with suggestions for applications, see Steven Seidman, ed. *The Postmodern Turn: New Perspectives on Social Theory* (New York, NY: Cambridge University Press, 1994).

35 Falk, "Religion and Politics", p. 382.

36 I feel compelled to remind the reader that neither these authors, nor I, place any *value judgment* on these movements; that is, we cannot assume that a particular group is somehow "good" simply because it protests that which we think is "bad". I am not defending or in any way apologizing for the nature of the religious

resurgence in Iran (or elsewhere). I am merely arguing that it (they) bear(s) resemblance to other religious (and social) movements and should be analysed along more than its (their) Islamic dimension(s).

37 In a later piece entitled, "The Global Promise of Social Movements: Explorations at the Edge of Time" [*Alternatives*, 13 (1987), pp. 173–96], Falk notes that "the place of religion is . . . both uncertain and contradictory" (p. 174), but later in the paper he excludes "fundamentalisms" (providing no definitions/description for them) from his analysis, even though many groups (particularly in North Africa) identified as "fundamentalist" fit remarkably well into his hypothesis. Overcoming this kind of disciplinary/regional studies bias is one of the objectives of this paper.

38 See William H. Swatos, Jr., "Worldwide Religious Resurgence", *Religious Politics in Global and Comparative Perspective*, ed. William H. Swatos, Jr. (New York, NY: Greenwood Press, 1989).

39 "Worldwide Religious Resurgence", pp. 152–3.

40 Ibid., p. 153.

41 Echo E. Fields, "Understanding Activist Fundamentalism: Capitalist Crisis and the Colonization of the Lifeworld", *Sociological Analysis*, 52:2 (1991), p. 175.

42 I will not attempt to summarize Habermas; I will only point to the most relevant aspects of his concept. Habermas sees fundamental contradictions in the theory of modern state capitalism. More specifically, as Fields asserts, "the [legitimation] crises facing advanced capitalism are rooted in the inability of political and economic systems to deliver simultaneously on promises to increase wage and consumption levels, to ensure economic and community stability and to maintain rising profits and growth . . ." (p. 182). Habermas identifies the contradiction between mechanized production (public and for profit) and private accumulation (the market), and the ideology of continued growth. As (state-based) economic systems fail to deliver (because of the hierarchy within the international market), they lose credibility and become targets for social movements. In terms of the subject of this paper, the applicability lies in Habermas's contribution to an understanding of social protest as potentially both *human* (identity-driven) and *rational*. For the real thing, see Jurgen Habermas, *Legitimation Crisis* (Boston: Beacon Press, 1975); Jurgen Habermas, "What Does a Crisis Mean Today: Legitimation Problems in Late Capitalism", in *On Society and Politics*, ed. Steven Seidman (Boston: Beacon Press, 1989).

43 The "lifeworld" of which Habermas speaks is the "intersubjective realm of people's everyday life . . . [consisting] of all of the information that we create and share, such as language and values . . ." (Fields, p. 183). The family is an important site in the lifeworld, but as the state and the economic system create demands *vis-à-vis* the family, the latter becomes "colonized" – invaded by consumerism and rational utilitarianism, etc. See Jurgen Habermas, *Theory of Communicative Action, Vol. 2: Lifeworld and System* (Boston: Beacon Press, 1987), especially Chapter 2, "Marx and the Thesis of Internal Colonization".

44 John A. Hannigan, "Social Movement Theory and the Sociology of Religion: Toward a New Synthesis", *Sociological Analysis*, 52:4 (1991), p. 311.

45 While this is an admittedly nebulous term, a more precise one would have undermined the point I am trying to make. By employing the term "meaning-making", I am attempting to get at the process to which Alan Touraine refers as "historicity", or the overall system of meaning which sets dominant rules in a given society. See Alain Touraine, *The Voice and the Eye: An Analysis of Social Movements* (New York: Cambridge University Press, 1981); Alain Touraine, "An Introduction to the Study of Social Movements", *Social Research*, 52:4 (1985), pp. 749–97, especially pp. 766–70; and Alain Touraine, "Beyond Social Movement?", *Theory, Culture and Society*, 9 (1992), pp. 125–45.

46 Hannigan, "Social Movement Theory", p. 324.

47 Alberto Melucci, "The Symbolic Challenge of Contemporary Movements", *Social Research*, 52:14 (1985), pp. 807–8.

48 Feminists have addressed this issue as part of a critique of traditional perspectives on power and hierarchy for quite some time. Such critiques are just beginning to enter the mainstream. For an interesting series of essays addressing the issue of power and its reconceptualization, see Thomas E. Wartenburg, ed. *Rethinking Power* (New York: SUNY Press, 1992).

49 Hannigan, "Social Movement Theory", pp. 324–5.

50 Ibid., p. 325.

51 Political science has attempted to explain collective action by such methods as measuring grievances (relative deprivation), but has thus far not managed to establish the link between such grievances and "action". Furthermore, it offers little in the way of distinguishing one kind of action from another, riot activity from revolution, for example. Sociology tends to treat the phenomenon in a more holistic manner. Rather than worrying about the association between just two variables (grievances and propensity to act), sociologists look (generally) at the structural factors which create such grievances, and the meaning of that structural condition to a social actor or group of actors.

52 Surely there is a wide range within each perspective, but this use of this dichotomy for analytical purposes is well-grounded. See Jean L. Cohen, "Strategy or Identity: New Theoretical Paradigms and Contemporary Social Movements", *Social Research*, 52:4, pp. 669–716; Bert Klandermans, "Mobilization into Social Movements: Synthesizing European and American Approaches", in *From Structure to Action: Comparing Social Movement Research Across Cultures*, ed. Bert Klandermans, Hanspeter Kriesi and Sydney Tarrow (Greenwich, CT: JAI Press, 1988); and Alberto Melucci, *Nomads of the Present: Social Movements and Individual Needs in Contemporary Society* (London: Hutchinson Radius, 1989).

53 Cohen, "Strategy or Identity".

54 For an introduction to literature on social movements more generally, see Frances Fox Piven and Richard A. Cloward, *Poor People's Movements* (New York: Vintage Press, 1977) and Ralph H. Turner and Lewis M. Killian, *Collective Behavior* (Englewood Cliffs, NJ: Prentice-Hall, 1987). For RMT specifically, see John D. McCarthy and Mayer N. Zald, *The Trend of Social Movements in America: Professionalization and Resource Mobilization* (Morristown, NJ: General Learning

Press, 1973); Anthony Oberschall, *Social Conflict and Social Movements* (Englewood Cliffs, NJ: Prentice-Hall, 1973); and J. Craig Jenkins, "Resource Mobilization Theory and the Study of Social Movements", *Annual Review of Sociology*, 9 (1983), p. 527–53; William Gamson, *The Strategy of Social Protest* (Belmont, CA: Wadsworth, 1990). For newer theoretical approaches, see Aldon D. Morris and Carol McClurg Mueller, eds. *Frontiers in Social Movement Theory* (New Haven, CT: Yale University Press, 1992); Enrique Larana, Hank Johnston and Joseph R. Gusfield, eds. *New Social Movements: From Ideology to Identity* (Philadelphia, PA: Temple University Press, 1994); and Stanford M. Lyman, ed. *Social Movements: Critiques, Concepts, Case-Studies* (Washington Square, NY: New York University Press, 1995).

55  Mayer N. Zald, "Looking Backward to Look Forward: Reflections on the Past and Future of the Resource Mobilization Program", *Frontiers in Social Movement Theory*, ed. Aldon D. Morris and Carol McClurg Mueller (New Haven: Yale University Press, 1992), p. 330.

56  The reader will note that I willingly acquiesce to the use of gendered terminology here as (1) it is also gendered in the original texts; and (2) had the author(s) considered gender, their analysis might have been altogether different.

57  Carol McClurg Mueller, "Building Social Movement Theory", *Frontiers in Social Movement Theory*, ed. Aldon D. Morris and Carol McClurg Mueller (New Haven: Yale University Press, 1992), p. 3.

58  Mueller notes that, "[f]or the decade of the seventies, over half (56 percent) of the social movement and collective action articles in the *American Sociological Review*, the *American Journal of Sociology*, *Social Forces*, and the *Americana Political Science Review* were based on the theoretical approach of resource mobilization, but by the early eighties, it was almost three-quarters." Morris and Mueller, *Frontiers*, p. 3.

59  Alan Scott, *Ideology and the New Social Movements* (Boston: Unwin Hyman, 1990), p. 121. Emphasis in the original text.

60  Myra Marx Feree, "The Political Context of Rationality: Rational Choice Theory and Resource Mobilization", Morris and Mueller, *Frontiers*, p. 34.

61  Feree, p. 34, citing Michael Hechter, *Principles of Group Solidarity* (Berkeley, University of California Press, 1987).

62  Feree, p. 34, citing A. O. Hirschman, *Exit, Voice and Loyalty* (Cambridge, MA: Harvard University Press, 1970, p. 99).

63  Feree, p. 35.

64  See Michael Taylor, "Cooperation and Rationality: Notes on the Collective Action Problem and its Solution", *The Limits of Rationality*, ed. Karen Schwers Cook and Margaret Levi (Chicago: University of Chicago Press, 1990).

65  Feree, p. 36.

66  D. Kahneman, J. L. Knetch and R. Thaler, "Fairness as a Constraint on Profit-Seeking: Entitlements in the Market", *American Economic Review*, 76:4 (1986), pp. 728–41.

67  Marwell and Ames found one notable exception to their evidence against the existence of "free-riders". The group of economics graduate students was the *only*

group which consistently contributed less than half of the average contributions of other groups (to a public good). Moreover, although 3 of 4 participants in the experiment felt that 50% of personal investment in a public good was "fair"; of the economics graduate students, one-third refused to answer questions relating to fairness, or gave convoluted, uncodable reponses. The authors speculate that perhaps these individuals were students of economics *because of* their preoccupation with the rationality of personal investments; or that they may have simply taken on the behaviour of the good rational actor which their field demands of them.

68　David Sears and C. L. Funk, "Self-Interest in Americans' Political Opinions", *Interest and Ideology: The Foreign Policy Beliefs of American Businessmen*, ed. B. M. Russett and E. C. Hanson (San Francisco: W. H. Freeman, 1975).

69　See Axelrod (1984).

70　Feree, p. 37.

71　Specifically, it is racist, classist, gendered and Western-centric.

72　Augustus R. Norton associates (1) civility, (2) associability and (3) citizenship with the existence of civil society. There are huge problems with this term as an analytical construct, but such topics lie beyond the scope of the paper. For critical review, see Jean Cohen and Andrew Arato, *Civil Society and Political Theory* (Cambridge: MIT Press, 1992); John Keane, *Civil Society and the State* (London: Verso, 1988) and Carole Pateman, *The Disorder of Women* (Cambridge: Polity, 1989).

73　Alain Touraine, *The Voice and the Eye: An Analysis of Social Movements* (New York: Cambridge University Press, 1981), p. 29.

74　Nation-state, capitalism, etc. The reader will note that I use the term "structure" in different ways throughout this text. Here, it is invoked as an effort to be consistent with the original texts to which I refer; at other times the term implies "culture". I will indicate when necessary so as to avoid undue confusion.

75　Mario Diani, "The Concept of Social Movement", *The Sociological Review*, 38 (1992), p. 1.

76　While it is true that the convergence to which I refer here applies to the perspectives of those who adhere to the New Social Movement paradigm (and who therefore accept that the movements are "new" *a priori*), and that it refers to the content of "newness", it is nonetheless a valid point because there is a built-in bias in RMT which obscures changes in actors or groups of actors. As a result, it is quite likely that RM theorists would attribute changes in social movements to structures.

77　Touraine, "An Introduction", p. 780.

78　Habermas, "New Social Movements", p. 33.

79　Ibid.

80　Rudiger Schmitt-Beck, "A Myth Institutionalized: Theory and Research on New Social Movements in Germany", *European Journal of Political Research*, 21 (1992), p. 376.

81　Carl Boggs, *Social Movements and Political Power* (Philadelphia: Temple Press, 1986), p. 3.

82　Michael Dunn in an interview on *National Public Radio*, 15 November 1995.

83  Michael Hudson, "After the Gulf War: Prospects for Democratization in the Arab World", *Middle East Journal*, 45:3 (1991), p. 407.

84  Karen Pfeifer, "Economic Liberalization in the 1980s: Algeria in Comparative Perspective", p. 113.

85  Daniel Brumberg, "Prospects for a Democratic Bargain in Algeria", *American Arab Affairs*, 36 (1991), p. 25.

86  Islam, in fact, began as a sociopolitical movement.

87  By "modern" here, I refer to the 19th and 20th centuries when Islam began to be associated with the nation-state.

88  Hugh Roberts, "Radical Islamism and the Dilemma of Algerian Nationalism: The Embattled Arians of Algiers", *Third World Quarterly*, 10: 2 (1988).

89  I borrow this term from Rabia Bekkar, "Taking up Space in Tlemcen: The Islamist Occupation of Urban Algeria", *MERIP*, 22: 6 (1992).

90  BBC World Service on National Public Radio, Friday, 11 November 1994.

91  I have only anecdotal evidence to support this point as I was in Algiers the week such legislation was adopted. Indeed, it was among my first lessons in the power/deception potential of the Western media.

92  Mahfoud Bennoune, "Algeria's Façade of Democracy", *MERIP*, 20: 2 (1990), p. 9.

93  Brumberg, "Prospects for Democratic Bargain", p. 25.

94  The characterization of these two groups was borrowed from Brumberg.

95  There is a strong male bias here; women are not to be part of the egalitarian social order. On the other hand, there were a significant number of women, particularly among the highly educated and professional women, who supported the Islamists. Things are not always what they seem.

96  Fred Halliday, "Fundamentalism and the Contemporary World", *Contention*, 4:2 (1995), p. 42.

97  See various pieces in *The Christian Science Monitor, Middle East International* and *The New York Times*.

98  Brumberg (1992), pp. 25–7.

# 3

# Discursive Contentions in Islamic Terms: Fundamentalism versus Liberalism?

*Armando Salvatore*

In an era dominated by a widespread public and scholarly concern for things Islamic, their presumed "resurgence" or "revival"[1] or, as commonly known, "Islamic fundamentalism", has often been judged, explicitly or implicitly, in terms of the degree of its divergence from the values and standards of liberal secularism. In a more recent phase of this wave of attention, an option has emerged within the most general attitude, whose aim is to discover and support patterns of liberal responses to Islamic "fundamentalism" from within the Islamic public arena.[2]

The present contribution slightly differs from the last approach, to the extent that it attempts to avoid as far as possible any pre-constituted categories like "fundamentalism", liberalism and secularism, originating from the Western historical experience and not devoid of ambiguities, even if applied to Western phenomena.[3] The purpose here is to examine particularly relevant discursive contentions conducted in Islamic terms, in their dependence on an intellectual rationality which is probably similar but not reducible to the terms of discourse and categories that are familiar to a Western public. This option is motivated by the assumption that although patterns of intellectual modernity in the Muslim world are comparable with those in the West, and a permanent influence of the latter on the former is a matter of evidence, the terms and rationales of modern political discourses within an Islamic public space can produce a hermeneutic dynamic that is responsible for partly original options and forms of polarization. After delimiting the theoretical and historical background of the phenomenon, the analysis is to focus on a public intellectual dispute of the eighties.

This variability of discursive formulas in an Islamic context is due to the fact that at least since the end of last century "Islam", which is one major key word among others in the Qur'an, has been definitively reified as the label of what we can call a "framework of universal reference" in competition with other such frameworks like the "national" ones, that are more solidly rooted in the European than in the Islamic history, but also compatible with the reality of public communication in Muslim countries during both the colonial and post-colonial eras.

The concept of a framework of universal reference provides the least common denominator for a "minimalist" definition of modernity from the point of view of intellectual production and public communication. For it highlights the emergence of new modalities of production and communication of meaning that emancipate themselves from the compulsory reference to an established structure of domination. They seek instead reference and consensus towards a wider community and towards its intellectually receptive and publicly engaged components, on the basis of supposedly universal values, and with the aim of reforming the community by seeking inspiration from these values.

Each framework of universal reference has its own specificities, facilitating certain types of public discourse and excluding others, according to the symbolic power irradiating from its central key words and images. An Islamic framework of universal reference, or, as in this case, an "Arab-Islamic" one, originates from Arab authors, who have to take into account the value of *'uruba* with respect to Islam. It depends on an exercise of defining Islam which takes place within a hermeneutic spectrum that looks like a continuum. But within that there is some critical threshold that marks the separation of two different interpretative schemes: "conflationism" and "deconflationism". These correspond to the opposing attitudes towards the tense relationship, common to all Axial religions, between the two dimensions of the worldly and the after-worldly, the visible and the invisible, *al-manzur wa ghayr al-manzur*. For the scope of the present analysis, the type of social action that further defines the contention between conflationism and deconflationism is that which pertains to the political domain. The focus on the allegedly political dimension of Islam began to acquire prominence during the second half, and especially by the end, of last century. Then defining "Islam" as a reified ideological system, or as a framework for universal reference, became a major concern for both Western (Orientalist) and Islamic authors within a "transcultural" hermeneutic game. At this stage the polarization became one between the necessity and the contingency of the relation between "faith" and "politics" in Islam.

Conflationism and deconflationism are both dependent on the same process of seeing Qur'anic religion (*din*) in a highly reified form as "Islam". Reification is given by the capacity to distance oneself from an object, to objectify it as a target of analysis or an instrument for social action. This process certainly began with the theological-juridical disputes about the proper domains of reference of *iman* and Islam, which have animated the Islamic *umma* very early in its history. However, its high point was only reached with the maturation of a modern intellectual turn and the formation of a public sphere during the colonial era.[4]

One cannot establish *a priori* where the difference between a class of conflationist and deconflationist statements lies. It is only possible to point to two opposite poles, in terms of hermeneutic procedures, through comparing different statements, or analysing the internal dynamics of a textual clue in its basic dependence on one type of procedure, or, alternatively, in its oscillation between both. I will attempt to show how both interpretative schemes originate from the same discursive formation, which we may term "intellectualized" Islamic *'ilm*, the terrain of activity of modernized *'ulama'* seeking influence within the public arena, and how from a tendentially homogeneous framework of universal reference these two separate and polarizing kinds of dynamics unfold and consolidate for the obvious discursive constraint of "closing a circle". Deconflationism sees Islam as limited to *din* or as also encompassing the *dunya* or the "world" (according to the formula *Islam dunya wa din*), and sometimes as still strictly depending on the *iman*. The opposing scheme tends to conflate two poles that can be called Islam and politics, or Islam and the state, or Islam as *din* and Islam as *dawla* (*Islam din wa dawla*), and the like.

The basic tenets of the ("fundamentalist") conflationist formula, *Islam din wa dawla*, were established during the formative phase of an Islamic public space within and across Muslim societies under different degrees of colonial control towards the end of last century. However, the slogan acquired a particular prominence after the demise of the caliphate, and in particular from the thirties of this century.[5] There is more than one possible reading of this formula. The major difficulty, in historical perspective and in hermeneutic terms, lies in establishing in which phase it is legitimate to situate the genesis of one particular reading. The most basic meaning points to a reification of Islam followed by its predication, which consists in stating, almost programmatically, of what Islam should consist.

A further signification of the formula is related to the question of the differentiation of the meaning of *din*, which probably represents a more subtle and crucial signal of the making of an Islamic intellectual modernity than the more evident, preliminary reification of Islam. If *dawla* remains rather stable, from the end of last century, in representing the "state" as the vertical dimension of social organization, the shifting meaning of *din* is the variable responsible for the changing meaning of the entire formula. Pending careful investigations in the transformation of the meaning of both, the slogan as a whole and of *din* therein, which should also reveal the relationship between the shaping of the formula and the discourse of the *islah* ("Islamic reformism"), we can hypothesize that by the late seventies the agitation of *Islam din wa dawla* witnessed an affirmation. It is the affirmation of a capacity to invest the newly emerged public arena with a category loaded with power of mobilization and pointing to a feeling of externalization towards the existing state, and the opposition to it of a "we movement". Nonetheless, this meaning of the formula was not mature before the seventies, as discussed below.

Published shortly before the strong conflationist position began to take root in a "social movement" dimension with the grounding of the Ikhwan al-Muslimin (the Muslim Brethren), the book of the Egyptian *'alim*, 'Abd al-Raziq, *al-Islam wa al-hukm* (1925), is prominent for not simply countering a conflationist formula through the adoption of a rival framework transposed and adapted from European history, as it happened in the case of other famous authors in Egypt during the same period. The historical importance of 'Abd al-Raziq's essay is in its capacity to bring to the surface the potentialities and limits of the discursive formation of intellectualized *'alim* defined in the four previous decades under the umbrella of the *islah* ("Islamic reformism"). The author is conscious of arguing from within the *'ilm*, both institutionally and discursively. Although he writes under the influence of contingent inner-Islamic polemics about the caliphate, after its formal dismissal in Istanbul between 1922 and 1924, it would be reductive to locate his work hermeneutically in such a narrow context. We should at least accept that it represented the culmination of a trajectory of "reformist" *'ulama'* intellectual endeavour (from al-Afghani to Abduh to 'Abd al-Raziq's contemporary Rida). It had manifested, with Abduh but even more with al-Afghani, a slight, and mainly implicit, proto-conflationist leaning, and had touched, with Rida, a point where in spite of the clear admission of the contingent character of power in the Islamic community the reformist logic was invested in a congruent conflationist formula.

'Abd al-Raziq performed instead a sort of deconflationist *tabula rasa*, thereby redefining the terms of future discourse both for deconflationism and for conflationism. At the same time, as Rida was consolidating the reformist argument apologetically and doctrinally, the Egyptian *'alim* swiftly reappropriated the reformist "method of looking at [Islam] and the world".[6] He did that in order to disencumber the making of the Arab–Islamic framework of universal reference of the *salafi* incongruence of tendentially reading the whole of Islamic history as carrying a potential unity of "faith" and "politics". For such an interpretation overemphasized, as previous proto-modern political movements like the Wahhabites did, the importance of the genetic era of Islam. 'Abd al-Raziq's strategy was simple and straightforward: he objected to the possibility of saying that Islam *is* a blueprint for government. Thereby he opened the contention about what the relationship between Islam and the political domain *should be*.

Until now, however, 'Abd al-Raziq's work has been deemed important for the actual response he gave to the question of the relationship between Islam and politics. As we will see, this interpretation has been particularly successful during the last two decades, dominated by the contention between what may be called "solutionism" and "neutralism" with respect to Islam's political role. This interpretation of the work of 'Abd al-Raziq is also present in the classical work on Arab intellectuals written by Albert Hourani. In an effort to revise this assessment, Leonard Binder tests the appropriateness of assessing 'Abd al-Raziq's argument as a "liberal", westernized view of Islam, nothing else than an imitative reflex towards Western models. The admittedly normative charge of Binder's analysis, in search of an Islamic path to liberalism,[7] can be diluted in a perspective which allows us to recognize that what makes 'Abd al-Raziq's claim largely innovative is well beyond the intention to lay the groundwork for a deconflationist interpretative circle. What he was able to perform was an accurate work of checking and grounding anew the still fragile discursive formation of reformist, intellectualized *'ilm*, by emancipating it from the residual ahistorical perspective of traditional *'ilm*.

'Abd al-Raziq was certainly capable of formulating, in terms that were obviously argumentatively vulnerable, the claim that there was no religious legitimacy for the caliphate. While it remains undemonstrated that, *as a consequence*, he was denying any legitimation to the "Islamic *political* community",[8] all that we can say is that he tried to neutralize any political implication of the *ijma'*, the consensus of the community mediated by the *'ulama'*, at the same time as he not so much denied, but reinforced, the legitimation of the Islamic community as a unity of *din*. He still considers this community as given by, and bound to *kullu ma sharra'ahu al-Islam* (all that Islam prescribes), from which only *al-hukm al-siyasi*, the vertical dimension of organization of the community, is excluded.[9] So, if it is true that the attack he moved against the traditional consensus was first of all complemented by a rigorous checking of the logic of the conflationist argument, which considers the imamate or caliphate as co-essential to the religious obligation of "commanding good and forbidding evil",[10] the purpose of his move was the redefinition of a sound basis for a new kind of "consensus of communication" as the crucial medium for the viable functioning of a framework of universal reference.

The work of 'Abd al-Raziq has become an object of dispute in the post-Nasserist climate of the early seventies, in the context of the controversy on the legitimacy and necessity of an "Islamic state".[11] The second major presence in public debates taking place during the era of the "Islamic awakening" has been Sayyid Qutb, who has been considered the early inspirator of *al-sahwa al-Islamiyya*, or "Islamic awakening".[12] It is not surprising that 'Abd al-Raziq and Qutb have been juxtaposed by Leonard Binder, in his effort to judge the degree to which some liberal impulses of what he calls "the rejected alternative"[13] in constructing a relationship between Islam and politics, as epitomized by 'Abd al-Raziq, can even be found in the "fundamentalist" theoretical corpus delivered by Qutb.

For the scope of our investigation, however, the possible link between 'Abd al-Raziq and Qutb is interesting for a slightly different reason. Both the reception of 'Abd al-Raziq and the more immediate impact of Qutb have to be more carefully situated. They cannot be simply seen as the most illustrious precursors of contemporary Islamic liberalism and "fundamentalism" but as the shapers of the basic terms and rationales of political-intellectual discourse within an Arab–Islamic framework of universal reference. These terms have been reshaped by Muslim authors during the last twenty years according to contingent, and not generally valid, societal and discursive priorities. It is true that these two authors represent the two most prominent points, as to the radical character of their formulations, within the path of shaping of the Arab–Islamic framework of universal reference. At the same time, and precisely because of the radical character of their argumentation, they happened to fulfil complementary functions: the "minimalist" formulation of the lowest common denominator for the new consensus, in the case of 'Abd al-Raziq, and a "maximalist" intellectual elaboration of how this consensus should be filled, in the case of Qutb.

In particular, there is a logical link between the two authors in the passage from the hermeneutics which aim to purify *din* from what is *la dini* (non-religious), to a coherent redefinition of the hermeneutic range pertaining to *din* or emanating from it. Both sets of work are prominent in that they cannot be read as conflicting with each other; for they are not mere examples of "deconflationist" or "conflationist" hermeneutics, but rather embody the two extreme logical points in an ideal trajectory from the positing to the substantiating of the freedom and creativity of consciousness in Islamic terms. Both agree in saying that the *shar'* (God's legislative substance) has nothing to do with human government, and that no viable Arab–Islamic framework of universal reference can be grounded when arguing ahistorically, as traditional *'ilm* did, in postulating a religious legitimation of the exercise of power in Islamic history. Both agree in negating the existence in history of a government legitimated by *din*.

Qutb's argument is a step back from conflationism, as it renounces the exaggeratedly quick derivation of the necessity of the *dawla* for the sake of *din*, and concentrates on a work of derivation of all that *din* requires. This hermeneutics of *din* is centred on the individual being and its transformation. The resulting character of Islam as *haraki*, i.e. characterized by movement and development, is given by the permanent, creative reconstruction of the *shari'a* as inspired by the divine *shar'* but crafted by the individual consciousness. Qutb converges with 'Abd al-Raziq in positing God's intervention through His *shar'* as a preliminary condition for creating the movement, and in stressing that all that follows is determined by the efforts of individual Muslims. The unconditional submission of the Muslim to the *shar'* through an act of faith, the acceptance of the Islamic *din*, is the path of access to creative freedom.

A further characteristic accommodating 'Abd al-Raziq and the late Qutb is their high degree of isolation at the time they wrote, albeit for different reasons, within the public arena, along with a belated success of the terms of discourse they used. As for Qutb in particular, it is highly problematic to see in him the theoretician of the *sahwa*. There are simple historical and discursive reasons, some of which will be highlighted here, which explain why the strand of political-intellectual thought that has raised the banner of the *sahwa* cannot be regarded as a mere actualization of Qutbian motives. Whereas Qutb's thought, especially in its latest phase when it produced the most intriguing concepts for the neo-"fundamentalist" discourse, was embedded in the tragic political and existential fate of a limited group of committed "fundamentalist" activists, the slogan itself of the *sahwa* responds to a high need of reification within an intensive struggle conducted on the public arena since the late seventies.

The most immediate meaning of *sahwa*, and the way it is most commonly translated into English, is "awakening". One of the most representative theorists of *al-sahwa al-Islamiyya*, Yusuf al-Qaradawi, is straightforward in making clear that *sahwa* is simply "Islam awakened", "a return to the source".[14] The simplifying and homogenizing character of the concept of *sahwa* for the sake of public communication is here evident. However, the image used also shows plastic properties, as the *sahwa* is explicitly and directly related to the feeling of *naksa* (fall)[15] that marked the end of the *nahada* ("renaissance"). In spite of the apparent similarity of image and meaning between *sahwa* and *nahada*, the degree of assertiveness of the former is much higher. *Sahwa* is in fact not formulated as a will or feeling, but as a factual reality and an actual movement.[16] It is the "return of consciousness and vigilance" after sleep or drunkenness, two metaphors pointing to the two causal dimensions that determined the situation of crisis preceding the *sahwa*, the internal one, identified with the stagnation of the era of Ottoman rule, and the external one, represented by the cultural dimension of European colonialism, which is held responsible for having detached the *umma* from its essence, thereby alienating and depersonalizing it.

What is called "the politics of *sahwa*" has to be situated within the general communicative background of the consolidation of a common "Islamic idiom" in the public space, which has contributed to blur class differences, thereby fulfilling the function of reconciling differences within the gigantic middle class of countries like Egypt.[17] Within this process, a metamorphosed *'ilm* becomes the dominant form of legitimation of discourse, through remaining, in its formal constraints, general enough to be appropriated by as many types of social actors as to jeopardize the claim that it is the expression of defined social groups. The argumentative models allowed within this discursive formation can vary without any rigid corresponding difference in social location among representatives of different interpretative circles.

The curious phenomenon is, however, that only two models allowed within such an expanded *'ilm*, linked with each other through a hermeneutic polarization, seem to dominate the public arena. This polarization is due to the fact that the intellectual dispute revolves around the "Islamic state", *al-dawla al-Islamiyya*, or sometimes the "Islamic government", *al-hukuma al-Islamiyya*, where the shift in the substantive use does not modify the broader terms of the issue at stake.[18] The Islamic state does not represent a clear-cut "public issue" in a stricter, almost technical sense, as if it would refer to a debate concerning the requirements or the goals of the state, in terms familiar to us from constitutional theory or political philosophy (although the dispute can well take root, in particular cases, within such a terrain). An important clue to the wider problematizing range of the dispute is the enduring symbolic centrality within it of the slogan *Islam din wa dawla*, whose wide range of signification beyond the standard, simplifying translation has been previously elucidated.

The public arena referred to here is basically Egyptian, within which the polarizing dispute has been virtually continuous since the early seventies.[19] The contention has been often conceptualized by Western scholars under the ambiguous label of "secularism debate".[20] Against this procedure, I prefer not to translate the original patterns of this discursive contention conducted in Islamic terms into terms of discourse and categories originating from a different, though comparable, historical context.

A first sign of the polarization dates back to shortly before the early seventies, during a period which coincided with the vanishing of the public consensus previously crystallized around the Nasserist option. It seems that from this point on, the staging of the dispute saw some writers claiming that Islam can provide political solutions. These writers are referred to henceforth as the "solutionists", in order to avoid any short-circuit with concepts too heavily charged with references to

Western history. They were opposed by different claims by their challengers or the "neutralists". A similar scheme has regulated the debate throughout the eighties.[21] During this decade there has not been any significant shift in the basic terms of discourse used. Rather its crystallization has further progressed through also being carried out in the columns of leading daily newspapers and even in public debates, despite an extraordinary boom in the production of books on this and related topics.[22]

The two contenders here selected for the analysis of the controversy between "solutionism" and "neutralism" are Yusuf al-Qaradawi and Muhammad A. Khalafallah. An important parallel feature of their long-term engagement is that, although they have not disdained to directly participate in the everyday disputes in the Egyptian public arena of the eighties, they provide one of the best examples of an exchange. More or less directly, they performed at a higher hermeneutic level than usual, a level not exposed to the immediate pressure of persuading a wider public, and additionally situated within an explicitly Arab, not merely Egyptian, framework. The exchange took place in the framework of a conference held in Amman in 1987 on *al-sahwa al-Islamiyya wa humum al-watan al-'Arabi* (the Islamic awakening and the concerns of the Arab world). The separate analysis of both circles as represented by these two authors is to be based also on other writings contributed by them.

Al-Qaradawi is highly representative of the solutionist circle because he adds to an undeniable influence within the "fundamentalist" camp in Egypt and elsewhere and the corresponding theorizing of the basic tenets of solutionism beyond the sheer political slogan *al-Islam huwa al-hall* ("Islam is the solution").[23] This provides a capacity to preserve at least a common denominator between the highly innovative Qutbian claim of Islam as "movement" and the preservation of a privileged role for the *'ulama'–fuqaha'* in the hermeneutics of Islam. Besides the essay delivered at the Amman conference, the focus is on one major work that fully manifested the centrality of his position within the "fundamentalist" current.[24] The relevance of the responses he delivered in this book is probably due to the fact that at that time, during the early eighties, in the wake of the assassination of Sadat by the "fundamentalist" group al-Jihad, a strong pressure was put on him, as one of the major theorists of the *sahwa*, to clarify the independence of his solutionist position from the contingencies of political turmoil and from what al-Qaradawi himself agreed on calling "extremism" (*tatarruf*).

The *'ulama'* class, as supportive of or quiescent towards the power establishment, is notoriously not immune from the attacks of the "fundamentalist" youth. The reaffirmation and redefinition of the prerogatives of Islamic *'ilm* in general, and *fiqh* in particular, is therefore a recurrent issue for al-Qaradawi. It is symptomatic that this difficult task is carried out through highlighting the public, intellectual function of a rightly conceived *fiqh*. The operation of emphasizing the centrality of the *fuqaha'* does not result, as one may expect, in a confinement of *fikr* (intellectual thought) within the strict limits of "traditional" *fiqh*, as it would appear to be on the ground of the assertion that *fikr* is an emanation of the dogmas (*'aqa'id*).[25] Besides the well-known fact that the term for "dogma" or "doctrine" (*'aqida*) has widened its denotative field in modern "fundamentalist" discourse to encompass "theory", it is also intended in an intellectual sense.[26] This stress on the centrality of *fiqh* and of the science of *usul al-fiqh* ("the sources or fundamentals of jurisprudence" or "legal theory")[27] is more of a formal institutional nature, in the sense that it refers to the alleged absence, in Islamic history, of a major break in the discursive mediation of the *'ulama–fuqaha'* in spite of the emergence of Westernized intellectuals towards the end of last century.[28] Al-Qaradawi justifies this centrality by reference to their "technical" skills in the definition of "true Islam", by virtue of their capacity to select and identify the true fundamentals (*usul*), and differentiate these from the non-essential ramifications and contingent applications (*furu'*).[29] This is in fact a formula that, when read as it should be, in the context of public communication in which it is produced and not as a mere legal discourse, reflects with precision the essentializing function of selection and amplification of meaning that is a typical task of the modern intellectual.

It is however significant that al-Qaradawi can define the category of the Islamic "propagandists and intellectuals" (*al-du'at wa al-mufakkirun al-Islamiyyun*) only through stressing their belonging to *ahl al-'ilm*, scholars of Islamic science.[30] He thereby makes them almost a sub-category within *ahl al-'ilm*, more directly concerned with the actual social situation. The *'ulama'* are considered as the only legitimate leaders *and* interpreters of the "awakening". The public intellectual competence of other categories of authors in making sense of the *sahwa* is, accordingly, contested. This can be assessed as a synthetic formulation of the post-Qutbian normalization: to dilute the revolutionary appeal of Qutb in the reified scenario of the *sahwa*, and to fix the latter as intrinsically dependent on the mediation of the modern or modernized *'ulama'*.

The case of extremism is taken as proof for the necessary pre-eminence of the *'ulama'*. At the same time it shows the extent to which Qutb's own radical stance can be reabsorbed and accommodated, but not antagonized, by the reaffirmation of their centrality. On the one hand, there would be, as al-Qaradawi argues, no extremism if the "fundamentalist" youth were guided by people who are competent in questions of *'ilm*.[31] On the other hand, although it is indisputable that extremism is a concern for a wider range of social actors than the *'ulama'*, the attitude of merely judging on the basis of the category of "extremism", instead of considering first of all the impulse underlying the "awakening" of Islam, is responsible for the success of distorted interpretations of the phenomenon, which in turn legitimizes undue repression.[32]

The redefinition of the centrality of the carriers of *'ilm* is not an end in itself in al-Qaradawi's argumentation, but the crucial step for justifying a solutionist path. Through the reformulation of their role, the *'ulama'* are assigned a social task that fits our previous "minimalist" definition of the modern intellectual. *'Ulama'* are entitled to their public mediation in the interpretation and definition of Islam: any other unskilled mediation, as by journalists, cannot replace the *'ilm*.[33] More specifically, al-Qaradawi criticizes those ideological leaders of the extremist "fundamentalist" groups who reiterate the radical Qutbian reading of all Islamic history after its formative period, as well as of the historical institution of the caliphate, as not authentic.[34] This anti-radical critique is justified by reference to an evolutionist theory grounded on the allegedly supreme divine rule of graduation, which governs the coming about of the universe and of human society as well.[35]

Although this argument seems to lead one to regard the Qutbian theory as banal, and to its dilution to a generic "philosophy of history", there is no obstacle to taking up Qutb's motif of Islam as the complete and perfect *manhaj* (method) for human life, and to re-propose the principle of grounding the *hukm* (rule) in God alone. This operation, however, is carried out with much less emphasis than in the case of Qutb, in order not to prejudice the hermeneutic centrality of the *'ulama'*. This centrality is seen as deriving its legitimation from the *umma*, but is also hindered by the corrupt ruler, "whose Islam" is the product of an arbitrary selection of what suits his power, in disregard of the knowledge of the *imams* of *fiqh*.[36] The definition of true Islam should be the product of a publicly conducted, critical discussion under the guide of the leading *fuqaha*.[37] Freedom of opinion,[38] as well as of manifesting opposition, is advocated as perfectly compatible with the guiding function of the highest *fuqaha*.[39]

The rational legitimation of this interpretative-legislating leadership is dependent on the *fuqaha's* ability to produce an "enlightened *fiqh*" for the rulings of Islam, distilled from its "authentic sources". As a product of such a genuine hermeneutic effort, the *faqih* should "bring about such a kind of consciousness and *fiqh*" that escapes what is inessential and aims at reforming society.[40] The true *fiqh* is therefore always *al-fiqh al-wa'i*, the *fiqh* based on a deep hermeneutic consciousness. *Fiqh* and consciousness are inseparable from one another. It seems that the one defines the other, and the search for true meaning cannot depend on technical skills alone. If it did then the *fiqh* would drift away towards the handling of marginal issues or mere strivings of consciousness, which would produce distortions and extremism. The only way for understanding the *shari'a* is by differentiating in it what is essential and what is secondary.[41]

This should not, however, as al-Qaradawi warns, legitimize arbitrariness in the search for true Islam. A plurality of equally valid interpretations is excluded: *inna al-Islam huwa al-Islam* ("for Islam is Islam"). We believe that this strongly reifying assertion, and the corresponding argumentation, should be nonetheless interpreted as stating not so much that Islam *is* one, but that it should be interpreted and practised *on the assumption that* it is one. While al-Qaradawi highlights some firm certainties (*qut'iyyat*) in doctrine and intellectual thought (*'aqida wa fikr*), he makes them however the platform for change and for determining its direction and goals.[42]

The crucial point in the argumentation is that, along with the necessity that we recognize one "true Islam", we also acknowledge, i.e. develop, its socially all-encompassing character. This position is summarized in the statement that Islam – again used as the subject, where it replaces God – has posed a value and has legislated in every domain of human action.[43] Neglecting the obligations and the duties deriving from this regulating force would mean depriving Islam of its social dimension. The clearest example of this corruption is seen, coherently with the *islah* thinking since Abduh, in the lack of social engagement of the most *sufi* (mystical) brotherhoods, which reduce Islam to socially irrelevant rituals.[44] Al-Qaradawi's critique is also levelled, however, against the *du'at* (propagandists) who show insufficient concern "for the present problems, and the future aspirations".[45]

Even if al-Qaradawi advocates a fusion of *salafiyya* and renewal (*tajdid*), he tends to lay heavier emphasis on the latter, as this seems to be, at some points, equated with the *sahwa*. The evocation of the era of *al-salaf al-salih*, or the "good ancestors", is not the basis of a backward-looking attitude, but serves as a reference to an idealized model of "hermeneutic smoothness". For then Muslims were capable of shaping simply crafted, binding interpretations, while keeping the degree of conflict within the community to a minimum, and so allowing the unfolding of innovative capacities.[46] This is an idealization of the consensus in not merely traditional terms. According to al-Qaradawi what in fact characterizes the "age of backwardness", roughly identified with the Ottoman period, is, among other things, the lack of *ijtihd* (free reasoning) in *fiqh*.[47] The idealized consensus is viewed as based on essential questions, and obtained through the real participation of the legitimate holders of the keys for interpreting. This participation is after all a matter of subjective adherence, without which one cannot speak of the implementation of the *shari'a*, that is the symbolic core of the solutionist path. In one of the rare argumentative passages where a genuine Qutbian influence seems at work, al-Qaradawi stresses how this implementation is above all a responsibility of the people (*al-sha'b*), well before it becomes a concern for the state.[48] With an abrupt logical shift, this stress is however superimposed by the argument that, as there cannot be *'aqida* (doctrine) without *shari'a*, there cannot be *din* without *dawla* either.[49]

This jump unveils the hard nutshell of the solutionist version of neo-conflationism, argumentatively sustained by the resentment against those who misunderstand and reduce the Islamic *din* according to a Western view of religion – and this is certainly an older *islahi* motive. Al-Qaradawi crafts this argument in a direct polemic attitude against the Western view of a "political Islam" as centred on the formula of a "politicization of religion",[50] nurtured by explanations often based on socio-cultural, or even socio-psychological factors. Against this view al-Qaradawi is keen to reaffirm, again in a Qutbian vein, that Islam unifies theory and practice and spirit and form.[51]

The axial passage of al-Qaradawi's argumentation lies in the development of a balanced reading of the relationship between individual duties and the collective dimension. The former no doubt occupies a pre-eminent position in the doctrinally stricter terms of "obligation" (*fard*). But on this basis, the author is prompt to specify that individual duties affecting the collectivity precede those of strictly individual import. This narrowly juridical consideration is not sufficient, however, for establishing the primacy of the collective dimension. This only attains a definite primacy through resort to a logical argument grounded in the invocation of the concept of collective utility, sustained by the almost only ideological, no longer juridically grounded claim that Islam "gives pre-eminence to social relations over personal relations".[52]

This assertion is considered sufficient by al-Qaradawi for consecrating the "necessity" (*hatmiyya*) of the "Islamic solution" (*al-hall al-Islami*), as consisting in the implementation of the *shari'a* in all domains of life. The ensuing vision reflects a populist view of the *da'wa* (the "missionary" call for joining Islam, in this case the intellectually mediated "true Islam"), according to which concrete solutions to concrete problems are envisaged through direct contact with the "people".[53] This view almost automatically leads to the call for the establishment of the Islamic state, posited as a duty for the Islamic community and as a pivotal goal in the work of the *du'at*. But this assertion cannot, again, take advantage of any solid underpinning in the legal terms of *fiqh*. Al-Qaradawi uses here the word *farida*, and not *fard*. The former, although virtually identical to the latter in pointing to a dimension of obligation, has the advantage of not constituting a term of legal discourse. The obligatory character of the Islamic state is established through logical and ideological evidence and not through juridical argumentation.

More importantly, one can question whether there is a logical gap between the consideration of Islam as more or less synonymous with all that is socially good and endowed with normative force, hence worth being implemented, and the call for an Islamic state. The populist flavour and vocabulary of the entire discourse is the only element that fills the gap: its logic is that even in a gradualist optic, the reform (*islah*) of society cannot be achieved without bridging the gulf between the horizontal and the vertical levels of societal organization.[54] After having evaluated the contending neutralist circle, we will see that behind the populist colouring we can see an option that is, like any other politico-intellectual option, never fully justified by the path of argumentation followed.

As this is a truism, we should attempt to discover where the symbolic strength of the solutionist model lies, in spite of its logical incongruences. The appeal of a certain sort of hermeneutics is never a function of either logical strength or of underlying interests or in fact of both, even less so in the case of the "fundamentalist" discourse. The "re-enchanting", self-deceiving dimension of an argumentative path is what sustains it in the final analysis, and in the case of solutionism the category of *shari'a* is central in this respect. The call for the Islamic state, as is well-known, is strictly linked to the request for the implementation of the *shari'a*. The definition of this concept, which is not less subject to hermeneutic variability than *Islam* or *din*, is at the very core of the solutionist discourse, before this becomes overburdened, in purely logical terms, by the tension between the two dimensions, the vertical and the horizontal, of social organization.

According to the very essence of the *sahwa*, the *shari'a* cannot be reduced to "cutting off the hand of the thief", as al-Qaradawi stresses with bitter sarcasm, with evident reference to the most common, media-mediated views, in the West especially, of what the *shari'a* is. The implementation itself of the *shari'a* in its strictest sense does not exhaust what the Islamic "awakening" is or should be.[55] At this point al-Qaradawi suspends the definition of the *shari'a*, and it almost seems that its centrality is given precisely by this undetermined character.

It is difficult to establish what *shari'a* means in contemporary "fundamentalist" discourse as well as to define it univocally, since it is incorrect to translate it as "Islamic law". We can even say that the ambiguity of what *shari'a* is really about, is peculiar to its function. What is prominent in the concept is its "functional" abstraction and reification. In no way is *shari'a* identical with the legal system; occasionally it may have been its label. The ambiguous meaning of *shari'a* in the argumentation of al-Qaradawi seems to make it, in a Qutbian vein, the symbolic medium of Islam's unfolding in human history, or even of human history's unfolding as Islam. The reduced and diluted post-Qutbian version that intervenes in the framing model of the solutionist circle is finally centred, however, on the postulation of *sahwa* as a natural, spontaneous awakening of Islam in terms of a return of consciousness, as well as on the definition of *al-harka al-Islamiyya* (literally, the Islamic movement) as the activist core of the *sahwa*, bringing to full consciousness and articulating into a coherent vision the impulses inherent in it.[56] This view attenuates the revolutionary potentialities of a Qutbian reading of *shari'a*.

It is crucial to stress again that within this theoretical scenario the attainment of the level of the *dawla* (state) is not so abrupt as the slogan *Islam din wa dawla* would allow us to think. The presumption that this is the immediate, logical consequence of the request of the implementation of the *shari'a* should be reassessed with more caution than usual, in order not to deform the solutionist framing model. The recurrent accusation against solutionists, more from the Western side than from its neutralist contenders, is that the invocation of the Islamic state does not specify the constitutional model, hence the political specificity of such a state, so that one is allowed to fear that it will become the instrument of an arbitrary and despotic rule of a clerical oligarchy. In parallel, it has been questioned which concrete, relevant changes the implementation of the *shari'a* would introduce in the constitutional and legal system. On this point, it has been rightly claimed that "the argument over the *shari'a* is not purely legal. It has become more a symbol than anything else; for lack of any other acceptable shibboleth, its enforcement is considered a distinctive feature of an Islamic state."[57]

We should, however, try to modify this assessment, and in a certain sense to reverse it, by saying that the symbolic power of the call for the *shari'a* is the hard nutshell of the solutionist view. The invocation of the Islamic state is then an important corollary to it, to the extent that it symbolizes the end of the arbitrary violation, corruption and instrumentalization of *din* carried out by the existing *dawla*, which is what "arbitrary rule" from a "fundamentalist" point of view consists of. This obviously does not exclude that solutionists strive towards power and would enjoy a redefinition of the existing patterns of authority in order to achieve gains, as well as, if possible, an underpinning of these gains in the constitution, not unlike the Iranian case. The hermeneutic axis of the solutionist argument, as well as its capacity to appeal to individual consciences and achieving public resonance, is first in the symbolic construction and instrumentalization of the *shari'a*, and only secondarily in the accompanying call for an Islamic state. The invocation of the *shari'a* functions as the discursive medium for envisioning Islam as the solution.

The combination of logical vulnerability and symbolic strength of solutionism has been countered by a "neutralist" discourse, according to which Islam is politically neutral. We will see, however, how the corresponding framing model, while taking root on a logical terrain where it seems to be able to unveil the contradiction of solutionism, ends up by revealing some logical incongruences of its own that must be attended to with symbolic references. The neutralist circle seems to be less touched by the transformation of the last twenty years than it would appear when comparing its basic arguments with the standard reading of 'Abd al-Raziq – which is, as I attempted to show, highly reductive. Against this impression, it should be anticipated that, first of all, the neutralist argument cannot be properly understood when abstracted from the "politics of the *sahwa*" of the last two decades. Moreover, its argumentative path is given an added transcultural dimension for being generally assessed in the West as the area of reference for the "Islamic liberals", those who can express or translate Western values into an Islamic framework, thereby challenging the feared "fundamentalist" success.

Some representatives of the neutralist circle use the term *al-Islam as-siyasi* ("political Islam"), as in a famous book by al-'Ashmawi, for conveying the impression of corruption of true Islam: "God wanted Islam a religion; but [some] people want it to be politics."[58] If Islam makes an inroad into the political sphere, it is bound to corrupt its genuine nature. This appears to be, at first sight, the central formula of the neutralist circle. Neutralism distinguishes itself by the emphasis laid on the separation of Islam as a religion and way of life (*Islam din wa dunya*), on the one hand, and the realm of politics and government, on the other. It is problematic to equate neutralism with secularism, since this circle takes Islam seriously enough as a socio-cultural regulatory force or a "normative system". And, under the pressure of solutionism, it is even eager to discuss the extent to which it would be admissible or even arguable to define and construct an Islamic state or government. However, neutralist arguments are generally based on a higher degree of historical awareness than in the case of solutionism.[59]

Muhammad Ahmad Khalafallah shows a longer record of familiarity with such questions than most of the authors who have engaged in public contentions during the eighties. Khalafallah's elaboration on a deconflationist model dates back to at least 1973, when he published his book *al-Qur'an wa al-dawla*.[60] Six years earlier he had already dealt with some aspects that were crucial to the vision underlying conflationism, in the book *al-Qur'an wa mushkilat hayatina al-mu'asira*.[61] This work is, however, still inscribed in a perspective of refinement of 'Abd al-Raziq's argument, and the simplistic differentiation between the *al-dawla al-madaniyya* (a probably conscious translation of "secular state") and *al-dawla al-diniyya*[62] seems no longer to have been central in the later contributions that are examined below.

In the work published in 1973, Khalafallah openly challenges the argument in favour of the Islamic state, by focusing on its weakest points in logical terms. This challenge is based on the claim that if there is an Islamic way to the constitution of the state, this cannot be direct, but should follow the accomplishment of the principle of *islah*. What was already clear in the book of 1967 and is reiterated in the subsequent one, is, as also shown by the wording of their respective titles, that the author acknowledges only the Qur'an as the basis of justification of any social strategy inspired by Islam. In fact, he is keen to stress that, although the Qur'an does not prescribe anything concrete about the state, it provides some guidelines that should be taken into account.

In the context of the contention with the solutionist circle during the eighties, this fundamental claim has been reformulated by Khalafallah in a sharp and slightly provocative way. He has stated that using Islam for predicating something else through the adjectival form, such as *Islami/Islamiyya* or what might be called "attributional Islam", has hardly any basis in Islam as *din*. At least some of the concepts shaped through this attributional use of Islam have no textual basis, no footing in Scriptures. Among them there are key words in the solutionist circle such as *al-sahwa al-Islamiyya, al-hukuma al-Islamiyya, al-dawla al-Islamiyya* and, last but not least, *al-hall al-Islami* (the Islamic solution). The essay of Khalafallah, delivered at the already mentioned 1987 Amman conference and in some passages directly tackling al-Qaradawi's model, bears the significant title "*al-Islam bayna wahdat al-iman wa-ta'addudiyyat al-qira'at wa al-mumarasat*" (Islam between the unity of faith and the multiplicity of interpretations and practices). This title formulates the modern intellectual question of what "true Islam" is, or better should be, and hints at an answer by claiming that its hard shell is the *iman* (whose meaning is close to "faith"). This is supposed to embody what is unitary and untouchable, what is "sacred" in Islam, whereas all socially bound readings and practices inspired by it should be situated at a more profane level, their social relevance notwithstanding.[63]

This position is summarized by stating, through a formula which clearly echoes 'Abd al-Raziq, that in order to understand Islam one should try to differentiate between what belongs to the realm of *din* and what pertains to the domain of *la dini* ("non-religious" or "profane", more than just "secular").[64] Whereas the first realm seems to coincide with the *iman*,[65] this identification rapidly turns out to be a problem, as it appears in a passage of Khalafallah's argumentation where the major logical breach in the discursive path of neutralism is situated. Khalafallah shows here his awareness of how insidious the task is of sharply separating the two domains, which are variably linked in social reality.[66] However, he is inclined to ascribe the responsibility for this "contamination" of Islam as *din* to Western Orientalists, the alleged shapers of formulas such as "Islamic civilization" and even *Islam 'aqida wa shari'a*, instead of recognizing the socially endogenous reasons for the inherent complexity of any definition of "true Islam" as the basis for a framework of universal reference.

After this indictment of Orientalism, he promptly moves to tackling the problem of the Islamic state by addressing the rival solutionist circle. This abrupt passage is significant for two reasons: the first is that the author is incapable of pursuing in an autonomous, analytic way the question posed in the title and preliminarily approached at the beginning of the essay; the second is the apparent allusion to some strict continuity between the alleged Orientalist creation of "attributional" Islam and its use by solutionists. Among these he sees no difference between the wing represented by al-Qaradawi and the groups classified as extremist, such as al-Jihad. Khalafallah is eager to stress how the logical argument in favour of the Islamic state takes the upper hand in the framing model of the solutionist circle, to the detriment of the scriptural argument. Here he seems to have scored a point in favour of his position that tends to view true Islam as rooted in the Book, and even limitedly based on the *sunna* of the Prophet.

On this basis, Khalafallah seems to accuse al-Qaradawi of a too free exercise of *ijtihad*, as when the latter states that if one can perform a duty only in a given way, this way automatically becomes a duty, where the original duty is constituted by the obligations entailed by Islam. The "only way" refers to the institution of an Islamic state. This is, however, as we have seen, a simplification of the solutionist argument, to the extent that the call for an Islamic state is not independent of the more central call (loaded with symbolic, not merely logical significance) for the implementation of the *shari'a*. Through the ensuing argumentation, Khalafallah is not able or willing to capture this crucial and quite evident reason animating the rival claim. In fact, he insists on arguing on a merely logical level and raising the following question: while it is indisputable that Muslims belonging to a certain community need a state, are we really sure that we *need* an *Islamic* state? Why pose the question of the pursuit of true Islam in terms of government? Is this not rather a domain of purely social interaction, whose regulation God has permanently entrusted to man and his reason?[67]

Khalafallah's argumentation becomes more penetrating as he accuses the solutionist circle of overestimating the capacity of human reason to reproduce and represent the will of God. For Khalafallah is anxious not to deny, but to emphasize, the freedom of consciousness and the individual responsibility as rooted in *din*, and valid before God in the first instance. To immediately project into a vertical dimension the corresponding domain of reciprocal conduct (*mu'amalat*), i.e. in the sociological jargon, of "social interaction", is, however, an unjustified short cut.[68] The case of the particular rectitude and communal zeal of Muslims living in non-Muslim states is invoked as proof for countering the necessity of the projection of an Islamic state.[69]

Islam is deemed basically identical with other religions in that it is based on ethical principles; yet there is something more or something special in Islam. Khalafallah lists some Islamic ethical principles deemed as basic, and clearly transcending the level of *iman*. This is a point where he implicitly concedes that Islam is, beyond being an individual commitment to God, a blueprint for life conduct that inevitably affects the organization of the community. The list of principles culminates in the stress on *shura*, the mutual advice, which is necessary before taking decisions. This is undeniably a principle that also affects the methods of *hukm* (rule, or exercise of power), and Khalafallah is willing to praise its place in Islam, although there is no specification in the Qur'an of the proper modalities for its implementation. The resulting emphasis on the "enhanced" communal dimension of Islam, compared to other religions, is, nonetheless, in no way considered as a clue for formulating an Islamic doctrine concerning the power of the state. All principles, including *shura*, are rooted exclusively in consciousness.[70]

In another contribution Khalafallah expands this argument into a radical critique of the men of religion, accused of the arbitrary sacralization of extra-Qur'anic sources, in what happens to be a critique of the self-constitution of the *'ulama'* as the guardians of a sacred heritage. This is a passage that witnesses the importance of the conflict on the understanding of *'ilm* and the self-understanding of *'ulama'* that underlies the intellectual confrontation between solutionism and neutralism. Khalafallah asserts: "I shall have to do with God alone." Through direct contact with God and only in this way, one can creatively shape solutions. This implies a critique of solutionism as an unauthorized conflation between the human and a surreptitious divine realm arbitrarily confiscated by the *'ulama'*.[71] The precondition of any solution is consequently to sharply distinguish between the two realms.

Khalafallah carries the argument to its logical extreme, thereby shaping the final formula of neutralism. He claims that the necessary implementation of all basic Islamic principles including *shura*, is no prejudice against any form of government or constitutional profile of the state; the alternatives between monarchy or republic, democracy or dictatorship are an exclusively societal concern. Not all representatives of the neutralist circle would be willing to carry the argument so far. For al-'Ashmawi, for example, the principle of *shura* is the basis of "the government of the people; a government which they freely elect and in which they share; a government which they may change peacefully". This would be the "true Islamic government . . . not an Islamic government such as appeared in history but . . . another kind of government, one which would serve Islam rather than use it . . . [that] will offer Islam to all humankind as a way to God, a method for progress and a path of mercy. It will be the nucleus of a new ecumenical government, a core to a new united humanity."[72] This alternative model of closing the neutralist argumentation adopts in fact, in a slightly provocative way, an altered solutionist perspective, thereby defying the solutionism at the level of the actual profile of an Islamic state. Khalafallah is not far from a similar perspective, when he raises the question of social justice and distribution of wealth, thereby maintaining that a state that would endorse these issues could be legitimately called "Islamic". He uses this claim as a tool for accusing solutionism of not having any plausible solution to the most salient problem of communal relations.[73]

That the neutralist model is no dismissal of an autonomous, Arab–Islamic framework of universal reference is shown by the concluding claim that even without any reference to the actual form of state and government the Qur'an necessarily provides the basis of an "order" or "system" (nizam).[74] This affirmation, which echoes a central Qutbian motif, could be warmly supported by any solutionist and proves why the neutralist circle cannot be assimilated to liberalism in the Western sense.[75] Replying to the objections moved by the solutionist Hasan Turbi as well as by the Moroccan philosopher Muhammad 'Abid al-Jabiri in the discussion that followed the presentation of his paper at the Amman conference, Khalafallah added that his own plea was not against the Islamic state as such, but against propagating this as a religious duty. What is crucial for the neutralist position is to make clear that any discussion on the Islamic state is to be situated in the realm of human and historical contingency. Even if we may agree on the general formula of an Islamic state, its actual meaning depends on the orientation of the Muslims who run the state, as shown by the profound differences existing among the three existing approximations of Islamic states: Pakistan, Saudi Arabia and Iran.[76] In this way the neutralist circle eludes, however, the very core of the solutionist argument, centred on the symbolic power *and* the collective dimension of the call for the implementation of the shari'a. Here, the basic pitfall of neutralism is revealed: the difficulty of being neutral with regard to the vertical dimension of the organization of social life, just as one cannot be neutral when reference is made to the horizontal dimension.

The phenomenon of the apparent shifting of some leading authors from the orbit of the neutralist to that of the solutionist circle during the eighties, far from being a sign of a tendential exhaustion of the former, is a clue to the existence of a logical edge at the heart of the polarization. This edge makes the shift no dramatic jump in logical terms, on the one hand, and adds to the greater attractiveness of the solutionist circle for the higher strength of its symbolic references, on the other. Two recent cases, those of Khalid Muhammad Khalid and Muhammad 'Imara, have been widely read in terms of a mere "conversion" to the hegemonic argument of solutionism, as a pure matter of "going Islamist". However, it is more appropriate to look at the hermeneutic mechanism through which, within a possible pendulum between the two strictly interdependent forms of Islamic reformism that are basically *'ulama'*-mediated, the social and political situation of the last twenty years has favoured a swing of the pendulum towards solutionism.

The alleged shift of Khalid towards formal support of an Islamic state is certainly endowed with symbolic significance. In purely logical terms his argument[77] is nonetheless still virtually identical to that of some representatives of the neutralist circle, such as al-'Ashmawi, whose emphasis is on *shura* (the alleged Islamic equivalent of democracy) as the key for constructing a true Islamic government. The major difference is that Khalid does not use this argument for antagonizing the solutionists, as al-'Ashmawi does, but rather for accommodating or even joining them, by laying emphasis on the crucial properties of a future Islamic government, among which its democratic character is considered prominent.

There is a passage in Khalafallah that is of particular relevance for the direct approach of a crucial question underlying the hermeneutic legitimation of the reformed and intellectualized *'ilm*, and the new consensus grounded on it across the polarization between the two circles. Discussing the relationship between interest and interpretation, he claims that if the general interest (*maslaha 'amma* or simply *maslaha*) is at stake, the interpretation of the *faqih* (Islamic jurist) acquires a particular societal value. In posing the *maslaha* as a primary source, which can supersede the sacred texts in matters of *mu'amalat* (social interactions), he appeals to the Hanbalite *madhhab* (school) and in particular to Ibn Taymiyya.[78] This may sound surprising, to the extent that this medieval theologian-jurist, who represented a foremost authority for the proto-conflationism of Rashid Rida, has acquired during the last two decades the fame of a forerunner of solutionism, as he appears to be a source of inspiration for contemporary "fundamentalist" groups. This is however a distorted view, since Ibn Taymiyya provides a good "traditional" authoritative footing to the broader *islahi* strand, given that he posed the Qur'anic prescriptions, identified with the domain of *din*, as not legislating into the details of communal life, and highlighted instead how communal life should be at the service of *din*.[79]

This is a common terrain for the solutionist and the neutralist circles, and constitutes a further clue for showing how both circles are discursive derivations within the broader *islah*, and equally agree its emphasis on *ijtihad*. Their convergence lies in their support of the autonomous judgment of individual men and the need to take into account the requirements of the contemporary historical situation,[80] as well as in their emphasis on the "enhanced" social dimension of Islam, in comparison with other monotheistic religions. However, the terms of discourse used, common to both circles, have reached through the disputes of the eighties a degree of fixity and stagnation that is directly proportional to their incapacity to transcend the *islah* modalities of modern thinking or to take up the challenge of the cross-cultural commensurability of the political-intellectual modernity that sustains their efforts.

## NOTES

1 From the point of view of the Western perception, this era was inaugurated by the essay of Bernard Lewis, "The Return of Islam", *Commentary*, January 1976, pp. 39–49.

2 Leonard Binder, *Islamic Liberalism: A Critique of Development Ideologies* (Chicago and London: University of Chicago Press, 1988).

3 See Roland Robertson "Globalization, Politics, and Religion", *The Changing Face of Religion*, ed. James Beckford and Thomas Luckmann, (London: Sage Publications, 1989).

4 See Reinhard Schulze, "Mass Culture and Islamic Cultural Production in 19th Century Middle East", *Mass Culture, Popular Culture, and Social Life in the Middle East*, ed. George Stauth and Sami Zubaida (Frankfurt: Campus, 1987).

5 See Reinhard Schulze, "Muslimische Intellektuelle und die Moderne", *Feindbild Islam*, ed. Jochen Hippler und Andrea Lueg (Hamburg: Konkret, 1993), and Nazih Ayubi, *Political Islam: Religion and Politics in the Arab World* (London and New York: Routledge, 1991).

6 Albert Hourani, *Arabic Thought in the Liberal Age 1798–1939* (Cambridge: Cambridge University Press, 1983 [1962]), p. 163.

7 Binder, *Islamic Liberalism*.

8 Ibid., p. 138.

9 'Ali 'Abd al-Raziq, *al-Islam wa al hukm* (Cairo: Matba'at Misr, 1925), pp. 83–4.

10 Ibid., pp. 13–15.

11 Rotraut Wielandt, "Zeitgenössische ägyptische Stimmen zur Säkularisierungspolitik", *Die Welt des Islam*, 22 (1982), pp. 124–5.

12 On Qutb, see Yvonne Y. Haddad, "Sayyid Qutb: Ideologue of Islamic Revival", *Voices of Resurgent Islam*, John L. Esposito (New York and Oxford: Oxford University Press, 1991) and Ahmad S. Moussalli, *Radical Islamic Fundamentalism:*

*The Ideological and Political Discourse of Sayyid Qutb* (Beirut: American University of Beirut, 1992).

13  Binder, *Islamic Liberalism*, p. 128.

14  Yusuf al-Qaradawi, *al-Sahwa al-Islamiyya bayn al-juhud wa al-tatarruf* (Qatar: Matba'at al-Dawha al-Haditha, 1982), p. 201.

15  Yusuf al-Qaradawi, "al-'Itar al-'amm li al-sahwa al-Islamiyya al-mu'asira", *al-Sahwa al-Islamiyya wa humum al-watan al-'Arabi*, ed. Sa'id al-Din Ibrahim (Amman: Muntada al-Fikr al-'Arabi, 1988), p. 21.

16  Ibid., p. 17.

17  See Binder, *Islamic Liberalism*, pp. 16–17 and Ayubi, *Political Islam*, p. 228.

18  One could list several different definitions with the virtually equivalent denotative strength of "Islamic state", such as *al-khilafa, haqiqat al-Islam wa al-hukm, al-nazariyyat al-siyasiyya al-Islamiyya, nizam al-hukm fi al-Islam.* See Muhammad 'Abid al-Jabiri, *al-Khitab al-'Arabi al-mu'asir: dirasa tahliliyya naqdiyya* (Beirut: Dar al-Tali'a, 1982), p. 65.

19  Ayubi, *Political Islam*, p. 212.

20  See Wielandt, "Zeitgenössische", pp. 117–33 and Alexander Flores, "Secularism, Integralism and Political Islam", *Middle East Report* (July–August, 1993), pp. 32–8.

21  Flores, "Secularism", pp. 32–3.

22  See Nancy Gallager, "Islam v. Secularism in Cairo: An Account of the Dar al-Hikma Debate", *Middle Eastern Studies* 25 (1987), pp. 208–15 and Flores, "Secularism", pp. 37–8.

23  Yusuf al-Qaradawi, *al-Hall al-Islami farida wa darura* (Cairo: Maktabat Wahba, 1977 [Beirut 1974]).

24  al-Qaradawi, *al-Sahwa.*

25  Ibid., p. 131.

26  This expansion of meaning is however more difficult to demonstrate when the plural form is used, as in the mentioned excerpt.

27  al-Qaradawi, *al-Sahwa*, p. 150.

28  Schulze, *Islamischer Internationalismus*, pp. 34–46.

29  al-Qaradawi, *al-Sahwa*, p. 89.

30  Ibid., p. 17 and al-Qaradawi, "al-'Itar", p. 54.

31  al-Qaradawi, *al-Sahwa*, p. 89.

32  Ibid., pp. 11–20.

33  Ibid., p. 90.

34  Ibid., p. 100.

35  Ibid., p. 104.

36  Ibid., p. 133.

37  Ibid., p. 144.

38  The word used for "opinion", *ra'y*, also belongs to the traditional vocabulary of *fiqh*. In reformist *fiqh* the emphasis on the use of *ra'y* is a crucial tool for legitimizing the expansion of hermeneutic potentialities.

39  Evident is the closeness of this vision to the constitutional design of the Islamic Republic of Iran and its principle of the *wilayat-al-faqih*, the authority of the

*faqih*, all the doctrinal differences between Sunnism and Shi'ism notwithstanding. The Iranian case is, however, never explicitly mentioned by al-Qaradawi

40 al-Qaradawi, *al-Sahwa*, p. 145.
41 Ibid., p. 151.
42 al-Qaradawi, "al-'Itar", p. 55.
43 al-Qaradawi, *al-Sahwa*, p. 174.
44 Ibid., pp. 177–8.
45 Ibid., p. 29.
46 Ibid., pp. 27–8.
47 Ibid., p.19.
48 Ibid., p. 53.
49 Ibid., p. 134.
50 Ibid.
51 Ibid., p. 136.
52 Ibid., p. 176.
53 Ibid., pp. 218–21.
54 Ibid., pp. 222–3.
55 al-Qaradawi, "al-'Itar", p. 56.
56 Ibid., p. 107.
57 Flores, "Secularism", p. 35.
58 Quoted in Ayubi, *Political Islam*, p. 203.
59 For an extensive account of the production of the neutralist circle in Egypt during the eighties, see Ibid., pp. 201–15.
60 Muhammad Ahmad Khalafallah, *al-Qur'an wa al-dawla* (Cairo: Maktabat al-Anglo al-Misriyya, 1973).
61 Muhammad Ahmad Khalafallah, *al-Qur'an wa mushkilat hayatina al-mu 'asira* (Cairo: Maktabat al-Anglo al-Misriyya, 1967).
62 See Wielandt, "Zeitgenössische", p. 126.
63 Muhammad Ahmad Khalafallah "al-Islam bayna wahdat al-iman wa ta'addudiyyat al-qira'at wa al-mumarasat", *al-Sahwa al-Islamiyya wa humum*, pp. 149–50.
64 Ibid., p. 149.
65 Muhammad Ahmad Khalafallah, "al-Turath wa al-tajdid", *al-Mustaqbal al-'Arabi*, No. 28. 1981, p. 140.
66 Khalafallah, "al-Islam", p. 149.
67 Ibid., p. 151.
68 Khalafallah is particularly eager to recall that the amount of handling regulated by the Qur'an is low, whereas the highest number of suras concern dogma and worship ("al-Turath", p. 140).
69 Khalafallah, "al-Islam", p. 154.
70 The word here used for "consciousness", *admire*, attends a more individual domain than the word *wa'y* used by al-Qaradawi, more susceptible to be referred to as a collective dimension.
71 Khalafallah, "al-Turath", p. 139.
72 Sa'id al 'Ashmawi, "Islamic Government", *Middle East Review*, 18 (1986), pp. 12–13.

73 Khalafallah, "al-Islam", pp. 159–60.
74 Ibid., p. 157.
75 This obviously does not deny that some of its representatives can assume liberal (that is, compatible with Western liberalism) positions in political debates, but this is a side issue for the problematic tackled in this essay, which is concerned with the inner logic and terms of discourse of an Islamic dispute.
76 Khalafallah, "al-Islam", p. 164.
77 See Wielandt, "Zeitgenössische", p. 130.
78 Khalafallah, "al-Turath", pp. 140–1.
79 Louis Gardet "Din", *Encyclopédie de l'Islam*, New Edition, Vol. II, Leiden: Brill, 1978, p. 303.
80 Wielandt, "Zeitgenössische", pp. 128–9.

# 4

# Islamiyya and the Construction of the Human Being

*Ronald A. T. Judy*

In an interview published in the summer 1993 issue of *New Perspective Quarterly* entitled "Weak Ramparts of the Permissive West", the National Security Advisor to President Jimmy Carter, Zbigniew Brzezinski, offers a perplexing assessment of the post-Cold War struggle over human rights. Prompted by the interviewer's citing Malaysian Prime Minister Mohammad Mahathir's objection to what he calls the human rights imperialism of the West, Brzezinski remarks: "Some of that conflict is still a residue of the older era in which the political definition of human rights was part and parcel of the ideological conflict. As important as that may be, I am convinced that in the West we are moving beyond such conventional disputes to the much more complex question of what really is the human being and thus what really defines the scope of human rights."[1]

It should be borne in mind that the Brzezinski interview appears in an issue of *New Perspective Quarterly* that is focused on the question of religion's function in the New World Order, particularly Islam's, under the sectional rubric, "Civilization at Odds". The intent to echo Samuel Huntington's argument that this order is characterized by a "clash of civilizations" is explicitly emphasized throughout the interview, and by Huntington's contributing a piece entitled, "The Islamic–Confucian Connection", in the same section. That the question of human rights in Islam is of paramount concern in this issue is clearly indicated by the number of essays by prominent analysts and political players dedicated to the question. The range of contributors on this question is impressive, including Immanuel Wallerstein, Akbar Ahmed, Mahmoud Hussein, Edward Djerejian, Hassan al-Turabi, Abdullahi al-Naʿim, and Augustus Richard Norton.

Having put the Brzezinski interview in its context, which is admittedly by now well known, let us return to the perplexity of his assessment. There are two types of human rights discourse in Brzezinski's assessment, the political and that which is more complex than the political. Complexity is taken here as an index of this discourse being more fundamental and so beyond the discourse of political human rights. The West has superseded the political, *pace* ideological, conflict over human rights to consider the "truth" of the matter: "what really is the human being?"

Since the collapse of the Soviet Union as a state the West has required a coherent and compatible sense of stateless social formation. In this understanding, suppression of the political is a moment in the development of universal human consciousness, in our understanding of history. As Brzezinski puts it in the interview, "these are new dimensions of human rights." The problem is that up until the collapse, for the West as well as the Soviet Union, the state was the conceptual framework for development. The state was both the formation in which historical consciousness emerges as well as that which it develops towards. Accordingly, the purpose of the state is to enable the human subject that is possible in the state; that subject is in turn the protagonist for the state, and, thus the historical protagonist of the state. The more complex discourse of human rights is meant, then, to resolve a quandary in historical understanding: how to conceive of the stateless historical protagonist. In other words, does the human rights scheme belong to the political or to the human realm? Or, is it just a political discourse that is meaningful within the context of the state?

According to Brzezinski, situating the question of what really is the human beyond the political recasts what have been traditionally understood as geopolitical conflicts of interest as cultural or civilizational conflicts. In these terms, the issue of conflict is no longer the state, but civil society. And the struggle is over what will be the nature of civil society without the state. In the context of that struggle, Brzezinski's attempt at understanding "human rights in the broader sense" is concerned not with determining the possible conceptual schema for the stateless subject, but rescuing the subject of humanism from the collapse of its project by appropriating the emergent schemas to that project.

Here Brzezinski's assessment betrays itself as a residue of the older era political analysis. After all, since Hegel, civil society has been the conceptual shadow of the state; it is that which grows up into the state.

The acknowledgment of Muhammad Mahathir's concern with cultural imperialism as a remnant of geopolitics is attended by a tacit refusal to recognize that with the collapse of the geopolitical there emerge different possibilities of social formation with their attendant ways of thinking about history. In this regard, viewing Islam as a civilizational phenomenon is an exemplary instance of that refusal to recognize. Brzezinski is emphatic that the West not take the position that Islam is automatically its enemy and automatically against politically defined human rights. In fact, he remarks on the folly of the West's trying to impose on Islam a purely political definition of human rights while at the same time propagating a global culture characterized by a material hedonism that is much more detrimental to the human condition.

If Brzezinski reiterates in this way Edward Djerejian's caveat that Western powers must be able to differentiate between "militant" and acceptable or "moderate" Islam, he also echoes Djerejian's failure to define the latter except to the extent that it is identified with Western conceptualizations of "the human condition". Consequently, the questions that *New Perspective Quarterly* raises with Brzezinski about Islam return us to the concern of the Enlightenment with determining the rules governing the relationship between theoretical understanding (science and technology) and practical philosophy (morality). Asserting that the kind of questions that the broader understanding of human rights must address are those prompted by the discoveries of biotechnology and genetics research, Brzezinski delineates the field of dispute: "Who has the right to end a life, whether in the womb or in the hospital bed? A mother, a priest, a doctor, the state or the church? What about genetic self-alteration? Who has the right to determine its scope and its limits? A scientist or a theologian?"

Cast in these terms, the question of what really is the human being fails to escape the dualism that has characterized modernity since Descartes, separating physical history from the development of consciousness. This dualism is explicit in Brzezinski's assessment. The real human subject is universal, transcending the particular material manifestations of the political human subject. Although this difference has been made more apparent by the technological advancements in telecommunications, facilitating a global economy of consumption, that technology does not help us determine the rights of the transcendental human subject. These are found in morality, in a practical philosophy "inherent in the values of which we partake traditionally in the three great religions – Christianity, Judaism and Islam".

Leaving aside the retrograde notion of the sources of morality for the West (a notion that betrays a profound shallowness of historical understanding), the inclusion of Islam among the sources of a practical philosophy appropriate to the New World Order requires a reformulation in the assessment of the post-Cold War struggle over human rights. It is not a question of Islam and the West, but Islam and modernity. And, if Islam is recognizable as a part of modernity, albeit non-secular, in its conceptualization of humanness, in what way is it so? The answer Brzezinski and the *New Perspective Quarterly* suggest bears a striking resemblance to the project articulated by Dr Hassan Abdullah al-Turabi, who is generally regarded by Western analysts as a chief ideologue of global Islamism, as well as the architect of the course by which Sudan has become the only state in our age to formally establish *shari'a* as its system of government: in the face of the failure of Western liberalism to formulate a successful political theory for "how incommensurable civilizations can co-exist in a new world order" of global capital, Brzezinski says, "It is time to recognize that the spiritual dimension of life is as important as the material." As Turabi put it in his contribution to the same summer 1993 issue of *New Perspective Quarterly*,

> Awakened Islam today provides people with a sense of identity and direction in life, something shattered in Africa since colonialism . . . Islam provides a focus for unity and a minimum consensus in the face of the regionalism and tribalism which have been so devastatingly rampant in Africa. The idea of the "nation" has offered nothing in this regard . . . Moreover, the Islamic code of *shari'a* provides the people with higher laws and values, which they obey out of belief and not because they are enforced by government.

This resemblance warrants scrutiny. In arguing that the engagement with Islam must be as a counterbalance to the unbridled consumerism of the West – that is, as part of the moral counterpart to technology and capital – Brzezinski suggests the possibility of exploring the quandary of historical understanding in Islamist terms. Plainly put, much of the current Western policy towards and thinking about Islam clearly indicates how along with the collapse of the geopolitical understanding of history there is a concomitant failure of its categories of knowledge and value. It is due to the persistence in attempting to understand the emerging world according to the old categories that Islamism is regarded as a threat to the New World Order because it articulates an understanding of the human subject that is not somehow derivative of the historical project of Western humanism. Attending the emergence of a new world order is the necessity for new categories of knowledge and value. Determining whether or not Islamism is a threat to either requires giving some consideration to its own thinking: the apparent resemblance between Brzezinski's and Turabi's.

What is the status of the complex question of human being in relation to the concept of civil society for Islamism? According to Turabi, the Islamic Awakening, or Islamism, is a development of a mixture of different civilizations; it is a movement of unification led by intellectuals, many of whom were educated in Western countries and influenced by their intellectual culture (*al-thaqafa al-gharbiyya*). In this way, Islamism appears to be an intellectual project, whose agenda is to address the quandary of the historical subject – what is really the human being – by displacing historical understanding with a new practical philosophy. Turabi recognizes that as an intellectual project concerned with the conjunction of variegate categories of knowledge around the relationship of material history and the essence of humanity, Islamism cannot escape its own history.[2]

For some time now, Western analyses of the tension between Islam and modernity have been subject to the somewhat idealist view of Islam as a code-system (*aqa'id*) that, although accessible to rational critique, is not comprehensible for historical understanding. As was seen in Brzezinski's interview with *New Perspective Quarterly*, much is made of there being a "cultural" clash between Islam and the West, that the two consist of mutually incompatible categories of knowledge, of different systems of signification – i.e. codes – according to which value is determined. Although the difference between Islam and the West may very well be indicative of radically different cultural codes, it is not a given that those codes are incompatible. Were they incompatible, then cultural contact would result in their mutual destruction: both cultures would lose their "languages", as it were. The assumption of their compatibility, on the other hand, carries with it the thought that during cultural contact the two codes combine into a hybrid, resulting in a new comprehensive cultural code. Turabi has characterized the movement of Islamism in this way on numerous occasions.[3]

It is crucial that we do not lose sight of what happens in Turabi's characterization of Islamism to the familiar distinction between modernization as science-based material progress (*tahdith*), and modernity as an attitude of thought which aims at determining the absolute universal conditions of moral-being through reason (*hadatha*). Modernity in this sense is identifiable with the Enlightenment and post-Enlightenment projects of the rationalization of the world. Insofar as these projects claim to discover, along with material progress, the grounds for moral value in reason Turabi calls them Western civilization. Yet, because civilization is not only axiology but the everyday realization of moral values, these projects have succeeded as technology but failed as civilization. This failure is adduced from the way in which hypercommodification has undermined civil society in the West, resulting in an inability to reconcile individual sovereignty with social justice, getting a profound problematic of alienation manifest in collective crises of identity (ethnic conflict, fundamentalism, etc.).

The paradox of modernity is that its success as a mode of knowledge in which reality is theoretically (scientifically) thought, produces this crisis; the rationalization of nature, that is the global culture of technology-driven hypercommodification, is not civilization qua morality. Nonetheless, the successful dissemination of modernity in the course of reaching its impasse, i.e. colonialism, has brought about recognition of the historical limitations of all discursive knowledges which it has taken up into it. This includes the Islamic juridical discourse, *shari'a*. The challenge of the secular model of subjective experience has compelled the disassociation of Islam's juridical and ethical discourses, rupturing what had come to be treated as an inferential relationship between state and social formation. Consequently, Turabi approaches the contestation between *shari'a* and modernity as that between two heterogeneous modalities of knowledge. This in itself in not terribly insightful. That the difference between Islam and modernity is that of conflicting modalities of thought has been a tenet of Muslim analyses of the situation, arguably, since Rifa'a Rafi' al-Tahtawi published his *talkhis al-ibriz ila talkhis Bariz* (1834). Turabi's approach is, however, provocative in the attempt to think Islam as epistemology, rather than as an object of or the legitimate grounds for epistemology. He does this by elaborating an Islamic meta-narrative that historicizes the events of modernity as stages in the dialectical development of Islam.

Understanding the post-colonial Islamic world as being determined, in large part, by the disruptions of modernity, and so as an inextricable part of the emerging world of transnational capital, leads Turabi to define the tension between Islam and modernity epistemologically in a manner that organizes human action into heteronomous domains of knowledge: theory, moral, and juridical. The effect is a redefinition of Islam's relationship to modernity, the contest in terms of the struggle between Islam and the technology-driven hypercommodification of human existence. Although the state is still conceived of as *"veilleur de nuit"* in this redefinition, it is not the realization of aggregate individual or party sovereignty, but is the realization of divine sovereignty, expressed in the historical praxis of *shari'a*. *Shari'a*, thus, defines a purely legal discourse in which the source of law is transcendental – Allah. Accordingly, there are no valid transcendent historical sources of law such as inalienable human rights, inherent human sovereign will, or constitutional principles, except insofar as these derive from *shari'a*. The possibility of derivative rights is significant, in that it enables Turabi to entertain some notion of a public sphere of activity beyond the state in which critique and societal reform are possible. The important question becomes whether or not that public sphere is heterogeneous to the state, which is to ask: what are the possibilities for civil society? The distinction between modernity (*hadatha*) and modernization (*tahdith*) transcended in an understanding of *shari'a* as a legal function of the state, geared towards the re-establishment and sustaining of precisely the category of traditional socializing institutions that Western analysts like Brzezinski, and more recently Francis Fukuyama, identify with civil society. Crucial to any viable theory of civil society is how it addresses the problematics of value-transference across disparate domains of activity. This is all the more a necessary function of a theory of a global Islamic civil society where the domains are defined according to contesting and contested heterogeneous modalities of knowledge. Assuming that the paramount value at issue is what is or is not Muslim, the problematic of transference becomes, in short order, that of determining the authentic representation of Muslim subjectivity, which in turn is always a question of determining the "authentic" conception of experience. Turabi addresses this issue as a problematic of culture, or as he calls it civilization. Civilization is the agency of value. It could be said that it is "the enabling to distinguish values and to observe these values in daily conduct". This *imkaniya*, this enabling, is theoretical in the sense that it is a categorical discursive knowledge, an economy of signification in which meaning is valued in accordance with true unity (*tawhid*). As such, civilization is morality *in toto*: it is both theoretical understanding of truth and the derivative axiology that legitimates action. Hence Turabi can define morality as discretion in the exercise of individual sovereignty.[4]

Accordingly, the difference between Islam and modernity is not that one strives for and one negates individual sovereignty. Instead, it is in how they legitimize individual sovereignty. Modernity does so theoretically on the basis of reason, Islam does it literally on the basis of revelation. The most radical aspect of Turabi's project is his appropriating to Islam the post-Enlightenment theory of civil society as heteronomous domains of agency as though it had always been the dynamic force of Islamic development. What Turabi purposes is an Islamic concept of civil society that, while sustained by the same principal sources as *shari'a*, has the internal capacity to supersede its historical anachronisms.

Here, Turabi adheres to the established jurisprudence's division of Islamic practice into two spheres of legal action: *mu'amalat* (social transactions) and *'ibadat* (ritual praxis or worship). Maintaining that these two spheres of law constitute different aspects of the same general corpus of Islam with the difference between them being one of degree and not essence, Turabi extends the difference between these spheres of action to their textual basis in Qur'an. The laws of *mu'amalat* derive from readings in the *surat* of the Qur'an that were revealed in Medina, and dealt explicitly with the correct protocols of social interaction. The laws of *'ibadat* derive from the *surat* of the Qur'an revealed in Mecca, which focused principally on questions of theology and social justice. The Meccan *surat* of the Qur'an elaborate on Allah's uniqueness as the transcendental being, and the equality of each individual human's responsibility to worship Allah. This message of equal responsibility in worship is mirrored by the message of equality and individual responsibility between all men and women. For Turabi, the function of *mu'amalat* is to create a social structure in which every individual Muslim can realize the message of *'ibadat* in its fullness. It is supposed that prior to Western colonialism this was done through the careful and rigorous elaboration of *shari'a*. With colonialism a gap occurred between the capacity of *shari'a* to adequately account for and integrate into its discourse an ever increasing series of socially disruptive changes. What is required is an historical understanding of *shari'a*. The trick is to sublate *shari'a* Islamically, which, to say the least, seems paradoxical. Turabi's Islamism is predicated on the freedom of the individual to submit absolutely to divine law. In asserting that Islamism is the praxis of individual sovereignty, he focuses attention on the central issue at stake in the New World Order: the relation between subjective expression and objective possibility.

While employing the secularist opposition of reason to understanding, he does not identify *shari'a* with natural law; nor does he invest in *shari'a* as the inviolable basis for knowledge. Instead he sublates it with *sunna*, hence shifting the field of conflict from that of competing juridical discourses – *shari'a* and civil law – to that of axiology. What colonialism and modernity have demonstrated, beyond a doubt, is that *shari'a* is a historical construct that has reached its limits, and the result is not the projected individual of civilization. The significance of this lesson gets magnified by the fact that virtually every current movement of Islamic resurgence and political struggle for the return to *shari'a* is predicated on the inalienable right of self-determination. Given the heterogeneity constitutive of the Arab nation-states, the wholesale return to pre-colonial, pre-modern *shari'a*, rather than guaranteeing the sovereignty of the individual in civil society, would necessitate the disenfranchisement of many on the basis of irregular application of moral value. Still, Muslims should not be expected to forfeit their own right to self-determination and sovereignty. What is needed, then, is an Islamic discourse of individual rights that, while adhering to the foundational *'aqa'ida* of Islam, is universal enough to accommodate non-Muslims. For Turabi, *sunna* provides such a discourse. In opposition to modernity's economy of value based in an empirical phenomenology, *sunna* operates an economy based on phenomenal indeterminacy.

Individual sovereignty in Prophetic discourse is not determined by relations of propriety, but a theory of signification, according to which understanding is purely a priori; that is, it is essentially a fiat of belief, instantiated in a specific genealogy of thought. It is precisely the authority of this genealogy of thought (i.e., *ijma'*), which forms the basis of what is designated in Islam as *'ilm*, that is at issue for Turabi.[5] Simply put, Turabi is able to discern a viable philosophy of praxis through an inspired close reading of the Qur'an, enabled by the verifiable lines of oral transmission emanating from Muhammad's expressions and praxes, via his most trustworthy companions.

Verification implies at least the possibility of false witness, or worse, corrupt genealogy. In some sense, the formalization of the terms of verification into a methodological science – *'ilm-ur-rijal* – that combined ethical analysis with philology was a response to the danger of genealogical entropy, predicated on the recognition that verification was fundamentally a problem of indeterminate sign production.[6] In other words, the vast and highly complex system of Islamic knowledge is arranged according to a logic of culture in which every entity can become a semiotic phenomenon – every aspect of culture involves exchange value.

The traditional name for this logic is *'ilm-ul-kalam*, the paramount concern of which, from the time of its founding by Abu Hanifa (d. 150 AH/AD 767), was the axiology of the sign. Belief in the Qur'an's actually entailing *kalam Allah* (meaning that divine speech consisted of empirical signs) necessitated a theory of signification which differentiated logically between the materiality of the linguistic sign and the indeterminacy or incorporeality of what the sign conveys. This theory was given its most sophisticated formulation by al-Ghazali, who elaborated a doctrine of the sign as *modus ponens*. What is signified by the material text of the Qur'an (viz. the material *alfaz*) is an expression of relationship to the divine discourse and not the divine discourse itself. The signification is relational precisely because it is not concerned, *per se*, with the materiality of the text, instead it is concerned with the possibility of the inferential relationship occurring. What al-Ghazali established was the logical basis for jurisprudence in the axiomatic definition of the *necessary* correlation of the material Qur'an to a specific class of signifieds – *kalam Allah*. That necessity is called *sunna*, understood as the code of prophetic discourse.

Although working through the details of al-Ghazali's argument for the verifiability of prophecy is necessary for any thorough understanding of his system of thought, only two aspects of it are pertinent to the issue at hand. These are that determining the appropriate code of inference is a property unique to the prophet, and that, subsequent to the prophet's death, the authentic continuation of that code is the function of *ijma'*. In his *al-Mustasfa min 'ilm al-usul*, al-Ghazali defines *ijma'* as "the consensus of the community of Muhammad, particularly on a religious matter [*Ittifaq ummat Muhammad, salla Allah 'alayh wa sallam, khassatan 'ala amir min al-umur al-diniyya*]".[7] The issue of whether or not *ijma'* so defined, and its requisite mode of expression, are possible is beyond the scope of this paper. The identification of *ijma'* with the community (*ummat Muhammad*), however, goes directly to Turabi's argument for understanding Islam as a logic of culture in which every thing is a sign to be properly read.

For all *sunna* Muslim methodologies, and most *shi'a* methodologies, *ijma'* is recognized as a source of jurisprudence after Qur'an and *hadith*. There was no need for a theory of jurisprudence during Muhammad's lifetime, as his *sunna* was an ever-developing code, constantly adjusting to new events. Muhammad's death resulted in the truncation of the code's development. Consequently, when juridical issues arose for which there was no explicit Qur'anic injunction or prophetic proscription there was a need to extrapolate a rule adduced from these two source-texts. The earliest methods of adduction were *ijma'* and *qiyas*, analogy in aspect. Of these two methods *ijma'* functioned as the metonymic substitute of the dead prophet. Again, we need not be too concerned here with the finer arguments about the possibility of a truly collective consensus, or with the distinction between *ijma' sukuti* (implicit) and *ijma' qawli* (explicit). With regards to the status of the Qur'an as *kalam Allah*, that is a matter of *usul al-din*, and the consensus is universal.

As far as determining the authoritative code of reading the sign, then, we have a certain deductive inference: it is a recognized *ijma'* that the Qur'an is Allah's discourse; *ijma'* is infallible and binding; thus, the correlation of the Qur'an's material expression with Allah's eternal discourse is true and binding. What needs to be borne in mind is that this particular deductive inference is *qiyyas* in the sense of a syllogism, as opposed to juridical sense of analogy in aspect. The implication is that the materiality of the Qur'an in reading indicates a relationship with text, an activity of knowing. This activity is *shari'a* grounded in *ijma'*, which are grounded in the source-texts (Qur'an and *hadith*), *per se*, as these are the objects of the activity of knowing. This confusion of modalities of analogy with syllogistic reasoning itself is an index of the historical moment in which Islamic thinking and Hellenistic thought converge, generating a highly sophisticated social order characterized by the tensions of heterogeneity. Because of the problematic nature of the relationship between *qiyyas* as the syllogism legitimating *ijma'*, and as its mechanism of adjudication, there has never been a firm juridical definition of community; this is a failure that has always invested *shari'a* with a certain crisis of legitimacy. Consider that the activity of knowing as *ijma'* is legitimated on the assumption of the self-evident source-texts which are its objects. This is a formal fallacy of affirming the consequent, that the logical legitimacy of *ijma'* results from the logical error of inferring the truth of the premises from the truth of the conclusion. Al-Ghazali employed this formal fallacy in order to limit the critical (philosophical) inquiry of thought, which, unbridled, would subjugate the activity of Islam to the law of identity, and subvert the sanctity of our relation to the divine referent. His own case for the indexical sign-function carries the same potential, however. Therefore, an adjustment must be made in the case that will allow for the determination of the necessary correlation of the sign-function – i.e. *ijma'* – and *kalam Allah*. The crucial distinction here is between *qiyyas* as sign-function (syllogism), and *qiyyas* as symbol. As sign-function it is a relational term indicating an historical, material activity of inference that is recognized communicative behaviour. As symbol, on the other hand, it is not based on the model of inference but on the model of equivalence; it is a sort of signal which has an indeterminate relation to its agent. Both that relation and its agent are noumenal (essential), in the Kantian sense of being beyond our cognitive capacity to comprehend; they are "the unthought" of the sign-function (as al-Ghazali puts it *kalam Allah* is *sifatuh ul-qadim ul-qa'ima bi dhatihi*). It is in this sense that the material signs of the Qur'an are taken to be symbols of the unthought. But this unthought is thinkable only in terms of sign-functions which are indexical. Accordingly, the Qur'an legitimates *ijma'* which is its index. And in that indexical relation of sign-function *ijma'* engages the symbolic.

Another way of looking at *ijma'* is as the authorized way of thinking the unthought, because it lets the unthought be (*Gelassenheit*), that is, *Allah majhul*. By definition, then, *ijma'* is the collective activity of knowing that defines the community of legitimate readers. This means that the community is defined by an activity that is unthinkable in its taking place (al-Ghazali's principal complaint against the philosophers is that they fail to recognize *ijma'* as a conservative extension of prophetic discourse).[8] Questioning the legitimacy of *ijma'* as the activity defining community is tantamount to a lapse in faith, which is why al-Ghazali levels the serious juridico-theological charge of *zandaqa* (apostasy) against the philosophers for their theories of the eternality of the world, Allah's ignorance of particulars, and the denial of bodily resurrection.

It is precisely this axiomatic correlation of *sunna* and *shari'a* that Turabi means to dispose of, so that *ijma'* can be reinscribed as the collective process of reading instead of the product of reading. Once *ijma'* is reinscribed in this way, the question of communal identity and its derivative subjective identities is discovered to be at the heart of the issue of Islam's place in the new world order. What is at stake in determining the proper inferential relation of signifier to signified is the definition of the Muslim as the particular, subjective, historical expression of a collective cultural activity transcending the historical into history. Islamic *'ilm* is the correct way to think about value.

Even though both the Enlightenment and *'ilm* are characterized by their attempts to think the unthought, there are differences that at first glance place them at odds. Chief among these is the nature of the unthought. Whereas for *'ilm* it is Allah, for the Enlightenment it is the possibility of thought itself. This difference informs the difference in the way Enlightenment thinks the unthought. In contrast to *'ilm*'s letting be the unthought, for the Enlightenment the unthought is a *telos* that will eventually be known through the extension of reason in the world. Instead of the distinction Allah/appearance that subtends *'ilm*'s idea of signification, the Enlightenment puts the opposition natural/unnatural at the base of cultural activity. For the Enlightenment the world is real; there is no agent in absentia, whose intentionality can be discerned in the signs of nature. Indeed, there is an adamant resistance, on the part of the Enlightenment, to the very principle of the sign. The natural order is real, the order of signs is constructed and only appearance. Appearances are tangential, and serve the function of constructing a viable realm of cultural activity, whose only legitimate aim is to finally conceptualize the real. To comprehensively think the unthought through the extension of reason in the world is the Enlightenment project. Delineating natural law is an aspect of that project.

The tact among modernist Islamic reformers since at-Tahtawi has been to equate *shari'a* with natural law, thus appropriating Islam to the Enlightenment project. The cost for this appropriation has been Islam's engaging in trying to think the unthought rather than let it be. An engagement that has so undermined the authority of *shari'a* to provide value that Muslim society was condemned to unprecedented oppression.[9] Turabi's Islamic Awakening is an attempt to get some return on this investment by converting the relation of equivalence into one of inference – natural law is an expression of the divine principles of absolute individual freedom which subtends *sunna*. Inference is sublimated by analogy by aspect, or metonymy, so that the historical events of modernity can be read as preparatory stages in the universal advent of Islam's awakening. Turabi thus appropriates modernity to Islam. The effect is an idealist teleology. All historical phenomena, including *shari'a*'s marginalization by the colonial and postcolonial Muslim state, can be read as signs of Islam's development. This is why *shari'a* is the propaedeutic to the universal philosophy of praxis in which the activity of knowing that is Islam defines itself (comes to consciousness of its historicity) and realizes the world.

In a way perhaps more within the discursive field (*madhab*) of the Hanafi *mutakallimun* than he wished it to be Turabi reads the sign as an ahistorical index of the possibilities of history and power, such that any attempt to fix or erase any of these possibilities only assures their continuation as an inevitable resistance. There is a dialectic of bound doubles in Turabi's reading, according to which each realization of a certain power formation in a specific constellation of social structure anticipates its own overturning (here he follows Ibn Khaldun). Islam is an ideology of power that will reach a final end in the period of enlightenment when every subject of the community is competent to recognize the manifold possibilities of Being entailed in the sign. This collapsing of the distance between implied and explicit *ijma'* is achieved by democratizing knowledge. It appears, then, that Turabi is making a move beyond *shari'a*, in which the legitimating definition of the Muslim is no longer mitigated by a privileged discourse of power; instead the Muslim is recognized in the absolute freedom of thought. As he explained recently to Milton Viorst,

> Intellectual attitudes toward Islam are not going to be regulated or codified at all. The presumption is that people are free. The religious freedom not just of non-Muslims, but even of Muslims who have different views, is going to be guaranteed. I personally have views that run against all the orthodox schools of law on the status of women, on the court testimony of non-Muslims, on the law of apostasy. Some people say that I have been influenced by the

West and that I border on apostasy myself. But I don't accept the condemnation of Salman Rushdie. If a Muslim wakes up in the morning and says he doesn't believe any more, that's his business. There has never been any question of inhibiting people's freedom to express any understanding of Islam.[10]

It should be borne in mind that this is stated without irony by the man who was Attorney General of Sudan in 1985. Still, what does such a position mean for the more renowned Islamist's insistence on the Islamic state, on the rule of *shari'a*? Turabi's response is that "the scope of government is limited. Law is not the only agency of social control. Moral norms, individual conscience, all these are very important, and they are autonomous . . . The function of government is not total."[11] And it is not total "because it is Islam that is a total way of life, and if you reduce it to government, then government would be omnipotent, and that is not Islamic".[12] Yet while working towards the evolution of *shari'a* into a system of government, a new *ijma'* that does not confuse the legal with the moral, Turabi has demonstrated by his actions in government that he does not endorse pursuing a process of *ijtihad* in which *ilham* (epiphany) displaces *qiyyas* as the principal interpretive tool. What this means is that although the Islamist conception of the Muslim, as that subjectivity engaged in thinking the unthought of its own knowledge, liberates the individual from the constraints of historically limited legal doctrine, it is also a historicization of the activity of thinking as the unique final expression in the world of the transcendental unthought (Allah). Turabi is concerned with thinking the unthought of Islam as a horizon to be approached with the expectation of subjective fulfilment.

With this we return to the quandary in historical understanding with which we began. Turabi's Islamic Awakening aims for the stateless historical protagonist. To that extent it foregrounds a global crisis of memory, which is to say that what Turabi is struggling to do by forming an Islamic civil society is to achieve some control over memory in the face of the global economy of unbridled consumerism in which memory is commodified as nostalgia for a set of images that trade as identity. The traditional historical understanding of Islam, *shari'a*, unravels precisely because the Muslim subjectivity cannot be the presence of the unthought in humanity without a determinate memory. Turabi insists on the evolution of *shari'a* as opposed to its abandonment because he has no other historical conception of Islam. The call for evolution, then, is a bid to retain a specific collective memory as a viable possibility of human being in an emerging world order in which the inconstancy of memory heralds the end of the human being, or at least the concept of the human being as the protagonist of history. That concept is sustained in civil society as a "public" sphere of action, heterogeneous from, while enabled by, the Islamic state, precisely because the latter is based on *shari'a*. This, however, exacerbates rather than resolves the quandary of historical understanding. If the public sphere and the state are both derivative of a unified *shari'a*, then there is no civil society, in the sense that the public sphere and state are identical. Such unity of identity (*tawhid*) is the Islamist ideal; civil society is a categorical necessity whenever the Islamic state relates to a heterogeneous society, which, in light of Turabi's recognition of the multiplicities of intellectual attitudes toward Islam is always the case. Civil society here becomes the sphere of difference in which heterogeneous systems of identity interact. Insofar as the possibilities for exchange are determined by the historicity of each system, civil society cannot be natural, or identified with culture or civilization; instead it is the possibility of exchange itself. In this sense civil society is neither the possibility of collective identity (civilization) nor the historical outcome of collective identity (political society). Instead, it is the conceptual limit of identity – it is the moment of exchange in which civilization can be theorized as such. In the view of Turabi this exchange is both local and global. Locally, it is explicitly civilizational – what are the liberties of non-Muslims within the Islamist sphere? Globally, it is civilization mediated through economic interest – how can Muslims participate in transnational capital as Muslims? Granting the validity of this understanding of Turabi's project, Islamism, as he conceives it, is indeed no threat to the New World Order, *per se*.

## NOTES

1 Zbigniew Brzezinski, "Weak Ramparts of the Permissive West", interviewed by Nathan Gardels, *New Perspective Quarterly*,10, No. 3 (summer 1993), pp. 4–9.

2 For a systematic analysis of al-Turabi's major writings, see Ahmad S. Moussalli, "Hasan al-Turabi's Discourse on Democracy and Shura", *Middle Eastern Studies*, Vol. 30, No. 1, 1994, pp. 52–63.

3 Cf. Hassan al-Turabi, "The Islamic Awakening's New Wave", *New Perspective Quarterly*,10, No. 3 (summer 1993), pp. 42–5; Hassan al-Turabi, "Arafat is but a mayor, and Carlos was a mine we blew in Washington." Interview by Talal Kheris, *Ash-Shiraa* (October 1994), pp. 26–7; Milton Viorst, "Sudan's Islamic Experiment", *Foreign Affairs* (spring 1995), pp. 45–54.

4 Ibid., p. 45.

5 The polysemia of the term *'ilm* is best echoed in the Enlightenment concept of *Wissenschaften*, an interpretive translation that is not simply fortuitous, but speaks directly to the distinction of Turabi's principal assumption that Islam, like the Enlightenment, is an epistemological project for individual sovereignty.

6 This attention to the connectedness of ethical and theoretical values was a definitive feature of Islamic philological methodology. I have explored the specific implications of this methodological device for lexicography elsewhere; see R. Judy, *(Dis)forming the American Canon: African–Arabic Slave Narratives and the Vernacular* (Minneapolis: University of Minnesota Press, 1993), pp. 263–6.

7 This definition is somewhat more exclusive and precise than the one he gave in his earlier work, *al-Mankul min ta'liqat-il-usul*, where *ijma'* is defined as "the unanimity of the *mujtahidun* [*ahl al-hall wa 'l'aqd*]" (303).

8 At this point al-Ghazali makes the informal fallacy of *consensus gentium* in his argument that the Qur'an's being created and its symbolic value are facts of *ijma'*, and *ipso facto* true and binding.

9 al-Turabi, "The Islamic Awakening", p. 43.

10 Viorst, "Sudan's Islamic Experiment", p. 51.

11 Ibid.

12 Ibid.

# PART II

## CASE STUDIES

# 5

# State, Civil Society and the Question of Radical Fundamentalism in Algeria

*Yahia H. Zoubir*

## Introduction

While the new radical critics are routinely attacked, muzzled, and suppressed in most Arab regimes, fundamentalist spokespersons are not only allowed to proclaim their doctrines freely and publicly but are often provided with substantial aid by the state institutional machinery and media. Fundamentalism derives much of its strength from the vulnerability of the ruling classes, who invoke the same ideology as fundamentalism to validate their own uncertain legitimacy.[1]

The rise of radical fundamentalism in Algeria is a difficult phenomenon to explain, for, as in other Arab–Islamic societies, a close relationship between religion and politics has always existed. In Algeria, both civil society and the state are strongly permeated by Islam.[2] Islam is not merely a religion, but constitutes the basis of identity and culture. Not only does it regulate social behaviour, but, to a great extent, it also governs social relations. The state in the Middle East and North Africa has always resorted to Islamic symbols to establish and reproduce its legitimacy, whereas certain social movements have used Islam to wage their struggle against the established regimes. Today, radical fundamentalism has emerged as the most important and potent protest movement. Whatever one's assessment of the fundamentalist movement in Algeria, it is clear that neither Islam nor the fundamentalist phenomenon can be dissociated from the history of the Algerian nationalist movement.[3] It is no exaggeration to argue that the fundamentalist movement is one of the belated sequels of the nature of the colonial rule in that country.

Indeed, the brutality with which French colonial authorities expropriated the main local religious institutions (closing down of mosques and religious schools, expropriation of religious lands, etc.)[4] left an indelible mark in the Algerian psyche. The coercion to which France resorted in order to establish its cultural hegemony in Algeria[5] and the contempt with which the French treated the native population and its values[6] provides the explanation as to why Algerians clung to Islam as the most salient component of their national identity, on the one hand, and to the nationalist movement to use Arab–Islamic values as symbols for popular mobilization against the colonialists, on the other. Even if most of the leaders of the revolution were French-educated and carried a secular vision, the War of National Liberation (1954–62) was conducted as a *jihad* (holy war) and the fighters were designated *mujahidin* (holy warriors). In fact, not unlike the rest of the Arab world, in Algeria two antinomic currents, nationalism and the Islamic sentiment, dominated the system, whereby successive regimes would refer to revolutionary principles whose concrete application could not but be severely limited.[7]

## State and Society in Algeria

Before dealing with the question of fundamentalism in Algeria, it is crucial to give a brief description of the political system installed after the country's independence, the development strategy, and the position of civil society.

Despite the difficulty of defining with precision the Algerian political system, there is no doubt, however, as to its authoritarian character. The system was characterized by the absence of political pluralism and the presence of a small group, backed by the military, holding the reality of power.[8] Although the political system has presented the characteristics of both "Post Independence Mobilizational Authoritarian Regimes"[9] and "Bureaucratic-Military Authoritarian Regimes",[10] successive Algerian regimes have also been referred to as "popular sultanism".[11] However appealing the "populist sultanism" representation may be,[12] it needs to be qualified.[13] In a study by an Algerian political scientist,[14] it is clear that political power in Algeria has always been controlled by the military, in which a clan has usually surrounded the leader. The basis around which the clan has constituted itself is neither ideological nor essentially regionalist. The unity of the group is cemented by the leader (*za'im*) around whom emerges a nucleus of cronies as well as a disparate clientele.[15] The single party, officially charged with the task of ruling over civil society, played in fact only the role of transmission belt to the military, i.e. to the clan in power.[16] The party was no more than an instrument of control and repression in the hands of what A. Yefsah calls "l'Etat-clan".[17] The regime, aware of its lack of popular legitimacy, set up an entire administrative and political machinery in order to produce unanimous approval of its policies. This situation led to the transposition of rivalries and confrontations outside the political realm where dissident members of the clan were thrown to the wolves.[18] Civil society refused its domestication even if the clan wished to have *total* control over almost every aspect of state and society because it needed to stay in power whatever the means. The clan feared not only institutions but other rivals (i.e. rival clans awaiting their opportunity to achieve power), as well as societal strata that wished to share power. And, despite the clan's totalitarian attempts, parallel mechanisms (such as underground economy and the emergence of dissident groups) challenge the policies instituted by the regime. A divorce between the state and civil society has been the obvious result of the policies pursued by the successive clans.[19] The state of arbitrariness and the institutions it has established never represented the real interests of civil society. Rather, they existed only to give the illusion of legitimacy and to perpetuate the power of the clan and its supporters. The *Etat-clan* assigned clienteles within these institutions.[20] The obvious consequence was that, since the clan did not follow the rules it had itself decreed, civil society did not feel bound to obey them either. Therefore, everyone attempted to find a way to circumvent the rules. The *Etat-clan* is a state of *bakhshish* (tips) and of favouritism in which corruption and favouritism become widespread and affect the whole social body.[21] And, being arbitrary, the *Etat-clan* is by nature a repressive police state.[22]

The main problem in initiating a transition toward a more democratic order under such circumstances is, of course, that the overthrow of such a political system "without considerable prior social and economic change is not likely to lead to anything but another sultanistic regime or at best a more rational authoritarian rule with the support of the privileged oligarchies".[23] But, despite the unquestionable repressive nature of the regime, one may argue that the successive regimes in Algeria elicited a considerable degree of consensus and legitimacy, at least until the early 1980s. Both Ben Bella's and Boumédienne's regimes succeeded in creating a quasi-civil society, albeit one subordinate to the state and under the control of its watchdog the Party of the FLN. The state also succeeded in mobilizing the population around a development programme and in forging a relation of trust *vis-à-vis* the leadership of the country. The single party itself had to rely on a certain number of mass organizations: unions, peasant associations, youth organizations, women's associations, veterans' organizations, student unions, religious associations and individuals, etc. Progressively, however, these organizations were absorbed by the FLN and lost any kind of autonomy regardless of their influence. No association was authorized unless it obtained the authorities' approval. The main objective of the political system remained the elimination of any organized dissent and/or groups that have sought to seize power or to have, at least, a share of power. In terms of opposition and resistance to the state, what was left by the mid-1970s were merely isolated individuals forced to silence, co-opted by the system or to self-imposed exile. The state in Algeria drew its legitimacy not from any democratic process, but from a historic evolution, i.e. the war of liberation from French colonial rule and from a developmentalist strategy in which Islam held a privileged position. The main state's efforts concentrated in eliciting support for a vision of society carried by the co-opted elites and intellectuals. In reality, the unconvincing references to Islam and socialism rested on the notion of social justice of which Algerians were deprived during the colonial years. Yet, the clientelist system that was instituted did not coincide with the socialist discourse or with Islamic morality because only small segments of the population benefited from it despite the initial successes. It is conceivable that the original achievement of industrialization and the acquirement of some tangible social benefits (free care, free education, low taxation made possible by oil revenues, etc.), coupled with the promises for a better future, did for a time preserve the consensus and save the tacit social contract. Obviously, when such a state fails to deliver the goods it has promised, its legitimacy is inevitably undermined and the whole edifice begins to crumble. This is especially true in a country like Algeria, where there is little state tradition, for the state had always been a foreign entity imposed upon the society by outside powers. As correctly pointed out by a British scholar, "the main indigenous political tradition in Algeria is one of eternal resistance to these alien states by a fragmented population of self-governing tribes."[24] This tradition changed very little and the mutual suspicion between state and society has continued unabated until this day. The question of fundamentalism, therefore, cannot be dissociated from the process of nation and state building and its failures.[25]

## The State and Islam in Algeria

In order to build a modern identity/society and to gain legitimacy, the successive regimes in Algeria aspired to integrate what they described as a modern type of Islam into revolutionary perspectives. Thus, Islam, understood in its modernized/progressive form and decreed religion of the state in all the constitutions (1963, 1976, 1989), was seen as the foundation of the identity of the Algerian citizens, whereas the role of the state consisted in not only permitting the citizens to have access to the material benefits of the modern world (work, education, commodities, etc.), but also promoting Islamic principles and morality, through the erection of mosques, the teaching of the Arabic language, and the creation of religious institutions. Yet, Islam was accorded an influential role only insofar as it endorsed the regime's propagation[26] of an Islamic socialism. In other words, the country's leadership decided to incorporate Islam, again in its so-called modernistic/progressive version, as an essential element of the ideological and political apparatus of the regime in an attempt to build a modern nation-state through a developmentalist strategy. In this context, Islam, as a system of values, and modernity, or a set of rational principles, would coexist in a model defined by a French sociologist as *laïcité islamique* (Islamic secularism).[27] In addition, Islam played an ever greater role with respect to the legitimacy of the successive regimes since independence. Islam was used not only as an instrument of national integration in an ethnically heterogeneous society, but also as a tool of political legitimation. Indeed, the irreversible character attributed to Islam in the different constitutions inevitably paved the way to various interpretations, for, if some elites saw Islam as a religion open to modernity, others viewed it through a traditionalist prism, thus giving it the most conservative definition. This explains why the conservative forces, within the regime itself, used a certain interpretation of Islam as a force against the policies expounded by the state in the socio-economic and cultural fields. The state was infiltrated by many fundamentalists – including some influential 'ulama' who had joined the FLN against France only in 1956 (e.g. Tewfiq al-Madani, minister of religious affairs [Habous], 1962–5) – whose nationalist wartime credentials were often questionable.[28] Faced with an ideological struggle between 'progressives' and fundamentalists, the state could not but seek a balance between two irreconcilable visions, contenting itself with the exclusion of the most extremist among them so that it could preserve national unity and depict itself as an indispensable arbitrator.[29]

Even though the considerable growth of the radical fundamentalist movement in Algeria is a recent phenomenon, fundamentalist groups have challenged the regime at various degrees and periods since the country's independence in 1962.[30] The first association, al-Qiyam al-Islamiyya (Islamic Values), was founded in 1963 and became official in 1964. The organization's inarticulate aversion to Ben Bella's (Algeria's first president) socialist policies and to some secular aspects of the policies adopted by the single party at its Algiers Congress held in April 1964, mobilized a few religious figures, such as the Moroccan-born El-Hachemi Tidjani, the Imams Ahmed Sahnoun and Abdelatif Soltani, the forefathers of Algerian Islamic fundamentalism, Abbasi Madani, future leader of the Islamic Salvation Front in the late 1980s, but also some individuals from the wartime *Front de Libération Nationale* (FLN), such as Ahmed Mahsas, Safi Boudissa, and Muhammad S. Nekkache, all close associates of Ben Bella, and even Muhammad Khider,[31] one of the nine historic founding members of the wartime FLN. The most influential figure of the association, however, was the maverick Malek Bennabi, an outstanding, but often ignored, fundamentalist thinker. Because of his original and at times ambiguous views, it is not clear how much impact he had on the direction of al-Qiyam. What is certain is that he had a strong influence among the early, French-educated fundamentalists who attended the University of Algiers in the 1960s and early 1970s, i.e. until his death in 1973.[32] His ideas appeared in a review in the French language, "*Que sais-je de l'Islam?*" (What do I know about Islam?), whose popularity went well beyond the premises of the University of Algiers, on whose grounds the mosque (founded in 1968) attracted the most educated fundamentalists, especially physical scientists.[33] Malek Bennabi's views can best be described as gradualist and even intellectualist, which explains their little influence among the more radical fundamentalists.

In addition to its opposition to socialism, al-Qiyam demanded the full implementation of Islamic Law (*shari'a*). The association called on the state to close stores during Friday prayer (a demand satisfied in 1976 by the Houari Boumédienne regime), to ban the selling of alcohol, to exclude non-Muslims from public jobs, to create separate beaches for men and women, to introduce religious teaching in schools – which it obtained in 1964 – and to inhibit women's participation in sports events, and parades celebrating national holidays.[34] This 'cultural' association, perhaps reflecting its tenacious rejection of Ben Bella's flirtation with communist and secular groups, declared in its publication in French, *humanisme musulman*, that "any political party, any regime, or any leader that is not inspired by Islam, is dangerous and must therefore be banned. Any communist, secular, Marxist-socialist, or nationalist party (the latter putting in jeopardy the unity of the Arab world) cannot exist in the land of Islam."[35] This al-Qiyam association, whose leader acknowledged his affiliation with Jamal al-Din al-Afghani, Muhammad Abduh, Shakib Arslan, Hasan al-Banna, Sayyid Qutb, al-Ghazali and Abu al-A'la al-Mawdudi,[36] was disbanded in 1966 following the vehement opposition of its members to the sentencing to death and eventual execution of the Egyptian fundamentalist Sayyid Qutb by Gamal Abd al-Nasser's regime. The Algerian regime banned the association and its main publication, *Majallat al Ta'dib al-Islamiyya* (Journal of Muslim Education),[37] because of the diplomatic strain it was likely to cause in Algerian–Egyptian relations,[38] but also because the Algerian regime never tolerated any form of opposition regardless of the level of the threat it represented to its rule.[39] Despite the ban, al-Qiyam continued to exist, albeit in a more or less clandestine form, until its official dissolution in March 1970. Yet, this association did not disappear before performing the important task of paving the way for future fundamentalist organizations in the country.[40] Further, the dissolution of the religious association did not mean that its members left the political scene. Quite the contrary, they remained anchored within the system, thus exerting pressure to extract concessions from the state on moral, socio-economic (e.g. opposition to socialist policies; pushing for a family law based on *shari'a*, etc.), and cultural issues (acceleration of the teaching of the Arabic language, increase of religious programmes on television and so on).[41] In fact, the same year the association was dissolved, the state, through the minister of religious affairs, Mouloud Kassim, launched its own campaign to prevent the degradation of morals. The minister denounced the loosening of mores, alcoholism, and the attraction that the West exerted on some Algerians.[42]

The association al-Qiyam was in no way unique in using Islam as a form of resistance to the regime. A traditional current linked to the Jama'at al-'Ulama', the successor of the pre-independence "reformist" association founded in 1931 by Ibn Badis, and close to the al-Qiyam, expressed on several occasions its opposition to government policies and what it perceived as the Westernization of Algerian society and the degradation of Islamic values. One of the most bitter attacks against Boumédienne's socialist policies and the alleged degradation of morals in Algeria came from one of the forefathers of Algerian fundamentalism, the Imam Abdellatif Soltani. In a book he published in Morocco in 1974, entitled "*al-mazdaqiyya hiya 'asl al-ishtiraqiyya*" (*mazdaqism* is the source of socialism),[43] considered as the manifesto of Algerian fundamentalism, the imam criticized socialism, as a foreign ideology, which is incompatible with Islam, a religion that does not prohibit private ownership. In his view, although Islam is a doctrine of social justice, it has no relationship with the state's conception of Muslim socialism.[44] Shaykh Soltani also attacked the atheism that resulted from the secular teaching provided in the public schools. The book also included a severe diatribe against an Algerian feminist, Fadela Merabet, and against a Berber novelist, Kateb Yassine. Both were accused of spreading lies about Islam; the Imam went as far as disputing the "Algerianity" of the two individuals.[45] He saw the *shari'a* as the answer to all the problems faced by society, a perspective that is prevalent today among most fundamentalist factions. The regime was forced to reckon with the demands formulated by the fundamentalists by giving in on certain issues, such as the outlawing in 1976 of gambling and the promulgation of Friday as the Muslim weekend.

Another group of Algerian fundamentalists was made up of the Arabic teachers who were educated in Middle Eastern universities. The best representative is probably Mahfoudh Nahnah, leader of the non-violent fundamentalist association, al-Irshad wa al-Islah (Guidance and Reform), which gave birth in 1990 to a political party, Harakat al-Muqawama al-Islamiyya, known under the acronym Hamas. Nahnah belongs to the larger al-Da'wa wa al-Tabligh, linked to the Jama'at al-Ikhwan al-Muslimin (Muslim Brotherhood). This group waged a bitter ideological struggle against Boumédienne's regime – Nahnah was imprisoned from 1976 to 1980 for his participation in such acts. Although its leader resorted to acts of sabotage in the 1970s because of the opposition of the leader to the 1976 National Charter leftist orientation, Nahnah's association and party have held a moderate discourse (reference to human rights, non-violence, work for women, etc.). Nahnah's disciples endeavoured to re-Islamize Algerian society through persuasion and only reluctantly did it constitute itself as a political party in 1990.[46] In the 1970s, the followers of this movement chose the linguistic issue, as well as the family question (woman's rights, divorce, inheritance), as their battle-ground.[47] The linguistic subject had a utilitarian value, for the Arabic-trained students felt that their education was inadequate because it offered few job prospects, and that the French-educated groups enjoyed better employment opportunities. Thus, their emphasis on the importance of Arab–Islamic values was motivated primarily by socio-economic considerations. As to the family question, subject since Algeria's independence of bitter conflicts between secular and religious groups, this has remained much more complex and will in all certainty be an even more sensitive topic during a period of chaotic economic liberalization characterized by high unemployment.

## The Radicalization of Political Islam in the 1970s and 1980s

The reasons for the rise of political Islam in Algeria deserve elaboration, for they may help understand this phenomenon elsewhere in the Middle East. Undoubtedly, the radicalization of the fundamentalist movement took place at the end of the 1970s and early 1980s. The phenomenon found its importance in the wake of what sociologists, following Max Weber, call the 'disenchantment of the world'[48] provoked by modern science. Basing his analysis on Weber, the French anthropologist Bruno Étienne argues convincingly that the real detonator of fundamentalism in Algeria was the disenchantment subsequent to the first twenty years of independence.[49] A fundamentalist, therefore, is someone who has become conscious of the acute inequalities, but who is also convinced that the current strategies of development will not succeed in alleviating them, for he will never benefit from the fruits of development. In this case, then, the frustrations are even greater because the expectations were very high.[50] As pointed out earlier, fundamentalism is a consequence of anarchic modernity. The transition from *Gemeinschaft* to *Gesellschaft* proceeded without the state offering the newly urbanized, anonymous citizen any structures that could adequately replace the old, communitarian ones. Charitable fundamentalist associations, fulfilling the function of spiritual communities, provided such structures,[51] thus supplanting – and simultaneously discrediting – the state and undermining its populist discourse. In fundamentalism, the alienated individual·is able to regain a global image of the self within a community of believers who share a similar *Weltanschauung*. This situation is especially true in a country dominated by youth and where the populist state has increasingly been incapable of feeding, clothing, educating, housing, and employing its continuously growing population. Worse still, in a country where the state has established its almost total domination over the public sphere and hinders the blossoming of the private domain, only the mosque could offer an existential refuge and a moral substitute for alcohol, drugs and violence which had constituted the main pursuit hitherto. The state ceases to be seen as the provider; instead, society, especially its youth, feels betrayed. Not only does the youth communicate with the state through violence,[52] expressed in the form of cyclical riots, especially under Chadli Bendjedid's rule, but it also rejects all the founding myths and symbols of the Algerian nation. In other words, the state has lost its legitimacy and its *raison d'être* in the eyes of this disenchanted population.

The contention in this chapter is that, although the question of Islam in the political system has always been central, the recent phenomenon of fundamentalism as a radical protest movement is the result of a combination of factors, first and foremost of which has been the almost total failure of social, economic, and cultural modernization, coupled with the consequences of the painful colonial history which continues to have its effects on the evolution of Algerian society. Modernization in Algeria, as in many other Arab–Islamic countries, was understood in its material sense and failed to take into account the necessity for a process of secularization, which, despite fundamentalist claims to the contrary, is not necessarily antithetical to Islamic values.[53] Further, the post-independence FLN regime's ineffective developmental policies and the resolute refusal of the party and the state's personnel to acknowledge openly the shortcomings of the overall programme have led to a complete loss of legitimacy and credibility. The regime failed miserably in its attempt to reconcile a Western model of modernization, without its democratic principles to be sure, to a traditional, patriarchal society which, in many ways, it helped perpetuate as a neopatriarchy[54] because of its demagogic and equivocal position on religious and cultural issues. The total corruption and inefficiency of the regime, thus inhibiting any effective developmental policies, led to unbearable stagnation. Evidently, the blame for the failure of the developmentalist strategy cannot be put solely on the state, for the demographic explosion contributed a great deal to worsening the socio-economic problems. Worse still, the trauma that followed the chaotic urbanization resulting from the dislocation of traditional society debilitated the diffident modernization programme, especially in the socio-cultural realm, thus resulting in an identity crisis with disastrous consequences. The defeat of Arab nationalism and the concomitant humiliations suffered by Arab regimes against Israel, coupled with the Iranian revolution, provided the additional ingredients for the expansion of the fundamentalist movement.

Fundamentalism has always had a propitious terrain in Algeria even though the political system has been dominated by presumably secular elites. As has already been mentioned, fundamentalists have been present in the nationalist movement since its inception in the 1920s and continued to hold important positions in the state and party institutions at the end of colonial rule. Further, the presence, after Algeria's independence, of hundreds of Egyptian volunteers, primarily fundamentalists, sent by Gamal Abd al-Nasser – who was more than eager to get rid of them – to teach Arabic, had a major influence on large segments of Algerian educators. Another factor that facilitated the growth and rapid expansion of fundamentalism was the state's monopoly over religion and its decision to build thousands of mosques whose "volunteers", often self-proclaimed *imams*, it could not control. In 1962, there were only 2,000 mosques, whereas in 1992 their number reached 11,221, of which 6,000 were built by the state.[55] The existence of thousands of mosques is, of course, only natural in a country where the population is 99 per cent Muslim. But, the mosque performed another task than providing a place of prayer: it became the political base of the fundamentalist movement and the place where the future *amirs* were formed. By, then, of course, the state-appointed *imams* had lost their credibility because of their close identification with the regime and their pacifist inclinations. In the field of education, the state created its own grave-diggers, the Arabic-trained teachers with no real future, for the state failed – or was not willing – to create adequate structures to employ them. In 1975, Boumédienne sent home the Egyptian teachers and closed down the Islamic institutes, also built by the state. At the same time, however, he encouraged the construction of new mosques under the pretext that socialism helped the promotion of Islam in Algeria, for in each socialist village built, a mosque would be erected.[56] After 1988, the Islamic Salvation Front (FIS), founded in March 1989, was already in control of all the mosques in the country. These mosques were obviously the political forums of the fundamentalists. They constituted the embryo of a counter-power to the state and, had it not been for the totalitarian conception of the fundament-alists, they could have become the basis of a credible counter-hegemony, in the Gramscian sense.[57]

The FLN used Islam as part of its ideology in order to legitimize its rule. But, clearly, its attempt to produce a synthesis between Islam and socialism proved its limitations, for the political system continued to generate inequalities, especially under Bendjedid's rule, rather than the discursive egalitarianism trumpeted by the regime. In many ways, many of the fundamentalists were the orphans of Boumédienne, for unlike his successor, who lacked any vision, he succeeded in mobilizing the youth around a strategy of development that had the advantage of being essentially egalitarian in a relatively triumphant era in which corruption and clientelism never reached the proportions that developed under Bendjedid's regime.

The Algerian regime was instrumental in helping the expansion of the fundamentalist movement, for, despite its authoritarian nature, it never delineated the boundaries for the fundamentalists' activities and their allies within the state. As long as they did not threaten its rule, the regime allowed them to freely operate and even used them to curb the Left which also had its allies within the state bureaucracy. Whenever it opposed the fundamentalists' ideology, the regime did so in the name of Islam,[58] because religion was a necessary, albeit increasingly contested, component of its legitimacy. The regime, in fact, favoured the spread of fundamentalist ideology not only by allowing the building of thousands of public and private mosques, but also through founding Islamic institutes, and flooding television with religious programmes, and by allocating substantial resources to the holding of international seminars on Islamic thought. One cannot but concur with the Algerian journalist, A. Khelladi, when he raised the question: "How can one accuse the state of having fought Islam when most of its [state's] representatives have always been careful, often in a pathological fashion, to present themselves as 'irreproachable Muslims'?"[59] This is a legitimate question when one knows that Islam was one of the foundations of the hegemonic discourse and hegemonic rule of the successive regimes. It is in fact the state's contradictory policies *vis-à-vis* the fundamentalists which bolstered the audacious attitudes of the movement, especially in the aftermath of the October riots. Bendjedid was quite lenient toward the fundamentalist movement, which segments of the FLN unleashed against the leftist forces in the universities and elsewhere.

Fundamentalism in Algeria presented more violent forms in the 1970s and in the 1980s despite the rather complaisant attitude if not encouragement, at times, of Chadli Bendjedid's regime (1979–92) towards the movement in general. This violence was present in the universities and directed against students opposed to fundamentalists or mobilized around cultural and moralistic themes, against leftist/or secular students, Berberists, and people who did not share the fundamentalists' interpretation of Islam. Ironically, it was the acceleration of the Arabization campaign that led to further opposition owing to growing cultural distinctiveness, but also to the absence of opportunities for Arabic-educated emerging elites.[60] In other words, these groups couched their socio-economic demands through an ideological discourse garbed with religion. In fact, the fifth demand in the fundamentalist appeal of 12 November 1982, which included, *inter alia*, the full implementation of the *shari'a*, demanded from the authorities that citizens be given access to national wealth through legal means, such as agriculture, trade or industry. "But, this can be realized only if everyone is offered the same opportunities, without discrimination."[61]

Arabic-speaking students were not alone in using violence to express their frustration with a system that tended to marginalize them. In fact, the Iranian Revolution of 1979 bolstered some of the most radical voices of Algerian fundamentalism, such as Rachid Benaïssa, who had held an important position in the cabinet of Mouloud Kassim, minister of religious affairs in the 1970s.[62] The Iranian Revolution had a much greater impact on Algerian fundamentalists than observers are willing to admit. The Algerian fundamentalists used the opportunity – which coincided with the change of regime in Algeria – to make their demands on the new president more forcefully: the introduction of Islamic teaching from kindergarten to university, the creation of specialized Islamic sections in high schools and universities, the opening of Islamic universities, the teaching of the Qur'an by popular associations, the total freedom for religious associations under the supervision of the ministry of religious affairs in order to build mosques, the training of 'ulama' and imams, increase of religious programmes on TV and radio, the ban on selling any items offensive to Islam, ensuring that the population observed the precepts of Islam and penalizing those who violated them.[63] The regime could not ignore demands coming from members of the influential 'ulama's association who were well entrenched in important ministries (higher education, justice, education, religious affairs, etc.) and in the FLN.

But, the most violent fundamentalist small groups rallied around Mustapha Bouyali, founder in 1982 and amir of the Armed Islamic Movement (MIA) until his violent death in 1987. Holding a grudge against the regime for a trivial affair which caused the death of his brother by a policeman, Bouyali attempted to organize an all-out jihad against the regime. Former member of the first, Berberist-based, opposition party in Algeria, the Front des Forces Socialistes (FFS, created in 1963) and later member of the FLN until the early 1970s, Bouyali's actions epitomized the impulsive response by some Algerians to the lack of democratic channels to express their frustrations and disenchantment with modernization. The forerunner of the MIA was an organization, also created by Bouyali, the Group for the Struggle against the Illicit, which had conducted attacks against bars and individuals. The organization had little impact, though, and soon Bouyali was compelled to seek a more effective method against the regime, i.e. armed struggle. Even though many fundamentalists were in agreement with Bouyali regarding the foundation of an Islamic state in Algeria, many fundamentalist activists did not share the violence he and his followers (e.g. Muhammad Merah) advocated. Mahfoudh Nahnah, in particular, believed that the armed struggle against the regime was, in fact, harmful to Islam.[64] Bouyali's tactics resembled Blanquism in that the amir seemed to believe that a small, well-disciplined organization, made up of determined individuals, resorting to political assassinations and acts of sabotage, could seize power and hold on to it until they succeeded in swaying the population to their cause.[65] This belief was strengthened following the arrest in 1982 of fundamentalist figures, with no links to the MIA, such as A. Soltani, A. Sahnoun, and A. Madani, over incidents that took place at the University of Algiers. The authorities dismantled Bouyali's organization rather quickly, although it took years before they could trap Bouyali and a handful of his followers. His hard-core disciples were pardoned by Chadli Bendjedid in 1989 in the hope of preventing further radicalization of the movement; but, many of them eventually joined the guerrilla war currently waged by a much more extremist, better equipped and better organized fundamentalist movement in Algeria.

The fundamentalist movement in Algeria also includes a whole collection of smaller groupings with views ranging from the most peaceful to the most fanatic. Although some of them were little known before the October 1988 events, many have existed since the 1970s. The participation of some young Algerians alongside the Afghan *mujahidin* in their war against the Soviets bolstered the prestige of these daring groups, whose reputation is equalled only by their ruthlessness. They seem to act as autonomous bands, owing unconditional allegiance to an *amir*. In the 1970s and 1980s, al-Muwahhidun, Ansar Allah, Junud al-Allah, Da'wa of Sidi Bel Abbès (western city in Algeria), Ahl al-Da'wa of Laghouat (southern city), al-Takfir wa al-Hijra, and others, targeted bars, breweries, police stations, Soviet citizens and interests in Algeria, etc.[66] Further research will determine the nature of the relationship they have established with the Islamic Salvation Front and its armed branches.

In addition to these components of the movement, one should perhaps mention the *Mouvement pour la Démocratie en Algérie* (MDA), founded in 1984 by Algeria's first president (1962–5), Ahmed Ben Bella, who was released from house arrest in 1979. The literature of the party indicated some similarities between the party's – or one should say Ben Bella's[67] – demands and the political fundamentalists'. However, this example, albeit inconsequential with respect to the weight of this party in Algeria, is revealing insofar as it demonstrates the continuity between the Islamo-populism of the pre-independence nationalist movement and fundamentalism after 1962. Similarly, the second president of the Provisional Government of the Algerian Republic (GPRA, created in 1958), Youssef Benkhedda (1961–2), founded in October 1989 a fundamentalist party, al-Umma. During the liberalization period from 1989 to 1992, a multitude of other insignificant fundamentalist parties were created throughout the country.

In the 1980s, the fundamentalist movement remained atomized and ranged from very peaceful fundamentalists to quite extremist groups. Yet, despite the Bouyali affair, the regime did not seem to worry about the growth of radical fundamentalism and continued to either disregard its grievances or to make demagogic concessions (e.g. the Family Law of 1984). The regime made concessions by increasing religious programmes, organizing international symposia on Islam, and even "importing" in 1982 an Egyptian fundamentalist from the prestigious al-Azhar Mosque, Muhammad al-Ghazali, to give televised sermons, and to head from 1984 onwards the Department of Islamic Studies at the University of Constantine (eastern Algeria). This highly mediatized super *imam*, held in very high esteem by Chadli Bendjedid himself, served as an ideological cushion to the religious pretensions of the regime, but, through his ambiguous discourse, he also did much to encourage the growth of fundamentalism in the country.[68] His influence was immense, especially in a country still suffering from cultural schizophrenia – due to 132 years of brutal French colonial rule – and lacking well-trained native theologians. But, the influence of Ghazali and other fundamentalist figures in Algeria cannot account for the massive fundamentalist expansion in Algeria after the events of October 1988. Well before the riots, the fundamentalists were beginning to "re-appropriate" Islam, i.e. to take it away from the state, thus undermining the latter's legitimacy.

## October 1988: The Utterance of Disenchantment

In the 1980s, the economic reforms and the chaotic liberalization introduced by the regime aggravated the socio-economic conditions of the labouring masses. In particular, the industrial workers were denied the social benefits they had earned under Boumédienne's welfare-oriented regime. Furthermore, unemployment grew as a result of the dismantling of the state enterprises. The cut in food subsidies and the liberalization of prices in agriculture resulted in a considerable rise in prices with critical social ramifications, especially on the urban poor. Thus, the chaotic execution of Bendjedid's economic liberalization led Algerian society to organize itself, in an informal way, not around the production of goods and services, but around legal and illicit speculation. The underground economy [*marché parallèle*] imposed itself progressively as the essential mechanism, thus illegally determining the functioning of a drifting economy. The rapacious racketeering [*affairisme*] "has led ineluctably to corruption, a phenomenon which has seized the entire social body and generated in it an ethical malaise which has led to generalized cynicism and fed at the same time sermons in the mosques and reactions of religious fundamentalism".[69]

Indeed, under Bendjedid's rule, clientelist networks multiplied in a spectacular fashion and grew stronger; *affairisme* and the informal sector became widespread; and, a whole parallel economy was instituted, notably, the so called *trabendo*.[70] Moreover, due to its corrupt nature, the authoritarian state became more alienated from society. At the same time as corruption invaded the entire social body, the traditional forms of social resistance (strikes, urban riots, underground struggles, etc.) were replaced by more radical religious opposition.

The reforms, which applied to the educational and health sectors as well, led to the emergence of additional networks of privileges (e.g. selective schooling system, private vs. public hospitals, etc.), thus alienating large sections of Algerian society who used to benefit from the redistribution of part of the national income. In other words, economic liberalization benefited only the friends, relatives, and clients of those in power. Marginalization of large segments of society became evident and led to widespread anger, despair, banditry, and utter hatred toward the state and its clienteles.

Opposition to the economic reforms came from several sectors. Factions within the FLN party – whose members no longer benefited from the national income due to the reduced distributive capacity of the state[71] – were among its strongest opponents. Today even some radical fundamentalists, linked to the centre of power, thus to the national revenue,[72] are also antagonistic to it. The unions, communists and intellectuals constituted yet another section of the anti-reform camp. Popular indignation toward this disengagement of the state, which resulted in a conspicuous disarray that cut across Algerian society, was manifest through a return to the most archaic forms of solidarity (family, clan, tribe, region). Cultural struggles now superseded any ideological/political contest. Ideological strife was obscured by the rising cultural demands from fundamentalists, Berberists and the like. In other words, the political/ideological lines were blurred by cultural, identity issues which, in turn, rallied under the same banner social groups with antagonistic interests. The 1980s were thus characterized by intensifying demobilization and persistent atomization of an embryonic civil society.

The emergence of what seemed a new type of civil society was the result of a double process. The first, as seen above, came as the consequence of the abandonment of the welfare state policies, the pursuit of economic liberalization, implying the economic disengagement of the state from many sectors, the emphasis on profit, and the progressive withdrawal of the state from civil society. The traditional sense of egalitarianism was replaced by a thirst for profit and easy gain without any regard for rationality. A redefinition of the boundary between the public and the private spheres was drawn, thus making necessary the creation of associations standing between the two realms. The second factor relates to the crisis of the legitimacy drawn from the Algerian revolution. According to R. Babadji, the new movement towards associations accentuated the discord within the regime and the subsequent mutations that took place in Algeria, for it also contributed to calling into question the principle of the single party system.[73] As was predictable, the events of 1988 offered the opportunity for this movement to expand to proportions unimaginable hitherto.

In the summer of 1988, the socio-economic situation in Algeria was frightening: acute housing shortages, water problems, diminished food supply, high inflation, high unemployment, and so on. The social compromise established under Boumédienne's regime was broken. The widening disparity between the wealthy and the poor, the austerity programmes which affected mainly the impoverished masses and the low middle class, coupled with the impudent exhibition of wealth by the *nouveaux riches* who made their illicit fortunes with the assistance of state officials and/or through the underground economy, exacerbated social tensions in the country.

The regime's response to the grave socio-economic crisis was to insist on the necessity to carry out further austerity programmes which, of course, would have more devastating effects on the lower and middle strata by reducing their standards of living even further. This is probably why the masses and the underprivileged targeted their attacks against the new rich and those who used their public position to accumulate more wealth.

In October 1988, Algerian rioters violently expressed their revulsion for a political system founded on clientelism which favoured important segments, based on regionalism and clan/tribal/familiy solidarity; but, at the same time, this system marginalized millions. Algerians were also repulsed by the networks of patronage which provided so many benefits to those with access to them, while excluding those who have no alternative but to live an intolerable existence in the slums in and around the urban centres that eventually became the bases of radical fundamentalism. The logical effects of such a system were widespread cynicism, total removal from and apathy toward public affairs, absence of civic virtues, and absolute aversion toward the state and its symbols. Undoubtedly, it was within this context that fundamentalism found its propitious terrain. Yet, one should point out that, regardless of their yearning for freedom, social justice, and egalitarianism, the concern for democracy was not on the agenda during the October riots, except for a minority of intellectuals. At the same time, it is this crisis of the state which opened the door for pluralism in which fundamentalism could freely propagate its ideology.

The disastrous events of October 1988 demonstrated that the ruling bloc, which had begun to decompose in the mid-1980s, had reached a point of no return. The disintegration of the bloc was triggered by the general crisis of the rentier state due to prolonged socio-economic difficulties, an irreparable crisis of legitimacy and total demobilization of both elites and population. The ruling bloc was too confident as to its durability and seemed unwatchful of its diminished capacity as a welfare state or of the end of its historic legitimacy inherited from the prestigious war of independence. Unquestionably, the post-independence youth, which constitutes about 70 per cent of the population, shares few of the values that exemplified the wartime FLN and its army of liberation. Most Algerians lost all faith in the state's elites, accused of corruption and incompetence, and have rejected the over-utilized nationalist ideology propagated by the system for three decades. Algerians, the youth in particular, have been disenchanted because of the rise of a new bourgeoisie which has displayed conspicuously, against established ethics and teachings, its newly, often unlawfully, accumulated wealth. Worse still, the youth have lost all reference points and accord no credit to patriotic and national values.

Although the fundamentalists did not initiate the October riots,[74] they were able to play a mediating role between the regime and the rioters and to see the political vacuum available to them. Of major relevance here is the speed with which a considerable faction of the fundamentalist movement was able to constitute itself as a national party and use the opening in the political system to its own advantage.[75] The democratic parties that emerged following the liberalization of the political system, except for the FFS, had too little popular base to hope to compete against the FLN and the FIS.[76]

After 1988, some members of the Rabitat al-Da'wa (League of the Call), headed by Ahmed Sahnoun, which comprised important figures, such as Abbasi Madani, Mahfoudh Nahnah, Ali Benhadj, Muhammad Saïd, Hachemi Sahnouni, and many others, sought to unify the fundamentalist movement and structure it. The objective of the League was to be apolitical, limiting itself to moral issues, i.e. a league "in the service of God and of Islam [that] would struggle in the realm of thinking".[77] Yet, it was rather obvious very quickly that the mutual suspicions, the conflicting ambitions, and the different backgrounds of the leaders would make a unified movement rather unlikely. The most radical, the fiery activist, Ali Benhadj, recommended the creation of a mass organization which would be called the Islamic United Front. Theologians, such as Nahnah and Abdallah Djaballah, refused; but Abbasi Madani, a pure product of the nationalist movement, endorsed the idea and even substituted the term "salvation" for "united", because "we want to save this *umma* and this people."[78] Mahfoudh Nahnah rejected the creation of an Islamic party arguing that "an Islamic party must be led by an elite of religious scholars, not by immature kids."[79] He created his own association which eventually became a political party in 1990. Abdallah Djaballah, close to the ideas of Hasan al-Banna and Muhammed al-Ghazali, founded his own party in 1989, Harakat al-Nahda al-Islamiyya (the Movement for the Islamic Renaissance). Although close to Hamas and opposed to many of the ideas carried by the FIS, Djaballah, unlike Nahnah, maintained good relations with that party for quite some time.

The FIS drew its popularity from the simple fact that it was "a movement that succeeded in mobilizing a marginalized youth around an existential project, a moral order, an immanent justice where redemption is a permanent order".[80] This party gained immense support among the underprivileged sections of society. The largest component is a lumpenproletariat that grew out of the dislocation of traditional society and from the demobilization orchestrated by the state. The rest of the movement is made up of the unemployed; the *hittistes*, i.e. those who lean against walls all day long with no occupation; those with a diploma in Arabic but with no job (*Arabophones*); Arabic teachers; students and graduates in the physical sciences; and tradesmen hostile to state socialism who made financial contributions to the construction of numerous mosques and to the activities of the FIS; artisans, workers, jewellers, engineers, former FLN militants, some urban intellectuals, etc.[81] Ideological and social differences were blurred by religious solidarity, thus confusing the real nature of conflict within state and society.

Unquestionably, the now-banned FIS was not only the main party, but also the most popular and appealing organization to have emerged and gained from the liberalization of the political system. This mass party was the most mobilized and best structured fundamentalist party in the country. Prior to their arrest on 1 July 1991 and their condemnation a year later, Dr Abbasi Madani, a university professor, but by no means a theologian,[82] and Ali Benhadj, a high school teacher, dominated the party. The FIS's leaders contended that they expressed the general will of the Algerian people and promised to implement the *shari'a al Islamiyya* (Islamic law) once in power.[83] This, of course, implied total disregard for any republican constitution[84] and augured the divinization of politics, hence precluding the expression of secular views and the existence of a genuine civil society.[85]

Although the FIS was the main beneficiary of the democratization process, its activities (attacks on women, bars and the like) and the discourse of its main leaders revealed the aversion of the party to democratic principles. It is rather ironic that the fundamentalists condemned democracy even though they could freely express their hostility to it as a result of political liberalization within the context of democratization.

The FIS, however, cannot be viewed as a mere political party, but, as essentially a political movement. Its composite leadership was able to channel the leaderless protest movement, on the one hand, and to establish itself, due to the confusion of the regime during the riots, as the only interlocutor with the authorities, on the other. Undoubtedly, the success of the FIS was partially due to its ability to present itself as the heir of the "authentic" FLN of the revolution, i.e. the party which, in the eyes of Algerians, incarnated the unity of the Algerian people, egalitarianism, dignity, independence and so on. In other words, the FIS took up the FLN's ideological discourse and wrapped it with an Islamic cover, thus reducing the FLN to a party which has betrayed those ideals and accusing its members of having used the party to enrich themselves at the expense of the masses. Furthermore, in order to defeat its potential adversaries, the FIS, like the FLN in 1954, claimed to be the *only* force capable of offering salvation to the Algerian society. In practice, this meant developing not only a hegemonic discourse which it can use to fight its foes, mainly the democratic (secular) parties that reject its claims, but also to establish its hegemony *tout court*. By identifying itself with Islam, the FIS was able to discredit the other parties that resisted the movement's hegemonic domination and thus contributed to furthering the atomization of society sought by the regime.

Despite the violence exercised by the fundamentalist movement and its unveiled objectives, and despite resistance from the military[86] and important segments of civil society, the regime, in violation of its own Law on Political Associations, legalized the FIS in September 1989. In spite of its avowed opposition to the legal system and to republican principles and its promise to dismantle them once in office, the FIS was given a legal existence in violation of the constitution adopted in February the same year.[87] The legalization of this party was motivated by political considerations. First, it seems that the government of prime minister Mouloud Hamrouche encouraged the creation of an fundamentalist party because the fundamentalists, known for their pro-liberal views in the field of economics, would assist the regime in carrying out the reforms and help restrain a restless, agitated youth, attracted by Western consumerism. Second, a fundamentalist party could be utilized as a scarecrow against the middle classes suspicious *vis-à-vis* the regime. Further, the emergence of a well-organized fundamentalist party would certainly raise fears as to the future make-up of Algerian society, thus resurrecting republican sentiments favourable to the regime in place. Thirdly, it is quite plausible that the presence of a fundamentalist party was already perceived as an inevitable occurrence and that trying to circumvent it appeared to some factions in power more hazardous than giving it a legal status and thus a more controllable existence.

The FIS had by then already established its popularity among the youth and many other social strata. Its power of mobilization could not be matched by the highly discredited FLN. The democratic parties for their part were incapable of reaching any agreement to form a common front to counter the power of the fundamentalists and/or to prevent their manipulation by the old ruling party. Unlike the FIS, which concentrated its attacks against the state, they relied on the latter to contain the fundamentalist wave and to protect their interests against the advance of the fundamentalist "mob". The consequences of such political miscalculations were quite obvious: the democrats appeared as the objective allies of the authoritarian regime. The fundamentalists astutely sought to discredit them in the eyes of the population and to prove that the democrats were the carriers of a foreign ideology, whereas the FIS had the easy task of showing that it was the party of Algerian and Islamic authenticity.


## The Ideology of the Islamic Salvation Front

Although there is some continuity between *islahism* (reformism of the *salafiyya* movement) and fundamentalism in Algeria, the differences are much greater. *Islahism* was essentially reformist, intellectualist, and non-violent. The movement was led by *'ulama'* whose patrician social backgrounds differed considerably from those of the plebeians that make up the bulk of the radical fundamentalist wave. Whereas *islahism* rallies relatively small groups of religious scholars concerned with the moral values of their societies and intent on reforming them, fundamentalism is a social phenomenon resulting from modernity. Even if the movement seeks a return to the *shari'a*, it is not interested in a return to an archaic past. Rather, fundamentalism is a revolutionary movement, at least at its initial stages (i.e. before turning into mere "neofundamentalism"), that strives to re-appropriate society and modern technology through political means, i.e. seizing power in order to re-islamize a society allegedly corrupted by Western values.[88] The movement is, therefore, not theological, but essentially sociological. There ensues, at least for important sections of fundamentalism, an ideologization of Islam, whereby "'Islam' is not only a system of religious beliefs, but also a set of principles which should guide the general organization of the community."[89]

The difficulty in studying the fundamentalist movement in Algeria, especially its revolutionary component incarnated by the FIS, stems from its composite membership and structures. Indeed, since its creation in February 1989 until its ban in March 1992, the FIS comprised a variety of groups and ideological currents. The heterogeneous leadership of the FIS, combining radicalized salafists and new activist militants,[90] never really agreed on the means to achieve power – their principal preoccupation – in order to establish a vaguely defined fundamentalist state. The aspirations of the different groups included in the FIS diverged greatly. Some upheld a millenarian vision in which recourse to violence is an intrinsic part and whose major aim is the dismantling of the nation-state as it currently exists; for others, the objective is limited to a mere substitution of the fundamentalist elite for the one in charge of the state, which is perceived as having failed in both its modernizing tasks and in preserving Islamic values; still others have no clear strategy whatsoever. What is certain, however, is that the main objective is the appropriation of the state by legal (i.e. electoral) means for some or through violence for others. This explains the contadictory statements concerning the necessity or refusal of participating in the electoral process.

Despite the heterogeneous nature of the main fundamentalist party in Algeria, a dominant ideological discourse did, however, emerge regarding important political and social issues. One must insist, though, that because of the ideologization of Islam which has inevitably shifted the core of the debate from theological concerns to norms and values of the socio-political domain, the core beliefs of Islam have either regressed or been entirely cloaked.[91]

A reading of the FIS's leaders' pronouncements demonstrate very clearly the influence of Egyptian and Indo-Pakistani fundamentalists (al-Banna, Qutb, al-Mawdudi, al-Ghazali, etc.). The main commentaries concentrate on the "evils" that have plagued modern society and are leading to its "decadence": AIDS, sexually transmitted diseases, degeneration of morals, prostitution, mixing of the sexes in education in schools, universities, and workplaces, and contemporary ideologies (including liberalism, socialism, communism, feminism) which have, according to FIS leaders, replaced religion and corrupted societies. All of the evils of the *jahiliyya*, that is, those aspects that characterized pre-Islamic society, are said to be present in the Western world and have been blindly emulated in Islamic societies. The only solution to all these problems can be found in Islam.[92] The state in Islamic societies has not performed its duties, by deviating from the divine commandments, and has, in fact, contributed to the *jahiliyya*. The regimes in these societies may also be considered as infidels and should, consequently, be fought through a *jihad*; their killing (*qatl*) is lawful (*halal*). The other forces which have contributed to the decadence of Islamic societies are, according to leaders of the FIS, Ali Benhadj, in particular: journalists, writers, artists, state *'ulama'*, secularist parties which "militate with unequalled impudence for the separation of state and religion: they are the creatures of colonialism in our country".[93] These groups must be fought because they are opposed to *jihad*; in fact, "democracy is against *jihad* which it views as a manifestation of violence and interference in public liberties."[94]

## Fundamentalism and the Question of Democracy

In this context, it would be interesting to discuss the FIS's conception of democracy,[95] for it may shed some light on the place of civil society in the vision of this movement and will show whether this vision is favourable or inimical to the emergence of a genuine civil society.

Using their own radical interpretation of Islam, the FIS's leaders are opposed to the liberal version of Islam that advocates the separation of politics from religion. For the FIS, individual freedom itself is inconceivable outside the realm of religious notions. It is obvious, in this interpretation, that democracy and Islam are incompatible since the former allows freedom of conscience. One is a Muslim and must remain so or would face death in the event he/she decides to change religion or to become an atheist. Islam is seen as a holistic order whose societal organization is perfect and does not allow individual beliefs, for, according to this version of Islam, individualism would lead to a division within the *umma*. The introduction of any secular and/or imported ideas alien to divine revelation would destroy the foundation of the Islamic order. Democracy is viewed as an alien product belonging to a pagan society, Ancient Greece. The FIS's leaders present democracy as a religion that attempts to replace Islam. The inference, of course, is that democrats are Muslims who have converted to a new religion opposed to Islam – thus committing apostasy which is punishable by death. What the fundamentalists seek is an ideal political arrangement that rejects a conflictual society. Evidently, the leaders of the FIS, because of their "understanding of the divine revelation", claim to hold the key to entering – and ruling over – this ideal societal blueprint. Democracy, identified with homosexuality, drugs, Zionism, and many other evils, is, for its part, an order that has led to the decadence of moral and spiritual values in the West (including pornography, sleazy songs and trashy movies). The FIS's number two, Ali Benhadj, rejected pluralism by asking the rhetorical question: "Would Algeria, as has been the case in Europe, reach this moral dissolution under the dominance of democratic pluralism?"[96] Secularism (*laïcité*), the separation of state and religion, is seen as the biggest threat to Islamic societies. In all likelihood, the FIS's participation in the legislative elections of December 1991 was of a tactical nature, even if some segments within the party are believed to have been favourable to the democratic game.[97] Perhaps the greatest damage done by the fundamentalists was the way they have discredited democracy in the eyes of the youth they have indoctrinated. Their Manichean view only helped magnify the atomization of Algerian society and intensify the antagonisms within civil society. The most unfortunate aspect of the FIS's anti-democracy propaganda is that it presented democratic values as sacrilegious and totally antithetical to Islam. The impact of such an interpretation in a country that is profoundly Muslim is quite obvious. Democracy is, therefore, seen as the main factor of *fitna* (disorder). The FIS's leaders, it must be emphasized, did not derive their conclusions regarding democracy from any theological or serious political analysis of the concept, as did the symbolic figure of one of the FIS's small factions, Malek Bennabi,[98] but the "FIS utilizes the rejection of democracy as a propaganda tool in the context of a strategy of conquest of power".[99]

Owing to their political discourse and their strategy for the conquest of power, the leaders of the FIS made their societal project, quite ambiguous in many aspects, incompatible with that of millions of Algerians, even if Islam holds a supreme position among their overwhelming majority. Yet, one must recognize that the fundamentalists are not the only ones to be blamed for this deficiency. Tolerance and civility are not attributes of Algerian political culture. Each group, including the so-called democrats, seeks to cancel out the other. There exists little willingness to compromise or to provide guarantees for the ideological adversary. The absence of a democratic culture and the difficulty of expanding one is complicated by the neopatriarchal character of Algerian society. Undoubtedly, one cannot but agree with Camau that the main obstacle to the diffusion of democratic culture is not limited to what might be the political essence of Islam, but to the reproduction of the patriarchal system.[100] There is no reason to believe that Algerian associations and political parties have accepted the really important notion that there is no right answer.[101] The divinization of politics will certainly not facilitate the expansion of tolerance or the acceptance of compromise. If anything, it defeats the purpose of civil society. It should not be forgotten that Algerians did not rebel against the state in the name of democracy or because they sought to establish a democratic order, but they rose up, especially the youth, because this state was corrupt, unjust, stopped delivering the goods, and offered them no future. An authoritarian state that has the opposite qualities would, therefore, be acceptable.

Concerning the ideological struggle, some of the leaders of the FIS professed vigorously that when they come to power they would dispose of the republican constitution and outlaw the secular political parties altogether. Ali Benhadj repeated *ad infinitum* that democracy is incongruous with Islam and is *kufr* (unbelief). As he puts its:

> Article 6 [of the 1989 Algerian Constitution] proclaims that the people is the source of all power. This means that political parties which will emerge could, God forbid, lead the people in an anti-religious path. The only source of power is Allah, through the Qur'an. The people intervenes to choose a chief of state, and at this level only does it become a source of power. If the people votes against God's Law, this is nothing but blasphemy. In this eventuality, the '*ulama*' order the killing of the infidels because the latter wish to substitute their authority for that of God.[102]

Inevitably, the FIS' programme, its conception of "democracy", and its recourse to violence to institute its own interpretation of an ethical order, horrified not only the so called democratic forces and emancipated women, but large segments of practising Muslims, as well. Also, the FIS' programme, deliberately vague because of the existence of various currents which constituted it, did not help in appeasing the fears of several societal groups, which, incidentally, it could have won over as allies against the regime. The party was mostly concerned with the seizure of power rather than with any clear societal project[103] whose expression might have elicited a strong response from both the military and other social forces, but which would also have shattered the fundamentalist movement itself. The importance of the differences between the diverse groups inside the party cannot be underestimated. But, the radical discourse of the most radical among them is what frightened and alienated democrats and moderate fundamentalists alike.

It is necessary to point out that other fundamentalist or funda-mentalist-leaning parties held quite different conceptions of democracy from that of the FIS. Mahfoudh Nahnah held an exceptionally moderate position, especially regarding the question of women. Unlike the interpretation of the FIS, Nahnah argues that, based on the *shari'a*, a woman is man's equal "in struggle and at work, in education, in the building of civilization, and in the elaboration of a universal thought whose distinction is equity and the sense of moderation."[104] Hamas published a manifesto[105] in both French and Arabic, in which, unlike the FIS, it presents itself as an organic part of society rather than an alternative to it. What is also remarkable is the consistent emphasis put on pluralism.[106] In the manifesto, it is said that "geographical, linguistic, political and doctrinal diversity (provided such can be accommodated within an Islamic framework) is a natural and healthy phenomenon which enriches life and stimulates society by means of *shura*, dialogue, honest competition, exchange of ideas and constructive criticism."[107] According to this programme, any constitution would be inspired by Islamic principles in order to institute an "Islamic system of govern-ment", founded on *shura*, equality, freedom, and justice. It is also stated that individual and public liberties (of conscience, thought, expression, publication, association and so on) would be assured, "provided that these liberties are not exploited in order to destroy the bases of society, to conspire against the *umma* or to spread immorality among its members".[108] The objective is not to substitute a secular constitution for the *shari'a*, but to proceed with its incremental implementation, progressively abolishing the laws that are in opposition to it. In an interview he granted Kate Zebiri, Nahnah asserted that "Islam must be freely chosen by the people, who would always be able to vote for a non-Islamic party in future".[109] This is quite different from Benhadj's statement that "all the parties which are opposed to the Islamic solution are parties of the devil,"[110] although Madani did subscribe to the notion of political pluralism without, however, extending it to secular parties.[111]

Abdallah Djaballah's al-Nahda party was, like Hamas, opposed to the FIS's claims that it had won the June 1990 municipal and departmental elections on its own and that, consequently, it was the sole representative of Algerian fundamentalism. Al-Nahda strives for the erection of an Islamic state through the execution of the *shari'a*, but within a pluralist and democratic framework. However, like the FIS, the party opposes the legal representation of secular parties and would impose the wearing of the veil by women.[112] Djaballah's real objective is to found an alliance of fundamentalist parties that transcends the differences and in which the latter could be freely discussed. Needless to say, dissensions within the fundamentalist movement have always been of a political nature and/or stemmed from questions of tactics, but not from theological disputes. In fact, it is their ideologization of Islam which helps explain the rejection of these fundamentalist parties by many *'ulama'* and true fundamentalists.

## The FIS Economic Policy

Because of its numerical, political importance, and its looming victory in the 1992 legislative elections, a discussion of the FIS's economic policy is in order. In the section reserved for the economic sector, the leaders of the FIS insist that the party's doctrine is based on the "search for an equilibrium between consumption needs and production needs, on the necessary complementarity between quantity and quality in relation to demographic growth and civilizational evolution . . . and economic independence".[113] The policies pursued by the successive regimes are criticized because "they discouraged the entrepreneurial initiative [*esprit d'initiative*]", thus impeding productive projects and "penalizing small enterprises".[114] Statist policies favouring large industrial production units, considered by the FIS as big users of raw materials and requiring foreign experts, are said to have led the country to economic ruin. The FIS' economic programme consists of a series of "re-examinations" of the failed policies of the past. In agriculture, it proposes, "on the basis of the *shari'a*, to put an end to abusive expropriation and redistribution of feudal lands".[115] Lands should be distributed to those who deserve them and in conformity with the *shari'a*. The programme emphasizes the importance of the use of advanced technologies in agriculture, but does not make any tangible proposals beyond declaratory platitudes similar to the FLN's. As to industry, its importance is emphasized, while insisting that it should not be developed at the expense of agriculture "as was done in the past".[116] In conformity with the fundamentalists' pro-liberal views, the programme insists that small and medium enterprises should be encouraged. The objective of industry is to break Algeria's dependence on the outside world. In a passage reminiscent of

Boumédienne's economic nationalism, it is stated that Algeria's "natural resources require an industrializing industry adapted to technological evolution and capable of sustaining intense industrial competition in the field of armament as well as in that of trade or consumption".[117] In the domain of industrial management, the plan stipulates that "Islam advocates a collegial spirit, a type of management founded on the *shura* (consultation), and a sense of responsibility which all the workers should share in the application of the Prophet's instructions . . ."[118] Promotion of a free trade zone among Arab and Islamic states (especially the Great Maghreb) and the elimination of customs barriers, among other things, are also mentioned in the same programme. The main emphasis, however, is put on the private sector and, more importantly, on trade which constitutes "the nervous system of the economy that channels the production of wealth, coordinates the diverse interests, and achieves equilibrium . . . and must conform to the *shari'a*".[119] Further, "trade monopoly must be banned, except in cases where the state is compelled to intervene to safeguard *major* [emphasis in the original] political or economic interests."[120] In order to oversee price policy, it is suggested that a market police, the "*hisba* will thwart any prejudice and restore equity."[121] The importance of morality in the sphere of economics is also emphasized. The IMF and other financial institutions are blamed for the current world crisis, but there is barely any criticism, except to declare that the relationship with these organizations must be reviewed.

In short, the FIS' economic program is a concoction of rhetorical statements of economic nationalism (economic independence, social justice, self-reliance, etc.), economic liberalism, Islamic principles of morality in trade and human relations, basic economic principles found in the *shari'a*, elements of social justice meant to curb the ramifications of liberalism, pleas to Algerians to mobilize around a programme that would help them "re-establish [their] identity", doubtful propositions concerning the various fields of agriculture, industry, trade, and finance, and so on. The economic project, which occupies about one-third of the entire programme, contains trivialities due mostly to the framers' arduous job of reconciling a utopian scheme to complex realities. This was further complicated by their aspiration to visualize a third road between capitalism and socialism. Even though the economic programme betrays the party's preference for a mercantilist economy, it resorts to a populist language to answer the grievances of its rank and file.

## The Resurrection of Civil Society
## or "Movements of Rage"?

Although we may subscribe to the idea that civil society played a role in the shaking of the Algerian state, there is no question that civil society before October 1988 was weak. However, the post-October 1988 developments invigorated it. Yet, the presence of a powerful party with a totalitarian vision of the socio-political and cultural order would weaken civil society since, in face of the violence–repression cycle, the emerging civil society runs the risk of being re-absorbed by an ascending powerful state, i.e. a situation in which the state strikes back, by reinstating authoritarianism. The FIS was able to bolster what K. Jowitt so aptly calls "movements of rage", i.e. "violent nativist responses to failure, frustration, and perplexity".[122] The absence of peaceful means to fulfil their material and social aspirations partly explains the resort to violence, for as T. R. Gurr said, "only men who are enraged are likely to prefer violence despite the availability of effective nonviolent means for satisfying their expectations."[123] In the Algerian case, the predisposition towards violence is increased due to anthropological and historical factors.[124] This is why the transition to a more democratic system, understood in its most basic and universal sense, will be a long, bloody march rather than a simple, perhaps bumpy, transition. Whether civil society will continue pushing for a democratic transition is questionable as long as the socio-economic problems are not alleviated. One is tempted to suggest that although the concept of civil society is quite relevant in this context, its use should always be linked to the economic realities of the countries engaging in a process of democratization. Thus, the very concept of civil society has to be redefined in order to better account for the realities of youth-dominated societies subdued by failure and crushed by frustration and despair, where religion has been dangerously ideologized. Undoubtedly, the emphasis ought to be on the "interrelationship between the political and economic kingdoms, between challenges to authoritarian rule, emergent forms of mass participation, reinvigorated associational life, and new forms of social solidarity and action . . . on the one hand, and efforts to rehabilitate [the economy], on the other."[125] Therefore, we must avoid concentrating solely on the political and ideological realms of civil society because democratization does not evolve well or productively when the socio-economic conditions are unfavourable and are in constant deterioration. Perhaps we should agree with Callaghy and restrict the concept of civil society to the emergence of a consensus on norms defining a "civil sphere", that is "civil society would be not a set of *groups* but a *space* or *realm* defined by newly constituted norms about what the state should and should not do and by the rules of politics in that space, *including* politics by non state actors."[126] Even this minimum consensus could not be reached by the various actors in Algerian society, which partly explains the bumpy and now tragic evolution since October 1988 and the current political impasse.

## Conclusion: Algeria's Stalemate

The struggle between the state and the fundamentalists in Algeria since the interruption of the electoral process in January 1992 has been marked by perennial terrorism and repression. An unbearable stalemate has dominated life in the country ever since, especially in the absence of a strong democratic pole. The fierce struggle between the security forces and the fundamentalists – who were well-positioned to capture the absolute majority of the seats at the national assembly in the second round of the legislative elections – has reached a level unseen since the war of liberation (1954–62). The High State Council (HSC) put in place following the cancellation of the electoral process did not succeed in mobilizing the population around a genuine socio-economic and political programme or in re-establishing consequential channels of communication with the leadership of the FIS. The apparent existence of several centres of power prevented any positive evolution toward stability and a negotiated pact that would have helped create a modicum of consensus among the various societal forces. The five-man HSC, presided over by Muhammad Boudiaf (returned from exile to lead the country and assassinated in June 1992) and by his successor Ali Kafi until February 1994, did not fulfil its promise to establish order and create the proper atmosphere for a genuine transition toward a non-authoritarian, perhaps democratic order. The pledge to do so was in fact received with scepticism because of the apparent impotence of the regime to eradicate the terrorism and banditry that have plagued the country, and also because of the inability of the successive governments to break with the old political system and personnel to regain a minimum level of trust and some degree of legitimacy. The regime barely succeeded in eliciting the political parties' support in condemning terrorism before agreeing to a dialogue with them. The termination of the HSC's mandate and the subsequent appointment of a president, former retired general and defence minister, Liamine Zeroual, has not to this date produced any tangible results. Dialogue between the regime and some leaders of the banned Islamic Salvation Front (FIS), as well as the temporary quasi-liberation of its main chiefs, Dr Abbasi Madani and Ali Benhadj, has failed, thus leading to a radicalization on both sides. By the spring of 1995, it had become questionable whether the FIS leadership (in exile, in hiding, or in jail) has any effective control over the various armed groups, especially the most radical and most brutal, the Armed Islamic Group (GIA), which is totally opposed to any type of dialogue with the authorities. The Islamic Salvation Army (AIS), directly linked to the FIS, seems more inclined to negotiate with the regime, but due to vocal opposition within the regime itself, the so-called eradicators,[127] and the failure of dialogue with the two FIS leaders, earlier prospects for a definitive solution seem now remote. At the moment, it is doubtful whether the security forces will succeed in defeating the extremist and armed factions of the fundamentalists and whether the regime may in fact restart a dialogue with the FIS's members opposed to violence. It is also questionable whether the current regime will be able to win over the population, the main victim of the violence, whose support is needed if a governmental programme has any chance of success. This condition is predicated upon the degree of determination of the current powers in place to fight corruption and eliminate those individuals who have plundered the country's wealth and have led it to near bankruptcy and on the capacity of the regime to mobilize society, including the fundamentalists, around a genuine societal programme and the forging of national consensus; the HSC and the eight-member Commission for National Dialogue, instituted in October 1993,[128] the president, Liamine Zeroual, the National Commission of Transition (CNT), and many political parties, have all reached the same conclusion. The national dialogue initiated in August 1994 aimed at involving the political parties in the transition toward a democratic order through the formation of a government of national unity and the co-option of moderate fundamentalists, including members of the banned FIS, has also failed. And so has the platform signed by the opposition in Rome in late 1994 to which the FIS was a signatory. But there is no doubt that dialogue will have to be re-initiated at some point in order to stop the violence and to prevent the country from disintegrating. The regime, of course, is well aware of the divisions between the fundamentalists and will continue to exploit them. The possibility of a compromise between the military and the FIS leadership, long envisaged, is now almost close to nil. The eventuality of an alliance between the different fundamentalist factions and leaders to save a country from a wider civil war, although desirable, is not likely to occur either. The FIS never agreed to enter any kind of alliance before the interruption of the electoral process, not even with other fundamentalist parties, for it felt capable of ruling alone. Whether it would be willing to do so in the future is questionable.

Pessimism in the country stems from the regime's evident unwillingness to institute true democratization, to relinquish, or at least share, power, to allow the marginalized elite access to the state institutions, and to end its monopoly over national wealth. Whether the various clans in the political system will agree to end their proxy battles to allow the erection of a new order obviously depends on the determination of the men in power since February 1994 to neutralize those opposed to their policies.

For a while, that is from 1989 until 1992/3, the political system in place in Algeria resembled a form of "democrature", i.e. "an unstable mixture of democracy and dictatorship, of constitutionalism and authoritarianism . . .",[129] but now one can hardly speak of any degree of constitutionalism in view of the harsh repression that exists. Further, one may also wonder whether the state of siege put in place since February 1993 was not a manoeuvre to protect the middle class – an objective, albeit critical, ally of the regime – and to also give time to the old ruling party, the FLN, to revitalize itself and, as in Poland, come to power through democratic means. Only after a return to normalcy, that is the end of violence and the restoration of civil peace, can this question be satisfactorily answered. But, what is clear is that fundamentalism will remain a force to reckon with; the question is which type of fundamentalism, radical or moderate, will prevail.

In guise of conclusion, it is perhaps worth asking the question as to what brought about Algeria's democratic experiment to a standstill and why both state and society are in disarray. Unquestionably, the state has been fragmented, thus resulting in the existence of many centres of power following their own logic. This evolution adds to the difficulty for the analyst to provide a full understanding of the situation. Algerian society, for its part, has been somewhat lethargic, for it is utterly demor-alized and uncertain about the regime's ability to solve the country's problems, but is also terrorized by the terrorists be they fundamentalists or pawns of the various clans in or outside power. This partially explains why some sympathy for the FIS from many quarters has not completely faded. Algerian society remains divided between those who champion modernity, those who believe in a regressive, "ideal", mythological past, which they think is the only hope for solving society's multiform crisis, and, finally, those who strive to restore the *status quo ante* to preserve their considerable privileges. There is no clear evidence today that Algerians seek democracy – understood in its elementary, universalistic principles – or will only content themselves with the restrained political liberalization they have partly wrested from and partially been granted by the old authoritarian rulers. Yet, what is incontestable, is that Algerians in their overwhelming majority have lost faith in the FLN-produced elites and refuse, therefore, to give legitimacy to their rule. In the last two or three years, they have also lost faith in the FIS and what it initially stood for and give little credence to the other political parties. Their only concern is civil peace, physical and economic security. The way the cycle of violence is ended will probably indicate the form the Algerian state and society will take.

The description of the current situation has been highlighted in order to better reflect upon the conditions which have brought the country to such a stalemate. Understanding the reasons which have ended, at least in the short run, one of the most promising processes of democratization in the Arab and Islamic world is important because it may help comprehend the difficulties faced by other countries in the region in undergoing a genuine transition towards a more democratic order. One of the underlying working hypotheses in this chapter is that democratization in Algeria has failed mainly because it was initiated in an undemocratic fashion and because of the absence of a democratic political culture at all levels. Further, the transition was not of the protracted or of the negotiated type: the state did not seek to integrate the fundamentalists within a set framework, whereas the radical factions of the fundamentalists sought to replace one form of authoritarianism by another. One of the major obstacles to a true democratization was the absence of a negotiated pact between all the parties to set the basic rules of the political game before elections could have been organized.

Perhaps, the absence of a strong, well-organized civil society is also responsible for such a failure. If one follows Diamond's conception of civil society, it is clear that the FIS ought to have been excluded because it was definitely a millenarian movement that "seeks to monopolize a functional or political space in society, claiming that it represents the only legitimate path, [and] contradicts the pluralistic and market-oriented nature of civil society".[130] Worse still, the FIS was distinguished by its *partialness* in the sense that it claimed to represent the entire community's interests. In fact, unlike the Da'wa group headed by Mahfoudh Nahnah, who established good rapport with secular elements of civil society whom he sought to "lead in the right path of Allah", the FIS had, from its inception, alienated large segments of civil society.

The seeming pluralism that emerged on the morrow of the tragic events of October 1988 was not the result of a natural development, but was part and parcel of the scheme concocted by the regime to divide the opposition and to maintain the old system, albeit in somewhat altered form, and because of the segmentation of the rentier state. The vital question of time worked against democratic parties and associations. Years of repression by the regime and, since the 1980s, intimidation from the fundamentalists constituted a stumbling block to the formation of a genuine civil society. The democratic forces did not have sufficient time to "develop among themselves the relationships of mutual tolerance and trust and respect for law that can only emerge gradually, through years of competition and cooperation and repeated elections".[131] Neither the authoritarian state in place since independence in 1962, nor the socio-economic conditions, nor the political culture were favourable to the development of experienced democratic parties or of a strong, autonomous civil society capable of restricting state power. Today, this prerequisite has been made even less likely due to the terror that has pervaded Algerian society, the incredible intolerance of the fundamentalists, the harsh state repression, and the intolerable socio-economic conditions. Further, making politics sacred and politicizing the sacred has made the emergence of a strong civil society an eventuality that is hard to envision at the moment.

## NOTES

1 Hisham Sharabi, *Neopatriarchy: A Theory of Distorted Change in Arab Society* (Oxford and New York: Oxford University Press, 1988), p. 12.

2 An outstanding analysis of this phenomenon, see Mohammad Arkoun "Algeria" in Shireen Hunter, ed., *The Politics of Islamic Revivalism: Diversity and Unity* (Bloomington and Indianapolis, Indiana: Indiana University Press, 1988), pp. 171–86.

3 The best books on the Algerian nationalist movement are Mohammed Harbi, *Aux Origines du FLN* (Paris: Editions Bourgeois, 1975); Mahfoud Kaddache, *Histoire du mouvement nationaliste algérien. Question nationale et politique algérienne, 1919–1951* (2 Vols., Algiers: S.N.E.D., 1980–1); Mohammed Harbi, *Le FLN, mirage et réalité – des origines à la prise du pouvoir, 1945–1962* (Paris: Editions Jeune Afrique, 1980).

4 A reliable account can be found in John Ruedy, *Modern Algeria: The Origins and Development of a Nation* (Bloomington, IN: Indiana University Press, 1992).

5 An excellent treatment of the way the French strove to destroy the Algerian personality can be found in Yvonne Turin, *Affrontements culturels dans l'Algérie coloniale – écoles, médecines, religion, 1830–1880* (Algiers: Entreprise nationale du livre, ENAL, 1983).

6 See Jacques Berque and J. Paul Charnay, *Normes et valeurs dans l'Islam contemporain* (Paris: Payot, 1966), pp. 178–9. See also Mostefa Lacheraf, *L'Algérie – Nation et société* (Paris: Editions Maspéro, 1965), p. 107.

7 See Anouar Abdelmalek, *La Renaissance du monde arabe* (Gembloux, Belgium: Editions du Culot, 1972), p. 427.

8 The reference here is to Juan J. Linz's definition in "Totalitarian and Authoritarian Regimes", *Handbook of Political Science, Vol. III: Macro political Theory*, ed. Fred I. Greenstein and Nelson W. Polsby (Reading, MA: Addison-Wesley Publishing Company, 1975), p. 264.

9 Ibid., p. 321.

10 Ibid., p. 285.

11 Cf. the discussion in Michel Camau, "Les Régimes étatiques: le Maghreb" in Maurice Flory, Robert Mantran, *et al.*, *Les Régimes politiques arabes* (Paris: Presses Universitaires de France, 1990), esp. p. 430. Sultanistic regimes are "based on personal rulership with loyalty to the ruler based not on tradition, or on him embodying an ideology, or on a unique personal mission, or on charismatic qualities, but on a mixture of fear and rewards to his collaborators . . . The binding norms and relations of bureaucratic administration are constantly subverted by personal arbitrary decisions of the ruler, which he does not feel constrained to justify in ideological terms . . . The staff of such rulers is constituted . . . largely by men chosen directly by the ruler . . . Among them we very often find members of his family, friends, cronies, business associates, and men directly involved in the use of violence to sustain the regime." (Linz, pp. 259–60). Linz's discussion

draws heavily on Max Weber's *Economy and Society*, ed. and trans. Guenther Roth and Claus Wittich, (3 Vols., New York: Bedminster Press, 1968).

12 Jean Leca and J. C. Vatin, "Le Système politique algérien 1976–1978", *Annuaire de l'Afrique du Nord 1977* (Paris: CNRS, 1977), pp. 27–8. These authors, however, refute the view that the Algerian system was totalitarian. Lise Garon, rejecting such an interpretation, argues that, on the contrary, the Algerian FLN-state was definitely totalitarian; see her "Crise économique et consensus en état rentier: le cas de l'Algérie socialiste", *Revue d'Etudes Internationales*, 25, 1 (March 1994), p. 28.

13 See the refutation of Vatin's and Leca's thesis by Kuider Sami Naïr, "Algérie, 1954–1982: forces sociales et blocs au pouvoir", *Les Temps Modernes* (July–August, 1982), Nos. 432–3, p. 22.

14 Abdelkader Yefsah, *La Question du pouvoir en Algérie*, 2nd edn (Algiers: E.N.A.P., 1991), esp. pp. 447 ff. The author rejects the concept of "sultanism" as applied to Algeria by Leca and Vatin on the grounds that "in this case it is quite difficult to be really the arbiter among different groups that surround him [the president] or of those that helped him accede to the supreme magistracy. He finds himself prisoner of his membership to a clan and becomes the representative of the latter's interests despite, perhaps, his wish to be independent." (p. 326.)

15 Ibid., p. 448.

16 Ibid.

17 Ibid., p. 449.

18 Ibid., p. 452.

19 Ibid., p. 454. The author, however, is rather sceptical as to the current potential of Algerian civil society.

20 Ibid., p. 455. The Algerian psychiatrist Saïd Sadi provides an outstanding analysis of how the clan is organized and how it protects itself from the "Other". Cf. his *Algérie, l'échec recommencé* (Algiers: Editions Parenthèses, 1991), pp. 77ff.

21 Yefsah, *La Question du pouvoir*, p. 457. For an extensive description by an insider of how corruption, favouritism, and nepotism have operated at all levels of Algerian society, see Omar Aktouf, *Algérie: entre l'exil et la curée* (Paris: Editions L'Harmattan, 1989).

22 Ibid., pp. 458–9.

23 Linz, "Totalitarian and Authoritarian Regimes", p. 262.

24 Hugh Roberts, "The Algerian State and the Challenge to Democracy", *Government and Opposition*, 27, 4 (Autumn 1992), p. 442.

25 See Yahia H. Zoubir, "Algeria's Multi-Dimensional Crisis: The Story of a Failed State-Building Process", *Journal of Modern African Studies*, 32, 4 (December 1994), pp. 741–7.

26 See Muhammad-Cherif Salah Bey, "La Constitution et la théorie générale du droit", *Revue algérienne des sciences juridique, économique, et politique*, 15, 3 (September 1978), p. 448.

27 Henri Sanson, *Laïcité islamique en Algérie* (Paris: Editions du CNRS, 1983), p. 8. *Laïcité*, in this context, is also understood as the absence of a religious hierarchy

and that despite the preponderance of Islam, power is exercised in a secular fashion; see, pp. 52ff.

28  On the Jama'at al-'Ulama', the best account remains Ali Merad, *Le Mouvement réformiste en Algérie, 1925–1940, essai d'histoire religieuse et sociale* (Paris/The Hague: Mouton, 1967); Ben Bella, who appointed elements of this association in his government, denounced it 20 years later, making important revelations; see, Ahmed Ben Bella, *L'Itinéraire* (Algiers: Editions Maintenant, 1987), pp. 71–4. The book was originally published in Arabic under the title of *hadith ma'rifi shamil* (Beirut: al-Wahda Editions, 1985).

29  Bernard Cubertafond, *L'Algérie contemporaine*, 2nd edn (Paris: Presses universitaires de France, 1981), p. 21.

30  For a thorough chronological analysis of Islam's resistance to the State in Algeria, see, Jean-Claude Vatin, "Puissance d'état et résistances islamiques en Algérie, XIX-XXe siècles. Approche mécanique"; Ernest Gellner, Jean-Claude Vatin, *et al.*, *Islam et politique au Maghreb* (Paris: Editions du CNRS, 1981), pp. 243–69.

31  Hugh Roberts, "Radical Islamism and the Dilemma of Algerian Nationalism: The Embattled Arians of Algiers", *Third World Quarterly*, 10, 2 (April 1988), p. 563, included Khider as one of the members of al-Qiyam. However, Abbassi Madani asserted that Khider was not a member of the association. Cf. his interview in *Politique internationale*, No. 49 (autumn 1990), p. 181.

32  A biographical sketch of Malek Bennabi can be found in Khelladi, *Les Islamistes algériens face au pouvoir* (Algiers: Editions Alfa, 1992), pp. 37–44.

33  See, Khelladi, *Les Islamistes algériens*, p. 91. I was acquainted with many of Bennabi's followers. They were all French-educated, very tolerant, and exhibited no inclination towards violence whatsoever. Among Bennabi's works, which have yet to be carefully studied, one should refer to, *Le Phénomène coranique* and *Pour changer l'Algérie*. Malek Bennabi's books have been – or are in the process of being – reprinted under the editorship of Nourredine Boukrouh, leader of the *Parti pour le renouveau algérien* (PRA), founded in 1989.

34  Jean Leca and Jean-Claude Vatin, *L'Algérie politique: Institutions et régime* (Paris: Presse de la Fondation des Sciences Politiques, 1975), p. 308 and Saadi Nouredine, *La Femme et la loi en Algérie* (Algiers: Editions Bouchène, 1991), p. 45; Muhammad Harbi, ed. *L'Islamisme dans tous ses états* (Algiers: Editions Rahma, 1992), p. 134.

35  Cited in Leca and Vatin, "Le Système politique", p. 308.

36  François Burgat, *L'Islamisme au maghreb – la voix du sud* (Paris: Karthala, 1988), p. 150. This book is available in English, as François Burgat and William Dowell, *The Islamic Movement in North Africa* (Austin, Texas: Center for Middle Eastern Studies, 1993).

37  This publication and *Humanisme musulman* were both put out by the Algerian military's printing plant.

38  Aïssa Khelladi, *Les Islamistes algériens face au pouvoir* (Algiers: Editions Alfa, 1992), p. 19. The leaders of *al-Qiyam* sent letters to both Boumédienne and Gamal Abd al-Nasser.

39 On this point, see Yahia H. Zoubir, "The Concept of Civil Society and the Problems of the Transition to a Pluralist Political System: The Case of Algeria", Paper Presented at the 28th Middle East Studies Association Annual Convention, Phoenix, Arizona, November 1994, esp. pp. 13ff.

40 See Luc-Willy Deheuvels, *Islam et pensée contemporaine en Algérie: la revue al-Asala, 1971–1981* (Paris: CNRS, 1991).

41 For a detailed discussion, see Abderrahim Lamchichi, *Islam et contestation au Maghreb* (Paris: Editions L'Harmattan, 1989), pp. 151–3.

42 Bernard Cubertafond, *La République algérienne démocratique et populaire* (Paris: P.U.F., 1979), pp. 88–91.

43 Some commentaries and/or excerpts can be found in Burgat, *L'Islamisme au Maghreb*, pp. 147ff.; Harbi, *L'Islamisme dans tous ses états*, pp. 135ff. Mazdaq is in reference to a 5th century Persian leader of a tribe reputed to be heretic and communistic.

44 Harbi, p. 137.

45 See the text in Burgat, *L'Islamisme au Maghreb*, pp. 146ff. The fact that Merabet was married to a Frenchman, the philosopher M. Maschino, discredited her even more in the eyes of the *imam*.

46 For details, see Mustafa al-Ahnaf, Bernard Botiveau, and Franck Frégosi, *L'Algérie par ses islamistes* (Paris: Karthala, 1991), pp. 37–42; see also, Kate Zebiri, "Islamic Revival in Algeria: An Overview", *The Muslim World*, 83, 3–4 (July–October, 1993), pp. 215–17; Abderrahim Lamchichi, *L'Islamisme en Algérie* (Paris: Editions L'Harmattan, 1992), pp. 104–5.

47 Ibid., p. 155.

48 Max Weber, "Science as a Vocation", in H. H. Gerth and C. Wright Mills, eds. *From Max Weber: Essays in Sociology* (New York: Oxford University Press, 1978), esp. pp. 129ff. For a stimulating discussion of this concept, see "Rationalisation, modernité et avenir de la religion chez Max Weber", *Archives des Sciences sociales des Religions*, 61, 1 (January–March 1986), pp. 127–38.

49 Bruno Étienne, *L'Islam radical* (Paris: Hachette, 1987), p. 134.

50 Jean-François Clément, "Pour une compréhension des mouvements islamistes", *Esprit*, 1 (January 1980), p. 46.

51 Étienne, *L'Islam radical*, p. 135.

52 For an excellent, more detailed sociological analysis of the espousal of Islamism by the youth in Algeria in the 1980s, see Omar Carlier, "De 'islahisme' à l'islamisme: la thérapie politico-religieuse du FIS", *Cahiers d'études africaines*, 32 (2), No. 126 (1992), pp. 185–219. See also, Rémy Leveau, "La Culture des jeunes et la montée des mouvements islamistes", Paper presented at the Conference on The Political Role of Islamist Movements in the Contemporary World: Domestic, Regional, and International Dimensions", The Bologna Center, Johns Hopkins University, Bologna, Italy, 26–7 November 1993.

53 The most serious attempts to study this question, in my opinion, are those undertaken by the Egyptian Fouad Zakariya, *Laïcité ou islamisme: les Arabes*

*à l'heure du choix* (Paris and Cairo: La découverte/al-Fiqr, 1989); the Tunisian Muhammad-Cherif Ferjani, *Islamisme, laïcité et droits de l'homme* (Paris: Editions L'Harmattan, 1992); and the French Olivier Carré, *L'Islam laïque ou le retour à la grande tradition* (Paris: Armand Collin, 1993). See also, Yadh Ben Achour, "Islam et laïcité – propos sur la recomposition d'un système de normativité", *Pouvoirs*, 62 (1992), pp. 16–30.

54 This concept is used in the sense given to it by Hisham Sharabi, i.e. modernized patriarchy in which "material modernization . . . only served to remodel and reorganize patriarchal structures and relations and to reinforce them by giving them 'modern' forms and appearances." Sharabi, *Neopatriarchy: A Theory of Distorted Change*, p. 4.

55 Khelladi, *Les Islamistes algériens*, p. 29.

56 Ibid., p. 45.

57 See Gwyn Williams, "The Concept of 'Egemonia' in the Thought of Antonio Gramsci: Some Notes on Interpretation", *Journal of the History of Ideas*, 21 (1960). p. 593.

58 Ibid., p. 162.

59 Ibid.

60 For detailed accounts of the issues raised and the violence practised by the Islamists in that period, one should refer to Lamchichi, *Islam et contestation au Maghreb*, pp. 157ff; Khelladi, *Les Islamistes algériens*, pp. 51–6.

61 al-Ahnaf, *et al, L'Algérie par ses islamistes*, p. 47.

62 Harbi, *L'Islamisme*, p. 133. Rachid Benaïssa is one of the very few Algerians subscribing to *Shi'a* Islam; this information is reported by Khelladi, *Les Islamistes*, p. 41.

63 These demands were formulated by Ahmed Hamani, Director of the Superior Islamic Council at the 4th FLN Congress held in January 1979 to designate the new president of Algeria; they were reproduced in their integrity in the State-sponsored review, *al-Asala*, Nos. 65–6 (January–February 1979), pp. 59–67, an excerpt of which is cited in Luc Willy Deheuvels, "Islam officiel et Islam de contestation au Maghreb: l'Algérie et la révolution iranienne" in Dominique Chevallier, ed. *Renouvellements du monde arabe, 1952–1982* (Paris: Armand Collin, 1987), p. 138.

64 Khelladi, *Les Islamists*, p. 76.

65 On a definition of Blanquism, see Karl Marx, "The Civil War in France" in Robert C. Tucker, ed. *The Karl Marx Reader*, 2nd edn (New York: W. W. Norton & Co., 1978), p. 627. From the trial of its members, it appeared that the MIA had planned the assassination of the prime minister and the individual in charge of the FLN Party; see, Lamchichi, *Islam*, p. 159; Khelladi, *Les Islamistes*, pp. 78–9.

66 For a summary on these groups, see Khelladi, *Les Islamistes*, pp. 117–21.

67 Ben Bella's ideas are published in the forms of lengthy interviews in Ben Bella, *L'Itinéraire*. For his openly Islamist views and his admiration for the Khomeini

revolution, see Deheuvels, *Islam et pensée contemporaine en Algérie*, p. 264 and n. 83.

68 For a detailed discussion of Imam Ghazali's role in the rise of Islamism in Algeria, see Ahmed Rouadjia, *Les Frères et la Mosquée-Enquête sur le mouvement islamiste en Algérie* (Paris: Karthala, 1990), esp., pp. 197–208.

69 Mahfoud Bennoune, "Notre dernière chance – Comment on fait le lit de l'intégrisme, I", *Algérie–Actualité*, No. 1376, 27 February–4 March 1992, p. 19. Bennoune cites Ali El Kenz, "La société algérienne aujourd'hui: esquisse d'une phénoménologie de la conscience nationale" in Ali El Kenz, ed. *La Modernité et l'Algérie* (Dakar, Senegal: CODESRIA, 1989), pp. 24–5.

70 Illegal imports of foreign goods – especially those unavailable in the country – and their re-sale at prohibitive prices at home. Individuals involved in such a market have made huge fortunes. Their connections with the Algerian bureaucracy and with barons of successive regimes is certain. For an interesting study of this sector, see Karim Bouzourène, "L'économie informelle de distribution en Algérie", DEA Thesis, Institut d'Études Politiques, Paris, 1994

71 Mohammed Harbi, *L'Algérie et son Destin – Croyants ou citoyens* (Paris: Editions Arcantère, 1993), p. 204.

72 On this point, see Smaïl Goumeziane, *Le Mal algérien: Économie politique d'une transition inachevée, 1962–1994* (Paris: Fayard, 1994), p. 276. The author is well informed, for he was minister of commerce from 1989 to 1991.

73 Ramdane Babadji, "Le Phénomène associatif en Algérie: genèse et perspectives", *Annuaire de l'Afrique du Nord 1989*, (Paris: CNRS, 1991), Vol. 28, p. 231.

74 A serious analysis of the October events can be found in Abed Charef, *October 1988*, 2nd edn (Algiers: Éditions Laphomic, 1990) and the late Muhammad Boukhoubza, *Octobre 88 – Évolution ou rupture?* (Algiers: Éditions Bouchène, 1991).

75 For a detailed discussion of the process of political liberalization, see Yahia H. Zoubir, "Stalled Democratization of an Authoritarian Regime: The Case of Algeria", *Democratization* , Vol. 2, No. 2 (January 1995).

76 On this point, see ibid.

77 Cited in al-Ahnaf, *et al.*, *L'Algérie par ses islamistes*, p. 30.

78 Ibid.

79 Ibid., p. 31.

80 Ibid., p. 99.

81 See also the interesting analysis given by Benjamin Stora, "Algérie: huit clés pour comprendre", *Jeune Afrique*, No. 1539 (27 June–3 July 1990), p. 18.

82 This was admitted by Madani himself; see, "Pour une nouvelle légalité islamique – Entretien avec Abbasi Madani", *Politique Internationale*, No. 49 (autumn 1990), p. 188. In particular, he declared that "I am not a Doctor in [Islamic] Law. My job is political not religious or theological." At least until 1974, Dr Madani was a militant of the FLN. As such, he was elected in May 1969 to serve in the Algiers Popular *Wilaya* Assembly (APW). He finished his term in 1974. See the report, "Le Saviez-vous?", *al-Watan*, 7 April 1991.

83  See *Projet de Programme du Front Islamique du Salut* (Algiers, 7 March 1989).

84  For a full treatment of the FIS's attitude toward the 1989 Constitution, one should refer to Lavenue, "Le FIS et la Constitution Algérienne", *Praxis Juridique et Religion*, 10 (October 1993), pp. 127–43.

85  Civil society is here understood in the sense given to it by Larry Diamond, "Toward Democratic Consolidation", *Journal of Democracy*, 5, 3 (July 1994), pp. 5ff. "Civil society is conceived . . . as the *realm of organized social life that is voluntary, self-generating, (largely) self-supporting, autonomous from the state, and bound by a legal order or set of shared rules* . . . It involves citizens *acting collectively in a public sphere* to express their interests, passions, and ideas, exchange information, achieve mutual goals, make demands on the state, and hold state officials accountable. Civil society is an intermediary entity, standing between the private sphere and the state . . . It excludes . . . political efforts to take control of the state. Civil society not only restricts state power but legitimates state authority when that authority is based on the rule of law. When the state itself is lawless and contemptuous of individual and group autonomy, civil society may still exist . . . if its constituent elements operate by some set of shared rules (which, for example, eschew violence and respect pluralism)."

86  See "L'Armée au dessus de la mêlée", *Libération*, 11 June 1990, p. 20.

87  Jean-Jacques Lavenue, "Le FIS et la Constitution algérienne", pp. 130–1.

88  An outstanding discussion of the phenomenon can be found in Olivier Carré, *L'Echec de l'Islam politique* (Paris: Editions du Seuil, 1992).

89  Ali Merad, "The Ideologization of Islam in the Contemporary Muslim World," in Alexander S. Cudsi and Ali H. Dessouki, eds. *Islam and Power* (Baltimore and London: The Johns Hopkins Press, 1981), p. 38.

90  A very good study of the historical, generational and political differentiation with the FIS is Séverine Labat's "Islamismes et islamistes en Algérie: un nouveau militantisme" in Gilles Kepel, ed. *Exils et royaumes: les appartenances au monde arabo-islamique aujourd'hui. Études réunies pour Rémy Leveau* (Paris: Presses de la FNSP, 1994), pp. 41–67. The English version, "Islamism and Islamists: The Emergence of New Types of Politico-Religious Militants", can be found in John Ruedy, ed. *Islamism and Secularism in North Africa* (New York: St. Martin's Press, 1994), pp. 103–21.

91  Merad, "Ideologization", p. 37.

92  These points are drawn from Abbassi Madani's *Azmat al-fiqr al-hadith wa mubarrirat al-hal al-Islami* (Algiers: Imprimerie Meziane, 1989); commentaries on this book can be found in al-Ahnaf, *et al.*, *L'Algérie par ses islamistes*, pp. 77ff.; Sheikh Abu Abd al-Fatah Ali Ben Hadj (Ali Benhadj), *Fasl al-kalam fi muwajahat zulm al-hukkam* (n.p.: al-Jabha al-Islamiyya lil Inqadh [FIS], n.d.), 310 pages. The book is a gold mine for scholars interested in Benhadj's views. The influence of Qutb and Mawdudi, to whom he refers very frequently, is unmistakable.

93  Ali Benhadj, "Qui est responsable de la violence?", *El-Mounqid* (FIS's newspaper), No. 9, reproduced in al-Ahnaf, *et al*, *L'Algérie par ses islamistes*, p. 136.

94  *Ibid.*, p. 140.

95 In addition to the speeches of its leaders, this section draws heavily on Abdelasiem El-Difraoui, "La Critique du système démocratique par le Front islamique du salut" in Gilles Kepel, ed. *Exils et Royaumes: les appartenances au monde arabo-islamique aujourd'hui. Études réunies pour Rémy Leveau* (Paris: Presses de la FNSP, 1994); al-Ahnaf, *et al, L'Algérie par ses islamistes* is also a remarkable source.

96 Cited in ibid., p. 117.

97 This view is expounded among others by Séverine Labat, "Islamismes et Islamistes en Algérie".

98 Malek Bennabi, a francophone engineer, was influential among some Islamist university students until his death in 1973. He was a highly learned man, not prone to violence and quite nationalistic. His book written in 1965, *La Démocratie en Islam* (Algiers: Mosquée Beni-Messous, Imprimerie SARRI, n.d.) demonstrates his good knowledge of Western civilization and its classical and modern thinkers.

99 El-Difraoui, "*La Critique du système*", p. 123.

100 Michel Camau, "Democratisation et changements des régimes au Maghreb" in Bernabe Lopez Garcia, Gema Martin Muñoz, Miguel H. de Larramendi, eds. *Elecciones, participacion y transiciones politicas en el Norte de Africa* (Madrid: Agencia Española de Cooperacion Internacional, 1991), p. 77.

101 See Augustus Richard Norton, "The Future of Civil Society in the Middle East", *Middle East Journal*, 47, 2 (spring 1993), p. 214.

102 Ali Benhadj's declaration published in *Horizons* (Algiers), 23 February 1989. See also his writings on democracy reproduced in Mustapha al-Ahnaf, Bernard Botiveau, and Franck Frégosi. *L'Algérie par ses islamistes* (Paris: Karthala, 1991), pp. 87ff.

103 The reason why Islamists in general do not have a well-defined societal project is discussed in Fouad Zakariya, *Laïcité ou islamisme: Les arabes à l'heure du choix*, prefaced and translated by Richard Jacquemond (Paris: La Découverte 1991), pp. 73ff.

104 Cited in al-Ahnaf, *et al.*, *L'Algérie par ses islamistes*, p. 116.

105 "*Barnamij al-intikhabat al-tashri'iyya*" (1991) cited in Zebiri, "Islamic Revival in Algeria", p. 215. This section draws from Zebiri's and al-Ahnaf's discussions.

106 During the government political parties conference held in July 1991, which this author attended, Nahnah said: "Even Allah created Satan in order to have an opposition." Most of the *Hamas* members interviewed hold the same view on the necessity of pluralism. The membership of *Hamas* is highly educated and rejects violence as a means of action.

107 Cited in Zebiri, "Islamic Revival", p. 215.

108 Ibid., p. 216.

109 Ibid., p. 217.

110 Sermon at the Kouba mosque in 1990, cited in Khelladi, *Les Islamistes algériens*, p. 108.

111 See Madani's interview in *Politique internationale*, p. 186.

112 See al-Ahnaf, pp. 52–9

113 *Projet de Programme du Front Islamique du Salut*, p. 5.

114 Ibid.

115 Ibid., p. 6.

116 Ibid., p. 7.

117 Ibid.

118 Ibid.

119 Ibid., p. 8.

120 Ibid.

121 Ibid.

122 Ken Jowitt, *New World Disorder: The Leninist Extinction* (Los Angeles, CA: University of California Press, 1992), pp. 275–7.

123 Ted Robert Gurr, *Why Men Rebel* (Princeton, NJ: Princeton University Press, 1970), p. 317.

124 Youssef Nacib, "Anthropologie de la violence", *Confluences-Méditerranée* (Paris), No. 11 (summer 1994), pp. 69ff.

125 Thomas M. Callaghy, "Civil Society, Democracy, and Economic Change in Africa: A Dissenting Opinion about Resurgent Societies" in John Harbeson, Donald Rothchild, and Naomi Chazan, eds. *Civil Society and the State in Africa* (Boulder, CO: Lynne Rienner Publishers, 1994), p. 234.

126 Ibid., p. 235.

127 An interesting discussion, though questionable on the analysis of the Algerian military, can be found in Hugh Roberts, "Algeria between Eradicators and Conciliators", *Middle East Report* (July–August 1994), p. 24–7.

128 *Radio Algiers*, in French, 22:30 local time, 30 November 1993. Both the HSC and the CND declared that all currents must be associated to the national dialogue and that in order to achieve national consensus important segments cannot be excluded from the dialogue. There are signs, however, that some segments of the military are not enthusiastic about such an approach.

129 This concept was originally developed for Eastern Europe in the period 1989–90. See Pierre Hassner's "Conclusion: 'Démocrature' et 'Révolution' ou la transition bouleversée" in Pierre Grémion and Pierre Hassner, eds. *Vents d'Est – Vers l'Europe des États de droit?* (Paris: Presses universitaires de France, 1990), p. 116.

130 Diamond, "Toward Democratic Consolidation", p. 7.

131 Diamond, "Beyond Authoritarianism and Totalitarianism: Strategies for Democratization", *Washington Quarterly* (winter 1989), p. 145.

# 6

# Islamists under Liberalization in Jordan

### Glenn E. Robinson

I believe the Islamic movement is facing a real impasse. We, as a political party, reject violence. We are a moderate group. However, if the Islamic movement cannot pursue politics as a political party, the extremists and advocates of violence will be encouraged, and the leadership will not be able to maintain order.[1]

**Ishaq al-Farhan, Secretary-General of the Islamic Action Front Party, Jordan**

The past decade has witnessed an intense interest in the issues of democratic transition and civil society in the Middle East by specialists both inside and outside the region. Within this scholarly community, these issues represent perhaps the most studied set of questions in recent years. Such attention has not been replicated in the wider social science community, where the outpouring of publications on the "third wave" of democratization has largely ignored Middle Eastern and, more generally, Muslim societies. In the most prominent projects on democratization in the developing world – from the 1986 O'Donnell, Schmitter and Whitehead five-volume series on *Transitions from Authoritarian Rule* to the more recent multi-volume series on *Democracy in Developing Countries* by Diamond, Linz, and Lipset – the Middle East has been notable by its exclusion. In one of the few attempts to address the issue of democratic transition in the Middle East to a wider scholarly audience, a 1996 edition of the *Journal of Democracy* carried a series of articles on "Islam and Liberal Democracy".[2] But even here the lead article was by a scholar well-known for his essentialist views of Islam and his pessimistic outlook toward any real democratic opening in the Muslim world.

Much of the reason for the exclusion of the Middle East in the debate over democratization is the limited number of cases of democratic transition in the region and the limited extent of democracy in those extant cases. However, given the number of countries that have experienced some degree of sustained political opening in recent years – Jordan, Lebanon, Morocco, and Kuwait, for example – and the rich theoretical issues involved even in "blocked" cases – Egypt, Algeria, and Tunisia, for example – the exclusion of the region from the wider debate is remarkable. Given this state of affairs, one is tempted to draw the conclusion that the larger academy has reached the same judgement that the political establishment in Washington seemingly has: that democratic transition in the region is either impossible or, at least, undesirable, or both.

This present case study seeks to go beyond the rather stale question of whether democratization is possible in the Middle East. Both empirically and theoretically the answer to that question is obviously yes. The question I pose in this essay is whether an explicitly Islamist movement – usually viewed as the greatest threat to any democratic opening in the region – can be a force for democratization. Can Islamists be democrats? Using a case study of the Muslim Brethren in Jordan and its political party, the Islamic Action Front (IAF), during the political liberalization begun in 1989, I conclude that the answer is yes: that the Islamist movement in Jordan has been consistently in the forefront of democratizing the Jordanian polity. It has done so not because the movement is made up of Jeffersonian democrats, but rather because greater democratization has served its organizational interests. As the best-organized political movement in Jordan, the Muslim Brethren had the greatest interest in freeing its hands to pursue its various policy goals, from segregating the sexes at public schools to opposing the Jordan–Israel rapprochement. By focusing on interests and organizations, as opposed to political personality traits (i.e. "only democrats pursue democracy"), it is easier to conceive of ideologically "ademocratic" groups advocating greater democracy, and doing so for more than just short term tactical advantage.

This case study of the Islamist movement during Jordan's political liberalization programme is divided into four sections. The first section outlines how the Islamist movement in Jordan – primarily the Muslim Brethren and its offshoot, the Islamic Action Front – actually performed during liberalization, arguing that the Islamists "played" democratic politics reasonably effectively and by the rules, even when they lost on policy matters (which happened frequently). The second section analyses the major policy pronouncements of the Brethren and IAF since 1989, showing that ideologically the Islamists have been mainstream, establishment-oriented and widely accepting of democratic rules. The third section examines how and why the long and friendly relationship between the Muslim Brethren and the Hashemite monarchy worsened substantially during liberalization. Finally, in the fourth section I ask whether such centrist policies by the Islamists will be likely to continue given the internal political and ideological divisions within the movement and the changing nature of its relationship with the large Palestinian community in Jordan.

While the overarching argument shows a positive correlation between the Islamist movement and the democratization process in Jordan, I conclude more pessimistically that the volatile identity politics in Jordan among Palestinians in the post-peace era may well begin to radicalize the Islamist movement, limiting the possibilities of further democratic deepening.

## Islamists at the Polls

In response to a series of economic and political crises in the late 1980s, culminating in severe riots in the south in the spring of 1989, Jordan began a process of political liberalization.[3] A "pre-emptive democratization" in its origins, the process has been controlled in a top-down fashion, in large measure to forestall more serious challenges to the political order in Jordan. This political opening helped the regime in Jordan survive further upheaval, including the second Gulf war, the repatriation of scores of thousands of mostly Palestinian refugees from the Gulf, and the political uncertainties surrounding its reconciliation with Israel. In contrast with a number of its neighbours, Jordan included its powerful Islamist movement in the democratization process, directly challenging the idea that Islamists cannot effectively participate in democratic politics.[4]

Islamism in general and the Muslim Brethren organization in particular have been the most successful political movements in Jordan during liberalization. In both the 1989 and 1993 parliamentary elections the Islamist bloc won a plurality of seats, out-distancing its closest competitors by substantial margins. While the 1989 showing was not surprising (for reasons outlined below), the success of the Islamists in the 1993 elections – given changes in the electoral law clearly aimed at limiting their effectiveness – demonstrated the popularity of the movement and the capabilities of Islamists in electoral politics.

The 1989 elections – the first parliamentary elections since before the 1967 war – were prompted by the "bread riots" in the southern (usually strongly pro-Hashemite) part of Jordan in the spring of 1989. In the aftermath of the riots, the most serious threat to regime survival since the 1970 civil war, King Husayn called for new parliamentary elections. Since political parties were illegal (and had been outlawed for over three decades) candidates who participated in the 1989 elections had to run as individuals. Even so, ideological tendencies of candidates were widely known and publicized by the candidates themselves. In particular, unofficial Muslim Brethren candidates made their membership well known, believing it would help their candidacies. The short election period (25 days) and the fact that the Muslim Brethren was the only established political grouping in Jordan other than tribes, were to the distinct benefit of Brethren candidates.

The Islamist movement dominated the election results, winning 32 of the 80 seats in parliament. If one subtracts the various set-aside "quota seats" for minorities – Christians, Circassians, and Chechens – then the Islamists won 32 out of 68 available seats, or nearly half.[5] Candidates of the Muslim Brethren were particularly successful, winning 20 of the 26 contests they entered. In addition, 12 independent Islamist candidates likewise won seats.[6] Various tribal representatives, independents and centrists won 35 seats, and leftists took the remaining 13 seats. Turnout was relatively low, with 54 per cent of registered voters and 41 per cent of potential voters casting votes.[7]

The strength of the Islamist bloc forced other, often politically disparate, members of parliament to form a coalition which could defeat the Islamists on most issues. Thus, during the first session of parliament, while Islamists formed a plurality, they were denied the ability to form a government or even elect the Speaker of Parliament. Prime Minister Mudar Badran, appointed by the king, did negotiate with the Brethren on membership in the cabinet but failed to reach an agreement. However, three independent Islamists were included in the government.

The second session of parliament opened in 1990 in the midst of the crisis over Kuwait. This time the Islamists were more successful, electing the Speaker, US-educated 'Abd al-Latif 'Arabiyat. In addition, four members of the Muslim Brethren joined Badran's government. Having captured the Ministry of Education in the bargain, the Muslim Brethren announced its intention to segregate by gender all schools in Jordan, something for which it did not need parliamentary approval. King Husayn expressed his disapproval by dissolving the government.

A pattern was thus established by which the Islamist parliamentarians would raise an issue only to be defeated in one way or another by the king or the successive prime ministers appointed by the king: Mudar Badran, Zayd Bin Shakir, and 'Abd al-Salam al-Majali. On a number of issues, including the segregation of sexes at schools, the prohibition of alcohol, and opposition to the peace talks with Israel, the position of the Muslim Brethren was defeated. This was true even though the Muslim Brethren retained the Speaker's position after 1990.

In spite of the fact that the large Islamist bloc in parliament was effectively shut out of government during this period, the Muslim Brethren and its allies continued to play by the rules of democratic governance. As a whole they were outspoken in their opposition to some policies, especially the growing rapprochement between Jordan and Israel following the 1991 Madrid conference. Other Islamists, like Layth al-Shubaylat, conducted parliamentary investigations into political corruption, concentrating particularly on the practices of the former prime minister, Zayd al-Rifa'i. Thus, while engaging in active opposition to certain policies, the Islamist bloc in parliament remained a "loyal opposition", voicing dissent in democratically permissible ways.

Of the five major policies which the 1989–93 parliament approved – legalizing political parties, ratifying an International Monetary Fund agreement for economic restructuring, lifting martial law, passing the Press and Publications law, and endorsing the National Charter[8] – the latter was perhaps the most significant item that the Islamists supported. The National Charter (*al-Mithaq al-Watani al-Urduni*), written by 60 appointed members of a royal commission, was drafted in December 1990, and was designed to act as a blueprint for the democratization process. Included among the signers of the Charter were a number of the most prominent members of the Muslim Brethren in Jordan, including Ishaq al-Farhan (current head of the IAF), Yusuf al-'Azim, 'Abdallah al-'Akayila, 'Abd al-Latif 'Arabiyat (Speaker of Parliament, 1990–93), Majid Khalifa, and

Ahmad Qutaysh al-Azayida. In addition, several independent Islamists were members, including Jamal al-Sarayira, Muhammad al-Alawina, and Mahmud al-Sharif (chief editor of *al-Dustur* newspaper).

The Charter was a genuinely liberal and democratic document which espoused all of the rights commonly associated with democratic governance. In addition to individual rights, the Charter advocated the full equality of women. While most of the various democratic rights espoused in the Charter were likewise adopted by the Muslim Brethren and the IAF, the Islamists who helped draft the Charter endorsed some otherwise surprising principles. The most important of these principles was that Islam (as both religion and civilization) was seen as only one of four sources of political legitimacy to guide the polity. The three other sources of legitimacy – Jordanian nationalism (*wataniyya*), Arab nationalism (*qawmiyya*) and universal norms – were each given equal weight with Islam, something seemingly at odds with Islamist views of sovereignty.

Even though the Islamists had played by democratic rules during the 1989–93 parliament, they still represented a strong vocal opposition to key government policies. As a result, and with developments unfolding rapidly in the Arab–Israeli peace process in the autumn of 1993, King Husayn sought to create a more compliant parliament in the November 1993 elections. In particular, the king wanted to limit, as much as was practical, Islamist representation in parliament.

The single most important step in the attempt to engineer a more docile parliament was the adoption of the "one-person one-vote" system.[9] Such a system was forcefully mandated by the king over the objections of the Islamists and 16 of the 20 registered political parties. By limiting voters to one vote even in electoral districts with up to nine seats at stake, the king forced voters to choose between tribe and the now legal political parties. No more could a voter appease both familial and ideological impulses with multiple votes. Even those in government widely acknowledge that the change was principally aimed at undercutting the Muslim Brethren.[10]

As expected, tribal ties won out over party affiliation, with the Islamists being hit the hardest. Islamist representation dropped from 32 to 22 seats, 16 of which were IAF.[11] Two of the six independents were Muslim Brethren members. In what came to be known as the "tribal parliament", of the 80 parliament seats 46 were won by candidates with no party affiliation, and 90 per cent of all standing candidates likewise were independents. Even some parties themselves were little more than tribal groupings. The electoral gambit worked as designed, with a strongly pro-Hashemite parliament elected in 1993.

While Islamist representation was cut by a third, it is wrong to conclude, as many have, that the 1993 elections showed the waning influence of Islamism in Jordan. Rather, the elections show conclusively that electoral results can be openly and legally "managed" in advance by changing the rules of the game, something any first year student of politics knows. In spite of their handicap, Islamists still won a plurality of seats – over a quarter of all seats and a third of non-quota seats. The IAF won more than three times as many seats as the runner-up party, and an IAF candidate, 'Abd al-Munim Abu Zant, won the most votes of any candidate. Thus, the 1993 elections confirm rather than deny the continuing power and influence of Islamism in Jordan.

Once again, during the first two sessions of the 1993 parliament, the Islamists acted within the constraints of democratic politics, even as core beliefs were being attacked politically. In particular, the 1993 parliament was in session when Jordan and Israel signed their historic peace treaty in October 1994. The Islamists were outspoken in their criticism of the treaty, voting against it in parliament, and even boycotting President Clinton's address to the Jordanian parliament on the occasion of its signing. In the aftermath of the signing, the Islamists (and others) continued their vocal criticism of the agreement, both on principle and on what was seen as an unseemly rush to sign it. Even on an issue as central as that of Palestine and Israel, however, Jordan's Islamists were governed by the norms of acceptable democratic dissent. In response, the government hinted, without evidence, that the IAF might be in violation of the Political Parties Law, which bans any foreign funding, and that the Muslim Brethren might have overstepped its legal charter.[12]

In sum, the Islamist movement in Jordan was successful in terms of winning parliamentary representation in both the 1989 and 1993 elections and proved to be a capable opposition to the governing coalitions. On the other hand, the Islamists were largely unsuccessful in pushing specific policies, from school segregation and the banning of alcohol in Jordan to opposition to the treaty with Israel. In each major policy battle the Islamists lost. With the exception of the 'Arabiyat period, the Islamists were regularly outmanoeuvred for the Speakership as well, as

[175]

they were again most recently in December 1995. In both cases, however – winning pluralities but losing policies – the Islamists obeyed the rules of democratic life: more so, in fact, than the government did.

## Islamist Ideology during Liberalization

Mirroring its public behaviour during democratization, the Muslim Brethren has espoused an ideology which has been generally consistent with democratic values, even while being internally inconsistent. In fact, given the establishment orientation that the Muslim Brethren has traditionally had in Jordan, its published doctrine – as found in the 1989 Election Programme of the Muslim Brethren and the 1992 Party Platform of the Islamic Action Front[13] – contained few surprises: it was economically and socially rather conservative (but with a populist streak), supportive of Jordanian sovereignty and Hashemite rule, pro-*shari'a*, and strongly against corruption and ostentation. Again, if there was any surprise in the nature of Islamist ideology in this period, it was in the degree of support for democratic norms and practices.

The 1989 Programme of the Muslim Brethren was put together rapidly, given the short notice of parliamentary elections. Still, it is a relatively long and detailed platform that reflects the conservative and gradualist approach of many of its leading members. Economically, the Brethren espoused fiscal conservatism, but with a populist bent, unsurprising for a movement with close ties to the merchant community. The Programme called for the protection of private property, the reduction of government debt, lowering inflation, cutting government spending, stabilizing the currency, exploiting natural resources, and taking measures to boost investment confidence. Moreover, the Brethren sought a reform of the public sector, seeking to "purify it from corrupt thieves and lazy sloths".

However, it would be wrong to conclude that this was the work of the Chicago school of economics. The Brethren's platform also called for the protection of infant industries, a virtual ban on imports, national self-sufficiency even in sectors where Jordan enjoys no comparative advantage (such as agriculture), and the elimination of usury (which could undermine the banking sector).

Interestingly, the Brethren combined this contradictory but generally conservative economic platform with a healthy dose of economic populism.

In particular, it blasted the ostentatious wealthy in Jordan and their "sleek cars, worth tens of thousands of dinars, that their teenage sons and daughters drive, and . . . their villas, which cost millions". In fact, the great disparities in income along with high unemployment were cited as causes of "widespread hatred" which might lead to "angry explosions in society". Thus, in addition to the need for job creation, the Brethren supported the redistribution of wealth through tax reform (including zakat). Suggesting that the desperate and legitimate actions of the poor to survive were similar to those of criminals, the Brethren noted that "poverty can hardly be distinguished from heresy".

In social terms, the Brethren's platform was predictable. It repudiated "corruption in all its forms", including alcohol, gambling, drugs, dance halls, and "bawdiness and use of makeup". It called for equal rights for women, endorsing the woman's right to "own property, work and participate in developing the society within the limits set by Islam". However, these rights were further conditioned, to be applicable only insofar as they did not "overwhelm the duty of the woman toward her home, husband and children". The Programme urged the ending of illiteracy, and advocated compulsory education at all levels. It specifically called for "avoiding education by rote and adopting modern educational techniques based on encouraging research and exploration". Academic freedom was tempered by its need to be grounded in "faith in the Almighty God".

The Programme's political platform, especially the section on public liberties, stressed democratic freedoms. It called specifically for freedom of expression, freedom of thought, freedom of movement and travel, and freedom of worship and religion. All forms of torture and arbitrary arrest were likewise repudiated as banned by Islam. In a direct attack on the then prevailing and long-standing martial law in Jordan, the Programme emphasized that these various rights and freedoms "must not be confiscated under the cover of extraordinary laws, martial law, or emergency laws".

While personal freedoms were unencumbered by any caveats, views on the media were somewhat contradictory. In general, the Programme again was quite liberal, demanding the government "cancel any restrictions limiting the freedom of the press". It also sought to limit the ability of the government to withdraw a newspaper licence or to restrict new papers and magazines from being issued. On the other hand, the Programme went on to say: "We also believe that it is the right of every Muslim citizen, and in fact his duty to advocate Islam throughout the country. All news media must be devoted to achieving this noble objective." The tension between these views was left unexplored.

Much of the rest of the platform was predictable. It called for a *jihad* to liberate all of Palestine and condemned any Muslim who ceded any part of it,[14] and it supported the application of *shari'a* law by pushing for the implementation of Article 2 of Jordan's Constitution which stipulates that Islam is the religion of the state.

On the whole, the 1989 Programme of the Muslim Brethren was a reasonably liberal and democratic document, if not particularly consistent in its logic. One can entertain doubts about the democratic nature of the Programme by pointing out that, by arguing the *shari'a* needs to cover all aspects of "political, economic, military, financial, and educational life" a huge caveat undermining the liberal character of the Programme was adopted. Or, one could simply say that the Programme was a ruse. However, given the actual political behaviour of the Brethren in the years since this Programme was adopted, these criticisms do not seem justified. Moreover, given that pushing the political opening served the organizational interests of the Muslim Brethren – as it would any well-organized but politically restrained movement – it should not be surprising that the Muslim Brethren has been a force for democratic expansion in Jordan since 1989.

The Islamic Action Front was formed in 1992 immediately upon the legalization of political parties in Jordan. While it is technically independent of the Muslim Brethren – and its leaders stress this aspect – it was formed primarily by leading members of the Brethren and adopted a similar platform. Legally, the Brethren remains a social and cultural organization, dedicated to spreading the Call (*al-da'wa*), and not a political party. Despite the protestations of its leaders, however, the IAF is to all intents and purposes the political arm of the Brethren. Moreover, by separating itself from the IAF, the Brethren can distance itself from the vagaries of political life, including potential electoral defeats of the IAF. In addition, the separation allows the Islamist movement greater flexibility in dealing with a variety of issues, both domestic and international.[15]

The IAF's platform parallels that of the Brethren's 1989 Programme in most ways, and is, if anything, more liberal than the earlier version with fewer Islamic caveats. As with the earlier Programme, it calls for the implementation of *shari'a*, denounces corruption in all of its forms, advocates a *jihad* to liberate Palestine, stresses support for the Jordanian Armed Forces, and is more explicit in its call for public freedoms and democratic expansion. In an obvious reference to the East Bank–Palestinian ethnic schism in Jordan, the platform calls for "[r]einforcing unity among citizens; combating ethnic, regional, tribal and sectoral conflicts that threaten this unity".

Perhaps the most significant difference in the two programmes concerns the role of women. While the 1989 Programme advocated equal rights for women but in clearly circumscribed ways, the IAF platform was less restrictive. While again calling for equal rights "within the framework of Islamic virtues", the IAF explicitly advocated "broadening the role of women's leadership in political life". Thus, the Muslim Brethren through the IAF for the first time supported not only women's participation in public life, but also their assumption of leadership roles in the political sphere.

Establishment Islamists' views on other politically relevant topics are not well spelled out in either the 1989 Programme or the 1992 platform. However, interviews with key Islamists point to three central issues of interest: interpretations of democracy, notions of which polities should be emulated, and views on the role of the West in Islamist thinking.[16] Well aware that some Islamists, like members of the Islamic Salvation Front in Algeria, have publicly stated that they view democracy as a tactic, and once in power would abolish democracy in favour of an Islamic theocracy, Islamists associated with the IAF are careful to link Islam with democracy itself. For example, Ziad Abu Ghanima, while sceptical of the extent of democracy in Jordan, stated: "Democracy is a form of jihad for us. The sources of Islam encourage freedom of thought, freedom of action. Democracy is not a tactic for us, it is a strategy. The Islamic movement [in Jordan] is not totalitarian. We believe democracy is part and parcel of Islam. It is true that there are some Islamists who want a 'government of God,' but this is not our way."

The head of the IAF, Ishaq al-Farhan, viewed the link between Islam and democracy in similar terms: "The Islamist groups here do not themselves believe in using force to bring about an Islamic society. We believe in democracy – and as a strategy, not a tactic.[17] We accept freedom of thought and expression . . . Our strategic goal is to reclaim Islamic civilization, but that should be done gradually and democratically."

When asked if other parties – Ba'thists, for example – might prevent this from occurring, al-Farhan dismissed them: "the parties on the left – Ba'thists, communists, and others – just don't have cultural roots here for a long life. They have no real future, will always be marginal, and will just never represent a serious threat to us. There is nothing to worry about [from them]." Ironically, it was exactly with these parties that al-Farhan and the IAF united in common cause in 1995 to oppose further normalization of ties with Israel.

Interestingly, for Farhan there is no polity, past or present, which represents an ideal to be emulated. In other words, Islamist goals in Jordan are novel insofar as there is no reference country to guide appropriate political action. The Islamic Republic of Iran is certainly no model Islamic state: "Iran claims it is implementing Islam, but in reality it is just Shi'i Islam. The war with Iraq also destroyed the credibility of the Iranian regime. I do not think Iran is the ideal Islamic state – Iran needs to widen the concept of Islam, instead of being so narrow." Nor is Saudi Arabia, a self-proclaimed Islamic state, seen as a model:

> Saudi Arabia is not really an Islamic state either. They recently refused a human rights group from monitoring the situation there. We believe in human rights. More importantly, the way they could show that they are real Muslims is to share their enormous wealth for the benefit of all Muslims, and they have not. Why is it that Jordan has a $6 billion debt while the Gulf states have plenty of money, and still they refuse to come to the assistance of their fellow Muslims? The Islamic umma has more of a right, a claim, to the oil than the US, but that is not how the Saudis behave.

Only Turabi's Sudan is seen in a somewhat positive light, but not as a model for Jordan's Islamists:

> Sudan is trying to implement Islam, but has so many problems, especially in the south. They do not have the luxury [of experimentation], their concerns are much more concrete. If Sudan is able to overcome these problems, I think it can become the nucleus for civilization in Africa . . . But there is no other polity we view as the ideal. Jordan is unique and we will build here.

Even the so-called golden era of Islamic rule, the period of the four "rightly guided caliphs" is not a goal to strive for. Al-Farhan dismissed this model saying: "That was such a long time ago. We are not interested in utopia, just a gradual transition to a better Muslim polity."

Not surprisingly, both Abu Ghanima and al-Farhan viewed the West in general and the US in particular with suspicion, based primarily on political, not theological, reasons. For them, the West is out to destroy Islam, putting Muslims everywhere on the defensive. While al-Farhan stressed conciliation ("We all need to learn to live together") Abu Ghanima's comments were more pointed – and more representative of Islamist views of the West.

> The US has declared war on the whole of Islam – you can see that in Algeria, Bosnia, Iraq, Palestine, everywhere. The US supports regimes which are suppressing Islamic movement, especially in Egypt, Algeria, and Tunisia. Why? Probably because of the very strong Zionist influence on policy in the US, with the goal of dividing Muslims in order to make Israel strong . . . In general, Muslims have no particular problem with the West. Many good things come from the West – science, technology, industry. There is no fundamental reason for bad blood between Muslims and the West. The problem in relations comes from the West – from the hostility the West shows us . . . The Islamic movement is not intrinsically anti-West or anti-modern. We are responding to the fact that the West bolsters dictatorial regimes at the expense of Muslims. Look at Bosnia. The West is just letting Muslims die. You see Gorazde[18] now where the UN says this, and Clinton says that, and Major says this – and nothing gets done! Compare this with Iraq and the response of the US and the West . . . It is not possible to have good relations under these circumstances.

As a whole, Islamist ideology in Jordan during the liberalization period has been temperate in its language and sober in its analysis of what was politically possible and desirable. Reflecting its long history of close relations with the Hashemite throne and its rather privileged position in society, the Muslim Brethren in particular has shown a kind of political moderation which belies much of the rather hysterical rhetoric over Islamism heard commonly in the West. The Islamists in Jordan have shown, both in language and in action, a respect for the democratic process and support for the existing regime. Or, as the leader of the Muslim Brethren in Jordan, Muhammad al-Dhunaybat, stated bluntly recently: "There is nothing in the Brethren's strategy or policy that calls for toppling the regime. We are advocates of reform, gradual reform. We have always said that we will adopt peaceful means to bring about change. We never believed in violence or intellectual terrorism."[19] Calling criticism of the king a "red line" which will not be passed, al-Farhan has likewise viewed the king as "above all differences and disputes."[20]

## The Worsening Hashemite–Muslim Brethren Relationship

Since its legalization in Jordan in 1945 by King Abdallah, the Muslim Brethren has enjoyed a special relationship with the Hashemite monarchy. Abdallah knew personally the leader, or guide, of the Brethren, 'Abd al-Latif Abu Qura, and included the Brethren's secretary, 'Abd al-Hakim 'Abdin, as a minister in his government. In 1953 the Brethren's legal status changed from "charitable society" to "organized group", a step which allowed it to be politically active; that is, it became a de facto party. While all other political parties were banned in a general crackdown on political opposition in Jordan in the 1950s, the Muslim Brethren retained its legal status. In fact, all political parties remained illegal in Jordan until 1992. Thus, the Muslim Brethren enjoyed something of a political monopoly in the public sphere for over three decades.

The reason that the monarchy gave such a privileged position to the Muslim Brethren had far more to do with politics than religious devotion. Simply put, the Muslim Brethren was the most effective political force at countering both the pan-Arab left and the radical Islamist right. The greatest threat to the Hashemite monarchy in the 1950s and 1960s came from Ba'thists, Nasserists, and others advocating pan-Arab unity and Arab socialism. More recently, potent opposition to King Husayn was centred in radical Islamist circles – such as Jaysh Muhammad or the older Hizb al-Tahrir al-Islami – who viewed the Brethren as collaborators with an illegal monarchy. Ideologically bitterly opposed to the Arab left as well as to the violent tactics of Islamist radicals, the Muslim Brethren proved to be a strong ally of the Hashemite throne.

In return for such political support, the Brethren not only remained legal in Jordan (while it was banned in a number of other Arab countries) but was encouraged to prosper. Leaders of the Brethren regularly participated in the government, most often through the huge Ministry of Education. For the Brethren, the appeal of socializing Jordan's youth according to its own views was made more tempting by the fact that the Ministry of Education is among the largest employers in Jordan, thus providing substantial patronage resources for whoever controls it.[21] In fact, the current leader of the Islamic Action Front and the former Speaker of Parliament from the IAF were minister of education and secretary-general of the ministry of education, respectively, earlier in their careers.[22]

The relationship remained strong at first following the 1989 election. The Brethren abided by the political rules, and routinely repeated its loyalty to the king, the country, and the democratic process. Further, while Islamists were rarely part of the cabinet, they were involved politically. When Mudar Badran was prime minister, for example, he negotiated a document with the Brethren highlighting 14 points of common interest between the Brethren and the government. Half of these points were issues of a general nature like ending martial law, and the other half dealt with specific issues such as education, usury, and the like. Moreover, the Brethren proved to be a strong ally of the king during the second Gulf war, helping the monarchy survive a very difficult challenge.

The Islamists, of course, introduced a number of pieces of legislation that the king opposed, such as a bill to segregate the sexes at all schools and swimming pools, and one banning all alcohol in the country. These bills, as well as other pieces of legislation which attempted to implement *shari'a*, were all handily defeated in parliament.

The tension arose when some Islamists showed that they could legally use the democratic opening not just to espouse their own beliefs, but to attack centres of power in Jordan. In a top-down, controlled liberalization experiment such as was the case in Jordan, democratization was supposed to occur without any fundamental shifts in the social distribution of power. The most important legal threat to this power was the parliamentary hearing into government corruption, headed by MP Layth al-Shubaylat. Shubaylat, an Islamist from Amman's affluent third district, had won more votes than any other candidate in the 1989 elections, and was a widely popular reformer and government critic. Shubaylat's parliamentary hearings on corruption in government were the greatest challenge to the existing power structure in Jordan in the first years of political liberalization. The hearings exposed rampant corruption in government, particularly under the previous prime minister, Zayd al-Rifa'i. In fact, parliament came within one vote of the super-majority it needed to indict Rifa'i on corruption charges.

While parliament was in session, Shubaylat enjoyed parliamentary immunity. With the summer recess in 1992, however, he was arrested on charges of trying to overthrow the government through an Iranian-sponsored conspiracy. The charges were almost certainly fraudulent, as was the evidence provided by the state security services.[23] In addition, the prosecutor forbade Shubaylat from seeing his attorney, a practice legal in Jordan.[24] Shubaylat and his fellow MP, Ya'qub Qarrash, were tried in military court – not the relatively independent civilian courts – found guilty and sentenced to death.

The king pardoned the two deputies a few days later, fuelling the belief that this was a political show trial, designed to teach a lesson to the Islamists as to the limits of political opposition. Subsequently, Shubaylat decided not to seek re-election to parliament in 1993, instead opting for the leadership of the powerful Engineers Association. Many reformers in Jordan were understandably distraught at the whole episode, and not only because it showed the limits of the political opening. As prominent human rights activist Asma Khader noted, "His mistake – and others have made similar mistakes – was to go it alone. What we want to do is build societies, large groups, so that no one person will be hurt. He was trying to be too much of a hero."[25]

The year 1992 seemed to mark a break from the historically good relations between the king and the Muslim Brethren, as the monarch began to take a harder line against his opposition. The Shubaylat affair was a clear signal to the Islamists that not everything that is legal – e.g., the corruption hearings – would be tolerated. And while Shubaylat himself was an independent Islamist, the Brethren, as the most powerful and organized Islamist group, was the principal victim of the king's tougher stance. Husayn made no secret of his evolving attitude in a widely-noted address before the Royal Staff and Command College on 23 November 1992. In a thinly veiled reference he accused the Islamists of being "proponents of backwardness and oppression" and a vehicle for "interference by others in our affairs". In case they had missed his intent, he continued: "I wish to affirm our determination to stand up to those elements which seek to impair our country's image and take us back to the past. And if they outstep the limits at which they ought to draw the line, they will be faced with all that is necessary to protect democracy and ensure that they are stopped in their tracks and redirected to the proper path."[26]

The principal tool that the king used against the Brethren was noted above: a unilateral amendment of the electoral system in 1993 at the expense, primarily, of the Islamic Action Front. Led by the IAF, most parties decried this change and the way it was implemented, but backed down after the king made it clear that he would brook no opposition to this new format. As expected, the IAF was hit the hardest by this change, but still managed to hold by far the largest plurality in the new parliament. In addition, the government embarked on a wave of arrests of Islamists, particularly in the spring of 1994 and fall of 1995, sending a strong message to the Islamists – and to others in the opposition. In another case, IAF deputy 'Abd al-Munim Abu Zant was badly beaten by unknown assailants on 28 October 1994 following his denouncement of the peace accord with Israel in a public sermon. Suspicion immediately focused on the *mukhabarat*, the security police. Most ominously, Shubaylat was re-arrested in December 1995 on charges of slandering the king, an action that paralleled a general crackdown on professional associations in Jordan. In response, the Jordanian Engineers Association re-elected Shubaylat as president in February, 1996, while he was still behind bars. Shubaylat won 5,000 votes in the elections, while no other candidate received more than 90.[27]

While the government and the monarchy continued to try to limit Islamist power in a variety of ways, the Islamists, for their part, continued to play by democratic rules. Most Islamists were outspoken in their opposition to the October 1994 peace treaty with Israel, and showed their discontent by publicly condemning it, voting against it in parliament, and boycotting President Clinton's address to the parliament on the occasion of its signing. But neither the Muslim Brethren, nor the IAF, nor any prominent independent Islamist (including Layth al-Shubaylat) acted undemocratically in opposition to the treaty.

All of this begs the question why, given the peaceful actions of Jordan's mainstream Islamists, did the king crack down on what had been a pillar of Hashemite support? Why did these once strong relations worsen to such a degree? Three reasons stand out: the decline of a common enemy, the nature of the democratization process itself, and the changing demographics of the Islamist movement.

Much of what cemented relations between the Hashemites and the Muslim Brethren was common distrust of and opposition to the Nasserist left. It was from this quarter that the greatest threat was posed to the monarchy during the formative period of the Hashemite–Brethren relationship in the 1950s and 1960s. Moreover, the Nasserists were anathema to the Brethren, both ideologically and in practice: Nasir's persecution of Egypt's Brethren throughout his rule was well-known in Amman. Today, the left in Jordan is extinct, virtually unrepresented in parliament and in disarray over developments in Palestine. Thus, the mutual enemy of both the king and the Brethren has disappeared, no longer uniting the parties in common purpose. In addition, the more radical Islamists have been contained, and do not pose a threat to the ruling order, thus vitiating the king's need for the Brethren as a political buffer.

Second, the nature of the democratization process made it more difficult for the monarch to control the Brethren 'discreetly'. With a freer press and parliamentary immunity, Islamists had a public voice in a way they had not previously, and used these platforms to openly criticize key government policies. Of particular importance during much of the liberalization programme was the issue of peace with Israel. Since the 1991 Madrid conference, the king routinely emphasized publicly his goal of concluding a peace treaty with Israel, much to the outspoken dismay of the Islamists. In fact, this single issue explains many of the important contours in the post-1991 liberalization process, especially the deterioration of relations with the Brethren. In short, the king had to limit the Brethren's ability to derail the treaty (hence the 1993 electoral change), but could not completely marginalize the Islamists without ending the political opening. Furthermore, he needed the legitimacy that democratic approval of the treaty would provide in order to justify its conclusion; thus, ending liberalization was not the answer. In the end, then, the very exigencies of the democratic experiment made political control that much more difficult for the king.

Finally, the apparent changing demographic support of the Islamist movement in Jordan means that the Muslim Brethren can no longer be assumed to be the natural ally of the political and economic establishment. Sociologically, the Brethren is decreasingly a solid, East Bank-dominated, organization of establishment families. Rather, the Islamist movement is increasingly Palestinian-based, and appeals more and more to a younger, poorer, more precarious populace. While this transition is still in its early phase, the direction that Islamism is headed in Jordan seems clear. Thus, while the Islamists have played by the democratic rules, the kinds of people increasingly speaking on their behalf – and, by extension the political future of the Brethren – must represent a source of concern for the monarchy.

## Will the Islamist Centre Hold?

Two related developments cast doubt on the ability of the Islamist movement in Jordan to maintain its centrist course. First, there are growing political schisms within the mainstream Islamist movement that threaten to undermine its relative cohesion. Second, the Islamist movement in Jordan relies increasingly on Palestinian political support, which traditionally it has neglected. As Palestinian identity politics become more volatile in the years ahead, there could be a corresponding radicalization of Islamism. Both of these centrifugal forces may well transform the Islamist movement in Jordan from a well-integrated reform movement into a more activist, potentially destabilizing force.

I have argued above that in *political* terms the Islamist movement up to now has shown itself to be rather accommodating to the prevailing order in general and Hashemite rule in particular. Likewise, it can be shown *sociologically* that the Islamist movement has been a quintessential middle class movement of older, established males. For example, of the 353 founding members of the Islamic Action Front, 116, or 33 per cent, were professionals (doctors, lawyers, university professors, engineers, pharmacists and journalists); 179, or 51 per cent, were civil servants (many of whom worked in the Ministry of Education); and 37, or 10 per cent, were businessmen (mostly merchants).[28] Of these same founders, 56 per cent were over 41 years old.[29] The first Shura Council of the IAF – the governing body of the party – consisted of 120 people, 74 per cent of whom were over 40.[30] This in a country where half the population is under 16 years of age. Virtually the entire leadership of the IAF, including every member of the first Shura Council, and 342 of the 353 founders of the IAF, is male.

In the midst of this seeming political and sociological homogeneity, serious divisions have begun to plague the Islamist movement for the first time since liberalization began. The IAF in particular has suffered through a number of public schisms, principally involving internal elections to the Shura Council. When the IAF was first licensed in 1992 it held temporary (one year) elections for its governing Shura Council. The results of the elections led to a public letter of resignation from a number of leading figures within the IAF, some of whom had served as cabinet ministers in the past. Two issues were at stake. First, the elections were swept by members of the Brethren to the virtual exclusion of prominent independents, in violation of a tacit pre-election agreement to limit Brethren representation on the council to 60 per cent of the seats. More important, the elections were won by Islamist "hawks", hardliners on a number of significant issues. This did not sit well either with the government or with important members of the Brethren.

New elections were held in December 1993 for four year terms on the Shura Council. This time the elections were won by IAF "doves", handily, leading to charges by the defeated hawks of election engineering. Even as prominent a hawk as Shaykh Abu Zant – who won the largest number of votes in the 1993 parliamentary elections – failed to win election to the Shura Council. This time, the hardliners quit in protest, including six members of the 17-member Executive Committee.[31] Those who resigned from the IAF, including Ziad Abu Ghanima, were particularly critical both of the IAF's decision to participate in the 1993 elections after the mandated change in the electoral law which disadvantaged the IAF, and of the party's failure to adequately denounce the peace process with Israel. They saw this as "evidence of the leadership's complicity with the government in working to weaken and moderate the country's premier Islamist movement".[32]

The IAF was again racked by internal dissent along these same lines in the fall of 1995. The basis of the division was the IAF's consideration of joining the government. The centrist leadership of the IAF would not rule out such a possibility, while others strongly objected to joining any government that implemented normal ties with Israel. When the leadership awkwardly attempted to silence its internal critics by suspending their memberships in the IAF, the organizational integrity of the party came into question. Abu Ghanima, for his part, predicted the coming demise of the IAF.[33]

Other independent Islamists have been very critical of both the Muslim Brethren and the IAF, claiming, with justification, that the Brethren has had too cosy a relationship with the regime over the years – that it has, in effect, been "bought off". The most well-known Islamist making these kinds of charges has been Layth al-Shubaylat, the parliamentarian who led investigations into regime corruption. Even members within the Brethren have made similar criticisms in the past, including Dr Abdallah 'Azzam, who once fought for leadership of the organization.[34]

While these divisions have not yet led to pitched ideological battles, they are representative of a larger divide within the Islamist movement, between *cultural Islamists* and *political Islamists*. As with any broad categorization, there are exceptions to the generalizations about these two types of Islamists. Yet this distinction helps explain the schism within Jordan's – and other countries' – Islamist movement.

In brief, cultural Islamists tend to be East Bankers, not Palestinians, and have maintained the balance of power within both the Muslim Brethren and the IAF. While most cultural Islamists have modern educations, those individuals with some formal religious training are more apt to fall into this camp. In terms of politics, cultural Islamists tend to push moral and social issues such as banning alcohol, segregating the sexes, and "Islamizing" school curricula. It is this group of gradualist reformers which is most solidly pro-Hashemite, and is sometimes accused of being co-opted by the regime. While all Islamists reject the peace accord with Israel, the grounds for rejection vary. Cultural Islamists' opposition to the accord is based largely on fears of Israeli cultural and economic penetration of Jordan – and the subsequent assaults on Islam – in the post-peace era.

Conversely, the discourse of political Islamists on the issue of peace with Israel is quite different. For them, it is a question of Western and Zionist imperialism, and of social justice, not fears of cultural contamination of the Islamic *umma*. Likewise, gender segregation is not as important for the political Islamists as government corruption, torture, or IMF-mandated austerity measures. It follows, of course, that political Islamists are less enamoured of the monarchy and less likely to be members of the Brethren itself. Rather, they tend to be independents, or former members of the Brethren, or, in some cases, members of the second stratum within the Brethren. Sociologically, political Islamists are more likely to be ethnically Palestinian, and have modern, technical educations.[35]

Much of the current tension within the Islamist movement on a variety of issues can be traced to divisions between these two (unorganized) camps. While one can find exceptions, the generalization appears to hold. The question then becomes: do current trends favour the ascendancy of the cultural or political Islamists? The answer is the latter, largely because of the increasing importance of the Palestinian factor.

Palestinians probably constitute around 60 per cent of the population in Jordan; however, they have been effectively marginalized politically. While Palestinians enjoy Jordanian citizenship and technically possess rights equal to East Bank citizens, in practice East Bankers have dominated the political arena to the virtual exclusion of most Palestinians. Part of this exclusion is self-imposed, as many Palestinians do not view Jordan as their own national home even if they were born and raised in Jordan. Palestine itself is still the political focus for many Palestinians in Jordan. Moreover, a large measure of their political exclusion is based on East Bank views of Palestinians as ungrateful temporary residents of Jordan who have no "natural" claim to Jordan. Clearly the 1970-71 civil war between the PLO and the Hashemite army continues to be the memory benchmark for many East Bankers.

In the midst of such political exclusion, the Islamist movement in Jordan has provided a political home to Palestinians. The Islamic Action Front in particular has grown solid roots not only in East Bank areas but also amongst the Palestinians. Indicators of the relationship between the IAF and the Palestinian community are plentiful. For example, half of the IAF's current parliamentary delegation (8 of 16) has Palestinian ethnicity. There are only six other Palestinian members in the rest of the 80-member parliament, and one of the six is an "independent" Islamist who is a member of the Muslim Brethren. Thus, of the 14 Palestinian members of parliament, 9 are Islamists. Further, the secretary-general of the IAF is Palestinian, as are approximately one-third of the IAF's Shura Council and Executive Committee members.

Furthermore, electoral support for the IAF from Palestinians in the 1993 elections was strong, even though overall Palestinian participation in the elections was low. In fact, the IAF was clearly the party of choice amongst Palestinians. For example, in Zarqa, a heavily Palestinian city just northeast of Amman, IAF candidates were the top three vote getters, with 85 per cent of all votes for winning candidates going to the IAF. Likewise, in the mostly Palestinian eastern sector of Amman, the IAF garnered 43 per cent of all votes and 78 per cent of the votes for winning candidates.[36] Moreover, in some cases Palestinian voters tipped the scales from East Bank IAF candidates to Palestinian IAF candidates, as happened when the Speaker of Parliament, 'Abd al-Latif 'Arabiyat, was defeated in the Balqa' district.

While Palestinian support for the IAF was strong, overall Palestinian participation in the election was low. Of the more than 800,000 actual voters in the election it is estimated that only 30 per cent were Palestinian.[37] The lack of Palestinian participation explains in part the overall low turnout for the election: just 45 per cent of eligible voters. In the examples cited above, the turnout was just 28 per cent in Zarqa and less than 19 per cent in eastern Amman (second district) where only 42,670 of the 228,000 eligible voters participated.[38]

In spite of such low turnouts, there is a clear pattern of Palestinian political identification with the Islamist movement in Jordan that needs to be explained. For the 1993 elections a single proximate cause explained a great deal: the signing of the PLO–Israel ("Oslo") accords just two months earlier. The Oslo accords took Jordan by unwelcome surprise – the PLO and Jordan had been part of the same negotiating team in both Madrid and the Washington talks – and led to a great deal of public East Bank chauvinism and hostility. The animosity was directed at the Palestinians not because East Bankers opposed the peace (which they generally supported) but because of what was seen as PLO duplicity. One prominent East Bank nationalist, 'Abd al-Hadi Majali, leader of the al-'Ahd party and brother of the then prime minister, called for the cancellation of the elections because Palestinians should not be allowed to vote; to have Palestinians participate would lead to an "unrepresentative parliament".[39]

The Oslo accords also impacted Palestinian behaviour in the election. Those that opposed the accord were more likely to support the IAF, which denounced the agreement and campaigned in Palestinian areas on the slogan that "the PLO is abandoning you, your rights and Jerusalem."[40] Those that supported the Oslo accords were more likely to have seen their political futures in Palestine, not Jordan, and thus would be less likely to participate in the elections.

The proximate cause of the Oslo accords should not mask the more fundamental reason for Palestinian support of Islamists. *The Islamist movement is the only political current available in Jordan which allows Palestinians to participate in Jordanian politics without the "ethnic tag" applied to their activities.* A separate Palestinian political party would simply be dismissed by East Bankers as "merely Palestinian", and questions of "dual loyalty" or even disloyalty to Jordan would emerge. In contrast, the Muslim Brethren and the IAF have a legitimate political standing in the Jordanian body politic in spite of their significant Palestinian representation. Tahir al-Masri, a former prime minister and long-time player in Jordanian politics, will always be seen as just a Palestinian by most East Bankers; conversely, Ishaq al-Farhan of the IAF, born near Jerusalem, does not carry the ethnic tag with him. Thus, the Islamist movement is the only option by which a Palestinian in Jordan may maintain both a public interest in Palestine (because it is part of the Islamic umma and contains the holy city of Jerusalem) and a political legitimacy in Jordan. No other movement can satisfy both requirements for Palestinians, and as such, the Islamist–Palestinian relationship can be expected to remain strong.

In fact, the growing volatility of Palestinian identity politics in Jordan combined with the failure of Oslo to deliver tangible benefits – especially with the Likud's return to power in Israel – may well end up radicalizing the Islamist movement in Jordan in the coming years. Who are the Palestinians in Jordan? Are they short-term visitors waiting to return permanently to their homeland? Are they full-fledged Jordanians of Palestinian ancestry? Are they citizens of the emerging polity of Palestine who will maintain permanent residency in Jordan but without citizenship rights? It is likely that these kinds of questions will be asked by Palestinians (and East Bankers) increasingly as a final deal between the PLO and Israel takes shape. It is also likely that the kinds of existential uncertainty raised by these questions of identity will lead to emotionally charged and mercurial politics. As this identity decision draws closer, the Islamist movement is apt be the forum of Palestinian discontent in Jordan.

## Conclusion

The above case study has illustrated how an overtly Islamist movement can be a force for democratic expansion in the Middle East. Jordan's policy of political inclusion before and during its democratization programme led to the creation of an integrated, establishment-oriented and moderate Islamist movement. Moreover, Jordan's Islamists have proved themselves to be capable democrats, obeying the rules of the political game while parleying their strength in society into a parliamentary plurality. Such political moderation is reflected in the formal ideological declarations made by the Muslim Brethren and the Islamic Action Front since 1989, and in interviews by top Islamist leaders.

At the same time, the political opening has soured relations between the Muslim Brethren and the Hashemite throne. The Brethren has lost its privileged position as the only legal political grouping in Jordan and therefore feels less restrained in voicing opposition to key policy shifts, such as the peace treaty with Israel. Such criticism, in turn, combined with the strength of the Islamist movement, has led the regime to take measures to circumscribe the power of the Islamists. Without these restrictions, the Islamists might well have defeated certain key policies, or at least cast serious doubt on their legitimacy. Thus, the Muslim Brethren's special relationship with the Hashemites is over, and the extent to which any association will be reconstituted is a source of internal debate.

Finally, the growing Palestinian character of the Islamist movement in Jordan signals the potential for its radicalization, given the period of volatile identity politics which the Palestinians are now entering. If this happens, then Islamist relations with the Hashemites will likely reach a new nadir, with serious consequences for Jordan's experiment in democracy.

## NOTES

Author's note: Research for this essay was made possible by a grant from the United States Institute of Peace. An earlier version of this article appeared in *The Middle East Journal*, Vol. 51, No. 3 (summer 1997) under the title "Can Islamists be Democrats? The Case of Jordan".

1 *al-Watan al-'Arabi*, 22 December 1995, as cited in FBIS-NES-95-247, 22 December 1995.

2 *Journal of Democracy*, 7:2 (April 1996).

3 I have written about the causes and consequences of Jordan's political liberalization elsewhere. See my *Defensive Democratization in Jordan* (forthcoming).

4 The phrase "one-man, one-vote, one-time" has been used to encapsulate the supposedly necessarily democratic intolerance of Islamist groups – that wherever Islamists participate in multi-party politics they will both win and dispense with any further democratic politics.

5 There are 20 electoral districts in Jordan, and each elects from two to nine representatives, for a total of 80 seats. 68 seats are reserved for non-minority Muslim candidates, nine for Christian, two for Circassian, and one to be contested by Circassian and Chechen candidates. Data on the 1989 elections come from *Intikhabat 1989: haqa'iq wa arqam* [The 1989 elections: facts and figures] (Amman, Jordan: Markaz al-Urdun al-Jadid l'il-Dirasat, October, 1993).

6 Due to the obvious difficulty in labelling some candidates, reports vary slightly in the reported number of independent Islamicist candidates who won office. I am relying on the categorization made by the al-Urdun al-Jadid research centre cited above. Other reports give the Muslim Brethren 23 seats. However, all agree on the figure of 32 total Islamists.

7 Members of the military and the security services were not permitted to participate in the elections.

8 See Robinson's forthcoming *Defensive Democratization in Jordan*, for details on all of the measures.

9 In the prior election each citizen could vote for as many people as there were seats in the electoral district. Since districts ranged in size from two to nine seats, each voter in Jordan had between two and nine votes to distribute among candidates in that district.

10 This was confirmed in a number of interviews with leading members of the political establishment. The only one who volunteered this information on the record was Ibrahim Izzedine. Ambassador Izzedine was the minister of state for prime ministry affairs at the time this decision was made.

11 Unless otherwise noted, figures for the 1993 elections come from Markaz al-Urdun al-Jadid l'il-Dirasat, *Intikhabat 1993: dirasa tahliliya raqmiya* [The 1993 elections: an analytical and statistical study] (Amman, February 1994), and *Post-Election Seminar* (Amman, February 1994).

12 Ben Wedeman, "The King's Loyal Opposition?", *Middle East Insight* 11:2 (January-February 1995), p. 17.

13 The 1989 Programme can be found *al-Ra'i*, 25 October 1989, as cited in FBIS-NES 27 October, 1989. The IAF Platform can be found in *Hizb Jabhat al-'Amal al-Islami* [The Islamic Action Front Party] (Amman: Markaz al-Urdun al-Jadid l'il-Dirasat, 1993). Excerpts can also be found in Hani Hourani, Taleb Awad, Hamed Dabbas and Sa'eda Kilani, *Islamic Action Front Party* (Amman: al-Urdun al-Jadid Research Centre, 1993).

14 This programme was written less than a year after the 1988 Palestine National Council meeting in Algiers which explicitly accepted a two-state solution to the conflict, thus accepting the permanence of Israel. The PLO's acceptance of Israel was denounced by Islamists in Jordan, Palestine, and elsewhere.

15 Hourani, *et al.*, *Islamic Action Front Party*, p. 19.

16 Examples in this section are drawn from interviews with Dr Ishaq Farhan and Ziad Abu Ghanima. Farhan is currently Secretary-General of the IAF. A Palestinian by birth, he was raised in Salt, Jordan, and was educated at both the American University of Beirut and Columbia University (where he received his

Ph.D.). Farhan has a long history of working in both academia and government, primarily in the ministry of education. He is widely viewed as a dove within the IAF. I interviewed him in his IAF office in Amman, 17 April 1994.

Abu Ghanima was born in Irbid, Jordan, and received a BS in chemistry in Turkey. He also worked in the ministry of education and at the Islamic Hospital in Amman. A former spokesman for the Muslim Brethren, Abu Ghanima was on the Executive Committee of the IAF before resigning from the party. While still an establishment Islamist, he is seen as a hard-liner. I interviewed Abu Ghanima in his administrative office at the Islamic Hospital, Amman, 19 April 1994.

17  Interestingly, both Farhan and Ghanima used exactly this same phrase, the former in English, the latter in Arabic. Clearly this issue has been raised in the past.

18  The Serbian attack on the city of Gorazde – supposedly a UN-guaranteed safe haven – was ongoing at the time of the interview.

19  *Jordan Times*, 12–13 October 1995, as cited in FBIS-NES-95-198, 13 October 1995.

20  *al-Watan al-'Arabi*, 22 December 1995, as cited in FBIS-NES-95-247, 22 December 1995.

21  Hourani, *et al.*, *Islamic Action Front Party*. p. 13. They list the current number of employees as 60,000.

22  Ibid. pp. 13–14.

23  Political observers from all stripes share this sentiment. Even a high-ranking cabinet member at the time, Ibrahim Izzedine, has intimated that Shubaylat was framed. He referred to it as part of a "power struggle". Interview with Ambassador Izzedine, Amman, 12 April, 1994.

24  Interview with Asma Khader, lawyer and human rights activist, Amman, 19 April 1994. Khader, a Christian, has represented a number of Islamists charged with more violent crimes, including members of the Jaysh Muhammad, who were convicted of setting off a series of bombs. Many members of the Jaysh Muhammad are "Afghanis" – Jordanians who fought with the Mujahidin in Afghanistan.

25  Ibid.

26  The full text of the speech can be found in *Selected Speeches by His Majesty King Hussein I, The Hashemite Kingdom of Jordan, 1988-1993* (Amman: International Press Office of the Royal Hashemite Court, n.d.) pp. 89–104.

27  *Middle East International*, 15 March 1999.

28  *Hizb Jabhat al-'Amal al-Islami*, p. 29. The remaining 21 founders, or 6 per cent, had a variety of occupations.

29  Ibid. p. 30.

30  Ibid. p. 45.

31  *Post Election Seminar*, p. 56. Ziad Abu Ghanima was among those who resigned.

32  Ibid. p. 56.

33  *Jordan Times*, 23 October 1995, as cited in FBIS-NES-95-205, 23 October 1995.

34  After losing the leadership struggle to Shaykh Khalifa, 'Azzam fought with the Mujahidin in Afghanistan, before being killed in a bomb blast in Peshawar, Pakistan. He remains a very popular symbol for Islamist hawks today.

35 For a fuller discussion of this distinction, see Glenn E. Robinson, *Building a Palestinian State: The Unfinished Revolution* (Bloomington: Indiana University Press, 1997), chapter 6.
36 *Post Election Seminar*, p. 55.
37 Ibid. p. 47.
38 Ibid.
39 Ibid. p. 45.
40 Ibid. p. 48.

# 7

# Islamism and Civil Society
# in the Gaza Strip

*Michael Irving Jensen*

Political reform will be at the top of the agenda in the coming decades in the Middle East.[1] The main contenders for defining the political landscape of tomorrow, apart from the present-day rulers, is the Islamist opposition. Today, large segments of Muslims all over the Middle East are engaged in "politics of silence". They participate in everyday forms of resistance, such as making use of alternative Islamic banking and Islamic Non Governmental Organizations (NGOs) – actions that suggest some kind of dissatisfaction with the status quo.[2]

The Islamist opposition, or Islamism,[3] is of course not a monolith, and this is why a number of researchers have developed different categories for classifying the various Islamic oppositional movements and groups. Dekmejian, for instance, has divided the Sunni Islamist movements into six different, rather abstract, categories.[4] Other researchers only use two categories; namely, "accommodative" or "non-accommodative"[5] or, as Moussalli defines them, "moderates" and "radicals".[6] The main difference between the moderate and radical Islamists is that the radicals prove "resistant to dialogue and cooperation with the Arab regimes and the West in general",[7] while the moderate Islamists are "open to dialogue, compromise and more importantly, to universal rights, freedom, pluralism and civil society".[8] This article will deal solely with what Moussalli terms moderate Islamism.

First, this article outlines the modern history of the major Islamic social institutions in the Gaza Strip. Secondly, it investigates a specific item on the agenda of the Islamists, namely, an Islamic sports club. As has been pointed out by Morsy, "In considering the current proliferation of services offered by Islamic organisations, it is imperative to recognize the heterogeneity of such organisations and thereby avoid the orientalist tendency to reify Islam as a unitary force."[9] Thus, I am assuming that the users of an Islamic medical centre or a computer centre make to a larger extent non-religious decisions, than users of, for example, an Islamic football club or participants in religious reading groups. Sports activities usually include participation in a team sport on a continuous basis, a fact which on various levels will form part of the participant's identity. The same is true for participants of religious reading groups. In this article the focus is on young men playing football in an Islamic club, as an example of the work the Islamists carry out. Among the questions raised are: why do these young men choose to play in an Islamic club? What are their perceptions of the political situation in the Gaza Strip? How do they view the relation between Islam and politics in general?

The discourse of the moderate Islamists in the Gaza Strip (as elsewhere) is based on the Quranic verse (*al-Imran* 3:104), "Let there arise out of you a band of people inviting to all that is good, enjoining what is right and forbidding what is wrong. They are the ones to attain felicity".[10] This verse is used, for instance, in the opening paragraph of the statute of the Islamic Social institution, al-Mujamma' al-Islami. One way used by the Palestinian Islamists to implement the Islamic system (*al-nizam al-islami*) is by offering a number of services to the Palestinian people, channelled mainly through a number of Islamic social institutions. This paper tries to show that these Islamic social institutions are an integral part of Palestinian civil society.[11] Civil society is here defined as a place "where a melange of groups, clubs, guilds, syndicates, federations, unions, parties and groups come together to provide a buffer between the state and the citizen".[12] The Islamists are indeed part of civil society because they work within the system and alongside other groups, although the environment in which the Islamists operate is neither tolerant nor democratic.[13] Despite the fact that most Islamic social institutions in the Gaza Strip are close to Hamas they are considered as being moderate. Hamas has never given up 'Islamization from below', despite its armed struggle against Israeli occupation. Since the Palestinian uprising *(Intifada)*, Hamas has taken over the role and the institutions of the Muslim Brotherhood in Palestine. Thus, Hamas and the Brotherhood are synonymous.

Islamic medical clinics, kindergartens, schools, sporting clubs, computer centres, homes for the elderly and hospitals constitute the most important dispensers of the social services that the Islamists provide. Through a political strategy that is attempting to persuade individuals to embrace "true Islam" (*Islam al-hanif*), the moderate Islamists are seeking to create the foundation for an Islamic state. In other words, the moderate Islamists believe that the reform of the individual is a prerequisite for the transformation of society. Due to this conviction it is, of course, only natural for the Islamist leaders to operate at the grassroot level within civil society. Researchers within the field of political Islam mention this work as being of utmost importance to the Islamists. Emile Sahliyeh, for example, writes on the Palestinian Islamists:

> Many of the activities of Hamas in the West Bank and Gaza are centred on the mosques. A vast network of day-care agencies, religious schools, youth and sports clubs, clinics and nursing homes, and financial programmes were established. The creation of the Islamic Centre, Islamic University of Gaza and several Islamic colleges, in the West Bank provided the Muslim Brotherhood with additional means to advance their political agenda. These institutions served as mechanisms for the recruitment of new members and their indoctrination along Islamic lines.[14]

Although scholars acknowledge and emphasize the importance of the social institutions for the political strategy of the Islamists, most have failed to investigate and analyse how the Islamists carry out their work in a given socio-economic and historical context.[15] In this regard Augustus Richard Norton writes, "Scholarship on the Islamists has, however, been overly textual, too inclined to report words of the ideologues and the spokesmen, and insufficiently sociological, in terms of failing to look at the motives of those who lend their support to the Islamist movement."[16] Thus, apart from analysing how the Islamists work on the ground, it is important to focus on the motives of the supporters of the Islamic movements in order to achieve a more profound understanding of Islamism and its penetration of society. Robert Frenea writes in the preface of François Burgat's book, *The Islamic Movement in North Africa*:

> One cannot forget that it is men and women who give the movement its foundation, and not just the *suras* of a dogma that may be more accessible to the observer than the millions of individuals who claim it. And it is necessary to remember that none of these are

immune to their environment or to the human and sociological laws, despite the force of their affirmations.[17]

Because individuals are not immune from their socio-economic environment this article is not an attempt to generalize why Islamists act the way they do, but rather an attempt to arrive at a deeper understanding of why Palestinian Islamists in the Gaza Strip act as they do. The article is based on qualitative interviews with members of an Islamic football club in Gaza. What is presented is a first reading of a number of qualitative interviews conducted during preliminary fieldwork in the Gaza Strip during the period of December 1996–January 1997. Thus, this article forms part of an ongoing research, which may be summarized in the provisional title "The political strategy of moderate Islamists: an empirical analysis of Islamic social institutions in the Gaza Strip".[18]

## The Modern History of Islamic Social Institutions

Despite the fact that the Muslim Brotherhood established its first branches in Palestine in 1946 the main Islamic social institutions associated with the Brotherhood are of more recent origin. Contrary to what happened in the neighbouring Arab states, Islamism did not come to play a prominent role in the Palestinian society immediately after the Arab defeat of 1967.[19] Only by the end of the 1970s had the Muslim Brotherhood managed to set up an Islamic social infrastructure in the Gaza Strip. The first social institution established was al-Mujamma' al-Islami in 1973. The centre was set up by Ahmad Yasin, the leader of the Muslim Brotherhood in Gaza. Ahmad Yasin was born in Jawrat, a small village near present-day Asqelon in 1932. In 1948 he fled with his family and most villagers to the Gaza Strip. The paralysed Yasin studied in Egypt for a few years, and after his return, he taught at various UNRWA schools in the Strip. Furthermore, he was the imam in a number of mosques, including al-Abbas mosque. His political career began in the early 1970s when he founded al-Mujamma'. In 1984 he was sentenced to 13 years in prison by the Israelis, but was freed in 1985 in a prisoner exchange arranged by Ahmad Jibril of the PFLP-GC. Again in 1989 he was imprisoned in Israel, this time for life. Among the charges against him was the founding of Hamas two years earlier. Sheikh Yasin was released in early October 1997 in another prisoner exchange with Jordan. He is widely recognized as the spiritual leader of Hamas.

Al-Mujamma' al-Islami was located in the immediate vicinity of the home of Ahmad Yasin in the neighbourhood of Jawrat al-Shams in Gaza City. The aim of the Centre was to provide Islamic education and sports for the youth in Gaza, as well as to provide help and health care for the lonely and the poor.[20] Most researchers acknowledge that al-Mujamma' al-Islami played a significant role, not only socially, but also politically. This is partly due to the fact that a significant number of its leaders are at the same time prominent members of the Muslim Brotherhood. With the establishment of al-Mujamma' the Brotherhood acquired an institutional base from which to spread the message of Islam to large segments of the Palestinian population.[21]

In the mid 1970s other similar Islamic institutions were established. Among the most important ones was al-Jam'iyya al-Islamiyya (the Islamic society) which was founded by another influential Islamist, Ahmad Bahr, in 1976. Ahmad Bahr is a 'alim educated in the Sudan. A former imam at the Palestine mosque in central Gaza, he is currently associate professor at the Islamic University in Gaza. Moreover, he is a prominent figure within Hizb al-Khalas al-Watani al-Islami. Just like al-Mujamma' al-Islami, this institution was also located in the immediate vicinity of the home of the institution's founder, namely in the area of Nasr in Gaza City. Since its founding, al-Jam'iyya al-Islamiyya, like al-Mujamma' al-Islami, set up a number of branches in various towns throughout the Gaza Strip. Its aim is almost identical to that of its predecessor and is spelt out in article 3 of its statute: "The aim is to lead the people to the True Islam [Islam al-hanif] and to work spiritually through worship, and intellectually through science, and physically through sports, as well as socially through charity."[22] Another important Islamic social institution is the Jam'iyyat al-Salah al-Islamiyya, which was set up in the city of Deir al-Balah in 1978 by Ahmad al-Kurd. Ahmad al-Kurd was never a member of the Brotherhood and today the administrators of the institution stress that it has no relation whatsoever with the Islamic movement in Gaza. However, its statute is strikingly similar to, if not identical with, that of al-Jam'iyya al-Islamiyya.[23] Thus, there is no doubt that this institution, just like the other two, operates in line with the thought of Hasan al-Banna, the Egyptian founder of the Muslim Brotherhood. Another important organization, established in 1981, is Jam'iyat al-Shabbat al-Muslimat (Society of Young Muslim Women). In its four branches it offers a variety of services for women in the Gaza Strip such as Quran reading, computer training and sewing, etc.[24]

Apart from these virtually all-embracing institutions a large number of smaller and more specialized institutions exist in the Gaza Strip. There is, for example, al-Wafa li-Ra'iyya al-Musanin (established in 1980), which is an Islamic home for the elderly; Mabarrat al-Rahma, an Islamic home for orphans and Mustashfa Dar al-Salam, an Islamic hospital in Khan Younis established in 1995.[25] (see Figure 1.)

## FIGURE 1
## The Main Islamic Social Institutions in the Gaza Strip

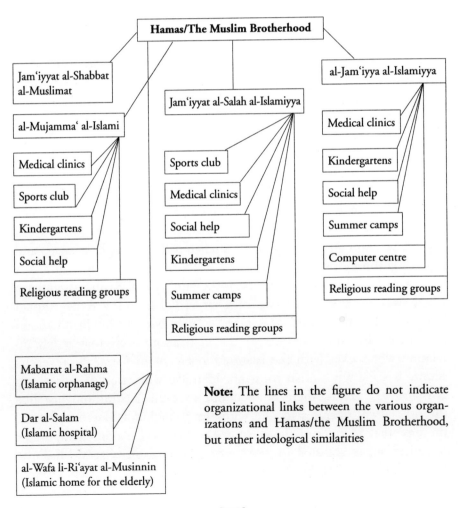

**Note:** The lines in the figure do not indicate organizational links between the various organizations and Hamas/the Muslim Brotherhood, but rather ideological similarities

It is a characteristic feature of all the Islamic NGOs in the Gaza Strip that they operate in the same fields as the Muslim Brotherhood in Egypt since the 1930s, namely education, social care, and health care.[26] This is, of course, no coincidence as all of the institutions adhere to the same line of thought as the Brotherhood.

Throughout the 1970s and 1980s the Islamists in the Gaza Strip were capable of making themselves visible, not only within the social sphere, but also within the field of education. In 1978, leading Islamists managed to establish the Islamic University of Gaza (IUG), which was the first university in the Strip. The ideology of the University is obviously Islamic as its name would indicate. According to Walid Amr, a professor of English at IUG, "The ideology of the IUG is Islamic. The main idea is to educate the Palestinian people. The strategy is to keep the basics of all individuals. These basics are derived deeply from Islam. We want people to return to our basics, i.e. Islam."[27] The IUG is properly the most important base for the Islamists.[28] According to Ali Jarbawi, the universities have generally been more important for the Islamic movement than the mosques due to their relatively greater autonomy during the Israeli occupation.[29] Recently, the Islamists in Gaza have set up a number of other institutions, such as a legal political party (Hizb al-Khalas al-Watani al-Islami), a weekly newspaper (*al-Risala*), and a bank (Bait al-Mal) (see Figure 2).

Several factors have influenced the visibly increasing activism of the Islamic movement during the past couple of decades in the Gaza Strip. The most important have been:

(a)  The failure of pan-Arabism, and later Palestinian nationalism, to fulfil the aspirations of the Palestinians' dream of creating a state.

(b)  The indirect Israeli assistance given to the Islamic movement in order to weaken the political power of the PLO in Palestinian society. In the early 1970s the moderate Islamists were not perceived as a threat by Israel because of the non-confrontational line the Brotherhood took at the time.

(c)  The assistance given to the Islamists by the government of Jordan for the same reason, that is to weaken the PLO with which Jordan has been engaged in a power struggle in the Occupied Palestinian Territories since the early 1970s.

(d)  The massive economic support granted to the Islamic movement from the *nouveaux riches* states in the Gulf since the 1973 oil boom. This support was primarily given in order to widen their legitimacy and influence.

(e)  The establishment of active Islamic movements in the surrounding countries, for example in Egypt and Syria. These movements became particularly active after the defeat of the front line states in 1967, in part due to the failure of the Arab left to fill the political vacuum which followed.

(f)  The military activities of the Hizbullah in Lebanon which were largely responsible for Israel's withdrawal from large parts of Lebanon in 1985. It convinced many Palestinians that Islam is capable of ending Israel's occupation of the West Bank and Gaza.

(g)  The Islamic revolution in Iran in 1978–9 showed that the creation of an Islamic state was not only possible but realizable.

The Islamic institutions did not compete with one another because of ideological affinity. Almost all the leaders of the various Islamic institutions are either members of, or closely connected to, the Muslim Brotherhood. Also the fact that all the institutions work locally and have been able to distribute their tasks in order to avoid overlapping, demonstrates the degree of their cooperation. Sullivan demonstrated in his study on what he calls Islamic Private Voluntary Organizations that 'small is better' and that NGOs working in local communities gain a higher degree of legitimacy.[30] This is also true in the Palestinian context, and Islamic leaders acknowledge this. In fact a leader of Hizb al-Khalas al-Watani al-Islami has argued that this is part of a deliberate strategy.[31] The ability to cooperate differs significantly from the experience of the organizations affiliated to the PLO which were weakened by competition and internal strife.[32]

Although the Islamists during the past two decades have been able to create a far-reaching network of social institutions, it is hard to judge how influential these institutions are in generating political support for Hamas and other Islamic parties in the Gaza Strip. There has undoubtedly been a tendency in the West to over-emphasize the strength of the Islamists in Gaza. This is largely because Israel and even the Palestinian Authority (PA) have portrayed them as being either extremely influential or extremely dangerous. The Islamists themselves have naturally worked hard to present the movement as being strong and influential in order to gain legitimacy. The PA has also made efforts to make the movement seem strong, albeit for another reason, namely to attract larger sums of donor money to enable them to take over most of the welfare activities of Islamic NGOs. The Israeli government has an interest – with or without the Likud in power – to make the world believe that the Islamists are extremely powerful so as to acquire a politically expedient leeway whereby it can postpone or even refuse to implement the signed agreements with the Palestinians on the pretext that Israeli security is being threatened.

## FIGURE 2
## The Islamist infrastructure in the Gaza Strip, 1997

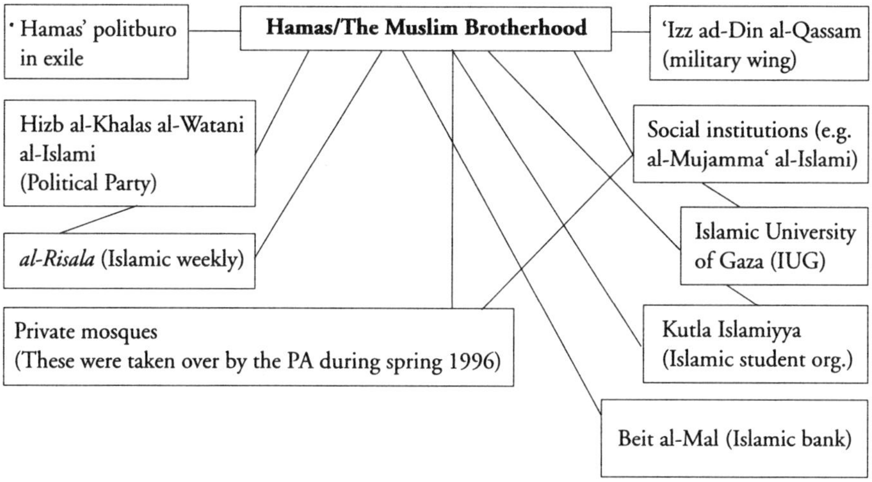

**Note:** The lines in this figure do not indicate organizational links between Hamas/The Muslim Brotherhood, but rather ideological links. However, Hamas leaders consider most of these institutions as being Hamas institutions.

## Islamists on the Ground

Sports are very popular in the Middle East. If football was not the most popular sport before 1982, it certainly became so after Algeria's sensational 2–1 victory in the same year over The Federal Republic of Germany at the World Cup in Spain. The popularity of football is not confined to secular Muslims, but also Islamists. The explosive growth in the number of satellite dishes – even in the numerous Palestinian refugee camps throughout the Gaza Strip – as well as the increasing number of sports channels have contributed crucially to the popularity of football and sports in general. A number of my interviewees declared that they often watched football on television and a number of them had encyclopaedic knowledge of football matched by only a few anywhere in the West. In the Gaza Strip there are 35 officially registered football clubs[33] of which four are Islamic, namely, Jam'iyyat al-Salah al-Islamiyya, al-Jam'iyya al-Islamiyya, al-Mujamma' al-Islami and Nadi al-Hilal al-Riyadi. The first three said that clubs were part of the social institutions bearing their names, whereas the latter was connected to the small, more or less pro-PA party, Harakat al-Nidal Islami.[34] Atef 'Adwan, a lecturer at the IUG and a Hamas supporter, claims in his bibliography of Ahmad Yasin, that sport is an important element in the attempt by the Islamists to attract the young Palestinians towards Islamic institutions and mosques.[35]

Within the health care sector, "Islamic health care does not appear to stand on its own, but is firmly supported by the well-entrenched pillars of high-tech, curative, individually centred biomedicine."[36] The same goes for other fields of Islamic activity. Thus, within the field of sports the Islamists do not try to revive the old traditional Islamic activities like horse racing and archery, but instead make use of "colonial games" such as football, volleyball, basketball and boxing. This seems to be an obvious example of their will and ability to cope with the modern world. Apart from the above-mentioned activities, the Islamists also offer training in karate and mon-cha-ko. These activities are in fact very popular with the youth as the following episode demonstrates. In December 1996 al-Jam'iyya al-Islamiyya held a party in order to celebrate its volleyball team, who had represented Palestine in an international tournament in Saudi Arabia. Some 500, mainly young men in their early twenties, as well as a large number of Islamist leaders, such as Ismail Haniyya, Ahmad Bahr, Hassan Shamma' and Imad Falouji, attended the festivities. Part of the programme consisted of a demonstration in karate and mon-cha-ko by some members of the Islamic club. Interestingly, more than half of the youngsters present left the party immediately after that demonstration. This shows that the spectators attended mainly to be entertained.

For an outsider it can be hard to see what differentiates 'Islamic sport' from 'non-islamic sport'; football for example is a universally popular game regardless of the players' political and religious convictions. The activists themselves do not make any differentiation between types of sport; to them, sport is about morals and attitudes, about how you treat and care about each other, regardless of the game played.

Because of the sensitivity of the research topic the names of the people quoted in the following part of this article are all pseudonyms. For the same reason all references to the name of the club in which these young men play has been omitted.

Mahmoud, one of the older (in his late twenties) and respected players of the team who, like all other interviewees, is a registered UNRWA refugee explains the Islamic nature of his club in the following way:

> We differ from other clubs first of all because of the morality of the players and also because of the way the team-mates treat each other.

Ahmad, a young man in his early twenties who has played in the club during the past six years, supplements this statement with these words:

> This club is different; it is Islamic; it represents Islamic men. In other clubs, morality is sometimes low; maybe they drink alcohol in other clubs, maybe they don't pray. There is a big difference.

Both Mahmoud and Ahmad emphasize morality. Morality in the Islamic club makes all the difference. To Ahmad, morality and Islam are almost synonymous. Thus, to those who are active, the basic nature of Islam is highly moral. It is tempting to see this attitude as a reflection of the way the Islamists are trying to differentiate themselves from others. Thus, it is an expression which signifies a wish to be different from the decadent and amoral West and especially from the westernized segments of the Palestinian population.[37] The Islamists define themselves exclusively in relation to their complete antithesis. It is worth noting how Ahmad describes his club as being different because "it represents Islamic men". The consequence of this attitude is the creation of a schism between "Islamic men" and the remainder of the Palestinians in Gaza. Thus, it seems as if the active participants in the Islamic sports club are trying to differentiate themselves from the rest of Palestinian society in as much as they are claiming to have a monopoly over Muslim morality.

When asked "what is specifically Islamic about the club?", the interviewees stressed the dress of the players as being of the utmost importance. Salim, one of the most experienced players who joined the club during the Intifada – after having been asked to do so by a representative of the institution – said:

> First and foremost, we wear long slacks when we play. Morals in the club are very high: we are all Muslims.

Mahmoud and Ahmad also emphasized dress as being of paramount importance. The Qur'an, as is well known, prescribes a number of rules on how both men and women ought to dress, i.e. modestly. Thus, the young players emphasized moral and religious aspects as being the club's specifically Islamic characteristics. Politics was not discussed.

However, while this writer attended the training sessions, none of the players were dressed according to Islamic principles. In fact, none of the players resembled the stereotype of an Islamist. No one wore a beard, and brown and olive-green were not among the dominant colours. On the contrary, most of the players were dressed like their counterparts in Ajax Amsterdam, al-Ahli and Mansoura football club in Egypt or in Italy's national team. The Mansoura strip is completely orange with a Pepsi advertisement in the middle of the chest. There is nothing archaic or particular in the way these young men dress and, as consumers, they do not differ from other young football players. As for the so-called long slacks, most players wore long shorts down to the knee under their fancy Adidas shorts. In this way they could claim that they were dressed according to the norms prescribed by the holy book.

## Choosing an Islamic Club

Morality is a central theme. The interviewees emphasized morality also when they were explaining why they had chosen an Islamic club. Several of them gave prominence to the term *intima'*. *Intima'* indicates an intimate relation or sense of belonging (identity), that almost takes on a family character.

In the words of Ayman, a player in his mid twenties, who recently joined the club:

> Intima' means that I will do everything for the club because I love the club; I would do everything for them, I would never hurt them. They are my friends, maybe even my brothers; I care about them.

At one point during the interview, Ayman gave another reason for playing in the club. When asked why he left his old club, which is conveniently situated next to his house, to join the present one he replied:

> I don't know; I did not have a big chance in the other club, you know. And there is some bias among the young men there; a lot of them belong to Fatah and some to the PFLP. Even though they are my friends, sometimes my position was uncomfortable there. I play in the forward line. There are many good players in the forward line in my former club but no good ones in the Islamic one.

Mahmoud explains his experience like this:

> Praise the Prophet! I believe in God and I chose to play in this club mainly for religious reasons.

Mahmoud, who has been playing for the club for more than ten years, stated that he chose the Islamic club for this simple reason: "It was close to my home, and because I always used to play in their playground."

As can be seen from the above statements the members have a very intimate relationship with the club because of its religious orientation. In other words, they chose the club because it is Islamic. However, this is only part of the truth. During the interviews, it was made clear that non-religious circumstances had an influence. In the case of Mahmoud it is evident that he began playing in the club mainly because since boyhood he lived next door to the playing ground of the Islamic club. As for Ayman, non-religious factors also influenced his choice of club. One strong motive was that he could play from the forward position in the Islamic club whereas he could not do so in his former club. This indicates that the players' motives are somewhat diffuse and that their personal ambitions play a part in their decisions. However, all the players argue that they play there mainly because of the religious dimension, including adherence to Islamic morality.

In the case of users of other Islamic services non-religious factors play a crucial role in people's decision to enrol. During my field work, five participants on a computer course at an Islamic computer centre with links to one of the three major Islamic institutions in Gaza were interviewed. Three out of five did not even know that ties existed with an Islamic institution. The main reason for taking the computer course, in this particular setting, was partly practical (two lived nearby and one had an uncle working there) and partly because of the centre's good reputation. The other two, who both considered themselves as being Islamists, pointed out that the most important consideration was not that the centre was Islamic – which was an advantage – but that it ran good courses. All agreed that their main motive in joining the centre was to develop skills in computer technique. Without such skills, they claimed, there was no chance of getting a job in the Gaza Strip, where unemployment has reached 50 per cent of the workforce.

Turning back to the subject of football clubs, although it is true that non-religious factors did influence these young men's choice to join, it is noteworthy that these clubs or institutions do not provide better training facilities or other advantages like, for example, better job opportunities or better housing conditions. All interviewees agreed that had they wanted better housing conditions and better job prospects and the like, they would have joined one of the many Fatah-dominated clubs.[38] According to them, the Fatah clubs offer a variety of benefits. This contradicts some of the assumptions that many researchers make regarding the popularity of the Islamist organizations, namely that they have vast amounts of money at their disposal. Judging by the young men's statements and the physical conditions of the clubs as well as the material benefits that the Islamist organizations are offering, one can safely say that they do not have anywhere near the economic resources they are alleged to have. Through interviews with Islamic leaders and secularly oriented Palestinian observers it was clear that the Islamic movement has been weakened economically during the past years, especially after an American law was passed some years ago prohibiting the collection of funds in the US for Islamic institutions and organizations in Palestine. Furthermore, Israel has been acting in ways which have made it more difficult to obtain money through Israel.

## We are all Hamas

Despite the fact that the club (to which my interviewees belong) does not require the members to be supporters of Hamas, all of the interviewees supported Hamas in one way or another.[39] One of them, Mahmoud, said: "I support 'Izz ad-Din al-Qassam, not Hamas". I interpret this radicalism regarding Mahmoud's support for the representative of the military wing of Hamas as being a sign of frustration about the social and political lot of the Palestinians, rather than pure radicalism *per se*. This view is based on the fact that Mahmoud was not engaged in any other Islamic activity, other than sport. Furthermore, it is important to take account of the political situation in the Gaza Strip at the time of the interview. The situation was quite critical at the beginning of 1997 due primarily to the Israeli government's reluctance to implement the agreements signed with the PLO. Not only were the political prospects bleak (and still are), but also the economy was suffering; the Gaza Strip is facing even worse hardship than before the signing of the Oslo accord in 1993.[40] According to a number of polls, the majority of the Palestinians feel that they are economically worse off now than before the accord. Partly because of these factors a larger number of Palestinians are now inclined to back the military actions carried out by 'Izz ad-Din al-Qassam and other militant groups.[41] In the course of my interview with Mahmoud, he said:

> We will have to be patient; we will wait for some five years. Then we will see if we could have our rights back; if not we have to prepare to fight for our rights. In my view, I don't think that things will be better; on the contrary, I think they will become worse.

Mahmoud also expressed his sympathy for the spiritual leader of Hamas, Ahmad Yasin, by saying that Sheikh Yasin is the most trustworthy Palestinian politician. Throughout the past years Yasin has been one of the most pragmatic Hamas leaders, one who is ready to reach a compromise with both Israel and the PA. Thus, he has argued for a de facto recognition of Israel and pledged reconciliation between Hamas and the PA.

My other interviewee, Ayman, expressed the frustration pervading the Gaza Strip in these words:

The PLO made peace. They told us they will take back all the land, that is the West Bank and Gaza. Okay, do it, we will wait; but, until now they have done nothing. They did not get Hebron back, the Jewish settlements in Gaza are still very big and the Jews control the areas near Khan Younis. Where is the peace? If we are in our country and live in the area which was defined by the peace agreement, why do the Jews still remain there and control the roads? I don't know about this peace; this is very strange. They have put us in a big prison. It is a joke.

Ayman's criticism of the PA went even further:

If you want to speak up or write an article in a Jerusalem paper, the PA would put you in prison. We are back in the dark ages. They simply don't want to move from the chairs and don't want anyone to ask them, "What are you doing here? What are you doing for your people, for your Palestinians?" They don't want us to ask them, "Where did you get this money from? And all these big buildings ? Have you forgotten the refugee camps? The people who struggled and those who were killed and wounded and imprisoned? Have you forgotten them? They don't want anybody to ask them these questions. So, how can we regain Jerusalem, Acre and Jaffa?

Not only Ayman is frustrated about the political situation, and as illustrated above, it is not only the Israelis that cause this frustration. Salim also criticized the PA in even stronger terms:

When the PA arrived we welcomed them back, singing and hailing. But when they settled down here they changed. The people that welcomed them were put in prison. The PA look for any excuse to stop the Muslims and imprison them. They consider the people who are still fighting the Jews as their enemy. The PA and the Jews are working together hand in hand; there is an agreement between them to fight the Muslim parties.

From these statements, it is evident that the activists are well-informed about corruption and repression committed by the PA.[42] The PA's supression of internal Palestinian elements naturally supports Hamas's criticism of the PA, making it seem convincing, and this in turn encourages these young men to follow the Islamist path.

## I have always been a Good Muslim

Most of the young Islamists playing in the club had been faithful believers in Islam. They have, according to their own statements, always been good Muslims. Ahmad describes how he first began to be attached to Islam:

> When I was a kid I lived near a mosque. I went there and listened to the Imam and read the Qur'an. So, it started a long time ago.

Mahmoud expresses himself by these words:

> I have always been a good Muslim. While I played in the club I heard about Islam, but I depended upon myself to learn about my religion; I also heard the preachers in the mosque and on television.

However, not all of the interviewees claimed that they had always been oriented towards Islam. Ayman is a good representative of the tendency that Legrain described at a conference in 1994, that a relatively large number of individuals close to the PLO began to support the Islamic movement during the Intifada.[43] Thus, Ayman has experienced a kind of religious revival, which I consider, at least partly, a result of powerlessness. This view is based primarily on the following facts: the socio-economic situation in the Gaza Strip (high unemployment, poverty, deprivation etc.); that Ayman is among the 700,000 registered refugees, who, after several generations, still have strong emotional connections with their original place of origin in the green line; the failure of the PLO to form even a mini-state for the Palestinians; and, not least, the arduous conditions experienced by the Palestinian youth during the Intifada.[44] In an environment like this, it is natural that large segments of the Palestinian youth feel powerless, and consequently seek comfort in religion, which offers them not only an alternative allegiance, but also a solution. To quote Ayman:

> I liked the PLO very much; I liked Abu Ammar [Yasir Arafat]. During the Intifada we suffered very much at the hands of the Israelis. They shot at us. They killed many of us. I wanted a change, I wanted to do something to redress this injustice and suffering. So then Hamas did something. During that time, when people were hurting daily, they sought comfort in religion. People went to religion,

to pray to God to help us during the Intifada. Even the children went to the mosques. At that time Hamas told the people that nobody except God can help. We are morally upright here; our customs and traditions tell us to go with God, pray to God to help us in this dangerous situation.


## Islamic Schooling

In spite of the fact that all the interviewees supported Hamas to some extent and had a clear sense of the close relationship between Islam and politics, they did not seem to be instructed to embrace an Islamist orientation. In his conversation with me, Mahmoud, who has played for the club for over ten years, bears this out:

> Truly, I don't know much about politics. I did not have much education; you see, I am just a poor man. If you ask a more educated man, he would be able to quote from the Qur'an, give examples from the Hadith and tell you that Islam is present in all aspects of life, including politics.

This statement suggests that no schooling or indoctrination takes place in the club, notwithstanding the stated aim of the organizers and the findings of a number of researchers. Though it was observed during some of the training sessions that when the muezzin called for prayer the players interrupted their training to perform their prayer, it was obvious that the prayer was short (four *rak'as*) enabling them to rush back to the field to resume their training as quickly as possible. A more convincing indicator to the lack of indoctrination taking place at the club is the fact that none of the interviewees participated in other organized Islamic activities. No one was engaged in religious group reading or any other kind of Islamic instruction. The players did not even attend the Friday prayer in the same mosque. Rather, they attended the prayer in the mosques which were closest to their homes, if they attended at all. In other words, given the harsh conditions that the Palestinians have to endure it seems that it is possible to be an active Islamist simply by playing football for an hour and a half three times a week.

## Conclusion

It can be seen that moderate Islamists are an integral part of Palestinian civil society. The Islamists in the Gaza Strip are engaged in a variety of activities, such as medical care in clinics, sports, education as well as social welfare. Although the Islamists oppose the status quo they work peacefully within the social system in the Gaza Strip alongside numerous other groups within civil society. Due to the conviction that transformation of society starts with the individual, civil society is then a natural space that occupies the minds of the Islamists.

Interviews with a number of players in an Islamic football club closely related to Hamas reveal that the young Islamists in the Gaza Strip are not dangerous fanatic terrorists as a number of researchers, the media and some Western politicians, especially in Israel and the USA, often point out. Anyone belonging to the Hamas infrastructure is automatically classified in this way. Furthermore, they are not young men with long beards, longing for bygone days. On the contrary, they are young men that are able and willing to adapt to the reality of the modern world. It is evident from the interviews that high moral standards are very attractive to the young men playing in the club. They believe that they have higher moral standards than the majority of Palestinians in the Gaza Strip. Thus, they seek to differentiate themselves from the Westernized segments of the Palestinian population. By dissociating themselves from them, the young Islamists are at the same time reaffirming their own cultural heritage: Islam. It seems as if the Islamists are seeking to adapt to the modern world on their own terms. Thus, they are attempting, to a large extent, to engage in the same activities as their secular counterparts, only they want to perform better. The young members do not only make their choices on the basis of religion. Non-religious circumstances also play an important role, especially in the case of people seeking professional training such as provided by the Islamic computer centre. This is less pronounced in the case of football players. This implies that the motivation of at least some players is closely related to personal dreams and ambition. With regard to the non-religious circumstances that influenced the players' decision to join, it was noteworthy that they were not related to the facilities that the club was able to provide nor to its ability to improve job prospects and the like. It seems that the Islamist organizations do not have large amounts of funds at their disposal, nor do they have a wide and effective network through which they can help their members find much needed employment.

Most of the Islamists interviewed did not experience a kind of Islamic awakening; rather, they stated that they had been good Muslims throughout their lives. This raises the question of whether the young Islamists of today (and of the future) are raised as Islamists. Their parents were the first among the Islamists and now they pass their political views on to next generations. However, it is important to stress that the picture is somewhat blurred; Ayman, for example, did experience a kind of religious awakening during the Intifada. Another interesting finding – based on the interviews and personal observation – is that no Islamist indoctrination is practised in the club (and certainly not in the computer centre). However, there is no doubt that the Islamists have an influential hand in persuading people to espouse the Islamist cause.

The Islamic institutions as a whole may be characterized as being a double-edged sword for the PA.[45] On the one hand, the PA needs the services that the Islamic (and other) NGOs provide for the people, and on the other hand, it does not want to see the Islamists gain too much ground. Such a development would ultimately have the effect of de-legitimizing the PA's authority. More importantly, the young participants in the Islamic institutions could, at a later stage, be mobilized against the PA. For the time being there are no signs of such a development.

## NOTES

1 A. Richard Norton, "Introduction" in A. Richard Norton, ed., *Civil Society in the Middle East*, vol. 1 (Leiden: E. J. Brill, 1995).

2 Dale Eickelman and James Piscatori, *Muslim Politics* (New Jersey: Princeton University Press, 1996), p. 108.

3 For a discussion of the term Islamism, see Jean François Clement, 'Journalists et chercheurs des sciences sociales face aux mouvements islamistes', *Archive science sociales des religions*, vol. 55, no. 1 (Jan.–Mar., 1983).

4 The six categories that Dekmejian uses are: (a) Puritan Traditionalist, (b) Mainstream Gradualist, (c) Revolutionary Messianist, (d) Revolutionary Jihadist, (e) Reformist Revisionist and (f) Modernist Rationalist. The two most important groups are the Mainstream Gradualists and the Revolutionary Jihadists. Hrair Dekmejian, "Multiple Faces of Islam" in A. Jerichow and J. Bæk Simonsen, eds.,

*Islam in a Changing World: Europe and the Middle East* (Surrey, UK: Curzon Press, 1997), pp. 4–9.

5  Eickelman and Piscatori, *Muslim Politics*, p. 109

6  Ahmad Moussalli, "Modern Islamic Fundamentalist Discourses on Civil Society, Pluralism and Democracy" in A. Richard Norton, ed., *Civil Society in the Middle East*, pp. 88–116.

7  Moussalli, "Modern Islamic Fundamentalist", p. 118.

8  Ibid.

9  Soheir Morsy, "Islamic Clinics in Egypt: The Cultural Elaboration of Biomedical Hegemony", *Medical Anthropology Quarterly* (1988), p. 358.

10  The translation of this Quranic verse is taken from Yusuf Ali. This verse has been used by several of the Islamic social institutions in the Gaza Strip in the introduction to their statutes; see for example, al-Mujamma' al-Islami, *Qanun asasi* (Gaza, 1973), p. 1.

11  It is worth noting that some researchers do not consider the work of the Islamists as being a part of civil society. Thus, for example, Sami Zubaida argues that Islamic groups and institutions are not sufficiently tolerant. See Sami Zubaida, "Islam, State and Democracy", *Middle East Report*, no. 179 (1992). Also the Egyptian scholar Saad Eddin Ibrahim is hesitant to include the Islamists in civil society. See Saad Eddin Ibrahim, "Civil Society and Prospects for Democratization in the Arab World" in A. Richard Norton, ed., *Civil Society in the Middle East* and Michael Hudson, "Obstacles to Democratization in the Middle East", *Contention*, vol. 5, no. 2 (Winter, 1996).

A basic thesis is that the more moderate line of Islamism will be strengthened at the expense of the radicals in so far as they are included in civil society as well as the political process in general. If that was to be the case they would turn out to be more pragmatic and oriented towards *realpolitik*. The development with regard to Hizbullah in Lebanon during the 1990s seems to support this thesis. See A. Richard Norton, "Lebanon: With Friends Like These . . ." *Current History* (January 1997). The same is true with regard to the Islamists in Jordan and Kuwait, for example. See Norton, "Introduction".

12  Ibid., p. 7.

13  Moussalli, "Modern Islamic Fundamentalist", p. 118 and Gudrun Krämer, "Islamist Notions of Democracy", *Middle East Report*, no. 183 (1993).

14  Emile Sahliyeh, "Religious Fundamentalisms Compared: Palestinian Islamists, Militant Lebanese Shi'ites and Radical Sikhs" in M. Marty and S. Appleby, eds., *Fundamentalism Comprehended*, The Fundamentalism Project vol. 5 (Chicago & London: University of Chicago Press, 1995), p. 142.

15  During the past few years a number of researchers within the field have worked on this particular issue. See, for instance, Denis J. Sullivan, *Private Voluntary Organizations in Egypt: Islamic Development, Private Initiatives and State Control* (Tampa: University Press of Florida, 1994) and Janine Astrid Clark, "Islamic Social-Welfare Organizations and the Legitimacy of the State in Egypt: Democratization or Islamization from Below?" (Ph.D. thesis, Department of

Political Science, University of Toronto, 1994). In both works Egypt has been used as a case study. My current research is a contribution to this particular field within the study of Islamism.

16 A. Richard Norton, *Political Reform in the Middle East*, Paper presented at the Seminar "State, Individual and Civil Society in the Middle East", Magleås, Denmark 13–14 November, 1995, p. 8.

17 François Burgat, *The Islamic Movement in North Africa* (Austin: University of Texas Press, 1993), p. 3.

18 My thesis is centred on three main issues: (1) the motivation on behalf of the Islamist leaders with regard to the setting up of a social infrastructure, (2) the motivation on behalf of the users of the Islamist networks and (3) an investigation of whether there are certain democratic structures within the Islamic institutions.

19 Beverley Milton-Edwards, *Islamic Politics in Palestine* (London: I. B. Tauris, 1995).

20 al-Mujammaʿ, *Qanun*, pp. 3–4.

21 Milton-Edwards, *Islamic Politics*. See also Ziad Abu Amr, *Islamic Fundamentalism in the West Bank and Gaza Strip: Muslim Brotherhood and Islamic Jihad* (Bloomington, Indiana: Indiana University Press, 1994) and Pinhas Inbari, *The Palestinians between Terrorism and Statehood* (Brighton, UK: Sussex Academic Press, 1996).

22 al-Jamʿiyya al-Islamiyya, *Qanun asasi* (Gaza, 1976), p. 1.

23 See Jamʿiyyat al-Salah al-Islamiyya, *Qanun asasi* (Deir al-Balah, 1978).

24 UNSCO, *Directory of Non-Governmental Organizations in the Gaza Strip* (Http:// www.arts.mcgill.ca/mepp/unsco/unfront.html, 1997).

25 Bowing to Israeli and American pressure, the PA closed down 16 Islamic NGOs in the Gaza Strip in late September 1997. Among them were: al-Mujammaʿ al-Islami, al-Jamʿiyya al-Islamiyya and Jamʿiyyat al-Shabbat al-Muslimat. See *al-Ayyam*, 26 September 1997.

26 Richard Mitchell, *The Society of the Muslim Brothers* (London: Oxford University Press, 1969).

27 Personal interview with this writer, IUG, 19 January 1997. See also Antony Sullivan, *Palestinian Universities under Occupation* (Cairo: Cairo Papers in Social Science, 1988).

28 A long list of teachers and administrators at the IUG are closely linked to the Islamic movement. For example: Ahmad Bahr, Yahya Moussa and Ahmad Saʿati (Hizb al-Khalas al-Watani al-Islami) and Mahmoud Zahar and Abdul Aziz al-Rantisi (both Hamas leaders). Also the majority of the students at IUG support the Islamic movement. At the latest election, for the student council at IUG, held in December 1996, the Kutla al-Islamiyya received some 75 per cent of the votes. In everyday language in Gaza, the IUG is called the Hamas University whereas al-Azhar, the only other university in Strip, is called the Fatah University.

29 Glenn Robinson, *Building a Palestinian State* (Indiana: Indiana University Press, 1997), p. 138.

30 Sullivan, *Private Voluntary Organizations*.

31 Personal interview with this writer, Gaza, January 1997.

32 Sarah Roy, "Civil Society in the Gaza Strip: Obstacles to Social Reconstruction" in A. Richard Norton, ed., *Civil Society in the Middle East*. See also Denis Sullivan, "NGOs in Palestine: Agents of Development and Foundation of Civil Society", *Journal of Palestine Studies*, vol. 25 no. 3 (1996).

33 Apart from the 35 officially registered clubs at the Ministry of Youth and Sports, there is a large number of unofficial clubs connected with over 200 mosques in the Gaza Strip. Also Hizb al-Khalas al-Watani al-Islami has a minor club called al-Muntada.

34 According to my informant there were prior to the establishment of the PA in 1994 other Islamic clubs. These have been taken over by Fatah. This is valid for Hridmat Khan Younis and al-Nadi al-Islam al-Riyadi (Beit Lahiya); the latter used to be related to Islamic Jihad. It is noteworthy that football clubs in the Gaza Strip are divided politically and, in tandem with the major political scene, Fatah is the most dominant power. Several of the Fatah clubs are directly connected to Arafat's huge security apparatus.

35 'Atef 'Adwan, *al-Sheikh Ahmad Yasin: hayatuhu wa jihaduhu* (Gaza: al-Jama'a al-Islamiyya, 1991), p. 73.

36 Morsy, *Islamic Clinics*, p. 355.

37 David Hirst, "Shameless in Gaza", *Guardian Weekly*, 27 April, 1997.

38 It is however important to stress that not all Fatah clubs are able to deliver goods. This is mainly true for the big clubs dominated by branches of PA's security apparatus. Furthermore, one needs to be a very good player in order to achieve these benefits. Fatah poaches the best players from other clubs in order to be the dominant power even on the football pitch.

39 In some of the Fatah clubs they are not as tolerant. The former head of one of the largest and most influential clubs in Gaza city stated in an informal conversation with this writer: "We only allow Fatah supporters to enter our club – no Hamas supporters." Because, as he explained it, "we don't want any troubles."

40 See for example UNSCO, *Economic and Social Conditions in the West Bank and Gaza Strip: Quarterly Reports* (http://www.arts.mcgill.ca/mepp/unsco/unfront.html, 1997).

41 It seems as if there is a direct link between the stalemate in the peace process and the support for armed attacks among the Palestinian masses. See Khalil Shakaki, *Transition to Democracy in Palestine: The Peace Process, National Reconstruction and Elections* (Nablus: Center for Palestine Research and Studies, 1996), p. 14–16.

42 See, for example, Amnesty International, *Palestinian Authority: Prolonged Detention, Torture and Unfair Trials* (MDE15/68/96, 1996).

43 Jean François Legrain, *Hamas, Legitimate Heir of Palestinian Nationalism*, Conference Paper: Political Islam in the Middle East, United States Institute of Peace, Washington, 2–3 March, 1994.

44 The harsh conditions experienced by the Palestinians both economically and politically throughout the past three decades has been well documented elsewhere. See, for instance, UNSCO, *Economic and Social Conditions* and Sarah Roy, *The Gaza Strip: The Political Economy of De-development* (Washington, D.C.:

Institute for Palestine Studies, 1995). See also, al-Haq, *Punishing a Nation* (Ramallah: al-Haq, 1988).

45 On double-edged swords see Guilain Denoeux, *Urban Unrest in the Middle East: A Comparative Study of Informal Networks in Egypt, Iran and Lebanon* (Albany: State of New York University Press, 1993).

# 8

# The Development Programmes of Islamic Fundamentalist Groups in Lebanon as a Source of Popular Legitimation

## *Hilal Khashan*

Social change has pressured Arab governments to launch broad development programmes. But corruption, resource misallocation, and inadequate technological capacity meant that most public demands would not be fulfilled. Frustrated expectations created an optimal environment for the emergence of opposition groups. Islamist groups equipped themselves with religious tenets which they raised as slogans for socio-political action, thus succeeding in building a base of wide public support. Lebanon provides an interesting case where Islamist groups compete with the government to provide badly needed public services. The paper advances an empirically testable hypothesis stating that Lebanese Muslims perceive fundamentalist groups as more legitimate than the national government. Legitimacy is treated as a function of ideological affinity and the provision of public services. The data come from a nationwide stratified random sample of 500 Muslim respondents, divided equally between Sunnis and Shi'is. The research instrument involves a questionnaire using closed-ended, mostly likert type questions. The analytical procedure comprises four variables: (1) the ideological affinity of the respondents, (2) the agency providing them with more public services, (3) the agency endowed with their political support, and (4) the agency having greater impact on their community life. The analysis utilizes statistical tools such as frequency distributions and bivariate measures. The results show that the respondents identify more with Islamic fundamentalist groups than with the government, and tend to give more political support to the former than to the latter.

Fundamentalist groups are seen as better providers of public goods and as having more impact on community life than the government.

## Introduction

The political objectives of Muslim fundamentalist groups are generally misunderstood in the West. Even the writings of European students of Arab affairs dating back to the 1930s evince a deterministic view about the focal role of Islam in Arab "national renewal".[1] The mixing of the spiritual and the temporal in the world of Islam, the failure of Muslim reform movements in the nineteenth century, and the immediate emergence of Muslim fundamentalist groups after the abrogation of the *khilafa* (political succession) in 1924 all seem to have fixed the Western mind on the central role of Islam in modern Arab politics. Shamsul Alam goes to the extent of describing the mainstream Western ideas about the Muslims from the perspective of an orientalist position viewing "the rise of Islamic fundamentalism as an historically sedimented antagonism between the West and Islam".[2] It is the contention of the present author that while the power of Islam is undeniably manifest in the political arenas of several Arab countries, it does not however constitute a link with political Islam of the past. The extent of social and political change during the last two centuries, first during the Ottoman reform period and later since the formation of the existing Middle Eastern state system, have left an irreversible impact on present Arab politics. Abu-Lughod accepts the reality of profound political transformation in Arabic-speaking countries, although incomplete by Western criteria. His remarks about the limits of secularism and the resurgence of Islamic trends do not usher a return to the Islamic period.[3] The demise of the Islamic state did not encroach on the continuity of the Islamic religion as the prevailing belief system in Muslim and Arab societies. The rise of Muslim fundamentalist groups in our present period simply means the activation of the political dimension of Islam – on the defensive since the last quarter of the previous century – as a belief system.[4]

The current use of political Islam as a weapon against narrowly based ruling elites in a number of Middle Eastern countries does not appear to be intended to accommodate universalistic ambitions. Quite to the contrary, political Islam is being applied by fundamentalist groups to seek recognition by the existing political orders. It can be said that

Islamic groups have adjusted themselves to operate as political forces within the framework of the de facto national boundaries. This situation does not exclude countries in which Islamist groups have been successful in assuming supreme political powers such as Iran and Sudan. Precht argues in an illuminating study that Iran's radical Islamists are fervently Iranian nationalists at heart. He says: "Their commitments rarely go beyond the historical national borders . . . [T]he current leaders follow much the same nationalism as their predecessor . . . Like the shah, today's rulers want Iran to be respected as a model and to exercise great influence in the region . . . [T]heir immediate agenda is political and economic independence at home, not dominion abroad."[5] Political Islam has been transformed into a vehicle of organized protest against inept, secularly structured but functionally ill-adjusted political systems. There is little evidence to support the surge of militant Islam in terms of organic attachment between religious belief and political action. Current Islamist trends are largely a translation of the frustration felt by the masses in connection with the regimes' failure to achieve political development, solve the riddle of political identity, and bring about balanced economic prosperity.

Recent years have witnessed a dramatic surge in the influence of Islamic fundamentalist groups in a number of Arab countries such as Egypt, Algeria, Jordan, Sudan, Tunisia, and Lebanon. Liberals and secularists in the Arab world see this type of change as unwholesome, since it sets back the tracks of political change to the first half of the nineteenth century when the forces of religious revival competed inconclusively with the agents of modernization. The depth of the present political divide in the Arab world lacks empirical support. This study will hopefully provide insights into the base of support which gives Lebanon's Islamic groups the sudden strength which they seem to enjoy.

This paper considers the pattern of popular legitimation among the Muslim segment of the Lebanese population. The main hypothesis states that the provision of public services plays a decisive role in the extension of political legitimacy by the beneficiaries to the agency providing the services. Thus the ability of Lebanese Islamic fundamentalist groups to exceed the national government in providing services to the public, and in the impact they exercise on community life, is expected to be reciprocated by political legitimacy. In connection with this, the recipient of services (1) should display greater ideological affinity with Islamic groups than with the government, and (2) extend more political support to the former than to the latter.

## The Status of Muslims in Lebanese Society

The main idea behind the creation of Greater Lebanon in 1920 was to found a Christian homeland in the Levant in which the Maronite community assumed a central role. The new arrangement traumatized the Muslim community and instantaneously shifted the political role of its members from prominence to subservience. Severance of affiliation with the now defunct Ottoman empire relegated Lebanese Muslims to political marginality. The concretization of the new Lebanese entity by advancing the National Covenant of 1943 which rested on the assumption of political partnership between Maronite Christians and Sunni Muslims did not bring about stability to the incipient country. Tension prevailed once it became obvious that the Christians were, by and large, faring better than the Muslims in terms of economic advantage and political influence. Excessive political rigidity ensured the maintenance of the system's weak distributive capacity and contributed mightily to the radicalization of disadvantaged (mostly Muslim) population strata. Lack of political accommodation caused the vast majority of Muslims to part ideologically from the concept of Lebanese statehood by immersing themselves in the then (i.e. during the 1950s and 1960s) fashionable notion of Arab nationalism.

The Six Day War in 1967 in which Israel scored a sweeping victory against the combined armies of Egypt, Syria, and Jordan altered the political equation in the Middle East and exacerbated political polarization in Lebanon. The consolidation of PLO power in Lebanon in the aftermath of the war caused an intensification of confrontation with Israel in the southern part of the country, and facilitated the rapid mobilization of the Shiʻi Muslim community. It is interesting to note that the emergence of active Islamist groups in Lebanon came relatively late. The first manifestations of Muslim opposition after the independence of this religiously divided country were inspired by secular slogans, not religious zeal. The tenets of Arab nationalism which were espoused by Lebanese Muslims were basically secular. Religion was generally looked down on, often associated with backwardness. The rise of Muslim fundamentalist groups waited until other forms of political opposition had demonstrated their total inadequacy. Would fundamentalist groups have gained breadth had secular modes of opposition succeeded in increasing the representativeness of the Lebanese system? Most likely not.

## Perspectives of Muslim Fundamentalist Groups in Lebanon

Lebanon, a country of numerous ethnic and religious minorities, does not offer a suitable ground for the origination of powerful Islamist groups. There are simply too many cultural and ideological crosscurrents in Lebanon to allow the dominance of a single idea, no matter how great it might be, in Lebanese society. Intellectual and ideological diversity abound even in each of the confessional groups comprising this unique political entity. Fundamentalist groups operating in Lebanon are invariably offshoots of powerful religious movements or trends originating in less ethnically and religiously divided Middle Eastern countries. A quick look at Islamic fundamentalist groups in Lebanon immediately shows their ideological affinity and linkages with larger movements in the region. There are two major fundamentalist groups in Lebanon, one Sunni and another Shi'i; they are respectively al-Jama'a al-Islamiyya and Hizbullah.[6] The political ideology of al-Jama'a is based on the doctrines of the Muslim Brethren (or Muslim Brothers) in Egypt and Syria. It should be recalled that the line of thinking of Fathi Yakan, the main ideologue of the Jama'a derives from the militant orientation of Sayyid Qutb.[7] In the parliamentary elections that were held in Lebanon during the summer of 1992 (the first in twenty years) the Jama'a captured, for the first time in the history of parliamentary elections in Lebanon, three seats in the 128-seat parliament. This was a remarkable achievement since only one of the four Jama'a contestants was not elected.

Hizbullah has been even more influenced by regional developments than the Sunni Jama'a. The architects of the Islamic revolution in Iran who have held the reins of power in Tehran since 1979 initially appeared keen on spreading their own revolutionary doctrines throughout the world of Islam. Esposito and Piscatori contend that although Iran's direct intervention in a number of Muslim countries has significantly altered the course of events in a few of them, Lebanon remains nevertheless the prime example of Iran's success. In fact they stress that "Iran's intervention has dramatically altered the political environment in which the local Shiʻi population has challenged the Lebanese state."[8] Khomeini's doctrinal changes regarding the interpretation of Twelver Shiʻism had a revolutionary effect on the conduct of Iranian politics. It was a shift from passivity to political dynamism that placed the ʻulamaʼ at the centre of Iranian public life. The need to wait idly for the appearance of the twelfth Imam has now been waived, since the faqihs (jurists) can assume temporal authority in the interim. Bill proposes that fundamental changes concerning the extent of the political role of the mullahs caused neo-Shiʻism to take root "in the Iranian political system as the political extremists among the ʻulamaʼ inexorably rode the tides of the times and the cresting social forces to direct rule".[9]

The politicization of the ʻulamaʼ in Iran led to a comparable consequence in Lebanon. The opportunity came during the course of the Israeli invasion in 1982. Shiʻis rose against their state of political submissiveness crystallized by the formation of a fundamentalist group under the name of Hizbullah. Abu-Khalil is convinced that "[t]he single most important event in the history of the emergence of Shiʻite fundamentalist groups in Lebanon was the creation of the Salvation Committee by president Ilyas Sarkis in June 1982 . . . to face the repercussions of the Israeli invasion."[10] Many Shiʻis viewed the main function of the committee, which was operating in the presence of Israeli troops near the presidential palace, as an effort to reassert Maronite dominance over Muslims in general, and Shiʻis in particular. The greater influence of Shiʻi fundamentalists within their own sect, compared to that of Sunni fundamentalists, appears to be related to the stronger religious and political authority of the ʻulamaʼ in Twelver Shiʻi Islam than in the Sunni tradition.[11] The extent of influence attained by Hizbullah within the Shiʻi community was revealed by the outcome of the 1992 parliamentary elections. All eight candidates running for the elections under the name of the party won the seats they contested by a wide margin of votes.

## Research Methodology

The data for this study come from a nationally selected, randomly stratified sample of 500 Muslim respondents, divided equally between Sunnis and Shiʻis. Men and women from each of the two religious groups were evenly represented in the sample of the respondents. The questionnaires were completed in 1993 between the months of April and October by six highly trained interviewers. Selection of the respondents was done in accordance with the realities of the demographic distribution of Sunnis and Shi'is in the five administrative regions comprising the Lebanese state.[12] An identical distribution of socio-economic status (SES) for both Sunnis and Shi'is was ensured. This was done in order to avoid skewed responses that may be caused by difference in social and economic conditions between the two groups. The respondents in each of the two religious groups were chosen according to the following socio-economic distribution: upper class (16 per cent), middle class (32 per cent), and working class (52 per cent).

The research instrument was developed by this researcher in consultation with four fundamentalist activists (two Sunnis and two Shi'is) who wished to maintain anonymity. The instrument included three independent variables pertaining to regional origin, socio-economic status, and religiosity. The socio-economic status of the respondents was measured by their occupation, level of education, income, place of residence, and self-description of status. Religiosity was measured by the frequency of praying, fasting, reading in the Qur'an, and attendance of religious study groups. The content validity of the SES and religiosity scales was verified by the use of factor analysis which showed high factor loading for all items. The four dimensions of the study were measured by twelve questions. The text and distribution of all items used in this study will appear in the appropriate sections of this paper. The formal administration of the research instrument was preceded by a pre-test which allowed the reformulation of some vague questions, and the elimination of a few seemingly irrelevant ones. Standard reliability procedures such as congruence with reality, non-bias, and consistency tests were applied to the data, and dubious responses were deleted from the analysis.

## Ideological Affinity

It may appear that the more than seventy years that have passed since the fall of the last Muslim state are sufficient to reconstruct the ideological mind of most Muslims away from the concepts of the Muslim *umma* (community), and *dawla* (state), towards that of the nation state and its secularly based nationalism. But one should not forget that the present period was preceded by thirteen hundred years of direct Islamic rule under the guidance of *shari'a*. The impact of that long historical experience on the formation of the political mind of Muslims certainly cannot be denied. Kelidar maintains a compatible view on this issue; he states that the nation-state has no historical "antecedent in the political culture of Islam; nor has it become a familiar term in the political vocabulary of the region. The concept has remained without an adequate definition ever since its importation, among a host of political ideas, from Western Europe during the nineteenth century."[13]

Is there ideological affinity between the respondents of this sample and the idea of the Lebanese political entity? Four related questions were formulated to measure the extent of the respondents' attachment to the concept of the Lebanese state:

(a)  Ideological orientation as expressed by the definition of the state in which they would like to live.

(b)  Perception of the variable that constitutes the major source of political legitimacy.

(c)  Views about the legitimacy of the present Lebanese government.

(d)  Ideological character of legitimate government.

Table 1 shows the respondents' ideological orientations as reflected by their perceptions about the ultimate political system which they would like to live in. Sunni and Shi'i responses differ significantly; more than 50 per cent of the latter believe in Lebanon as a final entity, as compared to less than 10 per cent only for the former. Sunni respondents express instead much stronger attachment to the notions of pan-Arabism and Islamic unity (one-third and 55 per cent of them respectively). Belief in the inevitability of Arab unity is weak among Shi'is, a finding which reinforces previous survey results.[14] Interestingly, 20 per cent more Sunnis than Shi'is manifest belief in the inevitability of unity among predominantly Muslim countries, even though Shi'i fundamentalism in Lebanon is – due to geopolitical factors – clearly stronger than its Sunni counterpart. The difference between Sunni and Shi'i responses on this issue can be readily explained. Sunni fundamentalist groups in the Arab East emerged with an eye on restoring the *khilafa*.

On the other hand, Shi'i fundamentalist groups, be they in Iran or else-where in the Middle East (Iraq, Lebanon, Bahrain), appeared essentially as protest groups against socio-economic and political injustices of a domestic nature.

## TABLE 1
### Ideological Orientation

Question:
Which of the following political entities express your ideological ori-entation?

|  | Sunnis n=250 % | Shi'is n=250 % |
|---|---|---|
| Belief in Lebanon as a final entity | 9.2 | 52.8 |
| Belief in the inevitability of Arab unity | 32.4 | 9.2 |
| Belief in the inevitability of Islamic unity | 55.2 | 36.4 |
| Undecided | 3.2 | 1.6 |
| Total | 100.0 | 100.0 |

It is not as difficult as it may seem to reconcile the gap between the presence of a highly active Hizbullah and the good percentage of Shi'is believing in the eternality of the Lebanese entity. Hizbullah remains after all, notwithstanding its Iranian connection, a manifestation of Shi'i social and political protest which took alternative forms among Lebanese Shi'is in the 1950s and 1960s (Arab and Syrian nationalisms, *Libanisme*, communism, etc.). Socio-political mobilization among the Shi'is led to its eventual embodiment in Shi'i sectarian political parties. Thus the rise of the Amal movement in 1975 was legitimated by its drive to represent the views of the "voiceless and dispossessed". The success of the Amal move-ment, which pursued narrow sectarian objectives, was made possible by a massive shift of Shi'i recruits from other, mostly illegal secular political parties. Lucrative ideological slogans were used as a vehicle to achieve certain political and social ends; otherwise it would not have been possible to undergo large scale shifts in party identification so easily. Similarly, the consolidation of the power of Hizbullah took place at the cost of continued erosion in Shi'i membership in non-confessional political parties. To be sure, a large percentage of Hizbullah's rank and file are drawn from the Amal movement itself. The following excerpt illustrates how political identification can sometimes alter in Lebanon: "The May 1988 fighting in the Beirut suburbs, which saw Hizb Allah's triumph over Amal militiamen, underlined Hizb Allah's steady success in enlisting the Shia, many of whom are ex-Amal members. It is symptomatic of Amal's decline in the suburbs that it was widely reported that Hizb Allah conquered some of the Amal positions through the simple expediency of paying off the local Amal defenders."[15]

On the other hand, Lebanese Sunnis are still politically inactive at the level of the masses. They have lacked both the motive and opportunity to develop a competitive politico-military apparatus similar to those of other confessional groups such as the Druze, the Maronites, and recently the Shi'is. Religious affinity with the dominant branch in Islam was always a source of assurance to Lebanese Sunnis who eschewed, in compliance with the authority of the caliph, direct involvement in political affairs. Political passivity persisted after the collapse of the Ottoman empire and the establishment of modern Lebanon, as they continued to identify with political leaderships outside the new geopolitical boundaries in which they found themselves immersed. It is possible that these seemingly nostalgic aspirations among the Sunnis may give way to increasing identification with the Lebanese state – if the existing regional order of states does not change – provided that they develop political organizations similar to those that operate on the Lebanese scene giving meaning and direction to its confessional politics.

Reactions to a question on the variable that constitutes the major source of political legitimacy show the weakness of some variables that normally command attention in Western democracies such as the promotion of democratic principles, respect of human rights, and enforcement of secular law. Instead, the responses evince, as can be seen from Table 2, attachment to Islamic *shari'a* and a wish that comprehensive public services be provided by the government.

## TABLE 2
### Sources of Political Legitimacy

**Question:**

What is the single most important variable that you use in determining the legitimacy of the political system in which you live?

| | Sunnis n=250 % | Shi'is n=250 % |
|---|---|---|
| Commitment to Islamic *shari'a* | 56.8 | 40.8 |
| Enforcement of secular law | 9.6 | 15.2 |
| Provision of comprehensive public services | 21.6 | 34.0 |
| Respect of human rights | 9.2 | 6.8 |
| Promotion of democratic principles | 2.8 | 3.2 |
| Total | 100.0 | 100.0 |

An examination of the pattern of choices reveals a clash of ideological orientations and demand priorities, and although commitment to Islamic *shari'a* prevails, it does so uneasily. One reason for this is probably the fact that the current religious drive in Islam differs from pre-colonial Islamic trends. Keddie posits that Islam then "tended to be conservative rather than militant or exclusivist".[16] It was the infusion of Western ideas and the pressure on Islam to adjust to the requirements of the age, as well as the onset of colonialism, that made Islam defensive and caused it to become militant. Commitment to *shari'a* does not necessarily imply the adoption of fundamentalism as a mode of political expression. Political behaviour is inherent in Islam; thus the routine display of political symbols by Muslim clerics is more ritualistic than a manifestation of fundamentalist tendencies. The mixing of politics with religion in Islam has invariably been labelled by Westerners as a demonstration of religious militancy which is not always the case. In fact the 1950s and 1960 witnessed – when the idea of Arab nationalism was in vogue – a conspicuous retreat in the role of Islam of Arab politics. Egypt's late charismatic leader Gamal Abd al-Nasser succeeded in convincing his numcrous followers that political Islam was reactionary. However, disillusionment with Abd al-Nasser and other Arab leaders, especially those labelled as progressive, and the failure of the state everywhere in the Arab East (with the exception of the oil-rich states) to improve socio-economic conditions allowed political Islam, fundamentalist or otherwise, to assert itself in the political arena. Whether influenced by Islamic fundamentalism or not, the respondents' choices attest to the weak distributive capacity of the Lebanese state. In fact, none of the respondents choose any of three other choices that were included among the forced-choice entries. These were the government's effort to maintain the country's confessional system, its attempt to reconcile former warring factions, and drive to improve the image of Lebanon abroad. There appears to be a dichotomy between the expectations of the respondents and the government's priorities. The respondents' choice of commitment to Islamic *shari'a* associates strongly with their ideological orientation (Cramer's V=0.68). But it is not yet clear if commitment to *shari'a* reveals a basic ideological demand, or whether it is a mere reaction to governmental inadequacy. This issue will become clearer as we proceed in the analysis.

A direct question requested the respondents to specify whether they considered the present Lebanese government as legitimate. More Sunnis (46 per cent) than Shi'is (30 per cent) answered that they considered the government as legitimate (see Table 3). Two readily available reasons may help explain why Shi'is are less supportive of the government. First, the current prime minister (this office is traditionally held by a Sunni Muslim) is powerful; actually he succeeded in becoming, unlike his predecessors, the most influential actor in the Lebanese political establishment. The rise of a political figure (no matter from what group) in this confessionally divided political system, beyond the narrow confines of the political game, threatens the base of support for politicians from other groups. Many Shi'i, as well as Christian politicians, seem threatened by the new political development. It is plausible to argue that opposition to the prime minister by members of the political elite has weakened the legitimacy of the government in the eyes of non-Sunnis. Second, the Shi'i s, who are the largest and most depressed religious group in Lebanon, make far more policy demands than the system has the capacity to deliver. Unfulfilled demands have the potential of reducing popular support for the government, leading eventually to withholding legitimacy from it. The widespread denial of legitimacy for the government by Shi'i respondents should not distract us from the fact that Sunni support for it is not universal, and is less than satisfactory for stable governance.

### TABLE 3
### Evaluation of the Legitimacy of
### the Lebanese Government

**Question:**

Do you agree that the present Lebanese government is legitimate?

|  | Sunnis n=250 % | Shi'is n=250 % |
|---|---|---|
| SA | 28.8 | 14.0 |
| A | 17.6 | 16.0 |
| U | 4.0 | 2.8 |
| D | 21.2 | 24.0 |
| SD | 28.4 | 43.2 |
| Total | 100.0 | 100.0 |

**Question:**

If the present government is not legitimate, what other forms of government would be legitimate in your view?

|  | Sunnis n=130 % | Shi'is n=173 % |
|---|---|---|
| A socialist government | 3.8 | 40.5 |
| A representative government | 23.8 | 16.2 |
| An Islamic government | 72.3 | 43.4 |
| Total | 99.9* | 100.1* |

*Due to rounding, percentages do not add up to 100.

Sunni and Shi'i respondents not believing in the legitimacy of the present government do not agree on what should replace it. More than 70 per cent of the Sunnis choose an Islamic government, and almost one-fourth of the rest prefer a representative government.

A word should be said here about political representation in Lebanon. The base of the Lebanese political system is narrow, and it accommodates almost exclusively feudal, militia, and technocrats according to a clientelistic formula. Many Lebanese feel that they are practically left outside the operations of the political system. Only 16 per cent of Shi'i respondents appear concerned about replacing the present government by a more representative one. Instead, the preferences of most of them are nearly equally divided between an Islamic and a socialist government. Inclination towards socialism makes sense for many Shi'is, since most of their demands cannot possibly be fulfilled by a government committed to privatization and economic deregulation. Finally, why do more Sunnis opt for an Islamic government than Shi'i counterparts? It is easier for Lebanese Sunnis, whose involvement in political parties has been minimal, to reveal identification with an Islamic-type government, being the only alternative one which they can draw upon from their collective memory. Incidentally, the Shi'is were historical opponents of the Sunni-dominated Muslim state. The beginnings of their identification with the Islamic concept of state are recent, and are inspired by the success of the Islamic revolution in Iran in 1979.


## Provision of Public Services

Developing countries, especially those in which the rate of migration within the country is high, are unable to provide badly needed public services. This situation is typical of Lebanon; bias in the allocation of resources by an excessively corrupt bureaucratic machinery has aided the formation of serious disparities between Muslim and Christian parts of the country. The protracted civil war demonstrated the conceptual problems of the Lebanese political model; it also disrupted, almost discontinued, the provision of the meagre public services provided by the government, particularly to predominantly Muslim-populated areas. The respondents were asked to assess the range of government services to their areas. The responses that appear in Table 4 indicate that 75 per cent of Sunnis and 90 per cent of Shi'is feel that the range, not to mention the quality, of government services is less than satisfactory. Cross tabulation shows association between place of residence and the perception of the range of the provided services among both Sunni (Cramer's V=0.42) and Shi'i (Cramer's V=0.36) respondents. Sunnis reporting positive remarks about the services are mostly residents of major urban centres where the government allocates significantly more resources than to semi-urban or rural areas. Among Shi'i respondents, access to leaders of the Amal movement holding positions in the government generates positive reactions about the range of services provided by the government. It should be mentioned here that the Lebanese political system operates on the basis of patron–client relations. The political reforms that were incorporated into the Tai'f agreement of 1989 do not seem to have impinged on the survival of clientelistic practices. Patron–client relations are especially manifest outside the major urban centres, where traditional contacts are stronger and government spending is sparser.

### TABLE 4
### Provision of Basic Public Services

**Question:**
How do you see, from your own experience, the range of essential public services (such as utilities, education, health care) as provided by the government?

|  | Sunnis n=247 % | Shi'is n=249 % |
|---|---|---|
| Good | 8.5 | 4.0 |
| Satisfactory | 12.9 | 5.6 |
| Unsure | 3.6 | 1.2 |
| Unsatisfactory | 36.0 | 39.4 |
| Poor | 38.9 | 49.8 |
| Total | 99.9* | 100.0 |

**Question:**
If you consider the range of the government-provided services as less than satisfactory, mention how you compensate for them?

|  | Sunnis n=197 % | Shi'is n=226 % |
|---|---|---|
| Personal resources | 46.7 | 19.0 |
| Aid by foreign relief agencies | 3.0 | 9.3 |
| Aid by local, non-sectarian agencies | 2.5 | 6.2 |
| Aid by local, sectarian agencies | 11.2 | 14.2 |
| Aid by local Islamic groups | 36.5 | 51.3 |
| Total | 99.9* | 100.0 |

*Due to rounding, percentages do not add up to 100.

The answers to a contingency question concerning the arrangements to compensate for unsatisfactory governmental services are quite important. To begin with, there is a basic difference between Sunni and Shi'i respondents with regard to the means of making up for deficient public services. While almost half of the Sunnis claim that they do so at their own personal expense, less than 20 per cent of the Shi'is say the same thing. Bivariate analysis results indicate that middle and working class Shi'i respondents seek outside help (Cramer's V=0.23); whereas only working-class respondents do the same among the Sunnis (Cramer's V=0.42). Mackey attempts to explain Shi'i "demanding" behaviour on the basis of the assumption that historical persecution has developed among many Shi'is a sense of deprivation, even when situational realities do not warrant it.[17] The verification of Mackey's assertion is, nevertheless, beyond the scope of this study. Shi'is seem to depend more than their Sunni counterparts on aid provided by local and foreign, private relief agencies. The single most important private provider of services for both Muslim groups (although noticeably more so among Shi'is) is obviously local Islamic groups. Another distinction exists between Sunnis and Shi'is as to the ideological orientation of Islamic groups providing them with aid. It should be mentioned here that not all Islamic groups are inspired by fundamentalist zeal. In Lebanon there are more Islamic groups advocating popular than fundamentalist Islam. In fact 80 per cent of Sunni respondents receiving aid from Islamic groups described the donor as a non-fundamentalist group.[18] Unlike the Sunnis, more than 90 per cent of Shiʻi respondents credit the aid they receive to Hizbullah, Lebanon's only credible Shiʻi fundamentalist group. Less than 10 per cent of Shiʻis acknowledged receiving aid from the Society of Islamic Projects, the major Shiʻi non-fundamentalist philanthropic organization. Trendle argues that the grass roots of Hizbullah's unprecedented success within the Shiʻi community is not due to the fundamentalist slogans it raises, but mainly to the comprehensive programme of social services it implements.

> A major reason for Hizbollah's successful move into the political mainstream is the backing it has procured through an extensive programme of social services for the Shia population, in place of the scant assistance provided by the Lebanese government . . . Hizbollah finances a wide-ranging welfare system in the [Biqaʻ] region which includes: a free taxi service for farm hands to reach remote fields and villages; sponsored supermarkets which sell food at reduced prices and where particularly impoverished families can get free food packages with ration cards; and low-cost or even free medicine and hospitalization . . . Residents in Hizbollah's other main area of influence, Beirut's teeming southern suburbs, have also enjoyed similar services. When Hizbollah seized control of the suburbs from rival Shia group Amal in 1988 it embarked on an aid programme to improve daily life of the residents of the woefully deprived area.[19]

## Endowment of Political Support

It is plausible to propose that the extension of support to the political programmes of Islamist groups is a function of dissatisfaction with the performance of the Lebanese political system. It is well known that Lebanese Muslims used to complain about the inequity of their country's political system which they accused of favouring the Christians. The former found difficulty integrating themselves in a non-Islamic order in which their status was that of a politically subservient minority group. Al-Sayyid observes that "Muslims joined the Lebanese entity from an oppositional standpoint . . . When they despaired of reuniting with Syria . . . they began to articulate the injustices of the system, and demanded more material benefits as well as better political representation."[20] Thanks to the political reforms of the Taiʻf agreement, the

Muslims are now strongly represented in the Lebanese government. Sectarian shifts in relative political strength in favour of Muslim groups have ensured a more equitable allocation of the material resources available to the system. It is known however that these resources are inadequate to reconstruct the war-damaged economic infrastructure, not to mention the achievement of a higher standard of living for the majority of the Lebanese. How do the respondents perceive the performance of the reformed Lebanese political system in relation to the one that existed on the eve of signing the Tai'f agreement? The results of the first question in Table 5 show that most respondents do not believe that the performance of the system has really improved, the Shi'is being somewhat more negative than the Sunnis. Similarly, the majority of respondents do not appear convinced that the present government is genuinely concerned about serving the real interests of the people; again more Shi'is than Sunnis provide a pessimistic assessment of the government's intentions. It is believed that the present government of Mr Rafic Hariri is less unpopular than the previous governments of the post-Tai'f period.[21] This probably justifies why noticeably more respondents are less negative about Hariri's particular administration than the general performance of the Lebanese system.

### TABLE 5
### Satisfaction with the Performance of
### the Lebanese Political System

**Question:**
How do you compare the overall performance of the Lebanese political system since the promulgation of the Tai'f Agreement with the previous period (1943–75)?

|  | Sunnis n=250 % | Shi'is n=250 % |
|---|---|---|
| It has significantly improved | 17.2 | 8.0 |
| It has improved | 10.0 | 10.0 |
| It has not changed | 61.6 | 44.8 |
| It has worsened | 2.8 | 14.4 |
| It has significantly worsened | 8.4 | 22.8 |
| Total | 100.0 | 100.0 |

**Question:**

Do you agree with the assertion that the government is showing real interest in serving public needs?

|       | Sunnis n=250 % | Shi'is n=250 % |
|-------|----------------|----------------|
| SA    | 15.2           | 9.2            |
| A     | 25.6           | 15.6           |
| U     | 1.6            | 0.8            |
| D     | 21.6           | 26.0           |
| SD    | 36.0           | 48.4           |
| Total | 100.0          | 100.0          |

By and large, the extent of the respondents' satisfaction with the performance of the post-Tai'f political system does not seem sufficient to generate broad political support. Therefore, it is highly likely that lack of satisfaction with the system would contribute to increasing the respondents' support for the political activities of local Muslim fundamentalist groups. To be sure, 70 per cent of Sunnis support such activities, while, quite surprisingly, not more than 45 per cent of the Shi'is do the same (see the first question in Table 6). The correlation between the belief that the government does not show real interest in serving the public and support for the political activities of Islamic fundamentalist groups is stronger among Sunni respondents (r=0.46) than among Shi'is (r=0.29). There is a striking association between receiving aid from Islamic groups and support for them among Shi'i respondents (Cramer's V=0.58); among the Sunnis this association drops clearly (Cramer's V=0.27). It appears also that support for the fundamentalists among the Shi'is is inversely related to SES (r=-0.64), whereas such a relationship is much weaker among the Sunnis (r=-0.15). Furthermore, cross tabulation reveals that the effect of aid provided by Muslim groups is stronger among the Sunnis than the Shi'is. In other words, among respondents who say they received aid from Islamist groups, more Sunnis than Shi'is view with favour the activities of such groups.

## TABLE 6
### Disbursement of Political Support

**Question:**

What is your position on the political activities of Muslim fundamentalist groups in Lebanon?

|  | Sunnis n=250 % | Shi'is n=250 % |
|---|---|---|
| I strongly support | 33.2 | 20.0 |
| I support | 36.8 | 25.2 |
| I am uncertain | 3.2 | 6.4 |
| I don't support | 16.4 | 22.0 |
| I strongly don't support | 10.4 | 26.4 |
| Total | 100.0 | 100.0 |

**Question:**

Do you support the overthrow of the existing Lebanese government in favour of an Islamic one?

|  | Sunnis n=250 % | Shi'is n=250 % |
|---|---|---|
| I strongly support | 15.2 | 18.0 |
| I support | 16.8 | 23.6 |
| I am uncertain | 10.0 | 7.6 |
| I don't support | 28.8 | 23.6 |
| I strongly don't support | 29.2 | 27.2 |
| Total | 100.0 | 100.0 |

Another surprise emerges from responses to a question concerning whether the respondents support the overthrow of the Lebanese government in favour of an Islamic one. Here about 10 per cent more Shi'is than Sunnis say so (see responses to the second question in Table 6). Although the percentage of Sunnis who support the political activities of Muslim fundamentalist groups exceeds that of the Shiʻis, members of the latter group apparently are more ideologically committed than members of the former group. While the underlying factors for this discrepancy are not discussed in this paper, one may argue that Shiʻi political radicalism receives reinforcement from involvement by the Iranian Islamic republic in Lebanese Shiʻi affairs, which has no equivalent for Sunni fundamentalist groups in Lebanon. Sunnis may be more willing to support Sunni fundamentalist groups, than Shiʻis to support theirs. Support of politico-religious groups does not necessarily imply condoning the overthrow of the regime. In the unlikely event of this happening in Lebanon, it would be Shiʻi fundamentalists (thanks to greater socio-political impact) who would prevail in the system; a development that would displease most Sunnis, including the fundamentalists among them.

## Impact on Community Life

Mueller considers the factors that improve elite–masses communication; he concludes that the "absence of a legitimating ideology leaves political and economic institutions . . . without a spiritual foundation."[22] A situation of this nature does not only weaken communication, but also encourages the emergence of latent ideological tendencies which in the Arab East are essentially of religious origin. Khashan and Palmer emphasize the strength of the confessionally based communal organization of Middle Eastern peoples, and argue that "loyalty to the communal groups, if not absolute, exceed[s] . . . loyalty to such a nebulous entity as the state."[23] Political instability and bureaucratic corruption have exacerbated the already tenuous linkages between the political elite and the masses. Political opposition groups – especially the Islamists – capitalize on the gap that exists between people's demands and the government's readiness to act on them, and in several Arab countries they seem to have made some gains in this regard. Lebanon does not appear to be an exception. The impact of the leaders on public life was measured by three questions related to leaders' accessibility to the people, the amount of information they seek about people's needs, and deference to them by the latter in matters of political importance. In fact the responses which appear in Table 7 about the leaders' impact on community life reveal the magnitude of influence wielded by the Islamist groups. For all three questions the respondents tend to place leaders of Islamic groups ahead of the government's as far as their impact on public political life. Although Shi'i respondents seem to indicate greater impact of Islamic leaders on their lives than their Sunni counterparts, these leaders assume more impact on both sectarian groups than any other set of leaders.

## TABLE 7
### Leaders' Impact on Community Life

**Question 1:**
Which category of leaders is most accessible to you?

| | Sunnis n=250 % | Shi'is n=250 % |
|---|---|---|
| Governmental | 10.0 | 12.8 |
| Sectarian | 15.6 | 15.6 |
| Secular | 7.2 | 14.0 |
| Islamist | 32.8 | 52.8 |
| None | 34.4 | 4.8 |
| Total | 100.0 | 100.0 |

**Question 2:**
Which leaders seek more information than the rest about the needs of people in your area?

| | Sunnis n=250 % | Shi'is n=250 % |
|---|---|---|
| Governmental | 17.1 | 24.6 |
| Sectarian | 4.1 | 9.3 |
| Secular | 2.8 | 8.9 |
| Islamist | 43.9 | 50.8 |
| None | 32.1 | 6.5 |
| Total | 100.0 | 100.1* |

**Question 3:**

To which leaders do you usually defer most in matters of political importance?

| | Sunnis n=250 % | Shi'is n=250 % |
|---|---|---|
| Governmental | 15.5 | 13.2 |
| Sectarian* | 8.2 | 4.9 |
| Secular* | 4.1 | 19.8 |
| Islamist* | 52.2 | 59.7 |
| None | 20.0 | 2.5 |
| Total | 100.0 | 100.1** |

* Opposition leaders.

**Due to rounding, percentages do not add up to 100.

The responses disclose a conspicuous difference between Sunnis and Shi'is with regard to the percentage of respondents who feel alienated from all brands of leaders active in the local political field. Far more Sunnis than Shi'is do not identify leaders with whom they can interact at the community level. It should be noted that while Shi'i political mobilization increased during the last two decades (thanks to the rise of exclusively Shi'i political movements), that of the Sunnis declined (due to the recession of the Arab nationalist movements with which they identified).[24] The political picture of these two religious groups looks like this: the Shi'is seem to have nearly completed the identification of the political panorama in which they operate, while many Sunnis have not. The implication is that Sunni political choices have not yet been fully explored. This is not to say that the present picture of Shi'i identifications is final. Experience in political activity in Lebanon tells us that consequential shifts in identification usually accompany major political developments. A shift that transforms the identifications of Lebanese Muslims towards the official political system is needed in order for the Tai'f agreement to succeed in ending entrenched primordial differences that continue to set most Lebanese apart. This is being said because it transpires from the responses that the impact of governmental leaders on community life is far less than satisfactory. The vacuum is filled by a plethora of traditional, secular and Islamic groups whose operations compete with those of the state to the detriment of the latter's influence. The machinery of the Lebanese state is weak and Table 7 provides plenty of supporting evidence.

## Implications of the Study

The findings demonstrate that in Lebanon the problems of effective governance are quite formidable. Officially, the civil war has ended, and the forces of "pernicious" opposition have either been removed or restrained. The government is restoring, although slowly, water and electricity services and is making plans for major economic reconstruction projects. In this connection, the most spectacular success has been the ability of a local construction company (linked to the prime minister) to collect $US 900 million from Lebanese investors for rebuilding the commercial sector in Beirut's central area. These successes aside, the basic problems that contributed to the ignition of the civil war in 1975 are still unresolved. Maronite Christians who previously gave meaning and impetus to a sovereign Lebanese entity are now disillusioned with the system, and generally unrepresented (by the sect's prominent political leaders) in the post-Tai'f arrangement, especially since the 1992 summer elections which they vehemently opposed.[25] Although Muslim political representation has increased – mainly by integrating their new, war-produced political elite in the core of political decision makers – it did not mean anything more than the extension of limited patronage prerogatives which left many rank and file Muslims literally untouched by the political changes. It appears that the vacuum in the linkage between the elites and the masses has been filled by politically aspiring Islamic (fundamentalist and popular) groups. This is most seriously evinced by the persisting tenuous concept of the Lebanese entity (particularly among the Sunnis), since most dissidents exhibit preference for integrating Lebanon in an all-encompassing Arab entity, and for enforcing the tenets of *shari'a*. As a result, the legitimacy of the Lebanese government receives low marks by the respondents, most of whom describe the scope of its public oriented services as less than satisfactory. The deficiency in government services is compensated by private organizations, the most active among them being Islamic groups. Alarmingly, most respondents do not feel that the performance of the reformed Lebanese political system of the second republic (since 1989) has improved in relation to performance during the first republic (1943–75). Thus it does not surprise us to discover that many respondents support the activities of Islamic groups, but not sufficiently to allow them to overthrow the existing government.

The implications of this study are clear: it is not too late for the Lebanese government to win the support of the people it is supposed to represent, but something positive must be done in this connection. More official attention needs to be given to the outlying regions of the country, particularly those in which Islamic groups are strongest, i.e. 'Aqqar (Sunni fundamentalists) and northern Biqa' (Shi'i fundamentalists). But the task is momentous since it entails a transformation from the patron–client relations that prevail in Lebanese politics into a genuinely representative political system. Compared to other Islamic groups in the Arab world, such as in Algeria and Egypt, Islamic groups are relatively quiescent in Lebanon. They have so far vented their military anger at Israeli occupation forces in southern Lebanon. However, the resolution of the Arab–Israeli conflict which seems to be underway means that the Islamists' potential for insurgency might shift to the arena of local politics, if the basic public issues that give momentum to their drive are not gratified. Finally, it is certain that the future of fundamentalist Islam in the Arab world, which is largely unclear, will have direct consequences on the status of Lebanon's Islamists.

## NOTES

1 G. Kampffmeyer, "Egypt and Western Asia", *Whither Islam?*, ed. H. A. R. Gibb (London: Victor Gollancz Ltd., 1932), p. 159.

2 S. M. Shamsul Alam, "Islam, Ideology, and the State in Bangladesh", *Journal of Asian and African Affairs*, 28:1–2 (1993), p. 89.

3 I. Abu-Lughod, "Retreat from the Secular Path? Islamic Dilemmas of Arab Politics", *The Review of Politics*, 28:4 (1966), pp. 447–76.

4 See B. Tibi, "The Renewed Role of Islam in the Political and Social Development of the Middle East", *The Middle East Journal*, 37:1 (1983), pp. 3–13.

5 H. Precht, "Ayatollah Realpolitik", *Foreign Policy*, No. 70, spring 1988, p. 113.

6 For descriptive information on these two, as well as lesser Islamic organizations, see A. N. Hamzeh, and H. Dekmejian, "The Islamic Spectrum of Lebanese

Politics", *Journal of South Asian and Middle Eastern Studies*, 15:3 (1993), pp. 25–42.

7  Ibid., p. 30.

8  J. L. Esposito and J. P. Piscatori, "The Global Impact of the Iranian Revolution: Policy Perspective", *The Iranian Revolution: Its Global Impact*, ed. J. L. Esposito, pp. 322–3.

9  J. A. Bill, "Power and Religion in Revolutionary Iran", *The Middle East Journal*, 36: 1 1982), p. 46.

10 Asad Abu-Khalil, "Ideology and Practice of Hizbullah in Lebanon: Islamization of Leninist Organizational Principles", *Middle Eastern Studies*, 27:4 (1991), p. 391.

11 Hentry Munson, Jr. *Islam and Revolution in the Middle East* (New Haven: Yale University Press, 1988), p. 29.

12 Sunni representation in the sample was as follows: 30 per cent from metropolitan Beirut, 34 per cent from the north, 12 per cent from the mountain region, the south, and the Biqa' respectively. Shi'i respondents included 40 per cent from the south, and 30 per cent from metropolitan Beirut and the Biqa' respectively.

13 Abbas Kelidar, "States without Foundations: The Political Evolution of State and Society in the Arab East", *Journal of Contemporary History*, 28:2 (1993), p. 316.

14 Hilal Khashan, "The Revival of Pan-Arabism", *Orbis*, 35:1 (1991), pp. 107–16.

15 R. A. Norton, "Lebanon: Conflict Without End?", *Middle East Insight*, 6:1–2 (1990), p. 45.

16 N. R. Keddie, "Ideology, Society and the State in Post-Colonial Muslim Societies", *State and Ideology in the Middle East and Pakistan*, ed. Fred Halliday and H. Alavi (New York: Monthly Review Press, 1988), p. 10.

17 See S. Mackey, *Lebanon: Death of a Nation* (New York: Congdon and Weed, 1989).

18 The fundamentalist group mentioned by 20 per cent of the respondents is *al-Jama'a al-Islamiyya*. The other 80 per cent listed the names of the nonfundamentalist *Society of Islamic Benevolent Intentions*, and the *Islamic Society of Philanthropic Projects*. It is rumoured that the last group is connected with the Syrian government which maintains strong political influence in Lebanon.

19 G. Trendle, "The Grass Roots of Success", *The Middle East*, February (1993), pp. 12–13.

20 R. al-Sayyid, "al-Harakat ad-diniyya al-masihiyya wa-l Islamiyya fi Lubnan wa mawqi'iha fil harb wa-l silm", *Ishkaliyat al-salam fi Lubnan wa afaqih* (Beirut: Manshurat Jami'iyyat Mutakharriji al-Maqasid, 1987), p. 88.

21 Mr Rafic Hariri is a multi-billionaire businessman. His appointment as prime minister in the summer of 1993 was seen by some Lebanese as the beginning of their country's economic recovery.

22 C. Mueller, *The Politics of Communication* (London: Oxford University Press, 1973), pp. 150–1.

23 H. Khashan and M. Palmer, "The Economic Basis of Civil Conflict in Lebanon: A Survey Analysis of Sunnite Muslims", *Journal of Arab Affairs*, 1:1 (1981), p. 113.

24 For additional information about shifts in Sunni and Shi'i political mobilization, see Khashan, "The Revival of Pan-Arabism", pp.107–16.

25 A comprehensive analysis of Maronite opposition to these elections is available in J. Harik and H. Khashan, "Lebanon's Divisive Democracy: The Parliamentary Elections of 1992", *Arab Studies Quarterly*, 15:3 (1993), pp. 41–59.

# 9

# The Future of Islamic Movements in Lebanon

## *A. Nizar Hamzeh*

For more than a decade, both the Islamic militant movements and the Islamic activist movements became an increasingly important and legitimate political force in Lebanon. The former includes such organizations as Hizbullah and al-Jama'a al-Islamiyya, while the latter includes al-Ahbash, officially known as Jam'iyyat al-Mashari' al-Khayriyya al-Islamiyya (The Society of Islamic Philanthropic Projects). In less than ten years, these movements created a political, social and economic presence within the Muslim community, whether in Beirut, the Biqa', the North or the South. More recently, these Islamic movements have been engaged in the difficult process of accommodating themselves to the country's new formula for inter-sectarian coexistence, forged in the Ta'if agreement of 1989. This formula represents the antithesis to the ideological goal of Islamic militants – the establishment of an Islamic Lebanese state.

In its present configuration, the Lebanese government has managed somewhat to overcome the resistance of Islamic militants with significant help from Syria. As for the long term fate of Islamic radicalism in Lebanon, it is likely to be influenced by three factors: the evolution of the Arab–Israeli peace process; the ebb and flow of political Islamism in Iran and Syria; and Lebanon's socio-economic problems. This paper sheds some light on the resurgence of radicalism among Lebanon's fundamentalist groups.

## The Fundamentalists' Profile

Given that Islamic movements have gained too much momentum and popular support in the Arab-Muslim world, political scientists researching the Middle East have explained the crises that led to the rise of Islamic revivalist movements. The crisis conditions explored and explained by researchers and writers can be condensed in six catalysts: (1) political stagnation leading to a weak central authority; (2) economic stagnation resulting in the gross maldistribution of wealth between the rich and poor; (3) failure of the nationalist elite to achieve balanced socio-economic development; (4) persuasiveness of political oppression; (5) the disorienting psycho-cultural impact of Westernization; and (6) the Arab defeats by Israel in 1948, 1956, 1967, 1973 and the Israeli invasion of Lebanon in 1982.[1]

These catalysts were particularly devastating to the balanced confessional system in Lebanon, which attempted to sustain an open society in a regional environment of endemic turbulence. Thus, the crisis conditions in the Arab world were exacerbated in the Lebanese sectarian context by problems inherent in the system itself; for example, the structural imbalance between Christians and Muslims according to the 6:5 ratio in favour of the former was a cause of the 1958 civil war and of the larger conflagration of the 1975–1989 war. Other factors contributing to Lebanese instability during the 1960s and 1970s were (a) the fighting between Israel and the Palestinians; (b) the increase in class differences in a market economy beset by official corruption; and (c) the proxy war fought by Arab countries on Lebanese soil. These catalysts helped shape the dynamics of Islamic militancy in Lebanon, which received further reinforcement from the victory of the Islamic cause in Iran.[2]

Far from being a monolithic reality, Lebanon's Islamic movements constitute highly complex entities in both ideological and organizational terms. They include a plethora of groups ranging from the activists to the militant revolutionary organizations (see Table 1 at the end of this essay).

Despite vast differences in their agendas and methods, Islamic movements share common ideological principles. John Esposito, in his latest work *Islamic Movements, Democratization and US Foreign Policy*, summarizes these principles in five broad categories.[3] First, Islam supplies comprehensive principles for personal life as well as for the society and the state. Second, Westernization, materialism and radical individualism are the causes of all the ills in Muslim societies. Though Westernization and secularization are condemned by Muslims, modernization as such is not. Science and technology are accepted but the direction and the frequency of the changes they cause are to be subjected to Islamic values and beliefs. Third, restoration of power and success requires a return to the correct path of Islam, a divinely mandated order. Fourth, the *shari'a* (Islamic law) inevitably produces a more moral and socially just society than other laws. A just society, though, is not a society of equal opportunity or economic equality but a society that lives according to the *shari'a* principles. Finally, fundamentalists believe that it is the duty of all Muslims to sacrifice and struggle against all odds, if necessary to die as martyrs in the way of God.[4] However, militant movements such as Hizbullah, al-Tawhid and al-Jama'a al-Islamiyya of Lebanon have gone beyond these principles. Their extreme militancy has made them preach that Islam and the West are locked in an ongoing historical battle that includes western crusaders and Zionism. The West, particularly the United States, is condemned for its support of unjust, un-Islamic regimes and for its support of Israel. Thus, violence against "un-Islamic rulers" and Western governments that support them is understood as a sacred duty, incumbent upon all believers.

Contrary to Islamic militant movements, activists, such as al-Ahbash, exhibit a low level of militancy directed against radical movements more than the West and Muslim rulers. Despite their call for the return to the correct path, al-Ahbash oppose the goal of all Islamists, particularly al-Jama'a al-Islamiyya, to establish an Islamic order. According to al-Ahbash, "the Muslims are neither prepared for that goal nor is there a way to appoint a caliph at the present time."[5] The mission of al-Ahbash is to promote a normal and stable society where social and religious pluralism is the mode of existence for Muslims among themselves and among non-Muslims.[6] Equally mild is the foreign policy orientation and worldview of al-Ahbash. They neither make reference to *jihad* nor are they angry at the West; on the contrary, they recommend that their members study Western thought and science to achieve a civilized Islamic society.[7]

The leadership and membership of both activist and militant fundamentalist organizations come from the lower and middle classes. Furthermore, the leadership of some organizations, such as al-Jama'a al-Islamiyya and al-Ahbash, consists of both lay and clerical figures. Although Hizbullah's *Shura* (Consultative Council) is led by clerics, its politburo is composed of laymen rather than clerics.[8] Many activists and members are graduates of faculties of law, science, medicine, education, engineering and economics rather than of religion.[9]

Responses to the Syrian influence in Lebanon, begun in 1976 and formalized by the 1989 Ta'if accord, took various forms on the part of the Islamic movements. The 1989 Ta'if accord, unique in some significant aspects, established Lebanon's "special" relations with Syria, and also called for the extension of Beirut Government's authority over all Lebanese territory, with Syrian assistance.[10] Al-Jama'a al-Islamiyya, for example, has postponed the quest for an Islamic order in Lebanon in favour of gaining a greater share of power for itself and the Sunni community. To ensure its survival in Lebanon the Jama'a, especially after Ta'if, has skilfully manoeuvred to separate itself from the Syrian Muslim Brotherhood's suicidal struggle against Asad's regime."[11] In contrast, al-Ahbash, who had already accepted Lebanon's confessional system and rejected violence and the politicization of Islam, has enjoyed excellent relations with most Arab countries, particularly with Syria, since the latter's intervention in Lebanon in 1976.[12]

As for Hizbullah, the party realized that the territories it holds are under Syrian rather than Iranian influence. Their response to Syria's undisputed influence in Lebanon since Ta'if has been a new strategy based on cooperation rather than on abolishing the system. The rank and file still aim to establish an Islamic order; however, the strategy used is an evolutionary rather than revolutionary model, in which the ballot box is used as an instrument for achieving social, economic and political changes.[13]

The parliamentary elections of 1992 marked the integration of some Islamic movements in the Lebanese political system for the first time. Hizbullah, the Jama'a and the Ahbash ran in the elections and did quite well (see Table 1). Regardless of whether the Islamic movements are committed to the Ta'if accord and its political processes, their participation in the electoral process is indicative of a new strategy. Today's strategy is to press for change in the name of political liberalization and democratization. The Islamic movements, especially those which won in the 1992 parliamentary elections, may not be swimming in Lebanon's political mainstream, but the water is surely tested.

## The Arab–Israeli Peace Process

Most scholars agree that an Arab–Israeli peace settlement would contribute greatly to the decline of Islamic militancy.[14] However, the Arab–Israeli conflict did not create the Islamic movements nor will peace between the Arabs and Israelis eradicate them.

Since the days of Hasan al-Banna, the founder of Egypt's Muslim Brotherhood, and the Ayatollah Muhammad Baqir al-Sadr, the founder of the Iraq's Party of Islamic Call (Hizb al-Da'wa al-Islamiyya, which inspired Iran's party of God), movements seeking to institute an Islamic, moral, social and political order in Lebanon have used the conflict as an instrument for promoting their goals. Sunni militants, such as Jama'a and the Tawhid, and Shi'a groups under Hizbullah identified Israel and the West as their enemy and advocated a holy struggle (with the exception of the Ahbash) to regain Muslim land, especially the holy city of Jerusalem.[15] Undoubtedly, they have gained some popular support as a result of using this approach especially since Israel's strongest supporter, the United States, remains deeply hostile to what it terms "Islamic fundamentalism". The real objectives of Islamic movements are not caused by the Arab–Israeli conflict, whether in Palestine or on other Islamic soil. They lie at home, rooted in the Muslim community itself.

Recruitment and mobilization by Lebanon's Islamic movements succeed because they address social and political issues like poverty and unemployment, class differences between rich and poor, insufficient government services, political corruption, perceived government subservience to "imperialism", led by the United States, and the Westernized or European lifestyle of the well-to-do. Lebanon's Islamists, as well as their counterparts in Egypt, Jordan, Syria, Gaza, and the Maghreb, address these issues through a comprehensive critique of modern life in the Muslim world and argue persuasively that a return to the "correct path" would bring social justice and equality to Muslim societies. Moreover, Islamic movements aim at transforming individuals at the grass roots level. They work in educational institutions, child care centres, youth camps, religious publishing, broadcasting, economic projects (Islamic banks, investments and real estate constructions), and social services (hospitals, clinics, water and power and legal aid).[16]

A significant example demonstrating that peace between the Arabs and the Israelis did not break the Islamic movements is the Egyptian experience. The peace accord signed by Sadat in 1978 slowed the Islamic movements, but not by much. On the contrary, since the assassination of Sadat the resurgence of Islamic movements such as al-Jama'a al-Islamiyya of Omar 'Abd al-Rahman occurred despite the oppression exercised by the Mubarak regime. More importantly, the 16 years of official recognition and diplomatic relations have yet failed to completely normalize Egypt's relations with Israel. The fundamentalist critique of the negative aspects of modern life in Egypt has gained too much momentum to succumb to peace treaties. Moderate Lebanese rulers, whether Muslim or Christian, will be confronting Islamic militant movements long after a Lebanese–Israeli peace treaty comes into being.

Second, Syria is reluctant to eradicate Hizbullah and other Islamic militants, an Israeli condition for peace in future agreements between Israel and Syria. A major reason for Syria's position is that the normalization of relations between Syria and Lebanon on the one hand and between Syria and Israel on the other hand, would allow anti-Syrians in Lebanon to mount the Israeli's horse against Syria's interest in Lebanon. Therefore, Syria will always need allies who ideologically and politically do not cooperate with Israel directly. But, Syria has also suppressed and continues to suppress militant movements that threaten its interests. For example, it suppressed the Sunni movement Tawhid in 1985; and in 1987, it evicted Hizbullah from Fathallah's Barracks in the Biqa' in Lebanon, allowing the Lebanese army to regain control over it. Furthermore, when fundamentalists mobilized by Hizbullah demonstrated against the so-called Gaza–Jericho agreement on 13 September 1993, and 13 demonstrators were killed by the Lebanese armed forces, Syria ordered Hizbullah not to retaliate in response.[17] Moreover, Syria may need Hizbullah to counter any possible coup by Syria's Muslim Brotherhood, whom Asad fears more than the Shi'a groups, the latter a minority in a predominantly Sunni world. Thus, it is to be expected that militancy will decline in the light of peace between Syria and Israel, bringing an end to the military control of Islamic movements whether that of Hizbullah or others. However, to reiterate, peace does not mean eradicating fundamentalists. They will continue to be political players in Lebanon and the region after the peace process takes its final form.

Third, the Syrian–Iranian alliance seems to be strategic rather than temporary. A study by Hizbullah extremists in Qum Iran, pointed out that the more Syria gets close to the United States and Israel, the more it will depart from Iran and regional–international policies.[18] The same study said "after signing a peace treaty with Israel, Syria will eradicate Hizbullah."[19] Although the above assumption may be correct, Iran's Rafsanjani has not transformed Iran's opposition to the Madrid conference and to developments in USA–Syrian relations into a political confrontation with Syria. In other words, Iran has not yet obstructed Syrian attempts to sign a peace treaty with Israel. On the contrary, Ali Akbar Wilayati, Rafsanjani's right hand and Iran's foreign minister, justified Syrian negotiations with Israel as due to regional and international pressure exercised by the United States.[20] Such justification illustrates that Damascus and Tehran know that confrontation between them would only serve Israeli interests. Furthermore, the leaders of Iran are not ignorant of modern political science. Though Iran is often portrayed as the most intransigent of all Islamic states, Tehran is questioning whether it makes sense to nurture eternal hatred and animosity toward Israel, while both the PLO and Jordan have shaken hands with it. After all, flexibility, pragmatism and even dealing with "unbelievers" can be justified by a *fatwa* (juridical opinion), provided that it comes from an eminent politico-religious authority such as Ali Khamene'i. Iran will continue to debate the peace process but no actual measures will be taken by Rafsanjani against Syria, Lebanon or other front-line Arab states.

Fourth, Iran's relative flexibility and pragmatism toward the West and Arab Gulf countries in the last few years have influenced fundamentalists and Hizbullah, especially the strategic ally of Iran. This group has changed its strategy in Lebanon, accepting the reality of its political system instead of calling for its abolition. In fact, beside participating in the Lebanese parliamentary elections of 1992, the fundamentalists submitted to all governmental decrees on public discipline. Fundamentalists have also ceased activities that belong to the state such as servicing public facilities.[21] The truce between Islamic militant movements and the Lebanese government has held since 1989, though it has witnessed tension from time to time. As in Iran, the fundamentalists in Lebanon will continue to debate the repercussions of peace but without seeking physical confrontation unless the Lebanese government triggers such confrontation. In fact, the emphasis has shifted from resisting peace to resisting normalization.[22] Confrontation with Syria as well as with the Lebanese government is deemed too great a risk to be taken by fundamentalist leaders such as Fadlallah, Nasrallah, Qasim and Fathi Yakan, the *murshid* of the Jama'a.

However, certain fundamentalist leaders, such as Shaykh Subhi Tufayli (Hizbullah's minority faction) and Shaykh Sa'id Sha'ban (Tawhid) are rejecting peace and normalization with Israel. The only option they accept is the liberation of Palestine through Islamic resistance, even if it would precipitate an open confrontation with the Lebanese government and Syria. In Shaykh Tufayli's words, "peace must be resisted at any cost even if it would lead to sacrificing one's soul."[23] Still, the great majority of fundamentalists are determined to gain more than lose in this peace process. Therefore, it should come as no surprise if rejection of the peace process gradually recedes from the rhetoric of some Islamic militants, once Israel withdraws from South Lebanon according to UN Resolution 425. Thus, these fundamentalists would offer the Lebanese government and Syria no excuse to eradicate them. Just as Iran will not recognize Israel until the peace process makes headway with Syria, Islamic movements in Lebanon will not engage in open confrontation with Syria but will bide their time and go quietly with the flow.

## The Ebb and Flow of Political Fundamentalism

The long-term fate of Islamic radicalism in Lebanon depends on the ebb and flow of political Islamism in the region. In other words, the ascendance of Islamic militants in Iran or the strengthening of fundamentalists in Syria may cause the resurgence of radicalism among Lebanon's fundamentalist groups. Thus it can be argued that radical Islam would not, without Iran's support of Hizbullah and other Sunni fundamentalists such as the Tawhid and Hamas, have emerged as a dominant factor in the politics of the region since 1980. As for Syria's geographic proximity to Lebanon, the Muslim Brotherhood could have strengthened the position of the Sunni Jama'a in Lebanon *vis-à-vis* the Lebanese state and other political factions had they succeeded in their revolts of 1978 and 1982 in Aleppo and Hama. Indeed, the coordination between fundamentalist movements in Iran, Sudan and elsewhere is still weak. Still, the two meetings that were held in the Sudan in April of 1991 and in Iran in October of 1991 suggest that there is a loose confederation among fundamentalist groups, despite their vast differences.[24] The need for more unity was expressed by Ayatollah Muhammad Husayn Fadlallah, who said that "the Islamic movements in the Arab world, which are highly segmented, will unite under government violence and oppression."[25] Nevertheless, Iran and Syria, more than any other countries in the region, continue to be active players in the future course of Lebanon's fundamentalist groups.

Until the death of Ayatollah Khomeini, militants supported by Iran dominated Islamic movements, particularly Hizbullah, Tawhid and Hamas. Iran's militant factions and revolutionaries, including Mahdi al-Hashimi (executed in 1987 by the Iranian Revolutionary Guard), Husayn Ali Muntaziri (deceased 1981) and his son Muhammad Muntazari, advocated exporting the Islamic revolution to the Muslim world. Their line of militancy has continued with Hujjat-al-Islam the former Interior Minister Ali Akbar Muhtashimi, who lately urged Lebanon's Hizbullah and Hamas "to hold to the principle of Islamic revolution, to strike at US interests in Lebanon and around the world, to spread its defensive and offensive line to Europe and the United States".[26] However, the death of Khomeini in 1988 and the succession of Rafsanjani to the presidency have changed the picture. Rafsanjani has charted a relatively pragmatic course which opposes Muhtashimi's. Far from being revolutionary, Rafsanjani's pragmatic approach leans towards rapprochement with the Gulf countries and the West.[27] Although he has so far not gained the trust of the West, he is often cited as another example figure of Islamic pragmatism and growing moderation.[28] A key indicator of Rafsanjani's control over Lebanon's Hizbullah was the complete release of the Western hostages in Lebanon in 1992. Another indicator was the decline of Shaykh Subhi Tufayli's militant faction, a group strongly supported by Muhtashimi. However, Rafsanjani is facing strong opposition in Iran and may fail because of three factors.

First, Rafsanjani has not yet succeeded in securing the majority's support for his programmes in the politico-religious arena. Despite Khamene'i's support, Rafsanjani has not been able to implement his policy because important decisions in Iran lie within the hands of various factions, thus limiting his ability to act. For example, the extremists led by Muhtashimi still hold authority with the Iranian people although they lost most of their parliamentary seats in the elections of 1992. Furthermore, the conservatives headed by Ayatollah Mahdawi Kini, who enjoy strong representation in the Iranian parliament, accuse Rafsanjani of turning the president's position into an "imperial presidency".[29] The Islamic Revolutionary Guards are also influential in limiting Rafsanjani's course of action. This is not to mention various leaders who remain Khomeini's disciples and ardent adherents to his principles. They have accused Rafsanjani of turning his back on the principles of the revolution.

Second, Rafsanjani has failed to institute his economic reforms and his reconstruction plan. He could neither rescue Iran from inflation and unemployment (30 per cent) nor publicly endorse policies of openness and realism that are necessary for reform and reconstruction.[30] Revolutionary fever and slogans still sell in Iran, attracting many Iranians more than Rafsanjani's policies of pragmatism and openness. He himself admitted this problem to *Time* magazine by saying, "if I turn my back to the revolution, the people would not support me."[31]

Third, the Iranian leadership has failed to win the confidence of the West, particularly that of the United States, because Rafsanjani has not been able to change the course and practices of his country. The United States still views Iran as the mentor of terrorism and assassinations in the world. Furthermore, for the United States, Iran consistently aims to kill the Middle East peace process with its support for Hamas and Hizbullah. Iran's relationship with the Sudan is another troubling factor for the United States since, through this relationship, Iran intends to destroy friendly Arab governments. What troubles the United States administration most is Iran's attempts to purchase and process nuclear weapons. All in all, the extremists regard the accusations as good material for their political speeches and good reason for the failure of Rafsanjani's open and pragmatic policies.

If Rafsanjani's pragmatism and openness towards the West and the gulf countries yield concrete economic and financial aid, helping the Iranian economy to recover, Khamene'i will continue to support Rafsanjani, thus preventing the rise of Muhtashimi's and Mehdi Karoubi's militant factions to power. Accordingly, the resurgence of Islamic radicalism in Lebanon is not likely to happen. However, if Rafsanjani fails to convince Western nations, particularly the United States, of his commitment to change the practices of his country, then it is likely that the militants will rise to power both in Iran and in Lebanon.

As for the Syrian Muslim Brotherhood, long regarded by the Sunni Jama'a of Lebanon as their brothers in faith and ideology, it is unlikely that this faction or any other underground movement will ascend to power in Syria at the present. First, Asad has used force and violence before, demonstrated in the bloody suppression of the two Muslim Brotherhood revolts in 1978 and 1982.[32] The significant result of both suppressions was the complete exile or eradication of cadres and of charismatic leaders such as Sa'id Hawwa, the chief ideologue, and

Marwan Hadid. According to Sivan, the future of any Islamic movement does not depend only on the objective conditions (i.e. socio-economic factor, ideology and organizational structure), but on the presence of some charismatic leaders and agitators.[33] In the case of Syria, Sivan's assumption holds since without charismatic leaders such as Hawwa, the Muslim Brotherhood would have had difficulty resurging. The military operations of Asad's regime, done with the precision of a scalpel, dealt the Muslim Brotherhood a deadly blow which will take them a long time to recover from. The Muslim Brotherhood has not even been given the chance to test the possibility of its integration in Asad's political regime since 1970. Where Lebanon is concerned, Asad may exercise stiff measures against Hizbullah, but he will not eradicate it completely as specified earlier. On the other hand, the Sunni Jama'a of Lebanon may be eradicated if Asad's regime establishes a connection between them and the underground fundamentalists in Syria. The threat of Lebanon's Sunni Jama'a to the Syrian regime is by far greater than Hizbullah's. It is thus no wonder that Lebanon's Jama'a leaders such as Fathi Yakan or Faysal Mawlawi, the general secretary, have denied publicly any connection with the Syrian Muslim Brotherhood.

Second, Syria's socio-economic situation is not as bad as Iran's. Although the regime has not succeeded economically, it has provided basic social services: schools, hospitals, medicine and public facilities. While Asad defended economic "open door" policy in Egypt, he only allowed privatization within controlled limits and under the supervision of the state in Syria. In this regard, Michael Hudson notes that the state is still a leviathan state going through transitory controlled stages.[34] Thus, the slogans of Syria's underground fundamentalists cover issues such as unemployment, social services, medical care, schools and hospitals but do not have as much of an impact on the Syrians as they have on the Egyptians or the Algerians. This is not to suggest that social justice and equal opportunity are recognized by the Syrian state for every single individual but to suggest that the lower and middle social classes are not as economically frustrated as in Iran, Egypt and Algeria.

Third, although Asad's regime embodies the Alawi's ascendance to power, the commitment of the regime is to "Arab nationalism" and not to religious fundamentalism. The charges against the Alawi sectarian regime have been balanced by a policy of accommodation, highlighting the appointment of Sunni officials to prominent positions. These positions include the prime minister, the minister of foreign affairs and the defence minister. Furthermore, the accusation that the Alawites are neither Muslim nor *dhimi* but *mushrikin* (infidels) was falsified by a validation of the Alawites' Islamic status by Iran's twelver Shi'ite clerical authorities. This religio-ideological factor has reinforced close strategic and common ties forged between Syria and Iran.[35]

Finally, until recently Asad pursued a militant policy towards Israel and the West in the name of "Arab nationalism". Even after the Madrid conference and the numerous rounds of negotiations with Israel under the United States' supervision, he has succeeded in remaining a key actor who does not yield easily. Asad is committed to peace but he insists on differentiating between peace and normalization of relations with Israel which Syria does not want in the meantime, a position praised by both Sunni and Shi'ite radicals, including Iran.[36] Should President Asad depart, the Ba'th is likely to become internally divided in a struggle of succession. Such an event may prove to be a landmark for the resurgence of the Syrian Muslim Brotherhood. However, the fundamentalists may find it difficult to assume power in the presence of the cultural heterogeneity of Christians, Druze, Isma'ilis and Kurds.

## Lebanon's Socio-Economic Problems

The future decline of Islamic radicalism in Lebanon will moreover depend on the ability of the Lebanese government to accommodate sectarian interests within a rapidly expanding economic system which can bring tangible benefits to Lebanon's poorer classes regardless of sectarian affiliation. The central problem for present and future Lebanese governments is how to achieve some measures of cross-sectarian justice. While the present government of al-Hariri has succeeded at the financial and monetary levels, it has unfortunately done poorly at the socio-economic level.

Lebanon emerged from its war with its basic infrastructure destroyed. As a result, the living conditions of the Lebanese deteriorated to a critical level, and, for a large segment of the population, to the subsistence level. Such a situation produced an ideal environment for Islamic movements to recruit many Muslims to the forefront, whether to fight against the Lebanese political system or Israel, promising them social justice and a better life.[37] By 1991, following the implementation of the Ta'if agreement and the subsequent improvements in the security and political situations, Karami's government was neither able to stabilize the Lebanese economy and currency (traded then at over two thousand Lebanese Liras to the US dollar), nor to advance some concrete plans to solve monetary and socio-economic problems. The result was the total frustration of the people expressed in demonstrations and civil disobedience, which led to the resignation of Karami's government.[38]

The government of Prime Minister Rafiq al-Hariri, which came to power in October 1992, won the support of the majority of the Lebanese people and Lebanese political factions with the exception of militant Islamic movements, particularly Hizbullah. Arguing that al-Hariri's programme is tailored to increase his own wealth and foreign businesses, Hizbullah has continued to oppose al-Hariri's reconstruction policy, even after some Syrian pressure in favour of al-Hariri and his government was applied.[39]

Nevertheless, the capital inflow to Lebanon increased as a result of improvements in the political and security situation. Also, al-Hariri's financial ability and international business connections have allowed him to gain confidence of international business investors and developers. Indeed, these improvements in Lebanon's political situation and its security would not have taken place without the strong pressure applied by the United States on both Syria and Israel. Thus, the capital supplied by al-Hariri or by foreign investors would not have survived without the presence of an international and regional political consensus on the need for stability in Lebanon after Ta'if. With that consensus, the inflow of capital increased from $1,073 million in the mid-1980s to $1,708 million in 1994. This inflow enabled the government to overcome the deficit in the balance of trade, over $1 billion in the last three years, and to achieve a surplus of $562 million in the balance of payments.[40] Likewise, the increased inflow of capital allowed for some appreciation of the Lebanese currency. The currency, which was traded at L£ 2,150 to one $ in 1992, improved to L£ 1,665 to one $ in 1994. However, the sharp depreciation of the Lebanese currency remains one of the major problems that the government has to deal with. Nonetheless, the Central Bank has increased its deposits in foreign currencies from $1,821 million to $2,800 million since 1992. It may reach $3,450 million if the deposits of Solidere, the real estate corporation responsible for the reconstruction of central Beirut, are counted. Moreover, the Central Bank's deposits may mount up to $6,750 million if the Central Bank's gold reserve (estimated at $3.3 billion) is taken into consideration.[41]

In addition, the Hariri government has increased its assets and financial capability through the government's revenue (taxes and bills), which has reached L£ 11 billion.[42] Recently, in order to attract more capital and investments, the government changed the tax system, reducing taxes on corporations and companies from 20 per cent to 10 per cent.[43]

In light of such financial improvement, the government of al-Hariri launched a number of projects for the reconstruction of Lebanon. The year 1994 witnessed the establishment of Solidere for the reconstruction of central Beirut. Solidere's investments will surpass $6 billion in five years.[44] The company is now working on removing the rubbles of the war from the central area in order to construct a new, modern city which will become the main business and trade centre in the Middle East, according to al-Hariri. At the same time, the government has signed a number of contracts with foreign telecommunication companies (from France, Finland, and Germany) in order to create one million telephone lines and 250,000 cellular lines.[45] Furthermore, the government has moved to rehabilitate water and power facilities, most of which were destroyed during the war. Also, plans for the expansion of Beirut's International Airport, local and international highways and railroad are already in motion. As for public schools, the national Lebanese university and public hospitals, plans and projects are still under study. In a nutshell, the estimated cost of all projects for the reconstruction of Lebanon has been placed at $18 billion by the Council of Development and Reconstruction.[46]

To be fair, between 1992 and 1994 al-Hariri has acted with determination as a catalyst for the reconstruction of Lebanon. He has succeeded in rebuilding Lebanon's destroyed infrastructure. Nevertheless, financing is slow in coming, and there are fears that the long-cherished aid and loans (estimated at 60 per cent of the total cost) from the Gulf countries and the European community might not materialize because of internal problems in these countries. One problem is lower oil prices in the Gulf countries; another is the economic recession in Europe.[47] Only 10 per cent of the aid has been received; the rest has to be raised through loans, leading to a large public debt. This approach has been strongly criticized by many Lebanese politicians, including the fundamentalist groups.

What make the fundamentalists' criticism of the Hariri cabinet acceptable to a sizable percentage of Muslims as well as Christians, not necessarily in favour of fundamentalist goals, are Hariri's seemingly misplaced priorities for reconstruction. Hariri is seen as treating Lebanon like a business acquisition simply added to his hefty portfolio. To the various opposing factions, his cabinet, including financiers, businessmen and some close aides and advisors, has been described as more of a "board of directors" than a cabinet of ministers.[48] More importantly, the inflow of capital and investments to Lebanon is concentrated in the sectors of real estate and construction and investment in treasury bank notes. Thus, prosperity has been limited to a few big businesses without expanding to other productive sectors, such as agriculture, industry and services. Certainly, this limited prosperity of the few introduced a new theme around which the fundamentalists can mobilize their constituency, and try to urge opposition to al-Hariri in other segments of the Lebanese population.

The al-Hariri cabinet is also seen negatively for its poor performance at the social level. Most Lebanese today suffer from the continuous decline of their financial status and the increasing deterioration of their living conditions. Despite the retreat of the inflationary rate from 487 per cent in 1987 to 40 per cent in 1994, a large number of citizens are not even able to cover basic expenses, such as housing, medication and education.[49] This situation is very well manipulated by the Islamists, who are increasing their popularity by offering social services, education, medicare and housing at very reasonable prices. For example, Hizbullah hospitals and clinics charge a nominal rate from those who seek their services. In Dar al-Hawra' hospital, for example, the cost of delivery and a complete checkup of the newborn does not exceed L£ 100,000 (about $50), in comparison to the thousands of dollars paid in private hospitals.[50] As for state hospitals, they remain inoperative, awaiting the government's reconstruction plan. Moreover, all schools operated by Hizbullah, the Jama'a, and the Ahbash are almost free.

Furthermore, housing and housing loans have been provided to people with limited incomes. Hizbullah's "development corporation", which operates under the supervision of the party's "Holy Construction Organ", has built hundreds of apartment buildings in the southern suburbs of Beirut and neighbouring areas, selling them at a low prices ($20,000 to $25,000) to the "oppressed".[51] In comparison, the average cost of an apartment similar to those provided by Hizbullah runs as high as $200,000 in similar areas of Beirut. However, Ras-Beirut, where the cost of an apartment runs to as high as $1 million, is an exception. Indeed, Hizbullah's construction companies are not selling luxurious apartments in comparison to those built by private contractors and construction companies. Nonetheless, they help those who are suffering from both the government's negligence and private contractors' hunger for profits. The fact remains that the government is so far unable to compete with the fundamentalist services at least at the level of providing basic services.

The most important indicator to reflect the acuity of social problems is the continuous decline of the minimum wage. Although the minimum wage has been increased three times since 1987 (the Hariri government increased the minimum wage from L£ 125,000 to L£ 200,000 which is about $100 per month) real income declined dramatically due to inflation, causing the minimum wage to fall below $60.[52] Such an income can barely cover the high bills resulting from deregulating the cost of public facilities, such as the telephone, water and electrical power, not to mention the cost of food, shelter, clothing and medicare, which cannot possibly be covered by such an income.

Overall, the government has succeeded in its financial and monetary policies; however, it has so far lagged behind in solving socio-economic problems, an important dimension of a successful public policy and political stability. As a result, social classes are highly differentiated as never before, a condition which the Islamists and the communists had earlier wanted very much. A policy of the rich getting richer and the poor getting poorer will prove to be devastating to Lebanon's reconstruction and, more importantly, to its political stability. Accordingly, the Islamists will be able to increase their representation in the next parliamentary election as long as the government is not able to compete with their services at the social level.

## Conclusion

Clearly, the Lebanese government has managed, with the help of Syria, to overcome the resistance of Islamic militant groups to some extent. Regardless of whether these groups are committed to the Ta'if agreement and its "democratization" process, participation by the Islamic movements in the last parliamentary elections in 1992 is indicative of a new strategy based on utilitarianism and accommodation rather than on complete integration in Lebanon's political system. The Islamic movements will always press for change in the name of democracy and freedom.

Thus, a possible scenario is that peace between Syria and Israel will contribute to the decline of Islamic militancy in Lebanon, but it will not eradicate the Islamic movements. The Islamic critique of the world has gained too much momentum to succumb to peace treaties. On the micro level, Syria will be reluctant to eradicate fundamentalists, especially Hizbullah, for they are needed to encounter future political imbalance with the anti-Syrian faction (mainly Christians), who will be more sympathetic to Israel than to Syria. Furthermore, the Syrian–Iranian alliance is another factor for which Syria will not eradicate Hizbullah and its affiliates. Despite Iran's rhetoric against the peace process and resulting agreements, it has not yet obstructed Syria's negotiations with Israel. On the contrary, Iran's Rafsanjani has justified Syria's actions as the natural result of pressure by the United States. Ultimately, Iran has influenced fundamentalist groups in Lebanon by directing them to avoid confrontation with both the Lebanese government and Syria. Iran and the fundamentalists will, thus, bide their time until Syria signs the peace agreement and then flow quietly with the mainstream in the Arab world. However, some extremist Shaykhs or factions, such as Subhi Tufayli and Shaykh Sha'ban's Tawhid will fight peace and normalization through available means, regardless of Syria's or Rafsanjani's influence.

Another possible scenario is that the ebb and flow of political fundamentalism in the region will finally cause Iran to fall under the control of the extremist factions of Muhtashimi and Karoubi. However, gaining the West's confidence means receiving concrete economic and financial aid from it to promote economic reform and prevent the militants' rise to power in Iran especially in Parliament. Conversely, Rafsanjani's failure means the resurgence of radicalism in both Iran and Lebanon since Iran is the guide for all fundamentalist groups.

Still another possible scenario is that Islamic radicalism in Syria will not grow in the meantime since the movement's leadership was eradicated in 1982 and since the state plays a strong role in welfare programmes, providing basic socio-economic needs for the people. In the negotiation process with Israel Asad played the fundamentalists' tune in rejecting normalization but not peace. Only in case of the absence or departure of president Asad will the fundamentalists, especially the Muslim Brotherhood, ascend to power in Syria.

The fundamentalists, now accommodated in the Lebanese parliament, have made social reform their political platform against the Hariri government. Their social and welfare activities, particularly Hizbullah's, demonstrate that the government's reconstruction policy has ignored the socio-economic dimension in its plans. While the Hariri government has succeeded at the financial and monetary levels, it has a poor record at the socio-economic level. It is true that the reconstruction of Lebanon may need ten years or so, but reconstruction should not be based on a corporate business mentality alone. The socio-economic dimension of any pubic policy is a key factor for stability in any country. Unless the Hariri government challenges the fundamentalist social and welfare programmes, providing basic and decent public facilities (water, power, telephones, transportation, schools and state hospitals), the present Lebanese government and future ones will have to deal with Islamic militant movements long after a Lebanese/Syrian–Israel peace treaty comes into being. As the great Greek historian Thucydides once said, "an excessive deprivation of one's basic value would lead to reckless pursuit of that value."

## Table 1: Islamic Movements in Lebanon

| | Name of Organization | Sect | Militancy | Leadership | Size | Current Status | Ties |
|---|---|---|---|---|---|---|---|
| 1. | Hizbullah (Party of God) | Shi'ite | High | Collective Ayatollah Muhammad Husayn Fadlallah (spiritual guide) Sayyid Hasan Nasrallah (General Secreatary) Shaykh Na'im Qasim (Vice-Secretary) | Large | Active, public since 1984 (won 6 parliamentary seats in the elections of 1992) | Iran |
| a. | al-Muqawama al-Islamiyya (Islamic Resistance) | Shi'ite after 1984 | High | Shaykh Nabil Qawouk (spokesman) | Small (trained fighters) | Hizbullah's combat organ, active since 1984 | Iran |
| b. | al-Jihad al-Islami (Islamic Holy War) | Shi'ite | High | Imad Mugniyyah (dismissed 1985) | Small | Hizbullah's assassination organ; held hostages Inactive since 1992 | Iran |
| c. | Munazzamat al-Adala al-Thawriyya (Revolutionary Justice Organization) | Shi'ite | High | Unknown | Small | Inactive since 1988; held hostages | Iran |
| d. | Munazzamat al-Mustad'afin fi'l-Ard (Organization of the Oppressed on Earth) | Shi'ite | High | Unknown | Small | Inactive since 1988; held hostages | Iran |
| 2. | Harakat Amal al-Islamiyya (Islamic Amal Movement) | Shi'ite | High | Charismatic Husayn al-Musawi | Small | Active, public since 1982 | Iran Syria Hizbullah |

| | Name of Organization | Sect | Militancy | Leadership | Size | Current Status | Ties |
|---|---|---|---|---|---|---|---|
| 3. | Majmuʿat Husayn al-Intihariyya (Husayn Suicide Squads) | Shiʿite | High | Charismatic Abu Haydar al-Musawi | Small | Inactive since 1982 | Iran |
| 4. | al-Haraka al-Islamiyya (Islamic Movement) | Shiʿite | High | Charismatic Sayyid Sadiq al-Musawi | Small | Inactive since 1989 | Iran |
| 5. | al-Muqawama al-Muʾmina (The Faithful Resistance) | Shiʿite | High | Collective Shaykh Adib Haydar and Mustapha al-Dirani (kidnapped by Israel 1994) | Small (trained fighters) | Active since 1986 | Iran Hizbullah |
| 6. | al-Jamaʿa al-Islamiyya (Islamic Association) | Sunni | High | Collective Fathi Yakan (spiritual guide) Faysal Mawlawi (General Secretary) | Large | Active, public since 1967 (won 3 seats in the elections of 1992) | Muslim Brethren (in Syria, Jordan, and Egypt) |
| 7. | Harakat al-Tawhid al-Islami (Islamic Unity Movement) | Sunni | High | Charismatic Shaykh Saʿid Shaʿban (Amir) | Small | Active since 1982 | Iran Sudan Hizbullah |

| Name of Organization | Sect | Militancy | Leadership | Size | Current Status | Ties |
|---|---|---|---|---|---|---|
| 8. Jam'iyyat al-Mashari' al-Khayriyya al-Islamiyya (Islamic Philanthropic Society of Projects) al-Ashbah | Sunni | Low (spiritual revivalist) | Charismatic/collective Shaykh Abdullah al-Habashi (spiritual guide) Shaykh Husam Karrakirah (President) | Large | Active since 1975 (won one seat in the elections of 1992) | Syria Jordan Egypt |
| 9. Jabhat al-Muqawama al-Islamiyya al-Lubnaniyya (Lebanese Islamic Resistance Front) | Sunni | High | Charismatic Shaykh 'Abd al-Hafiz Qasim | Medium/ small | Inactive since 1984 | Pro-Palestinian |
| 10. al-Harakat al-Islamiyya al-Mujahida (Islamic Struggle Movement) | Sunni | High | Charismatic Shaykh Abdallah al-Hallaq | Small | Semi-active since 1987 | Pro-Palestinian |
| 11. 'Ibad al-Rahman (Worshippers of the Compassionate) | Sunni | Low (spiritual revivalist) | Collective Abdel-Rahman al-Houri (spokesman) | Small | Active since 1958 | Egypt |
| 12. Harakat al-Muqawara al-Islamiyya (Hamas) | Sunni | High | Collective Ahmad Yassin (spiritual guide) Imad al-Ali (spokesman for Lebanon's branch) | Medium/ large | Active since 1986 | Palestinian Muslim Brethren (Syria, Jordan, Egypt) Iran & Sudan |

| Name of Organization | Sect | Militancy | Leadership | Size | Current Status | Ties |
|---|---|---|---|---|---|---|
| 13. Harakat al-Jihad al-Islami fi Filastin (Movement of the Islamic Struggle in Palestine) | Sunni | High | Collective Shaykh Ziad Nakhal (spiritual guide) Shaykh 'Abd al-'Aziz Awdeh (spokesman in Lebanon) Muhammad Abu Samra (General Secretary) | Medium/ small | Active since 1986 | Palestinian Iran Sudan |
| 14. Ansar al-Oussbah al-Islamiyya (Supporters of Islamic League) | Sunni | High | Ahmad El-Saadi (known as Abu Mehjen) | Small | New, active since 1995; assassinated Shaykh Nizar al-Hatabi (former president of al-Ahbash) | Palestinian Sudan al-Jama'a al-Islamiyya |
| 15. al-Jabhat al-Islamiyya (The Islamic Front) | Sunni and Shi'ite | High | Collective Shaykh Muharam al-Arifi (Sunni) (General Secretary) Sayyid Muhammad Hasan al-Amin (Shi'ite) | Small | Active since 1985 | Pro-Palestinian Iran Sudan |
| 16. Tajammu' al-'Ulama' al-Muslimin (Association of Muslim Clergy) | Sunni and Shi'ite | Low | Collective Shaykh Mahir Hammud (Sunni) (President) Shaykh Zuhair Kanj (Shi'ite) | Small | Active since 1982 | Sudan Iran All Islamic militant groups |

Source: Author's data

# NOTES

1  For further explanation of crisis conditions, see John Esposito, *Islam and Politics* (Syracuse, NY: Syracuse University Press, 1991); James Piscatori, ed. *Islam in the Political Process* (Cambridge: Cambridge University Press, 1983); R. Hrair Dekmejian, *Islam in Revolution* (Syracuse, NY: Syracuse University Press, 1985); Shireen T. Hunter, ed., *The Politics of Islamic Revivalism: Diversity and Unity* (Bloomington: Indiana University Press, 1988); Mary-Jane Deeb, "Militant Islam and Politics of Redemption", *Annals*, American Academy for Political Social Science (AAPSS), No. 524 (November 1992); Emmanuel Sivan, *Radical Islam* (New Haven, CT: Yale University Press, 1985); Michael C. Hudson, "Democratization in the Middle East", *American Arab Affairs*, No. 36 (spring 1991); Jihad 'Awda, "al-Haraka al-Islamiyya", (The Islamic Movement) *Al-Khahirah*, No. 130 (September 1993), pp. 46–55.

2  A. Nizar Hamzeh and R. Hrair Dekmejian, "Islamic Spectrum of Lebanese Politics", *Journal of South Asian and Middle Eastern Studies*, Vol. XVI, No. 3 (spring 1993), pp. 25–6.

3  John L. Esposito, "Islamic Movements, Democratization and US Foreign Policy", *Riding the Tiger: The Middle East Challenge After the Cold War*, ed. Phebe Mars and William Lewis (Boulder, Colorado: Westview Press, 1993), pp. 187–90.

4  Ibid.

5  On that point, see Shaykh Abdallah al-Habashi, *Sarih al-Bayan* (Beirut: Islamic Studies and Research section, Jami'yyat al-Mashari' al-Khayriyya al-Islamiyya,1990), p. 118.

6  *Manar al-Huda*, April–May 1993, p. 49.

7  Ibid., November 1992 , p. 6; April–May 1993, p. 6.

8  For further analysis of the leadership and membership of al-Jama'a al-Islamiyya and the *Tawhid*, see A. Nizar Hamzeh and R. Hrair Dekmejian, "Islamic Spectrum", pp. 29–32; as for Hizbullah's politburo, see A. Nizar Hamzeh, "Lebanon's Hizbullah: From Islamic Revolution to Parliamentary Accommodation", *Third World Quarterly*, Vol. 14, No. 2 (1993), pp. 325–6.

9  Ibid.; see also Esposito, "Islamic Movements, Democratization", p. 190.

10 For excellent analysis of the Ta'if Accord, see Augustus Richard Norton, "Lebanon after Ta'if: Is the Civil War over?", *The Middle East Journal*, 45:3 (summer 1991), pp. 471–3.

11 See interview with Zouhair al-Obeid, member of the Jama'a politburo in *al-Safir*, 2 September 1992, p. 4 and 13 July 1992, p. 4.

12 See *al-Safir*, 10 September 1992, p. 3 ; also *Manar al-Huda*, August–September, 1993, pp. 30–2.

13 See Martin Kramer, "Hizbullah: The Calculus of Jihad", *Bulletin, The American Academy of Arts and Sciences*, Vol. XLVII, No. 8 (May 1994), pp. 41–2; also Hamzeh, "Lebanon's Hizbullah", pp. 324–5.

14 For example, see Richard W. Bulliet, "The Israeli–PLO Accord: the Future of the Islamic Movement", *Foreign Affairs*, 72:5 (November–December 1993), pp. 43–4; Ghassan Salame, "Islam and the West", *Foreign Policy*, No. 90 (spring 1993), pp. 35–6; R. Hrair Dekmejian, *Islam in Revolution*, pp. 168–75.

15 See Hizbullah's open letter cited in Augustus Richard Norton, *Amal and the Shi'a: the Struggle for the Soul of Lebanon* (Texas, Austin: University of Texas Press, 1987) pp. 167–87; Fathi Yakan, *al-Mawsu'a al-harakiyya* (Aman: Dar al-Bashir, 1983), pp. 247–60; Marius Deeb, *Militant Islamic Movements in Lebanon: Origins, Social Basis and Ideologies* (Washington, DC: Center for Contemporary Arab Studies, 1986), pp. 7–8.

16 See Hamzeh and Dekmejian, "Islamic Spectrum", pp. 29–41; also Hamzeh, "Lebanon's Hizbullah", pp. 327–9; Esposito, "Islamic Movements, Democratization", p. 191.

17 See *al-Wasat*, 2 May 1994, p. 15.

18 Ibid., 24 January 1994, p. 17.

19 Ibid.

20 See interview with Ali Akbar Wilayati, *al-Wasat*, 14 March 1994, pp. 22–3; see also interview with Sayyid Muhammad Hussein Fadlallah in *al-Wasat*, 5 April 1994, p. 18.

21 Ibid., 2 April 1994, p. 16; see also Ali Jouny, "al-Haraka al-Islamiyya bayna al-muhadna wal-sidam", *Shu'un al-'Awsat*, No. 30, 1994, pp. 116–22.

22 See interview with Sayyid Muhammad Husayn Fadlallah in *al-Wasat*, 8 November 1993, p. 24; also an interview with Sayyid Hasan Nasrallah in *al-Wasat*, 25 September 1993, p. 27.

23 See interview with Shaykh Subhi Tufayli in *al-Hayat*, 25 January 1994, p. 3.

24 *al-'Alam* 26 October 1991, pp. 14–17; see also Judith Miller, "The Challenge of Radical Islam", *Foreign Affairs* (spring 1993), pp. 43–4.

25 See interview with Muhammad Husayn Fadlallah in *al-Wasat*, 8 September 1993, pp. 21–2.

26 Ali Akbar Muhtashimi's call was cited by Safa Husri, "Iran's Positive Attitude", *Middle East International*, No. 456, 6 August 1993, p. 6.

27 *al-Wasat* 31 May 1993, p. 29.

28 Hamzeh, "Lebanon's Hizbullah", p. 324.

29 *al-Wasat*, 7 June 1993, p. 14.

30 Ibid., p. 13.

31 Cited in ibid., p. 14.

32 Dekmejian, *Islam in Revolution*, pp. 118–25.

33 Sivan's analysis of the future of the Islamic movements in the Arab World in the meeting held with French officials was reported by *al-Wasat*, 29 March 1994, pp. 17–20; see also Sivan, *Radical Islam*, pp. 45–6.

34 See Michael Hudson, "After the Gulf War: Prospects for Democratization in the Arab World", *Middle East Journal*, 45:3 (summer 1991), p. 408; for Syria's case see Steven Heydemann "Can We Get There From Here? Lessons From the System Case", *American Arab Affairs* No. 36 (spring 1991), pp. 27–9.

35 Dekmejian, *Islam in Revolution.*

36 See interview with Hafiz al-Asad, *Al-Wasat*, 10 May 1993, pp. 14–15.

37 See Hamzeh and Dekmejian, "Islamic Spectrum", pp. 25–42; Salim al-Hoss, "Horizons of Prospective Change in Lebanon", *The Beirut Review*, No. 3 (spring 1992), pp. 4–5.

38 See *al-Shira'*, 11 May 1992, pp. 16–17.

39 *al-Safir*, 17 October 1992, p. 4.

40 Figures were obtained from *al-Wasat*, 7 July 1994, p. 38; see also Yusif al-Khalil, "Economic Development in Lebanon since 1982", *The Beirut Review*, No. 3 (spring 1992), pp. 83–94.

41 *al-Wasat*, 11 July 1994, p. 38.

42 Ibid.

43 Ibid.

44 Ibid.

45 Ibid., p. 39.

46 Ibid.

47 Ibid.

48 *al-Nahar*, 15 December 1994, pp. 4–5.

49 al-Khalil, "Economic Development", p. 87.

50 For more details of *Hizbullah*'s social review see Hamzeh, "Lebanon's Hizbullah", pp. 327 and 329.

51 *al-Wasat*, 2 May 1994, p. 13.

52 For more details see al-Khalil, "Economic Development", p. 100; *al-Shira'*, 11 May 1992, pp.18–19; *al-Nahar*, 22 August 1994, p. 7.

# 10

# The Islamic–Capitalist State of Saudi Arabia: The Surfacing of Fundamentalism

*Michel G. Nehme*

The purpose of this chapter is to present and analyse the actions and reactions of the Saudi state regarding the contention between two competing parties within the informal political establishment. On the one hand, there are the religious fundamentalists who still adhere to the strict application of the *shari'a* that was in use in the Muslim world before the onset of Westernizing reforms. On the other hand, there are the Muslim liberals who are essentially materialistic in their political conduct, are entrenched in the capitalist mode of economic behaviour and consumption, and solicit political and social reforms. The gap between the two groups has been growing wider and deeper ever since the implementation of the five-year development plans which, though they promote Islam, are nonetheless capitalist in scope and nature. While Islamic Wahhabi fundamentalism was the unifying force in the early Saudi state, it is now increasingly becoming an element of controversy. The royal family is doing all it can to enhance the cohesion between these two groups; however, the political, economic, and social reality is becoming too complex for them to cope with.

A few points should be clarified to avoid confusion. Wahhabism, originally, was indeed a fundamentalist militant phenomenon. However, since the Al Saud family established its power in the state, its version of Wahhabi fundamentalism has lost its original zeal. It is true that the Saudis are known to encourage and finance fundamentalist movements and programmes abroad, but this does not mean that the regime follows strict fundamentalist policies domestically.

## Wahhabi Fundamentalism

It was in Najd (a district in Saudi Arabia) that Islamic fundamentalism as an ideology and a political-military movement witnessed its birth and revival against the Ottomans who held the caliphate seat. The first sign was when Muhammad ibn Saud formed an alliance with the religious leader Muhammad ibn 'Abd al-Wahhab in 1745, and the second in 1912 when 'Abd al-'Aziz Al Saud formed a military movement called the Ikhwan (brethren) in an agricultural community at Artrawiya near Riyadh.

Historically, every time Saudi society witnessed a cultural challenge and an external intimidation, Wahhabism retorted by producing strong, brutal, fundamentalist and military organizations. An example of that is the Ikhwan movement of 1912–28, an Islamic reaction against the first Western infringement in the heart of the Arabian peninsula, especially in the Hijaz region. The Ikhwan assisted in the conquest and unification of what is now Saudi Arabia. They were the forerunners of men like Juhaiman al-Utaiby, leader of the group that led the armed revolt against the Saudi authorities, and seized the Great Mosque in 1979. Their indoctrination could be traced to the early Hanbali political theorist, Taqiy al-Din Ahmad ibn Taymiyya, who rejected the innovative practices of his day and called for a return to the original doctrines of Islam. The Ikhwan embraced one of the most revolutionary political ideologies in Islamic history, outrivalling by far, in purely intellectual terms, the Shi'ite Islamic fundamentalism of Iran after the Khomeini revolution. The Ikhwan claimed that political legitimacy came only from strict adherence to the fundamentalist teachings of the *shari'a* (Islamic law). Any ruler who did not follow God's law, Muslim or not, was not legitimate, and the Muslim community was obliged to rise against him in *jihad* (holy war). Muslim fundamentalists in the different states of the Middle East rely to a certain degree on the same teachings to justify their struggle against incumbent governments.

The Ikhwan's growing strength posed a threat to 'Abd al-'Aziz's ambition of establishing a moderate kingdom. He disbanded them and limited their strength. When they rebelled against him, he manipulated them and instigated their forces to fight against the British in the Southern parts of Iraq where they were totally crushed and defeated.[1] The Saudi regime has lost its Islamic revolutionary fervour of military adventurism beyond the Saudi state, but not its fundamentalist principles. The Wahhabi revival movement kept on shielding the regime against foreign and domestic threats. Saudi Arabia was never easily accessible to political upheaval from the leftist movements or from Shi'ite fundamentalism.

The Wahhabi doctrine saved the legitimacy of the regime against the chaotic reign of King Saud (1953–64), the peril of progressive movements in the late 1960s, the 1970s dissident left-wing Saudi groups operating out of Iraq where they were given safe asylum, the Shi'ite riots of 1979–80, and a ten year campaign of harsh propaganda against the royal family by the Shi'ite fundamentalists of Iran. The Wahhabis consider communism, socialism and Shi'ism as anathema to Islam, thus providing a strong justification for the regime to brutally crush any indication of such tendencies.

A return to the revolutionary tendencies of the Ikhwan and Juhaiman within the Wahhabi doctrine, which is deeply imbedded in the psyche and culture of some cliques, offers a far more serious threat to the status quo and its pro-Western capitalist position. Right after the 1991 Gulf war, the Wahhabi fundamentalists terrified many Saudis, including some in the royal family.[2] Even though they may be a minority (appropriate statistics are lacking), there is the belief that they are gaining strength. They base their resentments on the growing maldistribution of wealth. While no Saudi is suffering from hunger, the ever-growing gap between the wealthy few and the majority of salaried Saudis has bred envy that is exploited by fundamentalist forces. Recently, alarmed by their growing militarism, King Fahd dynamically and without using force constricted them to a defined framework within which they could function.[3] The demand of the fundamentalist Wahhabis to impose their convictions on the state poses a threat on the development strategy of the ruling elites. Thus, they have to be manipulated. It is conceivable that the fundamentalist, in using the regime's own Wahhabi ideology, might seek to overthrow the regime, not for the principles it espouses, but for its failure to live up to those principles. Opposition to the regime's ties with the secular United States and, by association, with Zionist Israel, and the introduction of Western values into the economic sector of Saudi Arabia could easily justify a rebellious act against the state.[4]

## Origin of Capitalism in Saudi Arabia

At the turn of the century, the Saudi family allied with Wahhabism were able to unite previously divided tribes. They forced sedentarization of certain tribes, and they attacked the nomadic structure of peninsular society. This was accomplished by British support and involvement in the internal affairs of Saudi Arabia.[5] The great increase in oil revenues paid to 'Abd al-'Aziz led to the rise of a newly strengthened state eager to advance its own interests and to exploit its collaboration with the capitalist West and Japan. Though the state was united on a traditional ideology, unity of religion and loyalty to one family, making Saudi Arabia the only state in the world that was ruled by a single dynasty, the general reorganization of the state economy prepared the ground for capitalism. What accelerated the introduction of capitalist economic values in the society was the unstable anachronistic status quo that required outside support to survive. Oil and Western investments fulfilled this function.[6]

In 1933 Saudi Arabia had to face a severe financial crisis because its vital source of income – funds generated from Muslim pilgrimage – had been undermined. Standard Oil of California offered 50,000 pounds in gold in return for oil concessions. This oil company later merged with three other American companies and formed the Arab-American Oil Company (ARAMCO). This company first initiated relations between the American government and the Saudi family. US officials occasionally had to scheme to justify their continuous support for the Saudi royal family. By 1947 Saudi Arabia received an estimated $100 million in American aid and much more in the following two decades.

In 1953, 'Abd al-'Aziz died, and he was succeeded by his son Saud. Though Saudi–US relations during the latter's reign were not at their best, capitalism, though not institutionalized, was already entrenched in the economic system of Saudi Arabia. It was with the coming of Faysal to power that capitalism was officially adopted as the economic trend in the Saudi system. Back in 1966, King Faysal said:

> We are going ahead with extensive planning, guided by our Islamic laws and beliefs . . . We have chosen an economic system based on free enterprise because it is our conviction that it fits perfectly with our Islamic laws and suits our country by granting every opportunity to the people, giving incentives to every individual and to every group to work for the common good. . . we will interfere when the government finds it necessary to do so, but without harming the basic principle involved.[7]

Faysal was the first to think seriously about economic planning. His first step was to create a planning apparatus with the help of the International Monetary Fund (IMF). The latter recommended the establishment of an economic development committee. Faysal, following this recommendation, established the Committee for Economic Development in 1959. This Committee evolved by 1965 into the Central Planning Organization (CPO).

In 1968, the CPO invited foreign advisory groups to assist Saudi Arabia in the fields of planning and development. One of these groups was the Stanford Research Institute (SRI) of California, which did not function as an independent body of the CPO but rather became a part of its staff.[8] In 1970, the CPO submitted to Faysal the first five-year plan. It included guidelines for systematic action in every field of the economic and social sectors of Saudi Arabia.[9]

In any global strategy of economic and social development major political choices have to be made. While the five-year plan became a programme adopted mostly by Third World countries to overcome their economic backwardness and move on the road to modernization, almost all of these countries applauded the experience of the Soviet Union and implemented a socialist or semi-socialist approach in their socio-economic schemes. However, in the case of Saudi Arabia it was different in the sense that the five-year plans were totally based on pure capitalist concepts. The plan, devised with the assistance of American consultants, could not have been different.

The manner in which the five-year plans were implemented accelerated the growth of urban areas, creating a massive concentration of population in less than ten big cities. At the same time, it enlarged the size of the middle class and created a relatively new type of lower class. Now, it is easy to distinguish classes according to their social status, profession and the way they earn their living.[10]

As a mandate of the development plans, the agricultural sector has been modernized. The government established large mechanized capitalist agricultural units, replacing the traditional labour-intensive system by modern capital intensive methods.[11] Most farmers and small agrarian landowners have been driven to the cities. This new class of city dwellers hold a social and economic location that pressures the system. Forming splinter-groups in their new locale, they compose potential forces for political reform. Those who are experiencing relative disadvantage from the existing order are apt to be much more resentful of the capitalist system. They nourish, each within his own group, religious tendencies in their fight for a better share in the economy.

The extensive, rapid, and abrupt socio-economic change that these new city dwellers are experiencing is an unsettling and perplexing human experience. It is creating a strain in their psyche and a crisis in their social order. Their old ways, familiar environments, long perpetuated habits, and old social and economic roles have become useless, while a new way of life and a new routine to suit the changes are not comprehended, liked, or fully adopted. Adapting to their refuge allowed old tribal values, such as those of hierarchy, obedience, and paterfamilias, to be transferred from tribal context to that of all-powerful religious symbols.[12]

Change, as a result of the capitalist five-year plans, has come to Saudi Arabia at a blinding pace. In 1950, there were virtually no college graduates, and few secondary school graduates. Now, tens of thousands have earned university degrees domestically and abroad. They have high expectations to fill important positions in their own society comparable to their educational status. They demand their economic share in the system; if this is not met, they turn to their Islamic rights to oppose the political and social process.

The ruling family, aware of this dilemma, has enlarged the government bureaucracy to absorb the ambition of the young to serve. But as the need for managerial posts in the government is declining, and lucrative positions in the private sector are limited, the frustration of the young educated urban class will translate itself into disaffection with the capitalist mode of development.[13]

Though the development plans were devised to encourage capitalist tendencies, i.e. to diversify the sources of national income, to create private investments independent of the state, and to reduce dependence on oil, national income became on the contrary more dependent on government spending out of oil revenues. The reason for this was the way in which the government utilized its funds. It contributed to the creation of the huge job market involving a large proportion of the population, all dependent on government-financed businesses and their subsidiaries; under those circumstances the capitalist mode of development was not successful by its own value-oriented logic. It has defeated its own purpose, that is, private and independent entrepreneurship and individual initiatives. Government spending in Saudi Arabia has proved to be the dominant moving force in the economy.[14] The private sector is now more than ever dependent on government expenditure, both directly through investments allocated for infrastructure, services and industrial projects, and indirectly through loans and subsidies. Revenues from oil export are still what holds the state economy and polity together. This means any reduction in the country's oil production could shock the Saudi economy and government.

## Side-Effects of Capitalism

From the beginning, the royal family planned to amalgamate Islamic values with capitalist modes of development. However, this plan produced non-regime-sponsored fundamentalist strains. These strains are manifested in several religious currents. There are a number of clerics that consider the official orthodoxy too lax in its tolerance of the market-oriented innovations brought about by capitalism and modernization. While discontent among these clerics seems to be tamed by the government, there runs within the urban areas a more radical fundamentalist current.[15]

The fundamentalist current stands firm against the institutionalization of Western capitalism, and denounces corruption among the royal family. Such a current was exemplified by the group that seized the Grand Mosque of Mecca in 1979. Though the band that seized the mosque numbered only around two hundred, nonetheless, what they did is significant and worth assessing.

The seizure of the Grand Mosque was led by Juhaiman bin Muhammad bin Saif al-Utaibi, who came from a well-known tribe, the Utaiba. Juhaiman entered al-Madina College of Technology in 1972 and came into contact with other Saudi and non-Saudi students who were all interested in learning about Islam. This college is one of many Islamic schools in Saudi Arabia which are sponsored and financed by the government for the purpose of promoting the religious values of Islam. Juhayman formed a group whose orientation towards Islamic teaching was similar to that of the Salafi movement. By the mid-1970s the group was easily recognized by its peculiar style. It was very active and openly preached strict adherence to Islam, an end to women's education, and the dangers of capitalist Western values to Saudi society; it also criticized the royal family.[16] Juhaiman and a large number of his group were arrested in June 1979, and then released on the grounds that they were young and misguided but nonetheless sincere Muslims.

When Juhaiman and his group seized the Grand Mosque of Mecca, their principal demand was the abolition of loyalty to the royal family for the following reasons:

1.   The Saudi family has strayed far from the teachings of Islam.

2.   The Saudi family is supplying the United States and Israel with oil and money.

3.   The Saudi family has harboured agents of the CIA.

4.   The Saudi state has deprived the Saudis of their right to self-expression.

5.   The government has become a source of corruption, bribery, and waste of the nation's money.

6.   The hypocrites who speak in the name of religion, especially the Shaykhs Harakan Louhaydan, Tantawi, Shawaf, and Sha'rawi, are considered puppets of the regime.[17]

The incident showed significant social dissatisfaction among some of the tribes, such as the Utaiba, Dawasir, the Yam tribes in Najran and some of the Qahtan and the Mutayr tribes. Historically, these tribes had opposed the Saudi family, but were coerced and drawn into the system as allies. The capitalist mode of development had alienated some members of these tribes enough for them to resort to armed struggle, the only way they know how to express their grievances against the emerging modern and Western capitalist mode of life.[18]

The speed with which the Saudi economy is being transformed from extremely traditional to capitalist and modern has created many contradictions, dualities and paradoxes in the personalities of Saudi individuals. The majority of Saudis have not changed their mentality as rapidly as they have changed their material conditions. The tribal system of values has not been totally forgotten. The capitalist reformers understand and relate to these values and try to tolerate them. They are convinced that it is in their best interest to keep politics as part of religion. However, Islam is a personal faith, a theological doctrine, and has never meant the same thing to all people. This diversity of understanding has caused numerous social and political conflicts in the Muslim world.

While some Islamic countries were affected by the stock of Western ideas first and then attempted to apply these ideas to their lives, the Saudis received the material components first; it was afterwards that these material components began to pose a challenge to their cultural and belief system. In response to this challenge, the Saudis split mainly into two Islamic orientational tendencies. Who is for and who is against Islamic adaptation of the capitalist mode of development is a complex question. The Saudi orientation is abstracted from a composite reality in which the attitudes and outlooks of the individual Saudi are more likely to shift from one tendency to the other, reflecting a paradoxical behaviour that can be linked to the issues involved, and the personal stake and private interests at hand.

As to the royal family, the senior members have traditionally been in favour of enforcing Wahhabi practices.[19]

If fundamentalism considers that the Qur'an is not the only source of value, that the conduct of the prophet Muhammad and the first generations of his followers is also normative, then many aspects of Saudi life failed to pass the test of fundamentalism.[20] The most obvious of these are the regulations on commerce which imply the legitimization of interest (usury), the oil concessions which were drawn up in terms of Western contract law, investing Saudi capitals in foreign societies according to Western principles, inviting non-Muslim armies to station troops, tolerance of the infidel Jews, and smoking.

It is appropriate to turn to the categories of capitalism and Islamic culture for an explanation of Saudi fundamentalism. Ever since the inception of the Saudi regime and the implementation of the development plans, the very organization of the adopted capitalist system and actions resulting from development have systematically promoted fundamentalism. While regime legitimacy in the Middle East is traditionally weak, the association between the Saudi family and Wahhabism appears to fulfil the old Islamic ideal of the legitimate state. The implication is that the ruler is a devout Muslim ruling with the advice of the *ulama* and in accordance with the *shari'a*. Islamic propaganda and values thus interfuse every aspect of social life. There is even a religious police (*Mutatawi'a*) to enforce Islamic traditions. Television and radio broadcasts are censored by the clerics and they exhibit a high Islamic content. Moreover, the religious authorities control much of the judicial system and control much of educational affairs.[21] But upholding the pure faith is a double-edged sword; while it defends the legitimacy of the royal family, it taps a powerful current of popular opinion critical of any contradiction with what is being advocated. Thus, pragmatism in conducting domestic and foreign policy, the Saudi royal family's reliance on temporal values and adoption of a Western outlook and behaviour are instigating the growth of fundamental tendencies.

## The Saudi System after the Second Gulf War

The difficulty in understanding the Saudi system is due to its conservative outward appearance despite the dramatic social, economic, and institutional changes since the consolidation of the state under Abd al-Aziz in the 1920s and 1930s. Oil wealth has provided immense resources to a country that as recently as the early 1970s was nearly bankrupt. While studying the impact of capitalism is necessary to understand some present-day realities, the role of Islamic fundamentalism and Islamic culture and values explains much of what is taking place in Saudi Arabia.[22]

The Gulf war of 1991, and the establishment of the Consultative Council associated with the announcement of the Basic System of Rules in 1992, have marked the upsurge of a new outlook in the kingdom of Saudi Arabia. Saudis of all strata are vigorously debating their future. There have not been such insecurities and fears in Saudi society since the discovery of oil. Anxiety, within their present political socialization, makes the majority concede to the rule of the Al Saud and to the strict mandate of Islamic laws. But for the first time, there is growing public demand for increased participation in decision-making.[23]

The phenomenon of increased demand for sharing in the decision-making process in Saudi Arabia is enshrined in Islamic doctrines. It challenges all existing Western hypotheses that correlate between economic growth, social change, modernization and democracy. The dynamics of social-cultural transformation at the level of the masses in a society that witnesses economic modernization are more complex in Saudi Arabia than Western paradigms of social and political development could explain – whether the dichotomy of traditionalism versus modernization or political economy theories.[24] The ruling elites are drawn from tribal-religious formations. The tribe in Saudi Arabia, far from being a rigid structure, as is often insinuated, has exhibited a significant capacity for adaptation to changing social conditions while maintaining the old symbols of religious cohesiveness and tenaciously adopting patriotic and religious-sectarian entitlement.[25] Most Saudis and specially the social elites, longing for change, do not challenge the legitimacy of their government. Instead, they direct their contentions towards the government's policy of confined participation and of elevating America's interests above its own. This by no means implies a deviation from Islamic convictions or the demand for a wholesale imposition of Western democracy. Neither the multi-party systems of the Western countries, nor the single-party regimes, command admiration among the Saudis.[26]

The Washington-based International Committee for Human Rights in the Gulf and Arabian Peninsula, made up largely of Saudi dissidents, asserts that the recent Gulf war and its concomitants in Saudi Arabia created a growing political awareness among the various religious factions of their civil rights and liberties as perceived by true Islamic teachings.[27] Many young Saudis living abroad see religious fraternity inside Saudi Arabia as the appropriate way to demand a better share in the state and to provoke the ruling family to action.[28]

## Pressures for Change

The global, regional and domestic thrust to develop and modernize left the Government in Saudi Arabia with no choice but to conform. As Huntington has noted:

> The principal threat to the stability of traditional society comes not from foreign invasions by foreign armies, but from invasion by foreign ideas . . . Nineteenth century monarchs modernized to thwart imperialism; twentieth century monarchs modernize to thwart revolution[29]

The boom in state oil revenues since 1973 provided the royal family with the leverage to maintain the kingdom integrated and stable. However, accelerating state-controlled capitalist modes of development dragged Saudi Arabia into profound exposure to the West. The backlash of the ruling elites was to intensify the promotion of Islamic values. They have been spending fat sums from their budget on building mosques and promoting Islamic indoctrination at all levels of educational institutions. Another chunky aggregate is spent on their Islamic propaganda in the state-financed mass media domestically and abroad.[30] There is a strong tendency among the elites of the royal family to maintain Saudi Arabia as a traditional Islamic kingdom and an absolute monarchy.

The profound exposure of Saudi Arabia to the West and especially its experience during and after the second Gulf war, undermined the old tribal formula whereby the king shared power with other tribal institutions and Islamic groups. In 1992, and under pressure from both traditionalists and reformers to be given a more active role in the decision making process, King Fahd established the Consultative Council in association with the initiation of the Basic System of Rule. This new step, if one is to thoroughly analyse the documents, may help in widening the base for discussion of policy but definitely it does not allow for sharing in politics; in reality the king's powers are absolute.[31]

Saudi kings have never intended to allow wider sharing in the power of the state and have never recognized elections of representatives. Before the unification of what now is Saudi Arabia, there used to be a system of municipal elections in the cities of the Hijaz region. They were abolished by the king in 1927 right after he established firm control over these cities.[32] For those steeped in Western traditions, it is difficult to understand the regime's source of legitimacy. The monarch proclaims that all important decisions are based on consensus, through informal institutions called Majalis al-Shura (Consultative Council). In reality, two separate procedures of consultation are followed depending on the nature of the issue at stake. If it is an important political issue, the king deliberates with a small orbit of members within the senior ranking royal family. If the issue is civil, conferrals by the king could involve a variety of elites: technocrats, personal associates and foreign consultants.

The initiation of the Basic System of Rules in March 1992 did not change the established political reality. The Saudi regime still forbids the formation of political parties and social organizations. There is no parliament (the Consultative Council is part of an Organizing Authority and not a Legislature Authority), no elections and no constitution. The usage of the term *dustur* (constitution) is blameworthy; it is always rejected by the ruling elite of Saudi Arabia. Saudis believe that there is only one divine constitution and that is the Qur'an. The new Basic System of Rules is not a constitution. It is an additional written document that legalizes the patriarchal principles of dominion. The other four documents are: the decree uniting the Hijaz and Najd (1927); the decree announcing the establishment of the Kingdom of Saudi Arabia (1932); the regulations of the Council of Ministers (1958); the decree of the Hijaz (1962).[33] The source of sovereign power is not mentioned in any of these decrees; it is assumed to rest on the right of conquest. The basic law of the country is the Islamic *shari'a* as interpreted within the *Hanbali* school. A second set of legal provisions governs affairs like the traffic code and the industrial accident code, etc. . . . The two types of law are administered separately; religious authorities enforce the basic law, the governor or the local emir administers the decrees.[34] Political opposition is strictly forbidden, and trade unions are illegal, as is the right to strike.

There are some traditional channels for the redress of grievances. Most Saudi rulers still hold the majlis which provides ordinary citizens with a chance to bring problems directly to the ruler's attention. Petitions are accepted and may be acted upon, but the majlis is in no way a forum for discussing national and political reforms or the limits of power.

The process, content, and outcome of the organizational and administrative reforms proclaimed by the Basic System of Rules in March 1992 do not represent a retreat from the tradition of the past nor do they negate the fundamental concepts of the conventional order. The people (including the opposition) as custom dictates, were not in any way involved in the making of these reforms.[35] The decree's rhetoric lacks substance and evades any concrete commitment in displaying the actual prerogatives and powers of these newly established institutions. Saudi Arabia was, and still is, governed by a central endowment – the king, assisted by the Council of Ministers which was formatively founded after the death of the kingdom's founder 'Abd al-'Aziz in 1953.

The establishment of a Consultative Council (Majlis al-Shura) is not relatively new in the history of Saudi Arabia. The People's Council (al-Majlis al-Ahli) was established right after the Hijaz region was conquered and annexed to the kingdom. This Council's by-laws including its name were amended several times to reflect its devalued power.[36] The new Consultative Council, in reality, enjoys negligible power. Like the old one, all of its members are appointed by the king. It reviews only matters submitted for its evaluation by the executive. All its recommendations are subject to the approval of the king, whose power extends to all legislative and executive undertakings.[37]

What is the significance of this new organizational package recently introduced to the political life of the Saudis? And how could it be compared to what existed before? To avoid falling foul of the complexity of explaining the three separate documents that comprise the reform package, answers to these two questions will entail only the components of the relevant documents:

1. The legitimacy of the Al Saudi in reigning over Saudi Arabia was known to be derived from the right of conquest. To provide a different and more solid justification for legitimacy, the king declared in the Basic System of Rules that

> The kingdom of Saudi Arabia is a sovereign Arab Islamic state with Islam as its religion; God's book and the *sunna* of his Prophet, God's prayers and peace be upon him, are its constitution. Legitimacy of the state is derived from the Islamic *shari'a*.[38]

But, there is no indication as to why the Al Saud holds the exclusive right to rule. Ostensibly, it still is the right of conquest.

2. Article 5 asserts that the state is a monarchy. All other articles directly or indirectly indicate that the essential powers are in the hands of the king. The traditional order of succession which it was feared would expire within approximately 25 years, creating uncertainty in the kingdom, was resolved. The eligible group of about forty privileged princes, the surviving sons of 'Abd al-'Aziz (the youngest is over 42 years of age), is widened to include about five hundred children of these brothers.[39] On the other hand, the religious establishment which has been traditionally recognized to endorse the succession to the throne was not mentioned in this Basic System of Rules. Perhaps it was deliberately done to accrue power to the royal family, because the new process requires the consultation of the additional princes when nominating a king.

3. The new reforms suggested in the Basic System of Rules are ambiguous in soliciting the prerogatives and powers of the old institutions in conjunction with the new ones. All vertical as well as horizontal divisions of command in the kingdom are currently overlapping. This was probably done intentionally to limit the power of the newly formed Consultative Council (legislative) and in the process to undermine the once established power enjoyed by the Council of Ministers (executive), not to mention the judicial authority. Once again, this overlapping allows the monarch to retain his authority as power of reference to which all divisions of the state have to report. This is clear in decree no. 90/A Basic System of Rules, section six, article 44:

The authorities of the state are to be composed of the judiciary, the executive and the organizing authorities [*al-sultat al-tanzimiyya*]. These are to cooperate in accordance with this order (*nizam*) and other laws, and the king is the reference for all these powers.

The third authority as indicated in this article is deliberately called "Organizing Authorities" not "legislature" because the Islamic *shari'a* superimposes itself on ordinary legislation. Again, the fact that there are three authorities does not mean that division of power emanating from checks and balances in the government is an applicable formula in the Saudi kingdom. State division of authority is based on unlike objectives. It is not power that is separated, since the absolute power is the king; it is the functions that are separated. The real balance of power in the kingdom remains in the traditional leverages that the different factions in the royal family are able to acquire.

4. The provincial regulations are enacted in the decrees of the Basic System of Rules to formalize the old relationship that governs the various parts of the kingdom from the centre. The kingdom as it is implied in the new regulations is to stay divided into fourteen main administrative regions (*muqata'at*), each headed by an emir appointed and relieved by a royal decree upon the recommendation of the minister of interior. Each of these regions is subdivided into smaller administrative units that in turn are subdivided into smaller ones. All of these administrative units are limited in their powers to review, advise and propose. Final endorsement is located in the central government which in turn is subject to the authority of the king.[40]

5. The judiciary system as proposed by the new decrees in the Basic System of Rules reaffirms the independence of the judiciary (article 46). However articles 50 and 52 indicate clearly that:

The king or some one acting for him are in charge of executing judicial verdicts, and that judges are appointed and dismissed by a royal decree upon the recommendation of the Supreme Council of Justice and in compliance with this Basic System of Rules.

The Basic System of Rules seems to have neglected the existing dualistic legal process in the judiciary system. Dualism exists in the fact that the functional law is to be applied by the Supreme Council of Justice which should in turn abide by the rules of the Islamic *shari'a* in accordance with what is indicated in the Qur'an and the *sunna*. On the other hand, the Board of Grievances has different prerogatives. Its courts "shall arbitrate in all disputes and crimes". This provision of arbitration power is known to have given leverage to courts of civil tribunals to apply a different civil order (*nizam*) better interpreted as the non-religious law.[41]

The Fifth Development Plan (1990–5) emphasized the need to increase the number of specialized courts under the Board of Grievances to settle disputes of a special nature – the Basic System of Rules does not negate the plan[42] (this term "special nature" means that there are issues that cannot be settled within religious law): labour and business disputes, traffic codes, juvenile problems, economic and commercial disputes. The Board of Grievances, however, is reminded that it cannot look into "petitions pertaining to acts of state" nor into "appeals from individuals against decisions or rulings of the courts in matters within their jurisdictions", and more importantly it is prohibited to look into "legality of administrative acts and regulations".

The Basic System of Rules is not really what the opposition has been aspiring for especially after the events of the Gulf crisis. Neither the progressive religious groups nor the more liberal Saudis are satisfied with this document. They argue that the Consultative Council has negligible powers and insignificant standing, especially since its 61 members are not elected, rather appointed by the king who has uncontested power to dissolve the Council at any time. Needless to say, its decisions are subject to the king's approval. *Al-Hayat* newspaper has listed a number of cases in Saudi Arabia where the government is intervening in the affairs of the Consultative Council causing its erosion; cases involving the budget, military expenditure, foreign policy and American presence in Saudi Arabia. Unless this process is controlled, it will paralyse the Council or cause its disappearance, as was the case previously.[43]

How can the Saudi citizen channel his opinion upward in the Saudi system? A Saudi student[44] posed this question and proceeded to answer. The Basic System of Rules completely ignored freedom of expression, the right to access information, and freedom of association and assembly. This means that political associations and public forums are forbidden in the kingdom. In other words, there are no channels for addressing the government and there is no room for political participation by the people.

It seems that the Basic System of Rules has raised expectations that are beginning to surface among the wider population. However, these new challenges do not constitute a force of unity among the various groups of opposition who are pulling the Saudi leadership in two opposite directions, Islamic fundamentalist revivalism versus the Islamic liberal trend.

## How Islamic is the State?

Any study of the Saudi system would show the considerable importance of the Islamic religious leaders, the *'ulama'*. The latter are authoritarian in attempting to impose the rules of social conduct: they have the upper hand in influencing the educational system, and they definitely ensure an Islamic orientation in Saudi policies, at least on the public level. The royal family has deftly managed to identify the *'ulama'* so closely within the system that any criticism of the rule of the Al Saud is portrayed as a challenge to Islam itself.[45]

On the other hand, the royal family has claims and interest in giving themselves the right to protect Islam because it was born into Saudi society, and among tribes that regarded unswerving loyalty to the community and unquestioned acceptance of authority as their highest values. Thus, the Qur'an and the laws based on the Qur'an (*shari'a*) were natural and practical rules for governing the different tribes in Arabia as they are a spiritual and moral code of behaviour. In other words, the concept of a differentiation between political and spiritual powers (division between church and state) does not exist as it does in Western capitalist societies. In Saudi Arabia the Islamic polity combines state and religious institution together.[46]

Saudi Arabia today is struggling to amalgamate the capitalist mode of development and Islam. Though a great number of Saudis now enjoy wealth and material achievements, the collective sense of insecurity going back for generations has not vanished yet. All development plans, since their execution in 1970, emphasize the need for maintaining security and social stability in the country and of upholding the religious and moral values of Islam as a means of ensuring these priorities. As one university official said:

The locus of legitimacy is not to be found in the people; instead, the good society emerges through a leadership imbued with Islamic values and a society governed by Islamic law and teachings . . . The Islamic system of Saudi Arabia is a close, real and practical expression of the general will . . . Islam is the most progressive system in the world.[47]

One Saudi observer asserted[48] that it is no denigration of Islam, or the sincerity with which almost all Saudis embrace their religion, to recognize that certain difficulties have arisen from traditional Islam's encounter with rapid capitalist social and economic change. One of the mistakes of the late Shah of Iran was to fight traditional Islam rather than allow himself to be seen as a defender of the faith.

It seems that the choice of mixing Islam with capitalism, as perceived by the Saudi ruling elite, was and still is the best solution to maintain the status quo. Any other alternative of economic development, especially those that were adopted by the other progressive Arab states or the Shah of Iran, would have led to the destruction of the existing regime. This means that whenever Islamic values clash with capitalist values the ruling elite, for the sake of maintaining stability, always tilt to the side of the Islamic belief system. As an example, in 1994 King Fahd had to face the two contending parties with regard to the issue of giving women the right to drive cars. Saudi women demonstrated for the right to drive and they actually drove their cars. Fundamentalists objected with rage to any attempt to give driving licences to women who were supported by the modernists. King Fahd preferred to stand on the side of the fundamentalists.[49] Women in Saudi Arabia are still banned from driving vehicles.

A close analysis of the Saudi Arabian system today reveals a number of substantial contradictions arising from the clashes between Islamic values and capitalism. Thus, there is a growing tendency among the new capitalists for a moderate political *action*, on the one hand, and an emerging rise of fundamentalism among the financially less privileged as a *reaction*, on the other. These contradictions are evidenced in:

1. The rising influx of demands for greater participation in decision-making from mainly two conflicting parties, the capitalist-reformers and the Islamic fundamentalists. Though the Saudi state is a closed system, nonetheless this led to covert and at times overt polemic debate between the two parties. Both parties are proponents of change in the political

process, but each pulls in a different direction. Both, however, do not dare to contest the demonstrable virtues of government along traditional lines, and their public debates in the kingdom are contained in an exclusively Islamic context: Islam is, in fact, the only vehicle for political opposition.[50] Criticism in the name of Islam cannot be silenced and must be rebutted in the same terms, a confrontation that is usually stacked against the capitalist-reformers.

In such an atmosphere, the intellectual and social elites who do look for change direct their arguments towards comparison with other Islamic Gulf societies and in retrospect advocate a substantially greater degree of popular participation in the process of government. This by no means implies an adventurous trend to associate Saudi capitalism with Western versions of democracy. Saudi capitalist-reformers discern that Western style democracy has its hurtful impact on the political and social stability in societies like Saudi Arabia. The king is acknowledged as the unquestioned arbiter.[51] The ruling family clearly opts to gear political reforms in the direction that pleases the Islamic-traditionalists and in doing so they compromise the demands put forward by the capitalist-reformers. This was evident in the king's proclamation that the documents presented in the Basic System of Rules are not permanent and are susceptible to modification.

> These modifications like the original must be orchestrated within the framework of our benevolent Islamic doctrine (King Fahd, 1992).[52]

2. Generally speaking, the reform debate in Saudi Arabia has been exploratory rather than revolutionary. Advocates of reform are found as much within the ruling elite as outside. By the same token, defenders of the traditions and the status quo are similarly distributed.[53] The debate in the government between the Islamic fundamentalists who strive hard to preserve the religious and moral values of Islam, and the capitalist-reformers who wish the country to progress along a capitalist mode of development, is always inclined in favour of the religious sentiments by the absolute powers invested in the king. As a business observer said:

> Through Islam, the Saudi family seeks a close political identity with the people, and it should never be forgotten that the Saudi public opinion is for the most part insular and introspective, concerned almost exclusively with Islam.[54]

3. The interests of the Saudi family, now more than ever, are dedicated to dynastic survival and this can only be achieved through an uninterrupted alliance with Islamic forces as the sole basis of legitimacy. Of course this appears at times as family interests versus those of the nation as a whole.

4. Science versus Islamic teaching and quantity versus quality in education are still issues under debate in Saudi Arabia. Evidence from the development plans indicate that priority has been given to Islamic indoctrination. The desire by the capitalist-reformers is to develop the nation's human resources (encourage women to become part of the working and producing force) and thus form a nationally relevant indigenous technology (to open up more scientific and technical schools and encourage fewer arts and theological degrees). The practice, as it stands now, restricts such demands. All text books taught in pre-college and university education are converted into literature compatible with that of Islamic teachings and values.[55]

5. The fears of Islamic traditionalists that foreign workers and employees are greatly contributing to the corruption of the Saudi social and political behaviour are being taken seriously by the royal family. By its policy of discouraging and prohibiting many foreign experts, technicians and workers, the government's stated aims of developing industry are hampered.[56] Another relevant factor is related to the demand of the 'ulama' that government should be formed by consensus, versus the desire of the capitalist-reformers for it to be formed by technocrats capable of fulfilling the decision-making requirements of a modern capitalist industrial society.[57]

6. There is also a debate between the Islamic fundamentalists who assert that economic development the Islamic way (restrictions on interests generated from loans and confining free market supply of commodities) is capable of ensuring political stability, and the capitalist-reformers who assert that new modern political institutions must be added and some must be changed to accommodate the growing complexity of society. The royal family is aware of the real forces lying behind the fundamentalist versus reformer conflicts. They recognize the Islamic-dynastic institutionalization of government versus nationalistic aspirations (social contract) under a capitalist mode of development. Their strategy in countering these problems is twofold: First, to work through Islam to keep society basically Saudi and Islamic. The philosophy behind this

is that the Wahhabi variant of Sunni Islam (the official doctrine in Saudi Arabia) strongly discourages rebellion against leaders.

> O you who believe! Obey God and obey the Prophet and those who hold authority.[58]

Second, to institute a policy of eliminating poverty among its Wahhabi citizens. There are government institutions in Saudi Arabia that provide the essential nutrition needs. Land, housing, internal air travel, education and medical care are either heavily subsidized or provided free. In fact the opportunities for most Saudis with an entrepreneurial flair to make fortunes are many and varied. It was only recently in 1995 that residents of Saudi Arabia were asked by the government to pay small fractions of taxes.[59]

## Diversified Islamic Discontent

Open political discontent in Saudi Arabia, though prohibited, has managed to speak loud along the process of economic development. However, it veiled itself with Islamic rhetoric. Suffice it to mention that any indication of political deviation from Islamic affirmation will automatically lead to fierce counteraction by the royal elite and the conservative groups. Thus the political arena is converted into a religious arena.

As a catalyst, the Gulf war of 1991 aided in revealing the hidden opposition and exacerbated the feuds between the existing two opposing views within the political arena in Saudi Arabia: (1) those among the religious establishment (mainly Wahhabis) who extend their postulate for political development by emphasizing religious practices, and (2) the more liberal Saudis who, though they are strong believers in Islam, nevertheless demand the reduction of the influence of the religious authority on Saudi society.

The first group feels that the political system needs to be reformed in a different direction than that adopted by the government. The memorandum calling for reforms in the kingdom is an evidence of their stand and an illustration of their views. The memorandum was given to King Fahd by the mufti, Ibn Baz (the paramount religious scholar of the kingdom), during a meeting on 18 May 1992.[60] It demanded the creation of the Consultative Council and that the members should be chosen (not elected) from the most competent individuals of the kingdom. It hinted at the restrictions of some of the powers enjoyed by the king and strongly advocated the Islamization of all economic, social, administrative and educational systems. The armed forces were not spared; all armed services and arms suppliers should abide by an Islamization process on the pattern of the prophet's armies. The memorandum called for the punishment of all corrupt elements – those who got rich by illegal means – and demanded a comprehensive Islamic improvement in the press and the media. It demanded the closure of the corrupt journalism that propagates non-Islamic values in Saudi society. This was the fundamentalists' response to the Western values expressed in the Saudi media. They called for purity and unity of society along the lines of Islamic pacts and treaties, and for the application of these two principles in the kingdom's embassies abroad.

This memorandum, to say the least, was daring by Saudi standards. It caused astonishment and anguish among the ruling elite not only for its content but for the way it was published and distributed to the people in mosques throughout the kingdom, for the law forbids that. It was condemned by the king, and under pressure it was disapproved by the senior Muslim scholars, including Ibn Baz.

The second group submitted another memorandum to the king. It was signed by 43 prominent Saudi politicians, who considered themselves as the reformers of Saudi society. They demanded the immediate creation of the Consultative Council and a comprehensive revision of the role and prerogative of the religious authorities. They asked for the review of the legal status of women and for giving them better roles to lift their status and enhance the Saudi potential for development. This group has American support and is backed by a faction from within the royal family. In its ideology, the Qur'an and the Islamic traditions are only guides to the affairs and well-being of societies. If they are trusted to the wrong ruler, they can be abused. This group demanded the approval of a constitution which will aid in limiting the Saudi government from going beyond the limits approved by the laws and the spirit of Islam.[61]

This reformers' group (modernizers) is a small yet powerful clique – the majority are Wahhabi in faith. It quickly climbed high above its original status. Its new location in society commands it to abide by the caste and class into which its new income bracket puts it, thus losing its ties with the old tribal social order.[62] The reformers are creating a new economic power structure domestically and internationally, inducing Western corporations to have a stake in Saudi economic viability.[63] The leaders of this new economic power structure, though grateful to the present political order, strove after the second Gulf war to achieve a political share commensurate with their economic status in the country. However, economic alterations in Saudi Arabia did not proceed through simple capital accumulation earned in long-term investment by this new economic elite, nor by the continuation of the old methods of production. They mushroomed swiftly by imposition from above, through government planning and financing. Thus, the dominating royal family holds in its hands the vital cards that promote the economic standard of this reformers' group.[64]

In general terms, the impact of the 1991 Gulf war as a catalyst in speeding up the political concomitants of about twenty years of accelerating intensive development, has had three divergent effects on Saudi Arabia: (1) remodelling a majority of the old traditional religious tendencies into politico-religious groups, (2) producing new socio-economic orientations among a group of modernizers, (3) undermining the tribal structure and yielding a non-coherent middle class that sways between religious rigidity and modernity.[65]

## Conclusion

The rapid acceleration of economic modernization that started at the end of the first five-year development plan in 1974 has been creating a paradox in the mind of the majority of Saudis that has delayed a corresponding socio-cultural change. The disintegration of the traditional tribal-religious order is attenuated rather than complete. The resistance of individuals to accept drastic change in their attitude and behaviour to meet their new modernized environment means that their existing psychological make-up still respects conformity to the old values and traditions.[66] These inherited emotions motivate them to conform, to some degree, to the native-born conservative political and religious leadership. The Saudis' need for a comprehensively ordered life cannot be totally dependent on their new activities within the immediate economic roles that they are pursuing. Social stratification, protection and security are gained from a well-rounded and integrated pattern of interaction. That is why religious sentiments are still strong among the majority of Saudis. They feel relatively deprived in comparison with a privileged minority. The latter exploited their family ties, and/or their educational potentials, to rise above their old ways. The majority feel deprived and alienated within their new roles. In their subconscious, they blame their alienation on the introduction of Western economic values and have developed a negative reaction and thus propagated a strong Islamic resistance to Western values associated with the modernization process.[67]

Accelerating economic development demanded vast changes in the methods of production, different types of labour and a new demographic configuration of production. This meant drastic transformation in the ways and places in which people live and work, as well as considerable alterations in the distribution of income. The fact that some younger Saudis earn much more than their elders develops an individualistic economic independence among the youth. Being in a state of paradox, the traditional bonds of class in the tribe become loose and religious-sectarian ties become fortified.[68]

The urban Saudis feel an intense need to assert a specific identity. Among all Arab societies, Saudis up to the early 1970s were the least exposed to Western cultures and values, and their loyalty to Islam has always remained strong. Some Saudis do not find their dealings with Western capitalist values uniformly gratifying. Moreover, it is only reasonable to see the Saudis' new oil wealth heightening pride in the country's specific identity – Islam.[69]

An important point to consider concerns changes in the political arena during the second Gulf war. This war has led to a resurgence of Islamic values thus strengthening the fundamentalists. While it may look as if this will enhance the stability of the Saudi polity, it may well bring along a destabilizing factor. These fundamentalists, though their spokesmen number fewer than a dozen and tend to be young, have come to be well-known among Saudis. They have organized a devout and devoted following. There is the belief that the fundamentalists are gaining strength. They are fuelled by resentment over the growing maldistribution of wealth and market-oriented practices. The government is unwilling to confront the extremists. The Saudi government, except in severe cases, has always been reluctant to crack down on Wahhabi groups. For this reason, in terms of development planning, things for Saudi Arabia will not be as clear. To continue with the capitalist mode of development, the government will eventually have to challenge the Islamic extremists. To do so the king will need the support of the technocrats, who do not enjoy the organizational base of the mosques.

Thus, the Saudi royal family, and for a very long time in the future, has to face the contending fundamentalists and reformers outside and within the political, economic and social establishments. Being aware of the dangers of confronting Islamic tendencies, the royal family continues to make efforts to magnetize the *ulama* and clerics. Though the recent reforms of 1992 by Fahd were meant as a compromise between the demands of both the Islamic traditionalists and the capitalist-reformers, in reality they strengthened the former. As a consequence, these reforms will intensify the disharmony between the monarch and the capitalist-reformers. In summary, the royal family is in an awkward position trying to balance the constraints of Islamic traditions and values against the proposed needs of the capitalist-reformers. On the one hand, Western-style modernization and development comes as a package that is hard to fractionalize; on the other hand, stability in the country demands stronger ties between the state and Islamic institutions.

Saudi internal stability is partially influenced by developments in the region. This fact explains the sensitivity of the ruling elite towards appeasing the religious establishment. Islamists are gaining popularity, not only inside the country but also throughout the Middle East. These Islamic traditionalists, including the fundamentalists, have access to a large audience through the Friday speech (*khutba*) in mosques, weekly meetings for believers, and above all, control over the channels of the mass media. Therefore the religious establishment in Saudi Arabia is the only entity that, relatively speaking, retains a legal base of power and influence which is partially independent of the government and the royal family.

## NOTES

1 For a thorough assessment of the *Ikhwan*, see John Habib, *Ibn Saud's Warriors of Islam: The Ikhwan of Najd and their Role in the Creation of the Saudi Kingdom 1910–1930*, (Leiden: Brill, 1978); see also David Howarth, *The Desert King: Ibn Saud and His Arabia* (New York, McGraw-Hill, 1964).

2 See *al-Wasat* (a weekly magazine published in Arabic); several issues from the end of 1991 to the beginning of 1992.

3 Ibid., issue No. 71, 7 June 1993, p. 4.

4 For a view on this pattern see James Piscatori, *Islam in a World of Nation-States* (Cambridge: Cambridge University Press, 1986), Chapter 3.

5 Fuad Hamzah, *The Interior of the Arabian Peninsula* (Cairo: al-Tawfiq Press, 1968) (published in Arabic).

6 Fred Halliday, *Arabia Without Sultans* (Baltimore, MD: Penguin Books, 1974), p. 49.

7 *Business International Research Report* (Library of Congress Card Number 81-68282, 1981), p. 27.

8 Fouad Al-Farsy, *Saudi Arabia: A Country Study in Development* (London: Kegan Paul, 1986), p. 74.

9 Helen Lackner, *A House Built on Sand* (London: Ithaca Press, 1978), pp. 27–31.

10 John Christie, "Stability Through Adaptability", *The Middle East* (Saudi Arabia Special Reports, 1994), p. v.

11 This information is derived from the introduction of the Fifth Development Plan 1990–5, in which the ministry of planning speaks about the achievements of the previous development plans.

12 Eric Hobsbawm and Terence Ranger (eds.), *The Invention of Tradition* (Cambridge: Cambridge University Press, 1987).

13 Joseph McMillan, "Saudi Arabia: Culture, Legitimacy, and Political Reform", *Global Affairs*, 7 (spring 1992), pp. 56–75.

14 Various authors, "Back on Course for Growth", *The Middle East* (Saudi Arabia Special Report, February 1992), pp. vi-viii.

15 Judith Miller, "Saudi Arabia is a Kingdom at War with Itself", *New York Times Magazine*, 10 March 1991, p. 31.

16 Bernard Lewis, "The Roots of Muslim Rage", *The Atlantic Monthly* (September 1990), pp. 47–59.

17 Ibid., p. 4.

18 Christine M. Helms, *The Cohesion of Saudi Arabia* (London: Croom Helm, 1981).

19 Ibid., Introduction.

20 Piscatori, *Islam*, Chapter 3.

21 'Urfan Nizam-al-Din, "Saudi Arabia after the Consultative Council", *al-Hayat* (Arabic newspaper), 1 January 1994, p. 15.

22 Judith Miller, "Saudi Arabia: The Struggle Within", *New York Times Magazine*, 10 March 1991, pp. 27–30.

23  Ibid., pp. 27–30.

24  Eric Davis, "Theorizing Statecraft and Social Change in Arab Oil-Producing Countries" in E. Davis and N. Gavrielides (eds.) *Statecraft in the Middle East* (The Board of Regents of the State of Florida, 1991), pp. 16–17.

25  The promulgation of adaptability of tribal forms of social organization are conferred by Dale Eickelman, *The Middle East: An Anthropological Approach* (Englewood Cliffs, NJ: Prentice Hall, 1981), pp. 85–104. See also Nicholas Gavrielides, "Tribal Democracy: The Anatomy of Parliamentary Democracy in Kuwait" in L. Layne (ed.) *Elections in the Middle East* (Boulder, CO: Westview Press, 1987), p. 157.

26  Christie, "Stability", p. v.

27  *The Washington Post*, 14 May 1993, p. A35.

28  Ibid.

29  Samuel Huntington, *Political Order in Changing Societies* (New Haven: Yale University Press, 1968 ), pp. 155.

30  Hilga Graham, "Saudi Secrets: Behind the Wall of Silence", *London Review*, 22 April 1993. Information taken from *Beirut al-Massa* (Arabic newspaper) 13 May 1993, p. 2.

31  For a thorough analysis of the role of the Consultative Council, see Rahshe Aba Namay, "Constitutional Reform: A Systemization of Saudi Politics", *Journal of South Asian and Middle Eastern Studies*, xvi, 3 (spring 1993, pp. 70–88.

32  Abdallah Hussein, *King Abd al-Aziz and the Saudi Kingdom 1880–1953*; see also, Hamzah, *The Interior of the Arabian Peninsula*.

33  Aba Namay, *Constitutional Reforms*, pp. 43–68.

34  Ibid.

35  See *Asharq al-Awsat* (Arabic Newspaper) 2 March 1992.

36  *Umm al-Qura*, (Arabic newspaper) 3–10 September 1926), cited in Aba Namay, *Constitutional Reforms*.

37  Article 44 of the Basic System of Rules.

38  Article 1 of the Basic System of Rules.

39  For more information on this point see, *al-Hawadith* (Arabic weekly magazine), an interview with Crown Prince Fahd, 19 January 1980.

40  See Ahmad H. Dahlan, ed. *Politics, Administration and Development in Saudi Arabia* (Jeddah: Dar al-Shuruq, 1990), pp. 85–96.

41  For more information on this issue see McMillan, "Saudi Arabia: Culture, Legitimacy, and Political Reform", pp. 56–75.

42  1990–1995 Fifth Development Plan, p. 364.

43  This point is included in the article by Nizam-al-Din, "Saudi Arabia after the Consultative Council", p. 15.

44  A Saudi student in Lebanon who did not wish to reveal his name.

45  John Christie, "Stability Through Adaptability", *The Middle East* (Saudi Arabia Special Report 1992), p. v.

46  Gavrielides, "Tribal Democracy", p. 157.

47  Michael Hudson, *Arab Politics: The Search for Legitimacy* (New Haven: Yale University Press 1977), p. 79.

48 *al-Wasat*, 9 March 1992, p. 7.
49 Ahmad H. Dahlan, (ed.) *Politics, Administration and Development in Saudi Arabia* (Jeddah: Dar al-Shuruq 1990), p. 3.
50 *The Washington Post*, 14 May 1993, p. A35.
51 Hussein Askari, *Saudi Arabia's Economy: Oil and the Search for Economic Development* (Greenwich, CN: JAI Press 1990), p. 2.
52 Abdallah Hussein, "Movements of Reform and Change and the Confessional Crisis of Saudi Arabia" (in Arabic), reviewed by the *al-Safir* newspaper, 4 April 1994, p. 11.
53 Aba Namay, *Constitutional Reforms*, pp. 70–88.
54 *Business International Research Report*, 1981, p. 17.
55 Dahlan, *Politics*, p. 43.
56 al-Farsy, *Saudi Arabia*, p. 56.
57 Hussein, "Movements of Reform", p. 12.
58 Qur'an, IV: 59.
59 *al-Safir*, 12 February 1995, p. 1.
60 *al-Wasat*, 9 March 1992, pp. 1–8.
61 Aba Namay, *Constitutional Reforms*, pp. 43–68.
62 See the statistics in the fourth five-year development plan, in the first part of the volume published by the Kingdom of Saudi Arabia, Ministry of Planning, Central Department of Statistics.
63 Various authors, "Back on Course for Growth", Eickelman, *The Middle East*, pp. vi-viii.
64 Iliya Harik, "Pluralism in the Arab World", *Journal of Democracy*, Vol. v, No. 3 (July 1994), pp. 43–5.
65 Various authors "Democratization in the Middle East", *American–Arab Affairs*, 36 (spring 1991), pp. 1–51.
66 Jacob M. Landau, *The Politics of Pan-Islam: Ideology and Organization* (Clarendon Press, Oxford, 1990), pp. 254–6.
67 "However Crisis in Gulf Plays Out: Arab Chiefs Face a Changed World", *Wall Street Journal*, 28 December 1990, pp. A–1; see also, Martin H. Sours, "Saudi Arabia's Role in the Middle East: Regional Stability within the New World Order", *Asian Affairs*, 18 (spring 1991), p. 50.
68 Eickelman, *The Middle East*, pp. 85–104; see also, Daniel Brumberg, "Islamic Fundamentalism, Democracy, and the Gulf War" in James Piscatori, ed. *Islamic Fundamentalism and the Gulf Crisis* (Chicago, American Academy of Arts and Sciences, 1991), pp. 187–94.
69 Ibid.

# 11

# Causes for Fundamentalist Popularity in Egypt

*Mirna Hammoud*

The rise of Islamic fundamentalism in Egypt has resulted from several factors. While some scholars argue that the rise of revolutionary Islam resulted from the accumulation of petro-dollar wealth by increasing class cleavages and discontent,[1] others attribute it to the availability of financial aid from oil-rich countries to Islamic groups.[2] Furthermore, the rapid pace of modernization is also seen as triggering the crisis of identity.[3] The crisis of legitimacy that has resulted from the failure of liberal, nationalist and socialist regimes to fulfil their promises is also considered responsible for the rising popularity of Islam as an alternative system.[4] However, some scholars stress the fact that economic crises such as high inflation, unemployment and housing shortages are the main factors behind the revival of Islam in politics.[5]

Saad Eddin Ibrahim summarizes the factors behind the rise of Islamic fundamentalism in Egypt under six issues: first, the "social question" which is related to the lack of social justice and equal opportunity for Egyptians; second, "the political question" or the degree of democracy and popular participation; third, "the economic question" in connection with the rulers' competence in ensuring development through the wise use of resources; fourth, "the patriotic question" or the system's degree of independence or dependence on a foreign power, especially that Islamic fundamentalists are interested in Egypt's sovereignty because only a country free from foreign control can be Muslim; fifth, "the nationalist question" in relation to the Egyptian nation and its role in the "greater Arab nation" and the solution to the Israeli problem; and sixth, "the civilization question" addressing the balance between the preservation of Egypt's historical traditions and Westernization.[6]

These six factors noted to be behind the upsurge of Islamic funda-mentalism in Egypt encompass the problem in its external and domestic aspect; however, the focus of this essay is exclusively on the current domestic factors behind the gradual build-up of pressure in Egyptian society, which implies the socio-economic and political questions in addition to the problem of the Coptic minority and the power of the Islamic discourse. Thus the following hypotheses are to be tested:

(1)   The Egyptian government is unable to provide adequate services.

(2)   Rising religious tensions increase the potential for extremist political movements.

(3)   Muslim fundamentalists function within the framework of an ideology that appeals to diverse strata of the population.

(4)   The repressive nature of the Egyptian political system causes disaffection and contempt toward the ruling elite.

Nowadays, several domestic factors are strengthening the appeal of fundamentalism in Egypt, other than the reality of the strength of Islam as an ideology and a certain belief system that the Egyptians possess in general. First, the socio-economic question represented by the state's economic retreat which provides the fundamentalists with the incentive to proliferate and affirm their existence at the social level. Second, the Coptic issue or the attempt by a minority to attain a solid base in a country where each crisis shakes it, leaving a situation where demagogic appeals are used to domesticate the "Coptic" presence in various ways. Third, the rhetorical power of the fundamentalists results from the many problems facing Egypt. This rhetorical power is derived from a discourse based on Islam which is a familiar creed, a powerful link with the past and a promise of a utopian future. This power gives the Islamic fundamentalists the chance to promise both a utopian future and to articulate solutions to all problems. Fourth, the political question where the effect of repression is examined. Actually, repression is a double-edged weapon which radicalizes families traumatized by violence, mass arrests, the loss of a son or a relative but also shows people the devastating effects of radicalism on property and social order. Thus this essay highlights these four domestic factors which are responsible for the increase in the fundamentalists' popularity as well as their radicalization as a movement.

## The Economic Crisis

The economic situation in Egypt is perhaps one of the main factors behind the increasing popularity of the Islamic fundamentalist movement. To understand this factor, it is necessary to trace it back to the Egyptian monarchic rule and the state's economic role since the 1952 revolution. Under the monarchy, a class of landowners controlled the Egyptian system through an extensive network of patron–client relationships whereby the citizens' welfare was subject to a contract between a patron and a client. This state of affairs came to an end with the coming of Gamal Abd al-Nasir who adopted socialism and initiated land reforms and industrialization. This chain of revolutionary changes gave paramount importance to the state which controlled religious institutions, mosques and courts. In essence, it eroded the basis of the class of landowners and ended the old patronage system because the changes were carried out by army officers, technocrats, and intellectuals. As a result, the welfare of citizens was placed under the direct responsibility of the state whose unlimited power and hegemonic control of the political and economic processes ended the wide margin of manoeuvring that Islamic fundamentalists enjoyed under the former regimes; the new order closed almost all loopholes,[7] linked the government and the people by a social "contract" centred on the commitment of the state to provide goods and services to the public in exchange for political docility and quiescence,[8] and developed a "utopia of well-being" with free medical care as one of its main symbols.[9]

After the 1973 war, Sadat turned rapidly towards the United States of America, forged a cordial relationship with the West and became amenable to Western political and economic pressures. As a result, Egypt witnessed an influx of Western goods and investments, and bridges were built between the newly emerging business community in Egypt and its Western counterparts. The West penetrated Egypt on all levels, governmental and private, and in 1974 Sadat launched the "open-door" economic policy or *infitah* and meant to allow private interests to flourish; however, these new steps introduced by Sadat were taken reluctantly, with a great deal of caution, and were subjected to government routine and bureaucratic procedures which inhibited a serious shift from a public-sector-controlled economy to a liberal one.

The *infitah* policy continued and reached a climax under President Mubarak, entailing a gradual retreat of the state from its social engagements to provide food, education, employment and social services. The funding agencies and the United States took advantage of Egypt's economic dependency to press it to dismantle its huge public sector. They considered the *infitah* a successful measure only if the "socialist" economic structure of the Nasir regime was eliminated.[10] This advocacy gives the *infitah* a centrality in the analysis of the dilemma of Egyptian society.

On 22 May 1987, the Egyptian government signed an agreement with the International Monetary Fund (IMF) under pressure from the international financial community. This development was the result of the precarious Egyptian situation that presented an important increase of its external debt[11] due to the large gap between its resources and the patron role played by the state towards society.[12] The economic situation was worsened by the existence of an imbalanced economic network run by an incompetent administration which resulted in increased inequality and decreased productivity. The agreement with IMF gave Egypt a loan which amounted to $250 million in exchange for the devaluation of the Egyptian pound and the progressive decrease of subsidies for basic products.[13] In 1987, some measures to put the agreement into practice were taken, but the results were judged to be insufficient. In 1988, a number of price rises and taxes were decided on; however, not all of them were applied. Energy prices rose at a rate of 330 per cent between 1986 and 1990 but remained 45 per cent lower than world prices. Since 1991, the economic reforms gained significant momentum and significant policy changes were implemented; especially, an agreement with IMF was reached in order to modify the functioning of the economy because since the mid-1980s, GDP per capita had fallen from $750 in 1985/86 to $640 in 1989/90 and real income stagnated or declined. Moreover, unemployment continued to grow and in the 1990s became twice the level of the mid-1970s. Between 1980 and 1989, the foreign debt increased from $20 billion to $49 billion, revealing that the "rents" earned from oil and from the country's strategic position were insufficient to maintain an acceptable external balance.

This domestic situation witnessed the fall of real incomes and the rise of unemployment which threatened the stability of the country. Furthermore, the revolution of Eastern Europe made long-term expectations about further foreign-exchange inflows gloomy, because the elimination of the West's main political protagonist (USSR) threatened Egypt's long-term ability to bargain for aid. In 1990, Egypt was reclassified as belonging to the group of the world's poorest countries. As a result of the economic reform decisions, important modifications were undertaken in four important areas. First, the foreign exchange system was modified and the first legal, private money-changers emerged in Cairo. Moreover, the government merged three foreign-exchange rates for the US dollar into one largely market-determined rate. Second, the interest rates area was freed from state control. These rates were to be set freely by the banks. Moreover, weekly treasury-bill auctions were issued providing an anchor for the market-based interest rates used by the banks. Third, the government budget deficit and the money supply areas were affected by a reduction in the deficit due to the introduction of a general sales tax in May 1991 and the imposition of tight restrictions on the money supply related to loans. Fourth, the pricing policies area was touched by the reforms when subsidies were reduced on a large variety of goods like energy products whose prices were increased by 50 to 170 per cent in 1990/1: basic foods, cigarettes, and fertilizers. These measures contributed to the reduction in the budget deficit and in the distortions in the incentive system and thereby encouraged a more efficient resource allocation. Furthermore, policies in the areas of investment and foreign trade were modified to encourage economic activities. In fact, the government presented in 1991 a shortened "negative list" of areas in which private investments banned it and also guaranteed automatic approval of investments that did not appear on the list. This meant that the anti-competition motion was dropped. (When existing capacity covers domestic needs, investment should be prevented.) Privatization and the public sector were also areas where the economic reforms have been felt but in a more limited fashion.[14]

In 1991, a programme of privatization was launched by the government. The difficulty of such a step lay in the fact that the public sector represented 70 per cent of the fixed investments, 80 per cent of external exchanges and 90 per cent of banking and insurances. This meant that large amounts of money in the form of loans were needed to complete the step of reforming the structure of public enterprises in order to privatize it. Privatization began in 1991 with the selling of 851 small enterprises, valued between £E50,000 and £E100,000.[15] In 1994, the director of the World Bank's Middle East and North Africa Department, Ram Chopra, declared that the World Bank was satisfied because Egypt had met its privatization targets so far. The state had sold three public sector companies (El Nasr Bottling, the Egyptian Bottling Company, and El Nasr Boilers and Pressure Vessels Company) and had placed about 50 companies under sale. As a result of the Egyptian state's commitment to implement the IMF agreement, its disengagement or retrenchment was expressed through a number of forms such as the reduction of state subsidies, whereby taxi fares, electricity (which was to be brought up to world prices by 1 July 1995),[16] petrol, cooking oil, sugar, meat, rice, and some types of bread rose in cost, while salaries remained stagnant.[17] Moreover, all agricultural products were freed from compulsory price controls, except cotton, rice and sugar cane. Consequently, the economic situation worsened, leading to massive unemployment (estimated at around 20 per cent of the 15 million work force)[18] and lack of affordable housing, obliging thousands of Egyptians to postpone marriage, and forcing a large number of salaried workers to look for additional income in order to cope with the changing situation.[19] In the domain of social services, services regressed in quality and increased in price.[20] The state's social disengagement is mostly observed in the health sector, one with direct social implications. Faced with a serious future financial crisis, and in an attempt to achieve its social role, the state was forced to encourage private capital to take over some responsibilities.[21] This fact led to the establishment of a mixed health system whereby private capital was invested to develop health insurance, pharmaceutical industries, and the construction of private hospitals. At this point it is important to note that the insurance system is still in its initial stages. It used to cover only 7 per cent of the population in 1982 and is expected to cover up to 50 to 60 per cent of the population in the next 10 or 15 years, although the government's objective was to achieve total coverage by 1990.[22] The pharmaceutical industry is of particular importance in reflecting the impact of reforms on the life of ordinary Egyptians. In this important branch, the public sector held 60 per cent of the market but the government is encouraging private investment especially since local production covers 85 per cent of total consumption. Private organizations were able to pressure the government and extract a 30 to 50 per cent increase in the prices of 500 medicines in March 1988 and another 35 per cent increase in May of the same year; these increases related mainly to antibiotics and anti-diarrhoea medicines. As a result, the "utopia of well-being" and free medical treatment were replaced by "economic" care – meaning "low cost" services provided by the ministry of health.[23]

The economic reform Egypt adopted had three main positive results: first, it made the Egyptian currency convertible;[24] second, it was one of the factors which helped in lowering the Egyptian external debt from $51.69bn in 1989 to $38.3bn in 1993;[25] and third, it reduced some import duties. However, the reforms created new wealth among the upper classes and the poor were affected by price increases caused by inflation and the elimination of state subsidies.[26] Moreover, it caused a recession and reduced the growth rate to 2.5 per cent in 1992.[27] The public sector underwent trimming, free education and the right to jobs for graduates were called into question, and the governmental control of economic and financial flows, prices and wages diminished considerably. The difficulties that have resulted (and may continue to be encountered) were not unexpected. The authorities feared that social unrest might develop, especially since the reforms engendered radical changes in the structure and functioning of the economy. This fear may be explained by the fact that subsidies for basic products like oil, sugar and wheat are considered to be social and political instruments with the objective of maintaining a certain degree of basic subsistence for all Egyptians. In 1977 when the price of bread was raised, two days of social unrest followed which resulted in 44 dead and 600 injured. In 1984, when the price of bread was raised by one piastre, as recommended by the IMF, serious disturbances took place in Kafr al-Dawar (to the south of Alexandria) forcing the government to back off. To avoid this danger of social unrest, the International Bank created a social fund of $400 million to alleviate the results of the economic reforms that were about to be undertaken; for example, to provide compensation for the rise in prices and also to create new jobs because it anticipated an increase in unemployment.[28]

President Mubarak warned Egyptians as of May 1990 that they would have to face the difficulties that were to come, and "tighten their belt" because there was no alternative but to pay the price that would secure the support of the international community.[29] However, he anticipated the minimization of economic hardships by the end of 1995 when the economic reform package to which the government was committed vis-à-vis the international financial institutions would be fully implemented.[30]

As economic reforms are forcing ordinary Egyptians to make major sacrifices the government and the ruling party (the National Democratic party) grow uneasy as they can see that further democratization of the political system would favour the Islamic fundamentalist opposition in these circumstances.[31] Counterbalancing the economic retreat of the state, many private institutions have taken the initiative to provide alternatives to the inefficient governmental services and high-priced services of private institutions. This alternative is mainly advocated by Islamic fundamentalists who saw their room for manoeuvre becoming wider and Islam becoming a salient phenomenon at the social level.[32] For example, the social organizations with Islamic referents showed an increase in their percentage compared to organizations of general interest. Islamic social organizations amounted to 24 per cent in 1969 and doubled in 1975 to reach 48 per cent. In 1985, 13 out of 17 social organizations bore names with Islamic referent. In 1992, Islamic organizations constituted 28 per cent of the total number of organizations created that year.[33] Various Islamic societies have established hundreds of medical clinics and schools, a fact that bolsters the Islamic movement. As a result, individual clinics are facing stiff competition from religious establishments, since mosques as well as churches have created clinics in popular and peripheral zones and are well-equipped to offer services and at prices lower than those charged by private clinics (£E1.5 to £E2 as compared to £E3 to £E5 and more), absorbing an important number of young doctors unable to have their own clinics (only 25 per cent of doctors have private surgeries).[34] An example of this phenomenon is the famous Mosque "Moustafa Mahmoud" that offers health, educational, and charitable services.[35] Moreover, mosques play an important role in collecting and redistributing "zakat" to the needy in surrounding neighbourhoods.[36] Through these services, ranging from schools and libraries, services for students (such as photocopying) to medical clinics, Islamic fundamentalists are trying to replace state control and that of the traditional elites by their own. However, the role they play with members and outsiders is based on the same role as was played by the traditional notables; one of clientelism and mediation between citizens and public authorities. In brief, this situation arose as a result of the harsh impact of the economic situation on the life of most Egyptians.

The importance of the economic situation in the life of Egyptians may be detected and measured by the level of stability and the degree of the fundamentalists' popularity in relation to economic issues. The relation of the economic factor to stability is evident from the timing and ways in which unpopular policy changes have been introduced. In contrast to the manner in which subsidy cuts were announced in 1977 (as part of an agreement with the IMF), in 1991 the planned price hikes and general sales tax were announced at the start of an important feast, 'Id al-Fitr, presumably on the assumption that people are less likely to take to the streets and riot on a major festive occasion. The government has also practised what has been referred to as "reform by stealth" or gradualism, meaning that subsidies are maintained but the subsidized items gradually disappear and are replaced by slightly modified and costlier items.[37] This practice is related to a policy of conditioning whereby the failure to deliver products and services of poor quality makes the public lose interest in acquiring them, and those who can afford them are driven to purchasing goods exchanged on the free market. For instance, in recent years the Mubarak regime introduced a 5-piastre loaf of bread and phased out the production of the 2-piastre loaf so that people became gradually used to the 5-piastre loaf.[38] Another government practice is to give the economic reforms an Egyptian stamp by presenting them as though they are designed in Egypt. For example, in December 1990, five months before the conclusion of the agreement with the IMF, the government announced a "1000-day" programme of economic liberalization, and President Mubarak insisted that the ideas behind the reforms were Egyptian.[39] The economic effect is also reflected in the degree of the fundamentalists' popularity which can be measured by two important factors: first, the "money investment companies (MIC)"; and second, the fundamentalists' relief services offered during times of crisis. First, "money investment companies" emerged in the 1980s as a result of the economic liberalization initiated by the state. These companies are deposit-takers and direct investors. They are "Islamic" in the most tenuous of meanings. Their Islamic label was used to impart a sense of respectability and appeal to the conservative inclinations of holders of small sums of foreign currency; they are especially influenced by the growing Islamic religiosity which decries investment in banks that offer "interest" on deposits because taking interest (regarded as usury) is prohibited by Islam.[40] However, despite their "Islamic" appellation, some of the MIC were run by non-Muslims and had non-Muslim depositors. "We are an MIC, not a mosque", said one of the major owners. Investors in these companies had no right to inspect their activities, projects or budgets. Many of the owners of such companies were known for their illegal practices such as currency and metals speculation as well as drug trading. Examples of these companies are al-Rayyan (Ahmad al-Rayyan was a member of al-Jama'at al-Islamiyya), al-Sharif ('Abd al-Latif al-Sharif was a member of the Muslim Brothers), al-Huda and al-Hilal groups. MICs contributed financially in support of fundamentalist candidates in the April 1987 elections and co-opted a number of influential political figures like ex-ministers and governors and important editors and journalists, some of whom were far from being sympathetic to the moderate Islamic movements.[41] MICs assumed a central role in the Islamic economic sector since the 1980s and claimed to have 2.5 million depositors which were attracted by high rates of return (or "Islamic profit") of 24 per cent and even 35 per cent as opposed to the Egyptian state which gave 12 per cent interest only – and this due to a high rate of inflation of 20 to 30 per cent per year.[42] This economic sector was a major asset for the expansion of the fundamentalists' ranks, the Muslim Brothers in particular.[43] Moreover, it was only in 1988 when the financial crisis of these companies became acute, coinciding with the spectacular bankruptcy of some of them (e.g. al-Rayyan), that the state interfered and liquidated them. The state had not intervened earlier because the MICs had been popularly regarded as successful businesses before the crises.[44] The 1987/88 and 1988/89 university elections revealed a certain distancing from Islamic groups, while the left did not advance. In 1986, the Jama'at list had won all seats, but their withdrawal in 1988 and 1989 (the rate of participation was only 40 per cent) was mainly due to the scandals of the MICs especially since the campaigns of the Jama'at were financed by these companies.[45]

Second, the fundamentalists' relief services offered during times of crisis (like the earthquake of 1992 and the flood of 1994) were a continuation of their various social services and of major importance to their popularity. After the earthquake of 1992, thousands of homeless Egyptians were moved by the government to new settlement areas. In these areas Islamic associations took over the responsibility of filling in the gaps left by the state. They distributed water, gathered rubbish and offered many other services essential to make the new settlements more viable.[46] After the flood that occurred in November 1994, the Muslim Brothers were the first to rescue the inhabitants of Darnaka. The same thing happened in Asyut where they provided people with food, clothing, money amounting to £E50,000 for rescue operations, organized daily medical missions to visit the destroyed areas and provided care and medication. Moreover, they supplied Asyut with food and 1,500 blankets and Sohaj with 500 blankets during the first two days of the catastrophe when no one was able to reach the devastated areas. As a result, it was obvious that these initiatives would create feelings of gratitude for the Muslim Brothers, a sentiment which was forcefully reported by the Egyptian magazine *Rose al-Youssef*.[47]

The increase of the popularity of Islamic fundamentalism in Egypt and its Islamic call is a response to a familiar authentic creed, but also a rational choice for a good health care, for example. Therefore, the revival of religiosity among Muslims is not to be minimized, but there is no doubt that the network of private voluntary organizations under the fundamentalists' control has enhanced and strengthened support among Muslim believers. But this popular support for the Islamic call is variable in the sense that if the Islamic social welfare and health activities are reduced, popular support diminishes in tandem.

## The Coptic Choice

The economic hardships faced by Egyptian society added to the existing psychological disposition to confessional tension between Muslims and Copts. This "Coptic factor" can be regarded as an important catalyst for the increase in popularity of Islamic fundamentalism, especially in the light of the late Coptic resurgence demonstrated by increased militarization, increased investments in the social field, by new political alliances with secular Egyptian political forces, by a wide movement in the political sphere and an increased support for the state. The objective is to exhibit and stress the loyalty of the Coptic community to Egypt.

In dealing with the Coptic issue as a factor behind the increase in popularity of the Islamic fundamentalist movement in Egypt, we should consider one particular form of Islam that is especially relevant to popular attitudes. This form of Islam is the "communalist" idea and sentiment, or Islam as an "ethnic marker", marking the boundaries of one community against another which is identified in terms of religious differences. This is due to the fact that there are many forms of Islamic political ideas as well as different ways in which they are represented as political ideas and movements. Communalist models do not presuppose any specific Islamic political ideas and are quite distinct, at the level of political programmes, from modern political Islam; however, they can mobilize sentiments in favour of a particular movement and provide a stimulus for support of Islamic movements, calling for the restoration of Islamic superiority versus the inferiority and separateness of other religions.[48] Such a stimulus is effective, especially in that cultural perceptions of the "other" become sharper, and rejection more categorical in times of crisis.[49] The Islamic groups' perception of the Copts is essentially that of the religious other. For them, the main source of religious antagonism is attributed to a Coptic conspiracy to prevent Egypt from becoming an Islamic state. Moreover, the Coptic church is perceived as scheming to convert as many Muslims as possible through an aggressive missionary effort and the building of churches.[50]

A brief review of the Copts' most important periods of tension with Muslims may show that communalist appeals in Egypt play a role, openly or covertly, in demagogic political appeals.

Actually, the first period of extreme hostility between Copts and Muslims occurred in the first decade of the century when acrimonious statements made by the press, political groups and political activists culminated in the assassination of the Coptic prime minister, Boutros Ghali, and the holding of a Coptic conference to discuss the situation, followed by a Muslim conference to counter it. After the First World War, nationalist fever peaked and led to the creation of an Egyptian nationalist movement based on liberal and egalitarian beliefs which instigated a revolution in 1919 with a great deal of Coptic participation. As a result, all tensions were forgotten in an attempt to attain independence from Britain and forge a new and just society. This was supported by the Copts who participated actively in demonstrations. The reward of Copts for participating in the independence movement was their incorporation into the post-independence political system in which they were accorded a degree of equality in the constitution and theoretically were given equal opportunity to participate in representative bodies.[51]

Egyptian nationalism launched a new trend of general mobilization, leaving behind all kinds of cleavages between Copts and Muslims. This period was characterized by the rise of new consciousness among the Egyptian youth of both Copts and Muslims under the impact of national education, religious education, communal organizations and other activities and services. This new consciousness was the result of a synthesis between the religious identity and modern sense of national belonging that manifested itself in the massive involvement of university students in the 1930s to the national movement which was then represented by the Wafd Party. In this party the Copts were strongly represented even at the leadership level. For example, the party's executive committee consisted of six Copts and eight Muslims.[52] This high degree of representation of a minority group gave the Copts hope of future access to and participation in the political system. In 1936, after the Wafd Party, acting in the name of Egypt, signed the Treaty of Friendship and Alliance with Great Britain, it was perceived as the voice of the whole nation. However, several political players feared the strength of the Wafd and aimed at discrediting its nationalist call. Thus the British together with the Egyptian royal family as well as the religious establishment, al-Azhar, wielded the "Coptic" weapon to intimidate the Wafd Party; they accused it of neglecting its Islamic foundation and allowing the Coptic element to steer it in a direction that would secure Coptic domination of Egypt. Such atttacks had the effect of setting back the establishment of a secular, democratic polity and traumatizing the Copts.[53] Moreover, the importance of Islam and Islamic groups increased as a result of the economic dislocations of the depression and the inability of the parliamentary system to solve pressing problems. The Wafd Party did not defend its principles of equality and national unity. Copts began to be excluded from a large area of political activity and became estranged from the polity and from the Wafd Party which negotiated an alliance with the Muslim Brothers in 1948 in preparation for parliamentary elections.[54] In fact, this move had a great impact on the Coptic community and prompted the creation of its "opaque" and secretive institutions and politics. This in turn had the effect of causing the Egyptian state and Muslim groups to mistrust it. As a consequence of the changes in the Egyptian political line of nationalism, the Coptic community withdrew from the political arena and formed Coptic parties with a confessional nature like the "Kutla" and the "National Democratic party".[55]

In the late 1940s, after a temporary calm due to the Second World War and the imposition of martial law, intercommunal relations again deteriorated as a result of economic and social instability. Copts found themselves out of power although Muslims accused them of using the system to dominate Egypt. As a result of this polarization, fewer Copts were willing to undergo the perils of political leadership. After the overthrow of the monarchy in 1952, the new revolutionary leader,

Gamal Abd al-Nasser halted the deterioration in intercommunal relations and the destructive hostilities and their communal expressions. In fact, Abd al-Nasser was not interested in religious questions, and Copts presented no real threat. However, no Coptic participation in the revolutionary leadership was registered. In order to fill the gap, the regime appointed a single Christian minister in each government in addition to appointing eight or ten Copts among the non-elected members of the Assembly.[56] The revolution of Abd al-Nasser had a positive as well as a negative effect on Copts: positive, given that the Nasserist ideology was secular as evidenced by the suppression of the Muslim Brothers; and negative, given that the Copts suffered financially along with Muslims as a result of the land reform that split up large estates and the nationalization of large businesses dominated once by the Copts. The squeezing of the private sector and the reduction in recruitment of Copts in teaching institutions and medical faculties resulted in the emigration of thousands of middle-class Copts to the US, Canada and Australia.[57] In general and over the years the Copts had lost prestige in the eyes of many Muslims because of their perceived association with the colonial powers and the previous regimes. Furthermore, their prestige decreased because of the tensions caused by the confrontation with Israel and the West. Coincidentally, this period witnessed the emigration of small minorities like Jews, Greeks and Western Europeans.[58] Thus from the point of view of the Islamists that era experienced little confessional tension or, to put it another way, relative confessional peace, because of the firm grip exercised by the regime and fear of Abd al-Nasser's displeasure. This was also due to the character of the Patriarch Kyrillos, a reserved man who tended to avoid involvement in politics. This meant that a degree of mutual respect characterized the relationship between the patriarch and Abd al-Nasser. On the other hand, religious feelings on the part of the Copts experienced a revival which was reflected in the growing number of people attending church, the rise of Sunday schools and youth groups, and faculty associations for religious and social activities formed by Coptic students whose main social outlet was the church and voluntary organizations. The defeat of Egypt by Israel in 1967 accentuated this trend, which somehow prompted a series of apparitions of the Virgin Mary in the Zeitoun district in Cairo in 1968 and 1969.[59]

Abd al-Nasser's death coincided with that of the Coptic Patriarch Kyrillos. President Sadat was elected in 1970 and Pope Shenouda III in

1971. These two events marked a definite change in the regime's policies, and the relationship between the Copts and the state.[60] The attitude of the state was in many ways the reverse of the one under Nasser. It is true that Sadat encouraged the development of a liberal economy, one which mainly served the interest of businessmen and shopkeepers, many of whom were Copts, and also revitalized the private sector creating new opportunities for employment.[61] However, Sadat abandoned the Nasserist formula of political mobilization based on secular ideas and adopted instead a formula designed to win the support of the traditional and conservative elements with whom he allied himself in his struggle with the left. Consequently, he released most Muslim Brother cadres who had been imprisoned by Abd al-Nasser to enlist their support and demonstrate his Islamic piety. However, discrimination against Copts in the public sector, the civil service and in the university teaching profession continued unabated.[62] In sum, Sadat's formula had two disastrous consequences on the stability of the political system: first, it alienated the Copts and second, it forced them to take a militant stand under the leadership of the church.[63] This importance of the church in organized militancy was due to the Copts' historical attachment to it, the Copts' lack of seclusive concentration at the geographical and occupational levels, and their migration to the West.[64] With the appointment of the young patriarch Shenouda III Coptic involvement in politics was revived after a long period of inaction. Thus, Shenouda's appointment signified the beginning of an activist church, the "porte parole" and the main representative of the community, which was ready to negotiate for a new kind of relationship with the state and was determined to protect the rights of the community as a whole. Two factors were responsible for the activism of the Coptic church: Shenouda's personality and the Egyptian political climate during this period. First, Shenouda was more politicized than his predecessors, had a new perception of the role of the church and was known for his radical position *vis-à-vis* the authorities on some problems even before his appointment as patriarch. Second, Sadat's weak beginning and the Nasserist regime before him – weakened after the 1967 defeat – prepared the ground for an activist church. In fact, not only the Coptic church, but all political and social forces that had been excluded from political participation under Nasser, wanted to benefit from this new opportunity by attempting to regain access to the political arena. It is within this framework that we can explain Shenouda's policy during the first ten years of his pontificate which consisted of confirming the Coptic identity and confronting the state publicly as a new mode of political action. His policy contrasted sharply with the submissiveness of his predecessors.

The first major confrontation between the new regime and the church centred on the governmental policy of restricting the construction of churches. Under pressure from the sudden revival of the church, a population explosion and migration to Cairo from the villages, Copts resorted to building churches illegally and presenting the government with a *fait accompli*. In 1972 in Khanka, Muslims set fire to an illegally built church.[65] The next day one hundred priests were sent from Cairo by the patriarch to march through the town in protest, which alarmed the government and pushed Sadat to promise the construction of fifty churches. After this incident, the government accused the American imperialists and the Zionists of instigating religious strife in order to destabilize the country, and prevent Egypt from facing up to the "Israeli enemy" after seizing a number of letters addressed from the USA to various persons and groups, both Muslims and Copts, playing one against the other.

In 1977, relations between church and state entered a new difficult phase. Coptic anxieties began to reflect the increasing strength of the Islamic right in Egypt and especially the Islamic direction of the regime. Moreover, the Sadat regime showed clear signs of toleration towards Islamic fundamentalist groups in the universities and its willingness to accept a wide-ranging application of the *shari'a* laws to cases of libel, theft and apostasy; however this was stopped by Coptic protests in 1977. But the situation alarmed the Copts, especially after the attacks on churches in Fayoum and Asyut which raised confessional tension further. More trouble took place in early 1978 in Asyut and in the universities at Minya with Islamic groups harassing Coptic students. In 1979 the ancient Qasriyat al-Rihan church in old Cairo was burned down. In 1980, due to mounting harassment of Copts, the patriarch declared the cancellation of the Easter celebrations, and during Sadat's visit to the United States Coptic immigrants voiced their protests. On 14 May 1980 President Sadat himself declared that the religious strife was initiated by the Coptic leadership and that Pope Shenouda was conspiring to make the church a state within the state, to transform the Copts into an alien "foreign" minority, to mobilize other Christian sects into a unified front under his leadership, to arouse antagonism of foreign states – mainly the United States – towards his regime, and to establish links with the Lebanese Phalangists in the Lebanese civil war. Moreover, President Sadat charged the Coptic leadership with trying to prevent the constitutional amendment concerning the change of the second article, that is from Islam as a major source of legislation to Islamic law as the basic legislative source. He also implied that the Coptic leadership was connected to a foreign plot dating back to the 1960s, aimed at the secession of the Copts from Islamic Egypt and the formation of a Coptic state in Upper Egypt with Asyut as its capital. While these accusations put Shenouda under pressure, the government proposed a constitutional amendment making Islam the basic legislative source instead of a major source. In June 1981, confessional violence was renewed in the Cairo suburb of Zawiat al-Hamra where eighteen people died and more than a hundred were injured, this in addition to the explosion of a bomb in the Cairo suburb of Shubra at a Coptic wedding. Deteriorating relations manifested themselves on another level, through attacks and counter-attacks in journals, books, sermons, and personal exchanges. That year in Sadat's speech at the People's Assembly, the Coptic church leadership was harshly accused of conspiring with the Christian Lebanese in a scheme aimed at partitioning the Arab States into religious states and trying to build an inter-Arab Christian organization modelled on that of the Muslim Brothers, of providing military training to Copts in Southern Lebanon in order to carry out military operations in Egypt with the ultimate goal of creating an independent Coptic state in Upper Egypt. This plan was to be carried out with active cooperation of Israel, with finance from the American Central Intelligence Agency, the West German Intelligence and the German Christian Democratic Party in addition to the channelling of funds from the World Council of Churches. At the same time, the Soviet Union and some Arab countries were accused of inducing Islamic groups to attack the government and providing them with finance. However, the Coptic leadership was accused of initiating and continuing the religious strife while the Islamic groups were absolved of any direct responsibility since they were simply reacting to the constant provocations from the Coptic leadership. Finally, Pope Shenouda was banished to a monastery in Wadi Natroun and a committee of five bishops was appointed in his place.[66] Thus, since the appointment of Shenouda, the church aimed at the reconstruction of national identity in such a way as to promote national equality between Copts and Muslims; however, this whole process resulted in clashes with the political players or Islamic elements[67] who applied to the Copts the stereotype generally assigned to minorities: the plotting with foreign powers against the nation, secession schemes, sinister plots to weaken the nation of Islam, attempts to wrest power from the majority or at least to prevent it from exercising its collective will.

Today, there is an atmosphere of heightened confessional tension, based on a continuation of the conspiracy theory of the 1970s. Attacks against the Copts are the main strategy used by a number of Islamic groups which view this kind of "civil war" as a useful method to initiate popular mobilization around them and thus create a possible confrontation with the state.[68]

In 1991 the most serious incident took place in Imbaba, a poor suburb in Cairo. The incident was said to have begun when a Coptic woman ran a tape of Christian prayers while Muslims were praying nearby. A "mob of fanatics" tried to set fire to two churches and burned down several shops belonging to Copts.[69] The year 1992 witnessed the worst sectarian clash in Egypt during the previous ten years. On 4 May thirteen Copts were massacred by radical Islamic fundamentalists in an Upper Egyptian village in the governorate of Asyut. Two explanations were given for the incident: first, the massacre was perhaps an act of revenge for the death of a Muslim extremist in early March; secondly, it was possible that the attack was prompted by the refusal of a Coptic tradesman to pay the *jizya*, or poll tax, imposed by local Muslim extremists of the Jama'at al-Islamiyya on Coptic citizens.[70] Violence in this area was again revived on 19 and 20 June, when security forces attempted to prevent the attacks against shops and homes owned by Copts. Nine people were killed and several were wounded. On 26 October, a Coptic jeweller and his assistant were killed by Islamic fundamentalist gunmen who robbed his shop to raise funds for their militant activities. Similarly, a bus carrying Copts returning from a visit to religious sites in Upper Egypt became a target of Islamist fire south of Cairo where ten people were wounded.[71] On 19 May 1993, a Coptic mayor was killed near Asyut and on 16 July a Coptic shopkeeper was killed by radical Islamic fundamentalists. That year witnessed the killing of six Copts at the final count.[72] In March 1994, the first attack directed specifically against Copts took place when a gunman shot at a crowd outside a monastery near Asyut in March. Six people were killed and three were wounded.[73]

Apart from physical violence against Copts, the fundamentalists' strategy touches also the social level and specifically the development of social organizations with Islamic referents at the time of the state's social disengagement.[74] It is quite interesting to see that in 1992, areas where the Coptic population is at its highest compared to the national average, such as Minia and Asyut, were the ones that witnessed the strongest development of Islamic social organizations or social associations with Islamic referents. In counting social associations with Islamic referents, two criteria were taken into consideration: the name and the domain of activity. This included every association whose name contained the word "Islam" or one of its derivations, whose name or activity was related to an Islamic religious practice, whose name contained expressions with Islamic connotations (e.g. the Ka'ba Association), whose name referred to an Islamic personality or a saint (Sayyida Zaynab), and whose name contained the word "mosque".[75] The percentage of associations using a Muslim referent in areas with an important Coptic presence was significantly higher than the national average estimated around 28 per cent: 57 per cent in Minia, 45 in Asyut. On the other hand, the most heavily populated governorates such as Cairo, Giza and Daqahlia dropped in percentage behind the national average. Against this wave of Islamic penetration, Copts are setting up their own social organizations: first, because the state's retreat led to an autonomy within social space, and second, because the Islamic social organizations, which Copts have no access to, have increased their own activities. Coptic investment includes educational, economic and medical assistance and housing.[76]

Another aspect of this factor may be revealed by the assassination of Farag Foda, who was accused of being manipulated by Copts, and of having certain connections with Israel. On 8 June 1992, Farag Foda was assassinated by al-Jihad organization, the same organization that assassinated Sadat in 1981 and the president of the Egyptian Parliament in 1990. Foda was a secular leader who advocated a radical separation between the state and religion and called for the establishment of freedom of faith. His importance did not lie in his rejection of the Islamic state but rather in the position he occupied in the cultural as well as in the political debate. He played an active role in mobilizing public activities like conferences and debates on television which enabled him to articulate ideological views along with political actions. Before his death, he occupied an important position at different levels. Foda was one of the founders of the popular committee of national union which included a number of intellectuals, actors and political personalities, like Judge al-Ashmawi who is the head of Egypt's state security court, the actor Adel Imam, the former minister of the interior, Hassan Abou Bacha, and the Copt, Milad Hanna. This committee had an objective to enhance national unity and mobilize public opinion against fundamentalist attacks on Copts. Foda also requested permission to create a new political party, Hizb al-Mustaqbal (Party of the Future). Moreover, he pressured the public authorities to issue an anti-terrorist law in a public suggestion to the president of the republic during a meeting with the press, because, according to Foda, the emergency law which had been active for the past ten years had failed to curtail the activities of radical fundamentalist groups.[77] This new law was adopted in mid-July 1992, and as a consequence, introduced the death penalty for members of "terrorist" organizations and enabled the security authorities to detain suspects for three days without informing the prosecutor's office.[78] During the sectarian confrontation in Asyut, he wrote several articles warning against the development of civil war and criticized the silence prevailing in the face of the old anti-Coptic discrimination.[79] His "portrait" gave his assassination little importance and gave his murderers an excuse and an explanation. Moreover, it intimidated intellectuals and journalists who expressed their opposition to the Islamic fundamentalists and to the application of the *shari'a*. Even after his death, Abdel-Ghaffar Aziz, an old professor at the Faculty of al-Da'wa at al-Azhar University attacked him and accused him of complicity with local and external Christians,[80] implying that the Copts were plotting with foreign powers against the Egyptian nation and conspiring against Islam.

## The Rhetorical Power of the Islamic Fundamentalist Discourse

In discussing the factors underlying the popularity of the Islamic trend in Egypt, it is essential to take into consideration the rhetorical power of Islam. Islam is a rich and complex cultural system which has developed over centuries offering a vast symbolic network, a means of interpreting reality, and has provided meaning for believers.[81] In fact, Islamic fundamentalist thought has contributed to the intellectual discourse which has been going on for hundreds of years in the East and West, especially in that it constitutes a critique of philosophy, of political ideology, and of the sciences. In dealing with the truth and knowledge it rejects the claim made by man to be the possessor of truth and the claim that all knowledge is relative. Moreover, it offers a way of life and thought, a way that is regulated by God's laws and by nature. Politically, it considers that authority belongs to God only and rejects the notion that societies are no more than places where desires are satisfied. It also strives to erect societies based on justice, virtue, and equality. Islamic fundamentalism is a movement that aims at making the two fundamentals, the *Qur'an* and the *shari'a*, the basis of Muslim life and society and of the Islamic state.[82] As a result, Islamic fundamentalism is a language, a discourse performing a cognitive function and a way of talking. In fact, the fundamentalists benefit from this important *atout* and it would be to their advantage to reintroduce the old Islamic vocabulary of their ancestors into the political arena after it had been restricted to private circles. Therefore, the success or popularity of Islamic fundamentalism may be explained in terms of Islam's glorious history especially since it possesses a holistic and all-encompassing view of life. This fact provides Islam with a rich quasi-political vocabulary and literature that may be of great value in political as well as economic issues.[83] In examining this factor in a more detailed fashion two aspects of the fundamentalists' discourse should be mentioned: first, their anti-state discourse; second, their economic discourse.

First, the fundamentalists' discourse is distinguished by its anti-state sentiments which hold the secular state to be responsible for the dismal situation experienced by all Egyptians. This attitude is strengthened by the fact that the fundamentalists are not in power and so have the opportunity to make weighty promises and paint a colourful and favourable picture of their model.[84] In fact, the modern secular state is held responsible for the condition of alienation and exclusion that Egyptians are suffering from. Accordingly, Islam is considered to be an effective weapon against the "cultural dependency" that results from the policy of Westernization adopted by various Middle Eastern rulers as part of their modernization and development programmes, an aspect that alienated a major part of the people who never really benefited from them. This alienation pushed the people to look for an alternative, and this was found in Islam and its glorious history; especially under Abd al-Nasser,

Sadat and others, Egyptians in general and the young generation in particular were excluded by the closed nature of the system. This political exclusion prompted those unable to express themselves to search for various means of participation through the word of God, the Almighty. This sense of political exclusion was accompanied by an economic "exclusion" felt by very many Egyptians because of the lack of jobs, housing and commodities they could afford to buy. This kind of alienation forced them to look for higher degrees of participation by embracing Islam. These two major grievances over "exclusion" and "alienation" and the related quest for authenticity as an alternative, led to the quest for participation in the political and economic life. Such dissatisfaction was translated into confrontation between the radical fundamentalists and the modern secular bureaucratic state which, in the final analysis, failed to provide political and economic opportunities.[85]

Second, the fundamentalists' discourse is distinguished by a concern for the socio-economic aspect of society which further enhances their rhetorical appeal. The modern fundamentalist discourse takes the pious individual as an essential unit and a starting point to attain a virtuous society. Hasan al-Banna, the founder of the Society of the Muslim Brothers, saw the moral, spiritual and material comfort of the individual as constituting the foundations of a virtuous and just society and therefore the primary concern of the state, all individuals, in particular, being equal except in their degree of religiosity and faith. Thus, his view on economic organization gave the state full responsibility in promoting equality, closing material gaps between classes and preventing class conflicts. Within this framework, the state is required to provide social security and comfort for all its citizens through the use of the religious tax, zakat. Private property is considered to be within the rights of the individual as long as he works and produces in accordance with Islam and the public interest. But a more equitable distribution of wealth meant ending foreign monopolies, providing health care and general education for the citizens and reducing crime; building a decent army was mentioned as a secondary goal. As to how this might be achieved, he suggested three general means – deep faith, careful organization, and work. He encouraged the Muslim Brothers to think about these means and to elaborate on them, because he considered that the time for practical politics had not yet arrived. At this level, it is important to note that the language of Hasan al-Banna reveals a key element of the movement's appeal.

Al-Banna simply justified his teachings with the statement "Islam teaches", which reifies Islam into a fixed and eternal body of ideal doctrine, readily available to anyone who cares to know about it. Thus, the use of this statement is a call on the vague and powerful authority of an entire cultural tradition, an address to those whose fundamental identity is that of Muslim, especially threatened by the presence of alternative ideologies and ways of life. Moreover, the Muslim Brothers' literature is distinguished by the fact that the majority of its textual citations are drawn from the Qur'an. This is important because for the mass of Egyptians, the Qur'an was, and still is, embedded in everyday life and thought. Therefore, it possesses a tremendous impact and authority unmatched by any other book. This impact permits the Muslim Brothers to succeed in terms of moral values and to remain vague in terms of programmes. In effect, this is an assertion that Islam will restore national morality, economic prosperity, equality and justice, and withstand Zionist aggression. By addressing the people in terms of fear about cultural identity and fundamental values, the Muslim Brothers can maintain a broad audience without the need to present concrete social and economic programmes.

Like al-Banna, Sayyid Qutb viewed comprehensive social justice and equality as the main prerequisites for a moral society with a moralistic economic character. This view demands that the state should care about the material and moral welfare of individuals by providing them with the basic needs – beyond mere subsistence; also, that it should respect the right to private property which is to be interpreted as ownership of its benefits only and not a means of accumulating wealth. To close social gaps that are Islamically disapproved of, the state should impose religious taxes so as to provide some form of welfare for the whole of society. However, Qutb's concept of social justice remained abstract and its discussion was limited to the three foundations set forth in Islam. The first is that Islam provides man with absolute emotional freedom as well as freedom from all forms of subjugation. The second is that all human beings are equal, which means that no individual has a superior or divine birthright, and that equality is also established between the sexes except at the level of physical differences, customs, and differing responsibilities. The third is that Islam teaches mutual social responsibility which means that concern for others can limit individual freedom and that the community is responsible for the welfare of its weaker members: the means to achieve social justice in Islam are the exhortations to perform certain acts and the prohibition of others, as described in the Qur'an.[86]

Qutb's theory is closely linked to political and moral life, to the continuation of the same political climate where prevails a need to eradicate the unjust government, injustice and poverty and to encourage the creation and preservation of morality. Qutb's appeal may be explained by his extensive use of the Qur'an throughout his justification of how Muslims should conduct their government and life. All the basic notions he advocated – revolution, social justice or the Muslim's choice – were based on Qur'anic verses. Thus, he justified social justice and freedom in Islamic terms without adhering to democracy and socialism or referring to what he considered foreign ideologies that did not include God as underpinning their principles. He showed that Islam offered the principles of democracy (choice of the people) and socialism (social justice) before any other ideology; these principles made them religious as well as political duties, i.e. the principles of government in Islam. Thus, Qutb was able to gather the best in the Western tradition in a new Islamic ideology without negating Islam, to reinforce the notion that Islam was valid for all ages, that its principles could integrate changing conditions and be a guide which the majority of Muslims believe in.[87]

Modern radical fundamentalists also had their own rhetorical strategy based on simplicity and vagueness. According to Saad el-Din Ibrahim, modern radical fundamentalists claimed that Egypt's economic problems resulted from the mismanagement of resources, imported policies, corruption, conspicuous consumerism and low productivity. They envisioned a society where social justice and equity would prevail. To attain this kind of society, the state should be given tremendous leeway to engage in economic activities in the interest of the *umma*, and the ruler should be given the responsibility of promoting justice and equity. However, social differentiation is acceptable as long as it is the result of the labour of a person who follows the edicts of paying *zakat*, provides fair wages to labourers, works honestly and rigorously, and gives charity. Such a person should also refrain from taboos which include cheating, extravagance, hoarding and usury (charging interest). As a result, excessive wealth and excessive poverty would have no place in such a Muslim society.[88] This general outlook of the radicals on the economy was extracted from interviews with arrested militants in 1981. However, the writings of the leading Islamic radicals such as Shukri Mustafa, Abd al-Salam Faraj and Khalid al-Islambouli do not advocate a particular economic programme. Thus, the fundamentalists' message is simple: when true fundamentalists take over power, God's sovereignty will be declared and therefore social, economic, constitutional, technological and cultural problems will be resolved. This idea may be summarized simply with the statement: "Islam is the solution."[89] Islamic fundamentalist thinking attributes the difficulties experienced by society to the fact that greed, corruption and atheism were characteristics of the leaders and the fragmentation of society led to individuals drifting away from the path of Islam and to society's failure in confronting its external enemies. In essence, society is categorized in a way that gives a sense of group solidarity juxtaposing the community of the faithful to the community of unbelievers. As a result, the faithful are placed on a higher moral plane than other members of society and have a divine mission to serve, that is to espouse "Islam as the solution".[90] The vagueness of the doctrine, and the adoption of an attitude of moral hauteur and superiority (ta'ali) over any secular developmental option ensures its appeal to the broadest audience possible and gives it a degree of symbolic strength.[91]

The fundamentalists' rhetorical power and the resulting symbolic strength are mainly demonstrated by the reaction of the Egyptian state. It stresses the fact that it functions in the name of Islam and according to the shari'a and tries to include religion in its discourse and practices at the political and social levels.[92] At the political level, the government increasingly introduced religion into legislation, education, media and elsewhere.[93] Moreover, successive Egyptian regimes tried to strengthen the place of institutional Islam at the al-Azhar University which is one of the most important symbols of Islam; it also tried to increase religious terminologies in the official political discourse and the denunciation of radical violence. For example, the religious term of kharijite is always used to refer to radical fundamentalists.[94] As regards the role of al-Azhar, it is interesting to examine its answer to the argument put forward by the assassins of President Sadat in a pamphlet known as the Absent Duty written by Abd al-Salam Faraj. In his answer to al-Jihad's argument, the Mufti of Egypt, Shaykh Jad al-Haqq Ali Jad al-Haqq issued a fatwa rejecting the group's arguments. He considered that only errant polytheists can be considered apostates while persons who violate a core religious tenet are guilty of having committed a sin only, and not apostasy, since they did not renounce their belief in Islam. Thus, only Allah, not mortals, can punish a sinner. Moreover, he considered the *'ulama'* (not ordinay people) to be the source for the clarification of Islam's ordinances. As for *jihad*, he reasoned that after the Prophet's demise it devolved upon the community if a situation arose that called for it. Such situations refer to the occupation of Muslim lands by non-Muslims which necessitates a *jihad* by armed conflict, by means of wealth, words and heart. Furthermore, the Mufti held that Egypt is the abode of Islam because many aspects of the faith like prayer, alms-giving, pilgrimage to Mecca are observed, except for aspects that were replaced by positive law. This state of affairs implies that Egyptians are implementing Allah's law "within the limits of their capabilities" and therefore they are not apostates. From this premise he went on to argue that only counselling the ruler is allowed and not insurrection against him even if he only upholds prayer, because this means that he is a Muslim. Finally, the Mufti concluded that battles in defence of religion and the country should be fought by the army and not by a group of private individuals, that *jihad* is not lost but rather leads to continuous self-improvement and a constant fight against oneself and Satan. As a result, *jihad* does not signify pronouncing unbelief upon Muslims or attacking the community and its leaders nor interpreting Qur'anic texts in perverted ways which is prohibited by Allah. This answer to *al-Jihad's* argument demonstrates the importance of state institutions (such as al-Azhar) in political discussions, especially lately since the Mufti of Egypt called upon people to fight the radical fundamentalists.[95] At the social level, the state bank Nasir Ijtimai collected payments of *zakat* in 1991 which amounted to £E21 million to fund Islamic social services like centres for baby care in mosques and courses to help students.[96]

As a conclusion, the rise of the popularity of the Islamic fundamentalism can be attributed partially to its successful rhetorical power and the use of symbols which possess strong emotive power. This rhetorical power is based on two facts: first, the modern secular state failed to fulfil its promises of national honour and providing goods and services. This state pursued developmental plans which benefited only a minority while the majority was deprived of the benefits of capitalism and modernization;

second, the fundamentalists were excluded from participating in the execution of these development plans. It was therefore natural that they attributed these failures to the ungodly (secularist) nature of the state. Thus, the failure to attain economic modernization in the 1940s was due to capitalism and the presence of the "foreigner". In the 1960s and 1970s, evil was perceived to stem from socialism which was closely associated in people's minds with the Egyptian state, since the imperialist foreign power had long left Egypt. In their discourses, the fundamentalists have been tactically effective in providing only a vague idea about their alternative economic and political agenda or making wide-ranging promises though there is no evidence that they hold the solutions to the vexing social and economic problems of the country. Their call had great appeal and they were able to avoid possible embarrassment, since it remained pure, simple and abstract and based on Qur'anic verses, especially that Islamic groups are not on the defensive and that Islam is viewed by an "active minority as an emerging, durable, and appealing political ideology as well as a defense against the encroachments of 'Western decay' ".[97]

## The Egyptian Political System versus Islamic Fundamentalism

The growth of the Islamic fundamentalists' popularity stemmed from the popular discontent over the hardship caused by the country's economic reform programme involving a gradual move away from the Nasserist welfare state, the fundamentalists' exploitation of the Coptic presence to create confessional tension, and the strength of their discourse.

The fourth factor behind the increase in the popularity of Islamic fundamentalism emanates from the Egyptian government's concern that the exploitation of these issues may threaten the stability of the country. Therefore, the maintenance of law and order has been the main social priority of the Hosni Mubarak regime. This priority is closely related to three major defects in the Egyptian political environment. First, the presidential elections have always been plebiscitary rather than competitive, and since the 1953 revolution of the free officers movement no contender has run against the incumbent. The second major flaw is the fact that emergency laws have been in place since 1981 despite strong opposition. After the assassination of President Sadat in 1981, a law declaring a state of emergency was promulgated. This law gave the police unlimited powers to search, arrest, detain individuals without trial; the law also placed the media under government control. Moreover, it allowed the detention of suspects for sixty days without official charges being brought against them; in practice, many are detained indefinitely. These sweeping powers that were given to the security forces have been used against pro-Palestinian demonstrators, left wingers and others protesting against the deteriorating standard of living of most Egyptians. More importantly, these powers are commonly used to make blanket arrests of Islamic opponents of the regime especially since violence has been used increasingly by the fundamentalists. This has been countered by a harsh and indiscriminate response from the Egyptian security services, fuelling concerns that a vendetta-style confrontation is bound to develop from such harshness.[98] On 11 April 1994 parliament extended the country's emergency law for another three years, i.e. until 31 May 1997. Only 12 out of the 458 People's Assembly members voted against this extension.[99] Critics note that the courts may demand the release of detainees, but the emergency law allows the government to rearrest them immediately on grounds of national security.[100] Actually, 10,000 Islamic radicals were arrested in 1989 and hundreds of arrests took place in May and June 1994. Sometimes the police may detain up to 250 people a day on suspicion and hold them for at least three days. Moreover, a harsh anti-terrorism legislation was passed in July 1992, which introduced the death penalty for membership of a terrorist organization. It also empowered the security authorities to detain suspects for three days without informing the prosecutor's office. This law, like the emergency laws and the government's recent use of military courts to try radicals speedily, added momentum to state repression and violence. Third, the fight against Islamic insurgency has led to many human rights violations. Amnesty International reported that in 1993 different prisons in Egypt contained permanently no less than 2000 people because of the emergency law, and that many were executed outside the realm of law (eight people were executed in 1993 when the police attacked a mosque in Aswan). Amnesty asked President Mubarak to investigate the death penalty cases and to put an end to the military trials of civilians. In 1994, Amnesty reported an increase in repression and political violence since 1992, the death of 400 people, and the injury of 760. Moreover, in 1994 the Egyptian Human Rights Organization (EHRO) reported 20 cases of disappearance, 16 of which were documented. These cases exclude the (temporary) disappearance of those detained in unknown places for a week or even a month. On 10 May 1994 it also warned that brutal police methods such as mass arrests and curfews are alienating citizens of upper Egypt.[101] Actually, abuses committed by the security police like torturing detainees and arresting family members in order to coerce fugitive militants into surrendering, may alienate large parts of the population. Such practices prompt the Islamic groups to mount vendetta attacks on the police which may bolster their ability to enlist new recruits from among Egypt's angry youth.[102] Moreover, such suppression carried out by the government may radicalize the moderate or pragmatic wing of Islamic fundamentalist tendencies. Consequently, it could transform them into revolutionaries against the government and its allies – their main targets – in an atmosphere of violence and revolt which, according to the fundamentalists, is a legitimate self-defence tactic.[103]

It is thus the nature of the Egyptian political system that plays a major part in enhancing the appeal of Islamic fundamentalism. In trying to maintain law and order, the government uses any means with no holds barred. This made repression one of the characteristic ways of dealing with the fundamentalists, a fact that led to many human rights violations, and had the effect of radicalizing people who were subjected to violence, arrests or the loss of a son or a relative.[104]

In conclusion, there are four domestic factors which are responsible for the increasing popularity of the Islamic trend in Egypt. First, the economic situation witnessing a withdrawal of the state from its "welfare" role, a move that benefited the Islamic fundamentalists who enhanced their social role and appeal. Second, the psychological disposition for confessional tension between Muslims and Copts; when added to the existing economic crisis, this phenomenon can be considered an important catalyst favouring the popularity of the Islamic trend. The fundamentalists' claim that there is a Coptic conspiracy, accompanied by a series of confessional incidents, presented Copts as aggressors against Islam, a scheme that may make people sympathize with the fundamentalists and their cause. Third, the rhetoric of the fundamentalists emanating mainly from their Qur'anic discourses and their abstract appeals gives them a distinct advantage. As they are excluded from a position of authority they are free from any kind of responsibility. Fourth, the political climate characterized by repression of dissent and lack of freedom helps in radicalizing and alienating people who were subjected to oppression and coercion by the government. These four issues represent the current domestic factors behind the gradual build-up of pressure in Egyptian society. They constitute the dynamics of the Islamic movement in Egypt and place the Egyptian state in the awkward position of opposing a movement which is deeply rooted and highly developed in society. Thus, these factors play a crucial role in adding momentum to the popularity of the Islamic fundamentalist movement in Egypt, especially since the struggle between the state and the Islamic movement has led to a serious incoherence in the state's actions, putting it in contradiction with itself. In effect, the Islamic fundamentalist current in general has succeeded in sharing the geographic, social, and symbolic spaces with the state. Radical fundamentalists presented their opposition to the state through the scheme of *dar al-salam* (abode of peace and Islam) versus *dar al-harb* (abode of war and impiety), implying a confrontation that triggered repression by the state, which runs counter to its own established principles of government, such as freedom of the individual and respect for the law. Another more significant sign of incoherence may be found in the state's position which pretends to have religious laws as the foundation of its legitimacy, but at the same time refuses to apply the *shari'a* which, for example, imposes prohibition on alcohol consumption, the application of *hudud* (statutes for the offences and punishments defined in the Qur'an), and the separation of sexes. Such incoherence or inconsistencies may reveal an important contradiction within the state; however, they do not constitute a real threat to the security or stability of the system. As yet the state remains in control.

The conflict between the Egyptian government and the fundamentalist movements is still continuing. An abortive attempt against President Mubarak was carried out in June 1995; an attack on a group of tourists outside a hotel on the Pyramids Road resulted in the death of more than 20 people in April 1995. More recently, in November 1997, 58 tourists were massacred at Luxor. Although these bloody acts are abhorrent to the Egyptian public, the Islamic fundamentalist movement has not lost its advantage because of its social welfare schemes, the presence of the old Muslim–Coptic tensions, the familiarity of the Islamic discourse, and the repressive nature of the state. On the other hand, the Egyptian state is still maintaining the balance between liberalization and authoritarianism, enjoying the support of the army, using a policy of heavy patronage and co-option, and finally benefiting from the division within the Islamic movement itself.[105]

## NOTES

1 Ayman, Yassini, "Islamic Revival and National Development in the Arab World", *Journal of Asian and African Studies*, Vol. 21, No. 1–2 (1986), p. 105.

2 Daniel Pipes, "The World is Political: the Islamic Revival of the Seventies", *Orbis*, Vol. 24, No. 1 (1980), p. 41.

3 Ali Hillal Dessouki, "Islamic Resurgence: Sources, Dynamics, and Implications", *Islamic Resurgence in the Arab World*, ed. Ali Dessouki (New York: Praeger Publishers, 1982), p. 23.

4 Hrair Dekmejian, *Islam in Revolution: Fundamentalism in the Arab World* (New York: Syracuse University Press, 1985), p. 29.

5 Nazih Ayubi, "The Political Revival of Islam: the Case of Egypt", *International Journal of Middle East Studies*, Vol. 12 (1980), p. 484.

6 Barry Rubin, *Islamic Fundamentalism in Egyptian Politics* (New York: St Martin's Press, 1990), pp. 4–5.

7 Youssef Choueiri, *Islamic Fundamentalism* (Mass.: Twaynel/G.K. Hall, 1990), p. 74.

8 Hans Lofgren, "Economic Policy in Egypt: a Breakdown in Reform Resistance?", *International Journal of Middle East Studies*, No. 25 (1993), p. 412.

9 Sylvia Chiffoleau, "Le Désengagement de l'état et les transformations du système de santé", *Monde Arabe: Maghreb-Machrek*, No. 127 (1990), p. 84.

10 Richard V. Moench, "Oil, Ideology and State Autonomy in Egypt", *Arab Studies Quarterly* 10, No. 2 (1988), p. 180.

11 Jacques Séguin, "L'Economie égyptienne après la crise du golfe", *Monde Arabe: Maghreb-Machrek*, No. 133 (1991), p. 41.

12 Ali Hillal Dessouki, "L'Evolution politique de l'Egypte: pluralisme ou néo-Autoritarisme?", *Monde Arabe: Maghreb-Machrek*, No. 127 (1990), p. 13.

13 Séguin, "L'Economie égyptienne", p. 41.

14 Lofgren, "Economic Policy in Egypt", pp. 408–11.

15 Séguin, "L'Economie égyptienne", pp. 44–6.

16 "Egypt: Country Report", *Economist Intelligence Unit*, No. 2 (1994), p. 13.

17 Caryle Murphy, "Egypt: An Uneasy Portent of Change", *Current History*, 93, No. 580 (1994), p. 79.

18 "Egypt: Country Report", *Economist Intelligence Unit*, No. 3 (1994), p. 5.

19 Murphy, "Egypt".

20 Dessouki, "L'Evolution politique", p. 13.

21 Chiffoleau, "Le Désengagement de l'état", p. 84.

22 Ibid., pp. 90–1.

23  Ibid., pp. 92–6.
24  Murphy, "Egypt".
25  "Egypt: Country Report", p. 3.
26  Murphy, "Egypt".
27  Mustapha al-Sayyid, "A Civil Society in Egypt?", *The Middle East Journal*, 47, No. 2 (1993), p. 241.
28  Séguin, "L'Economie égyptienne", pp. 44–6.
29  Séguin, "L'Economie égyptienne", p. 46.
30  al-Sayyid, "A Civil Society in Egypt?".
31  Ibid.
32  Dessouki, "L'Evolution politique", p. 13.
33  Sarah Ben-Néfissa, "Le Mouvement associatif égyptien et l'Islam", *Monde Arabe: Maghreb-Machrek*, No. 135 (1992), p. 19.
34  Chiffoleau, "Le Désengagement de l'état et les transformations du système de santé", *Monde Arabe: Maghreb-Machrek*, No. 133 (1991), p. 98.
35  Ben-Néfissa, "Le Mouvement associatif", p. 19.
36  Dessouki, "L'Evolution politique", p. 13.
37  Lofgren, "Economic Policy in Egypt", p. 412.
38  Ilya Harik, "Subsidization Policies in Egypt: Neither Economic Growth Nor Distribution", *International Journal of Middle East Studies*, No. 24 (1992), p. 497.
39  Lofgren, "Economic Policy in Egypt".
40  Ayubi, *Political Islam*, p. 186.
41  Ibid., pp. 192–3.
42  Alain Roussillon, "Entre al-jihad et al-Rayyan: phénoménologie de l'islamisme égyptien", *Monde Arabe: Maghreb-Machrek*, No. 127 (1990), p. 35.
43  Mona Makram-Ebeid, "Political Opposition in Egypt: Democratic, Myth or Reality", *The Middle East Journal*, No. 3 (1989), p. 431.
44  Ayubi, *Political Islam*, p. 194.
45  Iman Farag, "L'Université égyptienne: enjeux et modes de mobilization", *Monde Arabe: Maghreb-Machrek*, No. 127 (1990), p. 82.
46  Galila El Kadi, "Le Caire: la ville spontanée sous contrôle", *Monde Arabe: Maghreb-Machrek*, No. 143 (1994), p. 35.
47  Issam El-Aryan, "Taharrakan raghm al-awamir al-askariyya," *Rose al-Youssef*, 21 November 1994, pp. 94–5.
48  Sami Zubaida, *Islam, the People and the State* (London: Biddles Ltd., 1989), pp. 152–3.
49  P. J. Vatikiotis, "Islamic Resurgence: A Critical Review", *Islam and Power*, ed. Alexander S. Cudsi and Ali E. Hillal Dessouki (London: Croom Helm Ltd., 1981), p. 195.
50  Nadia Ramsis Farah, *Religious Strife in Egypt* (Switzerland: Gordon & Breach Science, 1986), p. 94.
51  B. L. Carter, *The Copts in Egyptian Politics* (London: Croom Helm Ltd., 1986), pp. 10–19.

52  Ibid., p. 48.

53  Farah, *Religious Strife in Egypt*, p. 94.

54  Edward Wakin, *A Lonely Minority* (New York: William Morrow and Company, 1963), pp. 17–20.

55  Carter, *The Copts in Egyptian Politics*, pp. 279–81.

56  J. D. Pennington, "The Copts in Modern Egypt", *Middle Eastern Studies*, 18, No. 2 (1982), p. 164.

57  Wakin, *A Lonely Minority*, pp. 43–9.

58  Carter, *The Copts in Egyptian Politics*, p. 165.

59  Ibid., p. 166.

60  Farah, *Religious Strife*, p. 1.

61  Pennington, "The Copts in Modern Egypt", p. 168.

62  Ibid., p. 169.

63  Hamed Ansari, "Sectarian Conflict in Egypt and the Political Expediency of Religion", *The Middle East Journal*, 38, No. 3 (1984), p. 415.

64  Farah, *Religious Strife*, pp. 35–6.

65  Pennington, "The Copts in Modern Egypt", p. 167.

66  Farah, *Religious Strife*, pp. 2–21.

67  Ibid., pp. 35–6.

68  François Zabbal, "L'Assassinat de Farag Foda", *Les Cahiers de L'Orient*, No. 27 (1992), p. 194.

69  "Egypt: Country Report", *Economist Intelligence Unit*, No. 4 (1991), p. 20.

70  "Egypt: Country Report", *Economist Intelligence Unit*, No. 3 (1992), pp. 8–9.

71  "Egypt: Country Report", *Economist Intelligence Unit*, No. 4 (1992), p. 9.

72  "Egypt: Country Report", *Economist Intelligence Unit*, No. 3 (1993), p. 8.

73  "Egypt: Country Report", *Economist Intelligence Unit*, No. 1 (1994), p. 10.

74  Ben-Néfissa, "Le Mouvement Associatif", p. 35.

75  Ibid., p. 21.

76  Dina El-Khawaga, "Le Développement communautaire copte: un mode de participation au politique", *Monde Arabe: Maghreb-Machrek*, No. 135 (1992), p. 17.

77  François Zabbal, "L'Assassinat de Foda", *Le Cahiers de L'Orient*, No. 27 (1992), p. 193.

78  "Egypt: Country Report", *Economist Intelligence Unit*, No. 3 (1992), p. 10.

79  Zabbal, "L'Assassinat de Foda", p. 194.

80  Ibid., p. 195.

81  Eric Davis, "Ideology, Social Class and Islamic Radicalism", *From Nationalism to Revolutionary Islam*, ed. Said Amir Arjomand (London: The Macmillan Press, 1984), p. 140.

82  Ahmad Moussalli, *Radical Islamic Fundamentalism: The Ideological and Political Discourse of Sayyid Qutb* (Beirut: American University of Beirut, 1992), p. 13.

83  Ayubi, *Political Islam*, p. 227.

84  Dilip Hiro, *The Rise of Islamic Fundamentalism* (New York: Routledge, 1989), p. 85.

85  Ayubi, *Political Islam*, pp. 218–20.

86  Charles E. Butterworth, "Prudence Versus Legitimacy: The Persistent Theme in Islamic Political Thought", *Islamic Resurgence in the Arab World*, ed. Ali Hillal Dessouki (New York: Praeger Publishers, 1982), pp. 98–101.

87  Moussalli, *Radical Islamic Fundamentalism*, pp. 243–4.

88  Saad Eddin Ibrahim, "Anatomy of Egypt's Militant Islamic Groups: Methodological Note and Preliminary Findings", *International Journal of Middle Eastern Studies*, 12 (1976), pp. 432–3.

89  Ayubi, *Political Islam*, pp. 232–3.

90  Davis, "Ideology, Social Class and Islamic Radicalism", p.148.

91  Ayubi, *Political Islam*, pp. 234–5.

92  Ben-Néfissa, "Le Mouvement associatif", p. 30.

93  Ayubi, *Political Islam*, p. 86.

94  Khattar Abou-Diab, "Le Monde Arabe face à l'islamisme", *Les Cahiers de L'Orient*, No. 27 (1992), p. 17.

95  Shahrough Akhavi, "The Clergy's Concepts of Rule in Egypt and Iran", *The Annals of the American Academy of Political and Social Science*, 524 (November 1992), pp. 94–9.

96  Ben-Néfissa, "Le Mouvement associatif", p. 33.

97  Norton, *Civil Society in the Middle East*, p. 18.

98  "Egypt: Country Report", *Economist Intelligence Unit* (1990–1), p. 6.

99  "Egypt: Country Report", *Economist Intelligence Unit*, No. 2 (1994). p. 9.

100  "Egypt: Country Report", *Economist Intelligence Unit*, No. 2 (1991), p. 8.

101  "Egypt: Country Report", *Economist Intelligence Unit*, No. 3 (1994), p. 9.

102  Murphy, "Egypt", p. 80.

103  John Esposito, "Islamic Movements, Democratization, and US Foreign Policy", *The Middle East Challenges After the Cold War*, ed. Phebe Marr and William Lewis (Boulder, CO: Westview Press, 1993), p. 204.

104  Moench, "Oil, Ideology and State", p. 185.

105  For the latest reports and studies on the subject, see Sana Abed-Kotob, "The Accommodationist Speak: Goals and Strategies of the Muslim Brotherhood of Egypt", *International Journal of Middle East Studies*, No. 27 (August, 1995, pp. 321–39; "Egypt: Country Report", *Economist Intelligence Unit*, No. 4, 1995; Burhan Ghalioun, "L'Islamisme et l'impasse de la modernité", *Peuples Méditerranéens*, No. 70–1 (January–June, 1995), pp. 3–30.

# Notes on Contributors

**Mirna Hammoud** received her M.A. in Political Science from the American University of Beirut.

**A. Nizar Hamzeh** is Associate Professor of Political Science at the American University of Beirut. He has published many articles on the Islamic movements in Lebanon and on Qatar's legal system.

**Michael Irving Jensen** earned his M.A. in Arabic Studies from the University of Copenhagen and is currently Research Fellow at the Carsten Niebuhr Institute at the University of Copenhagen.

**Ronald A. T. Judy** is Assistant Professor at the Department of English at the University of Pittsburgh, teaching in the Program of Literary and Cultural Theory. He is the author of *(Dis)forming the American Canon: The Vernacular of African Arabic American Salve Narrative.*

**Hilal Khashan** is Associate Professor of Political Science at the American University of Beirut. His publications include *Inside the Confessional Mind* and *Arab Views of Peace and Normalization with Israel* and numerous other articles on politics of the Middle East.

**Ahmad S. Moussalli** is Associate Professor of Political Science at the American University of Beirut. His publications include *Radical Islamic Fundamentalism: The Ideological and Political Discourse of Sayyid Qutb* and *Islamic Fundamentalism: Radical and Moderate Discourses* as well as articles on modern Islamic political thought, Islamic fundamentalism and East–West relations.

**Michel G. Nehme** is Associate Professor of Political Science at the American University of Beirut. His numerous publications cover Saudi Arabia, Lebanon, the Kurds and the Middle East.

**Glenn E. Robinson** is Assistant Professor at the Department of National Security Affairs, Naval Postgraduate School, Monterey, California, and Research Fellow at the Center for Middle East Studies at Berkeley

University. His publications include articles on the Islamic movements in the Arab world.

**Armando Salvatore** is Researcher and Assistant Professor of Historical Sociology of Religion/Culture at Humboldt-University, Berlin. He has published *Islam and the Political Discourse of Modernity* and articles on Islam in Italian.

**Kristin Wolff** received her M.A. from the University of Arizona, Department of Political Science.

**Yahia H. Zoubir** is Associate Professor of International Studies at Thunderbird. He is the editor and main contributor to *International Dimensions of the Western Sahara Conflict* and has written many articles on the democratization of Algeria, US and Soviet policies toward France and the United Nations and the Sahara Question.

# Index